Industrial Enlightenment

MANCHESTER
1824

Manchester University Press

Industrial Enlightenment

Science, technology and culture
in Birmingham and the
West Midlands, 1760–1820

PETER M. JONES

Manchester University Press
Manchester and New York

distributed in the United States exclusively by Palgrave Macmillan

Published by Manchester University Press
Oxford Road, Manchester M13 9NR, UK
and Room 400, 175 Fifth Avenue, New York, NY 10010, USA
www.manchesteruniversitypress.co.uk

Distributed in the United States exclusively by
Palgrave Macmillan, 175 Fifth Avenue, New York,
NY 10010, USA

Distributed in Canada exclusively by
UBC Press, University of British Columbia, 2029 West Mall,
Vancouver, BC, Canada V6T 1Z2

British Library Cataloguing-in-Publication Data
A catalogue record for this book is available from the British Library

Library of Congress Cataloging-in-Publication Data applied for

ISBN 978 0 7190 7770 8 *hardback*

First published 2008

Typeset in 10.5/12.5pt New Baskerville
by Graphicraft Limited, Hong Kong
Printed in the UK
by the MPG Books Group

Contents

Figures

Tables

Preface and acknowledgements

This book is a product of chance, or perhaps I should say serendipity. In the summer of 1994 Birmingham City council announced that it had paid a little over one million pounds for a large quantity of personal and family papers relating to the steam engineer James Watt. At the time this was probably the biggest ever purchase of historic records by a local authority, but the expenditure was not difficult to justify. The City Library already possessed a remarkable archive of original documents arising from the business partnership formed in 1775 between Matthew Boulton of Soho near Birmingham and James Watt, and over the years it had also acquired the papers of the Boulton family and a substantial consignment of Watt papers which had descended through the family of James Watt junior's cousin. I sampled some of the material out of curiosity early in 1995, and quickly grasped its significance. The reconstituted Boulton and Watt archive seemed to open up a refreshingly new perspective on the cultural history of an urbanising provincial society in the late eighteenth century. However, another research project beckoned, and it was not until 2003 that I was able to give the very substantial contents of the 'Archives of Soho' the undivided attention they so clearly deserved.

It would be wrong to imply that the Archives of Soho have lain untouched. On the contrary, researchers tunnelled repeatedly during the course of the twentieth century into the small mountain of documents accumulated by the families who were the partners in the Soho undertakings. Even in the nineteenth century, Victorian hagiographers found moral purpose in exploring the 'remarkable lives' of Boulton and Watt. Investigators usually focused on one facet of the intellectual, industrial or business activities taking place at Soho, to the exclusion of all others, however. Thus, James Watt's role in the discovery of the compound nature of water was thoroughly aired and defended; his inventive 'genius' and that of his partner Boulton were co-opted into the energising myth of the Industrial Revolution; engineers and technologists diligently pieced together the developmental saga of the improved steam engine; economic historians highlighted the pioneering business practices of the partnership and the successful experiments with integrated production carried on at the

Soho Foundry site, and so forth. Perhaps unsurprisingly, therefore, the historiography of Boulton, Watt and Soho has developed in a staccato and somewhat lopsided fashion. The 1919 centenary of James Watt's death provided the occasion for an exhaustive scrutiny of his contribution to steam-power technology, and it was followed by the publication of a biography in 1935 in anticipation of the bicentenary year of his birth. Matthew Boulton, by contrast, has been much less well served, whether by historians or biographers. Watt's chronicler, H. W. Dickinson, produced a companion volume the year following, but issued it with the caveat that he had not attempted to capture the full range of Boulton's activities. As an engineer by training and with only limited contextual knowledge on which to draw, he concentrated his attention instead on his subject's technical achievements. Whilst James Watt has now received from Richard Hills an assessment which takes into account the recent additions to the archival corpus housed in Birmingham Central Library, Matthew Boulton – on the eve of the two hundredth anniversary of his death – awaits a biographer both willing and able to produce a rounded account of his life.

It is not hard to see why scholars should have jibbed at the challenge to provide an overall interpretation of the significance of Soho, of its partners, of the remarkable group of natural philosophers who gravitated around them, and of the provincial setting that was Birmingham and the West Midlands. Until 1974 the component parts of the present-day archive were dispersed, making research a test of stamina as well as of patience. Even after this date, systematic study was hampered by the inadequate and inconsistent listing of the sources – a situation temporarily exacerbated by the arrival in 1994 of the Watt family deposit, accompanied by no more than a rudimentary search guide. Only in 2003, following an extensive recataloguing and conservation project, did the material become fully and easily accessible to researchers. Yet fundamental problems remain, albeit ones of which scholars have no right to complain. The reconstituted Archives of Soho is immense and represents a veritable treasure trove which now fills a storage room the size of a small tennis court. And second, the researcher who wishes to do more than 'tunnel' has to find a frame of reference which will accommodate both the full spectrum of innovation and enterprise displayed at Soho between the years 1760 and 1820, and at the same time serve as a tool for analysis.

The present study cannot hope to provide a comprehensive account of the Soho undertakings, and even less a biography of Matthew Boulton, if only for the reason that it is angled towards the sciences. Yet I believe that it offers a more rounded picture of what went on in Soho, and more especially what went on in the minds of those associated with the enterprise, than anything written hitherto. Boulton's role as a political lobbyist, his role as a patron of the arts, or as a purveyor of consumer products, may only be mentioned in passing, but I have attempted to furnish the reader with a thorough account of the cultural context of his endeavours, whether local, national or international. I have eschewed tunnelling and, despite the originality of much of the material, have refrained from narrative or description for its own sake. The vantage-point of the sciences is helpful in this respect. In the second half of the eighteenth century the pursuit of natural philosophy became one of the defining cultural characteristics of the age we call the Enlightenment. To explore the activities of bodies such as the Lunar Society, or the reactions of those who came to visit the Soho Manufactory, is therefore to open a window on the cognitive landscape of an entire generation. On looking through that window we not only learn a good deal about how ambitious and self-made men in the West Midlands contrived to domesticate the Enlightenment, we are also able to capture the transition from scientific knowledge employed socially to scientific knowledge manipulated for increasingly utilitarian purposes.

Here lies the central problematic of this book. It sets out to explain how – in a particular provincial context – the widespread public consumption of science underpinned a very considerable expansion of know-how or technological capability; in other words, how conditions conducive to 'Industrial Enlightenment' came into being. The first chapter explores the historiography of the Enlightenment and puts forward the case for supposing that the practice of scientific enquiry was both central to those who considered themselves to be 'enlightened' and a connecting link to the industrialisation and modernisation of the western world. Chapter 2 introduces the case study, that is to say, the regional setting in which I seek to vindicate the notion of an Industrial Enlightenment. Chapter 3 deals with the production and diffusion of scientific knowledge and emphasises the porosity of Europe's science cultures in this regard, whereas Chapter 4 tackles the key question of how knowledge was actually conditioned for practical use. Diffusing knowledge among *savants* was not at all the same as embedding it in technological or industrial processes, as this chapter will show. In the matter of application as opposed to dissemination, Europe's science cultures are revealed as very far from being evenly permeable, or receptive. Chapter 5 returns to the case study. It asks whether the religious complexion of Birmingham and the West Midlands, and more especially the strength of protestant Nonconformity, might explain the precocious development of conditions favourable to Industrial Enlightenment across the region. In the final chapter the focus switches once more to the international ramifications of the knowledge economy, and to the very serious dislocation that it suffered at the century's end as a consequence of the French Revolution and the Napoleonic Wars. Whilst these late-century interruptions to the free flow of knowledge and technical know-how served mainly to thrust English provincial science in an ever more utilitarian direction, they signally retarded developments on the Continent. As a result, overseas visitors arriving in Birmingham and Soho after the signing of the peace treaties of 1814–15 were dismayed to discover that they faced a very considerable knowledge and know-how deficit.

This book could not have been written without the support of a number of institutions and individuals. I should therefore like to thank Birmingham City Archives for providing access to the sources in working conditions that enabled me to make the best possible use of my time. Financial assistance to fund a period of extended sabbatical leave from January to May 2007 was generously provided by the Arts and Humanities Research Council, and the Research Committee of the School of Historical Studies, University of Birmingham supported most of the costs arising from two short trips to consult printed sources in the British Library, London. Many individuals have facilitated this study, but I should particularly like to thank Sir Nicholas Goodison, Professors Maxine Berg, William Doyle, Roger Hahn, David Hill, David Miller and Jennifer Tann, who provided support at crucial moments; Dr Richard Hills formerly of the University of Manchester Institute of Science and Technology, Dr Jim Andrew of the Thinktank museum in Birmingham, and Dr Helen Smith, independent scholar. The archivists who carried out the recataloguing of the Soho collections, Adam Green, Tim Proctor and Fiona Tait, were hugely helpful in drawing attention to materials that I might otherwise have missed. However, my chief debt is owed to the late Professor John R. Harris of the University of Birmingham, who would bend my ear on the subject of Boulton and Watt long before I was even remotely interested in the cultural history of science and technology. A case of subliminal persuasion, or serendipity? In any event, it is to John that this book is dedicated.

1

The eighteenth-century
knowledge economy

Europe was becoming an information-rich society in the eighteenth
century and educated Europeans were increasingly conscious of the
fact. James Keir, a West Midlands factory owner and chemist, underlined
as much in an oft-quoted remark penned towards the century's end:
'the diffusion of general knowledge, and of a taste for science, over all
classes of men, in every nation of Europe, or of European origin, seems
to be the characteristic feature of the present age'.[1] Whether the consumption of knowledge was quite as widespread as Keir maintained
is open to question, but there can be little doubt about the process of
diffusion, or the fact that it owed a great deal to the enterprise of two
groups drawn from nearly opposite ends of the social spectrum: Europe's
well-travelled intelligentsia, and Europe's itinerant craftsmen. In the
peaceful and prosperous decade following the ending of the American War – a war which had embroiled France, Spain and the Dutch
Republic as well as Britain – Europe's highways teemed with the carriages of the well-to-do and with bands of working men trudging from
town to town in search of employment. Whilst leisured elites paid visits,
exchanged information, jotted down and, increasingly, analysed what
they heard or saw, ordinary journeymen and craftsmen also engaged
in knowledge transfer – albeit in ways which have left fewer traces in the
historical record. This literature of travel and of artisanal encounter
testifies to the interconnectedness of the eighteenth-century knowledge
economy. It also exposes to view a world of material consumption based
on sophisticated markets in which fashion and taste were increasingly
measured in pan-European, even trans-Atlantic terms.

---

[1] J. Keir, *The First Part of a Dictionary of Chemistry* (Birmingham: Pearson and Rollason,
1789), preface, p. iii.

Traditionally we know this 'knowledge economy' as the Enlighten-ment. Yet the term 'enlightenment' has scarcely any greater contem-porary application than the phrase 'knowledge economy': both are retrospective analytical constructs. The Enlightenment is said to have occurred in the chronological gap between the Scientific Revolution of the later seventeenth century and the Industrial Revolution of the early nineteenth century. Whilst some blurring at the edges might be allowed, those in charge of defining the Enlightenment (essentially literature specialists and historians of ideas) have invested a great deal of scholarly capital in maintaining its distinctiveness. This is not to make a partisan point, for very similar observations could be directed towards historians of science, historians of technology or even economic his-torians. The effort involved in establishing the credentials of a new field of research or specialism can easily lead to tunnel vision. Since the thesis on which this study will rest presupposes a breaking down of the traditional categories of analysis, it is important to explore in greater detail some of the historiographical issues raised by the way in which researchers have approached the eighteenth century.

Science history used to be written by scientists, in the main. As such it lacked autonomy as a discipline and borrowed from the historian's toolkit only that which was indispensable: a respect for chronology. The aim was to chart the process of cognitive development, via the way-stations of inventors and discoveries, until the moment when the human intellect finally grasped the (correct) explanations of natural phenomena. Neither context nor scientific practice was considered to be integral to this undertaking: 'science alone of the social activities of man, operates independently of its social environment',[2] claimed A. Hunter Dupree in 1964. Unsurprisingly, science historians working in accordance with this agenda favoured the medium of biography or thematic study applied to individual sciences. No less surprisingly, they tended to neglect the eighteenth century. Viewed from such a perspective, the eighteenth century resembled a post-Newtonian (or pre-Daltonian) black hole, inasmuch as no single figure stood out around whom a narrative of scientific progress could be constructed. Only in the 1970s did this situation begin to change, but even in the 1980s historians of science were not of one mind as to the methodological direction their subject should take. As late as 1987 Rachel Laudan[3] declared, in a book devoted

[2] A. Hunter Dupree, 'Nationalism and science: Sir Joseph Banks and the wars with France', in D. H. Pinkney and T. Ropp (eds), *A Festschrift for Frederick B. Artz* (Durham: Duke University Press, 1964), p. 39.

[3] R. Laudan, *From Mineralogy to Geology: the Foundations of a Science, 1650–1830* (Chicago: University of Chicago Press, 1987), p. 18.

to the foundations of modern geology, her conviction that the study of the cognitive development of the discipline must come first and should, moreover, be conducted independently of its social history. Similar tensions have riven the study of the Enlightenment, as we shall see.

The difficulty raised by contextualisation is that it undermines specificity. In the hands of the historian or the sociologist, scientific knowledge loses the talismanic value attached to it by the philosopher or the scientist. It becomes a mere subset of the general quantum of knowledge available to a society at any given time. And once the focus of scholarly interest shifts from ideas to practices and uses (the generation and consumption of information about natural phenomena), the special status of scientific knowledge acquisition is further eroded. Science history as traditionally conceived becomes, instead, a branch of cultural history. In the process the questions posed by researchers undergo an abrupt change of direction, too. If scientific knowledge is not transparent, but socially filtered like any other branch of knowledge, it behoves us to find out more about the practices involved in its acquisition, and how they varied over time and from place to place. We might also wish to examine more closely how knowledge was diffused and experiments replicated – in case it should turn out that 'invention' and 'discovery' can be better characterised as collaborative enterprises. The purposes for which scientific knowledge was imbibed also become a relevant area of investigation. As co-proprietor of a large chemical works producing alkalis for the glass and soap industries, Keir had small use for scientific knowledge as a social ornament, yet Franz-Xaver Swediaur – one of the most peripatetic of Europe's natural philosophers – reported that even in Edinburgh chemistry was 'more cultivated as an amusing exercise to the mind than as a useful practical art'.[4]

Confided in a letter to the Swedish chemist Torbern Bergman in 1780, this remark points the way to the huge explanatory potential in prospect when science history is reconceived as cultural history. It may hint at the limitations of the cultural approach, too, but that is an issue that we can set to one side for the time being. Once the 'cultivation' of science becomes a legitimate object of enquiry, the shortcomings of the eighteenth century as an area for investigation are substantially remedied. And, indeed, it is precisely in this theatre that research has reinvigorated the study of early modern science over the last two decades. Whilst some scholars have explored the multiple uses to which scientific

---

[4] F.-X. Swediaur to T. Bergman, London, 3 July 1780, cited in G. Carlid and J. Nordström (eds), *Torbern Bergman's Foreign Correspondence.* Volume 1: *Letters from Foreigners to Torbern Bergman* (Stockholm: Almqvist & Wiksell, 1965), p. 328.

knowledge was put, others have tried to map out the growth of what has been labelled 'scientific culture'. In each case the eighteenth century takes pride of place as the period when science finally escaped from the grip of the academy and became just one more source of freely traded knowledge. There are solid grounds for blurring, if not conflating, traditional categories and periodisation, therefore. Today, most scholars would extend the Scientific Revolution into the eighteenth century – the century which witnessed the banishment of earlier scientific languages and the incorporation of Galilean and Newtonian thinking about natural phenomena into the western European 'mind-set'. If, as Margaret Jacob and Larry Stewart have argued, the eighteenth century was the century in which Newtonian matter turned 'practical',[5] the agenda for future research is not difficult to sign-post. We will need to find out whether beliefs about the intelligibility of nature – the hallmark of the scientific mentality – were widely shared in the eighteenth century, and if so, where and by whom. We will need to specify and document how far the 'cultivation' of science could give rise to 'practical', that is to say, technological, applications. Finally, we will need to reexamine the status accorded to both the Enlightenment and the Industrial Revolution, since a culturally informed history of science cannot easily be demarcated from either.

As a topic of research which frequently doubles up as an analytical tool, the Enlightenment has also been the subject of a radical re-evaluation. In fact, a process of reappraisal not dissimilar to that undergone by the history of science has taken place. Until the 1970s, the majority of scholars were content to equate the Enlightenment with the activities of a small band of eighteenth-century intellectuals who were mostly French. In effect, the *philosophes* played the role of the great scientific thinkers, and the story of the Enlightenment was woven around what they thought, and wrote, and did. Peter Gay[6] performed a signal service in the 1960s when he rescued the subject from the hands of the philosophers, with their metaphysical emphasis on an overriding unity of 'mind'. Yet today, even his account reads more like modified intellectual history than a convincing social history of ideas. It is predicated on the notion of a hard core of dissident writers who waged intellectual warfare against Europe's *ancien régime* in the name of religious and political freedom. Even though he distances himself from the essentialist arguments of the philosopher-historians and makes an effort to contextualise, there remains in his analysis only one Enlightenment.

---

[5] M. C. Jacob and L. Stewart, *Practical Matter: Newton's Science in the Service of Industry and Empire, 1687–1851* (Cambridge, Mass: Harvard University Press, 2004).
[6] P. Gay, *The Enlightenment: an Interpretation*, 2 vols (New York: Vintage, 1966–69).

The challenge to this depiction took shape in the 1970s. As might be expected, it drew strength from the social historians' tendency to broaden and decentre the debate. With the emphasis placed squarely on human agency and with the determinism of ideas removed from the frame of analysis, the unity of the Enlightenment swiftly dissolved to leave in its place a discordant set of cultural practices. So much so, indeed, that many scholars seriously question whether the concept of Enlightenment – in the singular – retains any explanatory value. Lawrence Brockliss,[7] for example, prefers to use the umbrella phrase 'Republic of Letters', which at least has the merit of contemporaneity. Even so, he envisages the phenomenon as a vast federation of ill-defined and overlapping mini-republics. No doubt the *philosophes* formed the militant vanguard of one such republic, but the constituency of the enlightened embraced many other loose groupings too: antiquarians and collectors, natural philosophers and, we would argue, industrialist-*savants* such as James Keir and Matthew Boulton. Without unity of purpose and a vanguard, the Enlightenment is also deprived of momentum. Most specialists would find it hard nowadays to accept Gay's sense of a 'movement', whether based on motion deriving from the unfolding of the idea of rationality in philosophic vein, or provided by animus against the temporal status quo in Europe. Once again, the decentring of the *philosophes* causes the whole edifice of the Enlightenment as traditionally depicted to shatter.

A potentially fruitful way of coping with fragmentation is to turn the cultural approach to advantage, and to make allowance for specificity and diversity. Franco Venturi[8] had already pointed the way ahead in his attempts to broaden the spatial basis of the Enlightenment. He even suggested that a scrutiny of developments on the geographical margins of Europe, where new ideas often found it difficult to put down roots, might throw into relief the elusive common denominators of the phenomenon. Perhaps as a consequence, the 1980s witnessed a group of scholars making the case for discrete 'national' Enlightenments. This turn represents an interesting and important shift in the debate, if only for the reason that it helps to accommodate some of the arguments that will be outlined in the chapters to come. The 'Scottish' Enlightenment passed muster without too much difficulty. After all, Lowland Scotland was a powerhouse of reformist thinking in the eighteenth century. Its

---

[7] L. W. B. Brockliss, *Calvet's Web: Enlightenment and the Republic of Letters in Eighteenth-Century France* (Oxford: Oxford University Press, 2002), pp. 390–412.

[8] See F. Venturi, *The End of the Old Regime in Europe: the First Crisis, 1768–1776* (Princeton: Princeton University Press, 1989).

ancient universities occupied node points in the knowledge circuits of
the age. By contrast, the notion of a specifically 'English' Enlightenment
has proved a little harder to vindicate, notwithstanding a very large book
on the subject written by Roy Porter.[9] England lacked intellectual cru-
saders publicly engaged in struggle (against a church establishment;
an *ancien-régime* state), it is true. But it is doubtful, to say the least, whether
the posturings of the *philosophes* should still be regarded as typifying
the Enlightenment. Late eighteenth-century England certainly did not
lack an intelligentsia, many of whose members lived in and around
Birmingham, as we shall see. This intelligentsia, moreover, engaged self-
consciously and sociably in rational pursuits, and it lived in conditions
of easy familiarity with the currents of intellectual life emanating from
the continent of Europe. Indeed, travel in pursuit of useful knowledge
became one of the overriding characteristics of intellectual life in the
second half of the eighteenth century. Numerous continental visitors
would draw from the experience of travel the conclusion that Britain
approximated most closely to the *philosophes'* model of a tolerant secular
society.

Contextualisation and diversification are apt to produce diminishing returns, however. Pushed to extremes, this methodology risks over-
interpreting the Enlightenment to the point where the phenomenon
disappears from view altogether. Brockliss finds in the concept of a
Republic of Letters a far more promising analytical tool, as we have
already noted. He rejects the suggestion that the Enlightenment somehow replaced the Republic of Letters after the middle of the century;
in fact, he argues that it would be more appropriate to subsume the
Enlightenment – traditionally conceived – into his federation. He posits,
by the century's end, a creative community of seekers-after-knowledge
some 12,000 strong who were increasingly organising themselves into
disciplinary clusters. This is plausible, although the figure he proposes
seems far too low. Yet one wonders whether his approach brings any
greater clarity or coherence to the picture. Historians of science, who
are the group to make most use of the notion of a Republic of Letters,
have long questioned the integrity of the concept as part of their assault
on philosophical idealism. Nevertheless, there are signs that intellectual
and cultural historians are unwilling to allow the Enlightenment to be
contextualised out of existence. John Robertson[10] remains sceptical of

[9] R. Porter, *Enlightenment: Britain and the Creation of the Modern World* (London: Penguin,
2000).
[10] J. Robertson, 'The Enlightenment above national context: political economy in
eighteenth-century Scotland and Naples', *Historical Journal*, 40:3 (1997), 667–97; but see

the focus on 'national' contexts and has even asked whether it originated as anything more than a clever marketing ploy. Instead, he urges us not to lose sight of the threads connecting together the various communities of enquirers and reformers. One such, he argues, was the preoccupation with human betterment in the guise of political economy, which acquired the status of a pan-European discourse during the second half of the eighteenth century. Thomas Munck's[11] comparative social history of the Enlightenment also expresses regret at the degree to which decentred analysis has come to dominate. Like Venturi, he draws attention to the strength of cosmopolitanism and reminds us that the unity of the Enlightenment should be sought in a certain style of individual critical enquiry, and not in an 'end-product' set of beliefs to which all thinking men and women subscribed.

It is entirely possible, of course, that natural philosophy, or science, provided the anchor point. Indeed, the earliest historians of the Enlightenment gave pride of place to science in their metaphysical investigations of the eighteenth-century 'mind', as Jan Golinski[12] points out. But the 'science' of the philosopher-historians and the culturally informed 'science' history of modern practitioners are mutually incomprehensible, or very nearly so. And besides, a connected science narrative was one of the first casualties in the move to contextualise the Enlightenment. When, in 1985, Thomas Hankins[13] produced a textbook entitled *Science and the Enlightenment* there appeared to be an opportunity to reconnect the two narratives, therefore. But Hankins showed himself to belong to the older school of thought. His science history was of the great men/ great ideas type, whereas his Enlightenment was unrepentantly francophone in outlook. In a memorable review Golinski accused Hankins of merely juxtaposing science and the Enlightenment, before proceeding to some rather less satisfactory remarks of his own on how the two might be reconnected at the macroscopic level.

Yet, if we set to one side the abstraction of an Enlightenment 'mind' somehow schooling itself in the scientific method, is it really possible to combine the two in anything other than local contexts and situations? The hesitation that greeted Golinski's remarks suggested that

the author's recent *The Case for the Enlightenment: Scotland and Naples 1680–1760* (Cambridge: Cambridge University Press, 2007), pp. 21–8, which passes a more favourable verdict on this approach.

[11] T. Munck, *The Enlightenment: a Comparative Social History, 1721–1794* (London: Arnold, 2000).

[12] J. Golinski, 'Science *in* the Enlightenment', *History of Science*, 24 (1986), 413.

[13] T. L. Hankins, *Science and the Enlightenment* (Cambridge: Cambridge University Press, 1985).

embarrassment about how to link together the Scientific Revolution and the Enlightenment in a dynamic relationship was not Hankins's alone.[14] In fact, this is an area of enquiry which is full of pious hopes, and in which historians of science have only begun to make significant headway in the last few years.[15] The break-through occurred with the recognition that science, as practised in the eighteenth century, constituted an important – some would say the most important – cultural category of the Enlightenment. Scientific knowledge, the possession of scientific instruments and a taste for scientific experimentation all became signifiers of access to polite culture, a kind of behavioural language enabling enlightened gentlemen, and some gentlewomen, to recognise one another across the length and breadth of Europe. How else are we to interpret Sir Richard Steele's remark on first beholding a mechanical planetarium? The potential for improving conversation would, he enthused, 'encite any Numerous Family of Distinction to have an Orrery as necessarily as they would have a clock'.[16] Erasmus Darwin made the same point when writing to his Lunar associate James Watt, near the century's end. Requesting information on Watt's improvements to the steam engine for inclusion in his didactic poem 'Economy of Vegetation', he stressed that his need was for politely packaged knowledge: 'such facts, or things, as may be rather *agreeable*; I mean gentleman-like facts not abstruse calculations, only fit for philosophers'.[17]

The banter exchanged between Darwin and Watt serves to remind us that a vast and multi-levelled 'conversation' about science was taking place in the eighteenth century. It was facilitated by the itinerant habits of Europe's intelligentsia; by the growth of correspondence networks linking natural philosophers; and by the signal increase in the amount of encyclopaedic, periodical and even popular literature devoted to science that was now becoming available. Analysis of these sources of information suggests that they offer a promising way of restoring to science a central role in our attempt to understand the Enlightenment. But this analysis should reach beyond the hypothesis that a dilute knowledge of science conferred cultural legitimacy;

[14] T. Broman, 'The Habermasian Public Sphere and "Science *in* the Enlightenment"', *History of Science*, 36 (1998), 123–4.

[15] See W. Clark, J. Golinski and S. Schaffer (eds), *The Sciences in Enlightened Europe* (Chicago: Chicago University Press, 1999).

[16] Quoted in W. R. Shea (ed.), *Science and the Visual Image in the Enlightenment* (Canton: Science History Publications, 2000), p. 2.

[17] Birmingham Central Library [hereafter BCL] MS 3219/4/80B E. Darwin to J. Watt snr, Derby, 20 November 1789.

a hypothesis that is now reasonably well established – for Britain at least. Those historians who couple the Enlightenment with the spread of 'scientific culture' expect rather more, and quite rightly. We should not lose sight of Darwin's 'abstruse calculations, only fit for philosophers', for the claims currently being made presuppose a widening of the definition of 'scientific culture' to embrace the 'practical' as well as the 'polite'. According to Margaret Jacob,[18] who has been a pioneer in this field, the main reason why we should extend the Scientific Revolution into the eighteenth century so that it overlaps and fuses with the Enlightenment is because the century witnessed the infiltration of the science of Newtonian mechanics into sections of the community which could actually turn this knowledge to practical use. Some may question the extent to which Newtonianism embedded itself, even in eighteenth-century England. Nevertheless, this is potentially a very fruitful approach which wants only for case-study support. It provides a vector for the analysis of the large quantities of epistolary evidence that have become available to scholars since the 1980s, and it offers some remedy for the shortcomings of a purely cultural depiction of science mentioned earlier. In other words, her approach provides a means of bridging the gap between the 'cultural' and the 'practical'.

As the focus switches towards the practical applications of scientific knowledge, a host of questions concerning technology and its interface with science, the Enlightenment and the Industrial Revolution arise. The older histories of technology were at least clear on these issues: they largely ignored the scientific, the philosophical and the socio-economic. But the challenge of contextualisation will not go away and it has eroded long-held beliefs in this area, as in others. The pressure came from the economic historians, in the first instance, who warned that technology was not an actor: it required human agency and human institutions to make an impact. Innovation and invention do not take place in a social void and, by extension, the diffusion of a new process or an innovation (Darby's coke-smelting of iron ore; Watt's improvements to the steam engine) presupposes more than simply conditions of technical feasibility. In distinguishing between hardware and know-how, the economic historians also turned the spot-light onto the species of technological knowledge required to make a product, or to get it to work. In fact a lively debate ensued in the 1960s and 1970s between those who wished to keep 'knowledge' and 'skills' in separate compartments, and those like A. E. Musson and Eric Robinson who thought that such a differentiation

---

[18] See Jacob and Stewart, *Practical Matter*, chapters 1, 2, 3.

was quite untenable.[19] The object of the debate in this case was not the Enlightenment, but the contribution made by science to the causes of the Industrial Revolution. A. E. Musson, in particular, rejected out of hand the idea that a workable distinction could be drawn between the educated 'scientist' and the uneducated technologist. His view is substantially endorsed by Donald Cardwell in his depiction of the self-serving myth of the scientist who 'hands down his discoveries to the technologist who thereupon finds an application for them'.[20] In any case, evidence extracted from travel accounts and the epistolary correspondence of European *savants* scarcely allows this distinction to stand, as this study of 'industrial' Enlightenment in the English Midlands will demonstrate. Eighteenth-century visitors to Birmingham were in agreement that James Keir, James Watt and Matthew Boulton – to name only the individuals mentioned thus far – possessed both a great deal of 'pure' scientific knowledge and an uncommon level of technical skill.

Since the 1970s Musson's speculation about the degree to which the Industrial Revolution was 'knowledge induced'[21] has proved more fruitful than even he could have imagined. Why? Because this is the direction in which scholars as diverse as Joel Mokyr and Margaret Jacob have moved. Mokyr's views will be discussed below, but Jacob's conviction that the Enlightenment acted as the midwife to the modern world via the agency of 'scientific culture' owes much to Musson – even if it does not harness together the theory of science and the practice of technology in any neatly causal way. The problem that remains is one which Musson also anticipated. If, as Jacob and Stewart believe, the growth in the second half of the eighteenth century of 'a broad public audience interested in mechanical laws had significant consequences for the process of industrialization',[22] it ought to be possible to document the 'transitional'[23] phase. How did the to-ing and fro-ing from laboratory to workshop which T. S. Ashton[24] espied as long ago as 1948 actually take place? And how was the sophisticated understanding of mechanical laws and chemical reactions that a Keir, a Watt or a Boulton

[19] See A. E. Musson and Eric Robinson, *Science and Technology in the Industrial Revolution* (Manchester: Manchester University Press, 1969); A. E. Musson (ed.), *Science, Technology and Economic Growth in the Eighteenth Century* (London: Methuen, 1972).

[20] D. S. L. Cardwell, 'Science, technology and industry', in G. S. Rousseau and R. Porter (eds), *The Ferment of Knowledge: Studies in the Historiography of Eighteenth-Century Science* (Cambridge: Cambridge University Press, 1980), p. 480.

[21] Musson, *Science, Technology and Economic Growth*, p. 39.

[22] Jacob and Stewart, *Practical Matter*, p. 93.

[23] Musson, *Science, Technology and Economic Growth*, p. 66.

[24] T. S. Ashton, *The Industrial Revolution, 1760–1830* (Oxford: Oxford University Press, 1948), p. 16.

clearly possessed put there in the first place? The chapters that follow will attempt to answer these questions.

Underscoring all of these developments is the appealing image of the uninhibited eighteenth-century consumer who both drove demand and responded to entrepreneurial blandishments and initiatives. Whilst economic historians have tended to pooh-pooh the notion that the century gave birth to anything so specific as a 'consumer revolution', others remain convinced that they can detect significant shifts in patterns and habits of consumption – particularly towards the end of the period. In all of the fields of enquiry discussed thus far – the Scientific Revolution, the Enlightenment and that of industrial technology – the role of the consumer bulks large in scholarly investigations. It is obvious, for example, that much of what the historians of science have to say about the relevance of scientific knowledge in the eighteenth century presupposes the active presence of the consumer, whether as a subscriber to experimental philosophy lectures or as a devourer of scientific literature at the great continental book fairs. G. S. Rousseau[25] has reminded us that there was no archetypal customer. In the English-speaking world, at least, they were drawn from all literate backgrounds. Robert Darnton's[26] reconstruction of the commercial underpinnings of the Enlightenment also thrust the consumer onto centre stage. In fact, it was very largely his work that provided the spur and the incentive to relativise the phenomenon in the 1970s. Of greater interest in the present context, however, is the attempt by Maxine Berg[27] and others to bring the consumer back into the story of industrialisation. Since her approach helps to make sense of what was happening in eighteenth-century Birmingham and the West Midlands, it is worth exploring the arguments put forward in more detail.

During the century or so following the Restoration a new form of consumer behaviour took shape in England, or so we are told. It was rooted in enhanced levels of affluence permeating all social strata; in a more hedonistic approach towards material possessions, particularly textile, metallic, ceramic and cut-glass wares; in entrepreneurship; and in emulation. To those economic historians who have objected that

[25] G. S. Rousseau, 'Science books and their readers in the eighteenth century', in I. Rivers (ed.), *Books and their Readers in Eighteenth-Century England* (Leicester: Leicester University Press, 1982), pp. 197–255.

[26] R. Darnton, *The Business of the Enlightenment: a Publishing History of the Encyclopédie, 1776–1800* (Cambridge, Mass: Harvard University Press, 1979).

[27] M. Berg, 'In pursuit of luxury: global history and British consumer goods in the eighteenth century', *Past and Present*, 182 (February 2004), 85–142; *idem, Luxury and Pleasure in Eighteenth-Century Britain* (Oxford: Oxford University Press, 2005).

standards of living remained static throughout the early phase of industrialisation, the answer is given that aggregate data do not capture the
whole story and, in any case, the middling classes of provincial England
were manifestly increasing in numbers and spending power during this
period. Even if real incomes remained relatively stable for the bulk of
the population, it is further argued – on evidence drawn mainly from
the researches of Jan de Vries[28] – that ordinary families were learning
how to organise household economic activity more efficiently and to
reallocate expenditures. Entrepreneurs such as Matthew Boulton and
Josiah Wedgwood who were heavily engaged in the consumer-goods industries both responded to these commercial opportunities and actively
intervened in the market-place to stimulate and shape demand. A. E.
Musson[29] noted the reality of this speculative activity many years ago –
at a time when most economic historians thought of technological innovation as entirely demand led. But he did not draw out its implications
for consumer behaviour. Maxine Berg insists that the new propensity
to consume should be linked specifically to a taste for novelties, luxury
and semi-luxury products and, above all, fashion goods.

This is a plausible scenario, for England at least, and one in which
much of the qualitative and visual evidence appears to contradict the
macro-economic data. The Saxon traveller Christian Goede noted on
his arrival from Paris in 1802 that in the French capital it had been
easy to judge social status from dress, whereas 'in England it is scarcely
possible to know a lord from a tradesman, a man of letters from a
mechanic; and this seems to arise from the sovereignty of fashion in
the metropolis'.[30] Fashion and luxury consumption unquestionably
belong to the history of industrial technology and the eighteenth-
century knowledge economy, then. But whether they belong in any causal
sense to the history of the Industrial Revolution, as Maxine Berg con-
tends, is another matter. Fortunately this is not our primary concern.
When directed towards what we know was taking place in Birmingham
and the West Midlands, her cultural analysis of the 'product revolution'
makes good sense. As we will see, Matthew Boulton's Soho Manufactory
was not just a monument to Georgian England's consumer culture; it

---

[28] See J. de Vries, 'Between purchasing power and the world of goods: understanding the household economy in early modern Europe', in J. Brewer and R. Porter (eds),
Consumption and the World of Goods (London: Routledge, 1993), pp. 98–132; *idem*, 'The
Industrial Revolution and the industrious revolution', *Journal of Economic History*, 54 (1994),
249–70.

[29] Musson, *Science, Technology and Economic Growth*, p. 42.

[30] C. A. G. Goede, *The Stranger in England or Travels in Great Britain*, 3 vols (London,
1807), ii, p. 83.

was a place where science, technological dexterity and tastefulness were brought into close alignment. In common with other Birmingham manufacturers, Boulton and his several partners devoted a great deal of thought to the conception and creation of new products, and they would often customise their wares in order to sell them into different markets. Whilst some foreign visitors found Boulton's goods rather showy, even 'populuxe', all were impressed by the speed and ingenuity with which he was able to cater for, and even anticipate, the whim of fashion.

As the traditional categories within which scholars have conducted their investigations of the eighteenth century continue to shudder and slip, signs are beginning to emerge of a realignment. It is in this context that the views of Joel Mokyr,[31] who has written extensively about the processes attendant on industrialisation, merit consideration. Although historians of science such as Jacob and Stewart, students of the Enlightenment such as Porter and economic historians such as Berg each tackle the knowledge dynamic of the eighteenth century from a different angle, they share much in common with Mokyr in his effort to establish a set of technological preconditions for economic growth. The problem is how to explain the onset of sustained industrialisation in the early nineteenth century if economic demand factors are set to one side. This is a big 'if', many investigators would no doubt retort. After a decade of musing on this question, however, Mokyr responds by prioritising the role of knowledge, and, to a lesser degree, institutions. In his book *The Gifts of Athena* (2002) he sets out an argument which explains how 'useful knowledge' comes into being, is added to, and is, in due course, optimised for the purposes of industrialisation. The argument is largely theoretical, but certainly more rigorous than the murky generalisations that have often accompanied attempts to define the transcendent rationality of the Enlightenment 'mind'. Economists who are willing to attach some weight to 'applied' knowledge (technology) as an explanatory variable will be encouraged by the precision of Mokyr's thinking in this area. As for historians, they are more likely to want to know whether the theory can help to explain what they observe taking place in specific contexts.

If we are to understand properly the role of 'useful knowledge', it should be divided into its component parts: 'what' and 'how' knowledge. Propositional or 'what' knowledge Mokyr considers to be both formal, encoded scientific knowledge and informal, tacit or folk wisdom, whereas 'how' knowledge can best be understood as prescriptive or

[31] J. Mokyr, *The Gifts of Athena: Historical Origins of the Knowledge Economy* (Princeton: Princeton University Press, 2002).

instructional data. A discovery would be a contribution to the stock of 'what' knowledge, therefore. On the other hand, an invention adds to mankind's store of 'how' knowledge, since it embodies a recipe or technique. Additions to the latter can, and do, occur independently, he will allow, but when they do, they cannot evolve in a productive direction, since the fundamental understanding (i.e. why a technique works) is lacking. The breadth of the epistemic base is really the key, then, together with environmental conditions that conduce to the interaction of the two types of knowledge. In the right conditions, indeed, he envisages that 'positive feedback' will occur as improvements in techniques trigger a fresh round of advances in propositional knowledge. The 'useful knowledge' in pursuit of which so many members of Europe's travelling intelligentsia set out in the eighteenth century can be regarded, therefore, as a combination and amalgamation of these knowledge subsets.

In what historic conditions might such a combination take place? Here Mokyr joins forces with the historians of science and specialists in material culture such as Berg, for he looks to eighteenth-century Europe in order to find the 'tap-root'[32] of economic progress. The Scientific Revolution hugely enlarged the quantity of propositional knowledge in circulation and, thanks to the Enlightenment, accelerated the process whereby it could be converted into know-how. This conversion process or 'mapping function'[33] remains implicit rather than explicit in his theory and, as such, calls for further analysis. Nevertheless, Mokyr is so convinced that the crucial technological desiderata for self-sustaining growth came into alignment during this period that he creates a whole new analytical category dubbed 'industrial enlightenment'. In the eighteenth century – and more especially in its second half – a new, open-minded scientific culture came into being, as we have noted. The method of trial by experiment rather than by reference to authority or received wisdom triumphed, and access costs to indispensable propositional knowledge declined significantly. Industrial Enlightenment can therefore be said to have acted as midwife to Industrial Revolution.

And it did so first and foremost in Britain. This was not because Britain's propositional knowledge base was indisputably larger than that existing anywhere else in the western world by the end of the eighteenth century, but because England and Lowland Scotland possessed the greatest number of sites in which the interactions presupposed by the term Industrial Enlightenment could take place. Mokyr mentions in passing

---

[32] *Ibid.*, p. 28.
[33] *Ibid.*, p. 18.

some of the institutional advantages that Britain appears to have enjoyed to a greater degree than anywhere else (weak guilds, strong links between science practitioners and provincial elites, etc.), and it would be easy to list others. Late eighteenth-century Britain's public champions of science and scientific method would be a case in point. The first and foremost was Dr Joseph Priestley, who was indefatigable in his pronouncements on good practice in science, as on good practice in theology. Commenting sceptically on animal magnetism in 1791, he reminded a correspondent that 'everything should be brought to the test of fair and repeated experiment'.[34] The adumbration of useful knowledge was not significantly impeded by social constraints in Britain either. When the French astronomer Jérôme Lalande[35] arrived in London in 1763 he was struck by the fact that skilled craftsmen (clock-makers, jewellers, etc.) rubbed shoulders with *savants*. Indeed, he noted that some of the former had even been elected to the Royal Society. Since Mokyr's book appeared, Trevor Levere[36] and Gerard Turner have also published the proceedings of the Chapter Coffee House Philosophical Society, which contain hard evidence of how, in the London of the 1780s, 'conversations' about experimental philosophy brought natural philosophers and manufacturers into close contact with one another. This is an important, and probably the most important, interface if the Industrial Enlightenment thesis is to withstand scholarly scrutiny.

Many economic historians would rebel at the suggestion that the modern industrial economy finds its origins chiefly in the expansion of human knowledge rather than vice versa, of course. Knowledge determinism on this scale leaves little room for demand factors, or material incentives to keep the supply of technological improvements flowing. But for present purposes these large questions can be put to one side. It is the relevance of Mokyr's scenario to developments in the second half of the eighteenth and the early nineteenth centuries which is at issue here. In this connection three criticisms might be directed at the Industrial Enlightenment thesis. For a start, the neat distinction between propositional and prescriptive knowledge seems to belong more to the realm of theory than that of reality. Oral and hands-on knowledge, for instance, sits rather uneasily alongside 'pure' scientific knowledge

[34] J. T. Rutt, *Life and Correspondence of Joseph Priestley*, 2 vols (London: Hunter and Eaton, 1831–32), ii, p. 112, J. Priestley to Rev. J. Bretland, Birmingham, 26 June 1791.
[35] J. Lalande, *Journal d'un voyage en Angleterre 1763, publié avec introduction par Hélène Monod-Cassidy* (Oxford: Voltaire Foundation, 1980), p. 12.
[36] T. H. Levere and G. L'E. Turner, *Discussing Chemistry and Steam: the Minutes of a Coffee House Philosophical Society, 1780–1787* (Oxford: Oxford University Press, 2002).

– the more so as such wisdom would not be swiftly codified, whether in the eighteenth or the nineteenth centuries. Mokyr seems to acknowledge the difficulty, for in practice propositional knowledge is for most purposes depicted as 'science'.[37] But this raises the suspicion, in turn, that his formulation does not so much transcend the traditional 'science' versus 'technology' polarity as rephrase it.

A second criticism that empirically minded historians might choose to raise concerns the manner in which Mokyr tackles the issue of the contextualisation of knowledge. When compared with his early study of industrialisation in the Low Countries between 1795 and 1850,[38] *The Gifts of Athena* displays a much greater willingness to accept the role of cultural factors in the shaping and dissemination of knowledge. Yet throughout he holds on to his belief in the fundamental indivisibility of the western world, in which the size of the propositional knowledge base is the essential driver of progress. This introduces a tension into the book which surfaces, for example, in a reluctance to follow the science historians the whole of the way, whether in their relativising approach to knowledge or in their quest to uncover disparate scientific cultures. Mokyr's own view of the matter seems to be that 'tacit' knowledge was quickly incorporated into the canon of encoded and stored knowledge – thanks to the Industrial Enlightenment – and as a result the all-important data on which technological progress was predicated could easily move across boundaries and national frontiers. Cultural filters do not count for much, apparently, and nor does the fact that the know-how component of useful knowledge was often constituted in such a way as to prevent or deter transfer from person to person and from place to place. From an Enlightenment point of view the west European free-flow knowledge environment certainly *ought* to have existed, it is true. Our study of the social mechanics of Industrial Enlightenment in Birmingham and the West Midlands will show, however, that theory and practice were not always congruent in this area.

A third remark which comes to mind when putting Mokyr's scenario to the test is less a criticism than an observation, and a plea for greater flexibility in the analysis. As mentioned earlier, the critical proving ground for the Industrial Enlightenment thesis must be the interactive process whereby useful knowledge is generated, and which Mokyr embodies as 'communication between the *savants* and the *fabricants*'.[39]

---

[37] Mokyr, *The Gifts of Athena*, p. 35.

[38] J. Mokyr, *Industrialisation in the Low Countries, 1795–1850* (New Haven: Yale University Press, 1976).

[39] Mokyr, *The Gifts of Athena*, p. 54.

Yet he acknowledges that this process is not well understood, describing it as 'one of the more elusive historical phenomena'.[40] Part of the problem is undoubtedly the lack of case-study evidence capable of revealing how the latent potential of propositional knowledge could be transformed into inventions and innovative technological applications. But there is a problem of conception, too, inasmuch as he posits what may turn out to be a false dichotomy. The problem of communication through the interface is much reduced if the persona of the *savant* and the persona of the *fabricant* are one and the same. This seems likely, after all. Mokyr himself unhesitatingly labels Josiah Wedgwood 'the embodiment of the Industrial Enlightenment',[41] and it has long been known that the Staffordshire potter was also an accomplished chemist. If not actually a regular attender of Lunar Society soirées, he certainly met and corresponded with most of the members of the group. We know, too, that he tried to keep abreast of the Continent-wide debates among natural philosophers, albeit at one remove. In 1771 he informed his partner, Thomas Bentley, that he had purchased a copy of Macquer's chemical dictionary, which James Keir had just translated.[42]

Once we set off in search of individuals who combined the roles of *savant* and *fabricant*, they prove relatively straightforward to identify, in Britain at least. James Keir would be an obvious candidate, as would Matthew Boulton and James Watt. Foreign s*avants* visiting England knew perfectly well who these men were, and they tended to make a bee-line for them. On his arrival in Britain in the spring of 1782, Alessandro Volta[43] headed off to Birmingham in order to make the personal acquaintance of Priestley, Boulton and Watt. At Manchester he met Thomas Henry, industrial chemist and secretary of the newly established Literary and Philosophical Society, Henry Percival, and the industrial dyer, Charles Taylor. Thereafter, he proceeded to Ketley near Coalbrookdale in order to pay a call on William Reynolds, the Quaker ironmaster, who possessed a laboratory and collection of mineralogical specimens. If we leave to one side the West Midlands group whose role in the generation and

[40] *Ibid.*, p. 18.

[41] *Ibid.*, p. 52; in a subsequent revisiting of the question, he explicitly allows for this possibility, see J. Mokyr, 'The intellectual origins of modern economic growth', *Journal of Economic History*, 65 (2005), 321.

[42] *Letters of Wedgwood*, 3 vols (Manchester and Stoke-on-Trent: privately printed, n.d.), ii, p. 55.

[43] *Epistolario di Alessandro Volta. Edizione nazionale sotto gli auspice dell'Istituto Lombardo di scienze et lettere e della società italiana di fisic,* 5 vols. (Bologna, 1949–55), ii, p. 469; also G. Pancaldi, *Volta: Science and Culture in the Age of Enlightenment* (Princeton: Princeton University Press, 2003), pp. 160–3.

propagation of useful knowledge will be explored in the pages to follow, Charles Taylor,[44] the Manchester textile industrialist, probably best
personifies the qualities of both *savant* and *fabricant*. When seeking an
endorsement from Matthew Boulton for the secretaryship of the Society
of Arts in 1799, he recited his qualifications for the job: he spoke French
and German, he had toured Europe's textile districts and had established
personal contact with many luminaries of the Continent (Beaume,
Berthollet, Broussonet, Descroizilles, Guyot, Holker, Ingenhouz, Landriani, Lavoisier, Macquer, Magellan and Werner were all mentioned).
In addition, he claimed to have brought back the secret of Adrianople
Red from France, and to have introduced numerous improvements in
the preparation, bleaching and dyeing of cottons, linens and woollens.

If scientifically informed industrialists and entrepreneurs were as
numerous in late-eighteenth century England as these preliminary
remarks seem to indicate, it follows that sites where experimentation
and manufacturing took place must also have been quite common.
Mokyr's *savant–fabricant* interface starts to look a good deal less problematic, therefore. Or at the very least, it should be susceptible to analysis in those cases where collections of relevant family and business
papers have survived. In this respect as in others, specialists in the
cultural history of science are leading the way. Detailed research into
the Wedgwood and Boulton papers has already begun, and the hunt
is on for similar archival holdings that might enable us to put Mokyr's
thesis about the origins of the knowledge economy under the microscope.[45] Does this mean, therefore, that the concept of 'industrial
enlightenment' passes muster as a useful tool, notwithstanding the
caveats entered above? Yes, undoubtedly. Although *The Gifts of Athena*
has a remit that extends far beyond the scope of the present study,
it explores the destinies of Europeans at the end of the eighteenth
century in terms which the actors themselves would have understood.
Ideas were the common currency of the Enlightenment generation. Until
revolution and war sharply curtailed the cultural practices of Europe's
intelligentsia and shattered the myth of cosmopolitanism, the confident
belief that knowledge would take root, no matter what soil it was planted
in, was never seriously contested. As Samuel Galton junior, the longest
surviving member of the Lunar group, would put it in a remark to his
son which combined Bacon's dictum with a parental admonition to

---

[44] BCL MS 3782/12/44 Matthew Boulton: General Correspondence, C. Taylor to
M. Boulton, London, 12 November 1799.

[45] In this connection, see Jacob and Stewart, *Practical Matter*, pp. 127–38.

improve his grasp of French: 'songez-y mon cher Howard, Knowledge is Power'.[46]

Passing through Birmingham on his way back to Burslem, Josiah Wedgwood reported to his partner in the spring of 1767 that he had taken the opportunity to pay a call on Matthew Boulton. Two years earlier Boulton had completed the transfer of his workshops from the centre of the town to a purpose-built site at Soho on Handsworth Heath, two miles to the north-west. From his elegant residence adjacent to the manufactory, Boulton began to plan a diversification of his industrial activities to embrace a range of tasteful consumer products for which demand, on the morrow of the Seven Years' War, was booming. Wedgwood recognised in Boulton a man of his own stamp: 'He is I believe the first – or most complete manufacturer in England, in metal. He is very ingenious, Philosophical, Agreable.'[47] Both in fact were men of a new type. In their unfussy conviviality, their lack of dogmatism, their sponge-like capacity to absorb new ideas and new techniques and their commercial vision, they exemplified much that was typical of the way in which the Enlightenment manifested itself in Britain. Their outlook and activities encapsulate, moreover, the distinctive features of the phenomenon which Joel Mokyr and others have labelled 'industrial enlightenment' – Boulton even more so, perhaps, than Wedgwood. During the third and fourth quarters of the eighteenth century Birmingham and the West Midlands became one of the prime sites in the western world for the production of useful knowledge. How 'polite' science, 'hard' science and 'industrial' science were blended together in a context of confident Enlightenment consumerism will be the central problematic of this book, therefore.

The fact that the investigation can be undertaken at all owes everything to the survival of a rich archive pivoted on the activities that took place in and around the Soho Manufactory between 1765 and 1820.[48] Although the archive is remembered by scholars chiefly for its holdings of the papers and technical drawings of the Boulton & Watt steam-engine partnership, it also contains ample records of nearly all of the ornamental and consumer goods businesses in which Matthew Boulton

---

[46] BCL MS 3101/C/D/10/9 S. Galton jnr to J. H. Galton, Birmingham, 10 February 1811.

[47] *Letters of Josiah Wedgwood*, i, p. 141, J. Wedgwood to T. Bentley, 23 May 1767; also B. Dolan, *Josiah Wedgwood: Entrepreneur to the Enlightenment* (London: Harper, 2004), p. 227

[48] Known as the Archives of Soho, these materials can be found in the Birmingham City Archives, Floor 7, Central Library, Chamberlain Square, Birmingham, B3 3HQ, United Kingdom.

and his several partners were engaged. In addition, the archive brings
together the personal and family papers of the two key players: Matthew
Boulton and James Watt. This is the material that forms the bedrock
of our study. After much experimentation, in which James Keir was
also involved, Watt, in 1780, patented the first truly reliable means of
reproducing letters – with the result that the archive boasts substantial
runs of both outgoing and incoming correspondence. As John Heilbron[49]
has observed, letters provide a brilliant yet all too often under-utilised
means of gaining access to the scientific culture of a period, or a region.
In this case we have over 20,000 such items at our disposal. The same
point can be made with respect to foreign travellers' accounts and diaries,
of which large numbers exist for the latter part of the eighteenth century. Written for the most part in French, German, Italian, Danish and
Swedish, they, too, are a neglected source of information about the circulation of both natural and useful knowledge throughout Europe.

The Soho episode played out on the doorstep of Birmingham can
therefore be said to open a window onto the traffic of ideas, objects
and practices that all of Europe shared in, or wished to share in, during
the second half of the eighteenth century. Within a westerly radius of
perhaps twenty or thirty miles, a creative community of experimental
philosophers, liberal professionals, entrepreneurs and manufacturers
took shape, and it maintained close links, we know, with equivalent communities in Manchester, Glasgow, Edinburgh and London. But beyond
these centres the knowledge generators and circulators were scattered
and their impact dilute, or muffled. On the Continent, only Paris could
boast a critical mass that was comparable. Yet when Matthew Boulton
spent several weeks in the French capital during the winter of 1786–87
he found the apparent public interest in science and the no less apparent failure of scientific knowledge accumulation to trigger technological
improvement to be something of a conundrum. Some of Boulton's or
Watt's overseas correspondents would complain that they inhabited an
experimental wasteland, in fact. In Poland and parts of southern Italy
contact with a fellow Newtonian would have been extraordinary, and
interaction with a technologist or a manufacturer unthinkable. This
should give us pause for thought when we come to consider the suggestion that industrial progress on the Continent was driven forward
by a small group – no more than a few thousand in number – of knowledge facilitators and appliers. Such men could not have formed a community in any proximate, physical sense. Nor does it seem likely that

---

[49] J. L. Heilbron, 'Experimental natural philosophy', in Rousseau and Porter (eds),
The Ferment of Knowledge, p. 386.

they were the only agents involved in the process, save perhaps in the Scandinavian states, which were heavily reliant on technological knowledge transfer.[50] Industrial Enlightenment appears to fit best as a characterisation of what was taking place in eighteenth-century Britain, therefore. Yet it remains for us to demonstrate exactly how 'a nation of Newtons and Lockes became a nation of Boultons and Watts'.[51]

[50] See D. Ch. Christensen, *Det Moderne Projekt: Teknik & Kultur I Danmark-Norge, 1750–(1814)–1850* (Copenhagen: Gyldendal, 1996), p. 806.

[51] P. Langford, *Englishness Identified: Manners and Character, 1650–1850* (Oxford: Oxford University Press, 1992), p. 76.

2

Birmingham
and the West Midlands

The phrase 'Birmingham and the West Midlands' is an anachronism when applied to the period covered by this book. Whilst the expanding physical presence of the town of Birmingham drew frequent comment from travellers in the second half of the eighteenth century, none would have recognised an entity labelled the West Midlands. Indeed, it is doubtful whether contemporaries would even have acknowledged an area of the country called 'the Midlands'. Neither guide books nor trade directories shed much light in this respect, although the phrase 'Birmingham and District' appears to have been in fairly widespread use by the century's end. The notion of the Black Country, that is to say, a crude rectangle of territory bounded by Wolverhampton and Walsall to the north and Smethwick, Halesowen and Stourbridge to the south, is also an anachronism, since the expression cannot be traced back beyond the 1840s.[1] Without a clear-cut perception of physical space, there is no reason to suppose that a historic sense of regional identity existed either. Even historians of Birmingham – the most sharply etched feature in this otherwise indeterminate landscape – seem unconvinced of the case for an urban identity.[2] Only with the advent of parliamentary reform and anti-Corn Law agitation in the second decade of the nineteenth century did the townspeople of Birmingham grow accustomed to speaking with one voice. Why, then, do we couple together 'Birmingham'

[1] See W. Gresley, *Colton Green, a Tale of the Black Country* (London, 1847); also R. H. Trainor, *Black Country Elites: the Exercise of Authority in an Industrialised Area, 1830–1900* (Oxford: Clarendon Press, 1993), pp. 1–3 and figure.

[2] J. Money, *Experience and Identity: Birmingham and the West Midlands, 1760–1800* (Montreal: McGill-Queen's University Press, 1977) and the discussion in H. Berry and J. Gregory (eds), *Creating and Consuming Culture in North-East England, 1660–1830* (Aldershot: Ashgate, 2004), pp. 2–4.

and the 'West Midlands' in a single phrase? There are two possible answers, the second of which is the more persuasive. Historians, in common with geographers, like to identify regions for rhetorical purposes, that is to say, as convenient frameworks within which to carry out analysis. In so doing, however, they run the risk of assuming that which they are seeking to prove. The alternative is to use concepts which have a rather anachronistic ring to them as retrospective tools with which to mount an investigation. This is the approach adopted here. The West Midlands, it will be suggested, was a constructed, not a natural entity, and the motive force in the building process was the dynamism of the town of Birmingham. By the end of the eighteenth century Birmingham had become the hub of a highly integrated regional economy. The Black Country and the West Midlands as understood today should be regarded, therefore, as the product of a transition towards spatial and economic integration which culminated towards the middle decades of the nineteenth century.

The regional setting

The first point that needs to be borne in mind when discussing the regional context is that neither Birmingham nor the towns that would become its satellites were fashioned according to any pre-existing administrative template. In his study of the rise of the Midlands industries, W. H. B. Court[3] described 'Birmingham and District' as a smallish area of some 200 square miles made up of parts (parts of south Staffordshire, north Warwickshire, and east Worcestershire). Birmingham township grew up at the point where these three counties intersected, but he cautions that this district or mini-region was not sufficient unto itself. As an area increasingly defined by metal-working, its manufacturers maintained close links with the coal and iron industries of east Shropshire (Coalbrookdale) and, to a lesser extent, with the Warwickshire coal-field situated between Nuneaton and Coventry. Apart from the county towns (Stafford, Warwick, Worcester), about which more will be said in a moment, only Coventry offered an alternative regional focus and economic role model. But Coventry was a textile town (ribbon weaving) and by the eighteenth century was plainly living on its past. Most visitors to Birmingham and the West Midlands travelled through Coventry, if only

[3] W. H. B. Court, *The Rise of the Midlands Industries, 1600–1838* (Oxford: Oxford University Press, 1938), p. 2.

for the reason that the main London–Holyhead road passed along its high street, yet they had little reason to linger there. As recent research[4] has demonstrated, there existed a clear functional contrast between West and East Midlands by the end of the eighteenth century – even if those terms had yet to be invented. The notional line of differentiation skirted round the silk ribbon-weaving villages and crossed the highway at a point roughly equidistant between Coventry and Birmingham.

How, then, was this previously unrecognised collection of metal-working towns and villages fashioned into a region identifiable in its own terms? One approach might be to highlight a favourable natural resource endowment comprising coal, iron-ore, limestone and fireclays which established parameters for the development of an energy-rich regional economy along the lines proposed by Tony Wrigley.[5] The explosive population growth after mid century and the emergence of distinctively new types of towns within the orbit of Birmingham certainly conforms to the expectations of this model. Observations made at the time provide some support for an energy-driven explanation of growth as well. Barthélemy Faujas de Saint-Fond, who visited Matthew Boulton at Soho in 1784, concluded that it was the abundance of coal which had produced the 'miracle'[6] of Birmingham, while Alessandro Volta's[7] remarks on his tour through the Black Country and Coalbrookdale two years earlier can be construed in a similar vein.

Yet it should be remembered that Birmingham – at mid century – was not on the beaten track. Travellers had to leave the main highway about ten miles west of Coventry in order to gain access to the town. Nor did it enjoy the benefits of river communication, inasmuch as the Severn, whilst navigable as far as Shrewsbury, was nearly twenty miles distant. The natural endowment argument will only take us so far, then, as Wrigley himself acknowledges. The spur or trigger which helped to unlock this mineral wealth and launch the region upon an extraordinary industrial trajectory must be sought elsewhere. Economic geographers argue that transportation innovations provide the key to regional growth and differentiation in the late eighteenth and early nineteenth centuries.

---

[4] See J. Stobart and N. Raven (eds), *Towns, Regions and Industries: Urban and Industrial Change in the Midlands, c. 1700–1840* (Manchester: Manchester University Press, 2005), p. 16.

[5] E. A. Wrigley, *Continuity and Change: the Character of the Industrial Revolution* (Cambridge: Cambridge University Press, 1988), chapter 3.

[6] B. Faujas de Saint-Fond, *A Journey through England and Scotland to the Hebrides in 1784*, 2 vols. (Glasgow: Hopkins, 1907), ii, p. 346.

[7] *Epistolario di Alessandro Volta*, ii, pp. 119, 469–73; also Pancaldi, *Volta: Science and Culture*, pp. 160–2.

The turnpiking of highways and the construction of canals and river navigations promoted spatial integration, facilitated the expansion of intra-regional trade and credit networks, and improved long-distance communication beyond and between regional centres. According to this scenario Birmingham actively remedied its relative isolation, therefore, and in the process a dense 'region' with a specific hardware vocation came into being.

Disentangling the causal sequence linking transport improvements to urbanisation and industrialisation is not a straightforward matter, of course. Moreover, it could be objected that Birmingham, if not the still-microscopic Black Country industrial villages, was already firmly set upon a pattern of growth before the introduction, after the middle of the century, of significant improvements to land and water transportation. Nevertheless, this argument has much to recommend it at the regional level. Turnpiking came early and vigorously to the West Midlands, and it does seem to have been a response to pre-existing heavy road usage – particularly the roads frequented by the huge eight-horse wagons hauling industrial raw materials. Even though Birmingham required a detour, travellers had a choice of two fully turnpiked routes from London as early as 1740. The same may be said of canal building, in which the activism of local manufacturers such as Josiah Wedgwood, Matthew Boulton and Samuel Garbett was very much to the fore. All three had excellent commercial motives for promoting canal construction, whether to facilitate the movement of raw materials or to secure access to national and international markets for their finished products.

Work on the Grand Trunk canal, which was intended to link the Trent and the Mersey rivers, began in 1766. Wedgwood was one of its chief backers and took care to acquire land for his new factory at Etruria in Staffordshire on the proposed route of the waterway. Not until 1777, however, did unimpeded navigation along its entire 140-mile length become possible. In the meantime Boulton and the other Birmingham manufacturers lobbied for a navigable link of more immediate value, namely one which would connect the town's industries to their fuel sources in the Black Country. In 1768 the Birmingham Canal Bill passed both houses of Parliament, thereby enabling the construction of a water-way through the Black Country to Aldersley, north of Wolverhampton, with a view to joining up with the Staffordshire and Worcestershire canal. Whilst such a link would make it possible to bring in pit-coal, pig-iron and other raw materials by barge rather than by overland transport, it would also provide a convenient exit route for Birmingham wares via the Stour to the Severn and on to Bristol and, in due course, northwards via the Trent and Mersey to either Hull or Liverpool. Within two years the first cargoes were already tying up at the town's brand-new coal wharves and, with the completion of the Staffordshire and Worcestershire canal in 1772, the West Midlands gained its first point of access to the sea. The boost which the rapidly executed Birmingham Canal project gave to the regional economy is hard to over-estimate, likewise the Birmingham–Fazeley canal of 1783, which opened up a shorter route to the port of Hull and the markets of northern Europe. By contrast, the project to build a canal connecting Birmingham to the county town of Worcester, with which it had little in common, took over twenty years to bring to fruition.

The impact of these new arteries on the economic life of the region was immediate. William Hutton, Birmingham's first historian and a contemporary observer, noted how they brought relief to a road network groaning under the weight of industrial traffic. Before the opening of the Birmingham Canal 'it was common to see a train of carriages for miles, to the great destruction of the road, and annoyance of travellers'.[8] They also massively reduced transportation costs for heavy, bulky or, in Wedgwood's case, fragile goods. Wednesbury pit-coal, which had sold in Birmingham for about thirteen shillings per ton before the opening of the twenty-two mile cut, commanded just seven shillings in 1772 and eight shillings and four pence by the time Hutton published the third edition of *An History of Birmingham* in 1795. The capitalists who had financed the venture made the largest return, however. The original £140 shares were changing hands for about £370 in 1782 and £1,170 ten years later. Even allowing for the steady improvements to the road network, which reduced the quickest passenger journey times between London and Birmingham from around two or two and a half days at mid century to as little as fourteen hours from the summer of 1782, carriage by canal or river brought unmistakable cost benefits where goods needed to be moved over long distances. When, at the century's end, Anne Boulton – Matthew Boulton's spinster daughter – wished to transfer furniture she had purchased in London to Birmingham she was quoted eight shillings and sixpence per hundredweight for road haulage, or two shillings and sixpence for transportation entirely by water.[9]

It is important to emphasise that these improvements in the transportation network were regional in focus, however. As John Stobart[10]

    [8] W. Hutton, *An History of Birmingham* (Birmingham: Thomas Pearson, 3rd edn, 1795), p. 402.
    [9] S. Mason, *The Hardware Man's Daughter: Matthew Boulton and his 'Dear Girl'* (Chichester: Phillimore, 2005), p. 168.
    [10] J. Stobart, *The First Industrial Region: North-West England c. 1700–60* (Manchester: Manchester University Press, 2004).

has argued, specialised regional growth was not only generating highly distinctive patterns of industrialisation in this period, it was throwing into sharp relief less well-endowed or less well-developed parts of the country. Thanks to the turnpikes, Matthew Boulton and his partner, James Watt, were able to travel to the French capital via London and Dover in six days during the late autumn of 1786, and letters from Paris to Birmingham routinely took four. Yet the journey to oversee steam-engine erectors in Cornwall required a minimum of eight uncomfortable days on the road, and letters between Truro and Birmingham took up to fifteen. If improvements in communications, combined with a highly favourable natural resource endowment, provide the key explanation of how Birmingham and the Black Country were subsumed into a discrete West Midlands region, then, it is the interlocking quality of the transportation revolution that needs to be highlighted. The testimony of trade directories is particularly useful in this regard, for they enable us to take a look *inside* the embryonic West Midlands at a given moment in time. On this evidence, the principal industrial nodes by the 1790s were Birmingham, Wolverhampton, Walsall, Bilston, Dudley and Stourbridge, inasmuch as the working population of these towns generated nearly two-thirds of the region's output of iron and steel goods. These towns, moreover, were increasingly interconnected, whether by turnpikes, canal cuts, or wagon and carrier services. By the time Pigot's directory[11] was published in 1835, Birmingham boasted 594 carriage departures to thirty-seven destinations each week, and the best-served destinations were those located in its industrial hinterland to the west and the north-west. Communication *between* the towns of the Black Country had also become intensive, particularly between Wolverhampton and Dudley. Nevertheless, 83 per cent of Wolverhampton's scheduled carrier traffic continued to move in the direction of Birmingham.

The Wolverhampton–Birmingham axis was the region's main industrial artery, in fact. When the La Rochefoucauld brothers came to visit Dr Joseph Priestley in 1785, they reported that even at this date the fourteen-mile stretch of road resembled 'one continuous town'.[12] The French military engineer Charles-Pierre Dupin,[13] who had occasion to take the same route in 1816 but at night time, evoked a horizon lit

[11] N. Raven and J. Stobart, 'Networks and Hinterlands: Transport in the Midlands', in Stobart and Raven (eds), *Towns, Regions and Industries*, pp. 86–7.

[12] N. Scarfe, *Innocent Espionage: the La Rochefoucauld Brothers' Tour of England in 1785* (Woodbridge: Boydell, 1995), p. 106.

[13] C. Dupin, *Voyages dans la Grande-Bretagne entrepris relativement aux services publics de la Guerre, de la Marine, et des Ponts et Chaussées en 1816, 1817, 1818 et 1819*, 6 vols in 3 (Paris: Fain, 1820–24), iv, p. 22.

with fire. The nailers' cottages strewn along the highway had mostly been ousted by ironworks, brickworks and forges as a result of the opening of the Birmingham Canal. It was access to this canal that had prompted James Keir to select Tipton Green as the site for his new chemical works in 1781, and in 1795 the Boulton and Watt sons would choose Smethwick as the location for their steam-engine plant (the Soho Foundry) for the same reason. In a plateau district where groundwater was often in short supply, the canal network also fostered the expansion of steam-power technology, inasmuch as factory owners were encouraged to set up their operations canal-side by the prospect of cheap coals *and* a ready water source for their engines. Pumping engines were a virtual pre-requisite for canal development in the region, in any case. One of the earliest orders for Watt's improved steam engine was placed by the proprietors of the Birmingham Canal Company. It was installed at Smethwick in 1776 in order to replenish the supply of water to the locks. All in all, around 1,500 Black Country collieries and ironworks were linked to the canal network by 1798, and by the end of the Napoleonic Wars Birmingham could no longer be considered an out-of-the-way place. Dupin[14] reported eight major roads entering the town and a total of 348 kilometres of canal navigation within a radius of 32 kilometres.

If we shift the focus in order to view the regionalisation of the West Midlands from a demographic point of view, two clear patterns emerge: the explosive growth of the Black Country towns and villages, and the relative stagnation of the non-industrial 'county' towns (see Figure 2.0). The south Staffordshire landscape, which would form the kernel of the Black Country, was in a state of transition in the second half of the eighteenth century. A habitat based on fields, rural lanes, villages and isolated farms whose coherence was still largely agricultural was being gnawed away by unmistakable signs of industrial growth, which was impos-ing its own raison d'être in terms of turnpikes, canal basins and tram-ways. In 1843, at which point this transformation was approaching its zenith, Thomas Tancred described the environment thus:

> the traveller appears never to get out of an interminable village, com-posed of cottages and very ordinary houses. In some directions he may travel for miles, and never be out of sight of numerous two-storied houses . . . These houses, for the most part, are not arranged in continuous streets but are interspersed with blazing furnaces, heaps of burning coal in pro-cess of coking, piles of ironstone calcining, forges, pit-banks, and engine chimneys; the country being besides intersected with canals, crossing each other at different levels; and the small remaining patches of the surface

[14] *Ibid.*, pp. 225–6.

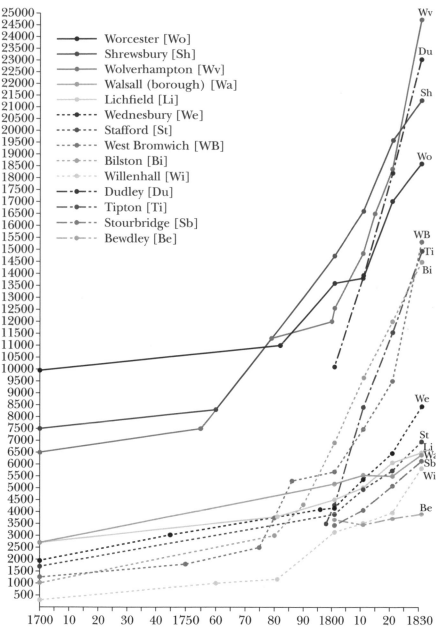

Sources: Census (www.histpop.org/ohpr); Whitehead, 'Georgian Worcester'; Adey, 'Seventeenth-Century Stafford'; Dilworth, *West Bromwich*; Ede, *History of Wednesbury*; Chalklin, *The Provincial Towns*; McInnes, 'The Emergence of a Leisure Town'; Price, *An Historical Account of Bilston*; Scott, *Stourbridge*; Tildesley, *History of Willenhall*; Hackwood, History of Tipton; Homeshaw, *The Corporation of Walsall*.

2.0 Population growth in the Black Country compared with county towns, 1700–1830

soil occupied with irregular fields of grass or corn, intermingled with heaps of of the refuse of mines or the slag from the blast furnaces.[15]

This picture of a disordered landscape of 'interminable villages' reflects very well one dimension of the process that completely altered the face of the Black Country in the space of five or six decades. Places such as Bilston, Tipton, Willenhall or West Bromwich, which were scarcely more than agricultural, or at best proto-industrial, parishes until the 1770s or the 1780s, suddenly experienced meteoric population growth as demand for basic hardwares soared, and money combined with entrepreneurship unlocked the resources of the subsoil and put into place infrastructure improvements. Bilston's vocation as a centre for the manufacture of ironmongery was settled in 1767, when John 'iron mad' Wilkinson erected the first blast furnace at nearby Bradley. Significantly, a traveller passing through the locality in 1790 described it as one of the largest villages in England, with more than 1,000 houses. Indeed, the population of the parish virtually quadrupled between 1780 and 1821. By this latter date no more than 20 out of 2,509 households were still engaged in agriculture.[16] Tipton, an insignificant parish containing nailers and edge-tool makers, experienced a similar pattern of growth with the arrival of large-scale coal-mining and iron-smelting operations. No census figures exist for the period prior to 1801, but by 1851 the population stood at 24,872, a sixfold increase over 50 years.[17] Willenhall remained a parish substantially made up of proto-industrial lock-makers, by contrast. Not until 1796 was production speeded up by the introduction of an adapted fly-press to stamp out lock parts. Even so a threefold population growth (to 3,523) occurred between 1780 and 1811.[18] Perhaps the starkest transformation happened to West Bromwich, however. A vast and thinly populated parish consisting of hamlets dotted across heathland, it benefited hugely from the kind of infrastructure investment already described. In 1725 the highway to Birmingham in one direction and to Wolverhampton in the other was turnpiked, and the prospect of water-borne transportation materialised in 1769 with the arrival of the canal. Yet the ribbon of nailers' cottages remarked upon by the brothers La Rochefoucauld remained the only visual evidence

[15] *Birmingham and its Regional Setting* (Birmingham: British Association for the Advancement of Science, 1950), p. 241.
[16] G. T. Lawley, *A History of Bilston, in the County of Stafford* (Bilston: Price, 1893), p. 171.
[17] *Birmingham and its Regional Setting*, p. 240.
[18] N. W. Tildesley, *A History of Willenhall* (Willenhall: Willenhall Urban District Council, 1951); also *The Birmingham, Wolverhampton, Walsall, Dudley, Bilston, and Willenhall Directory; or Tradesman's Useful Companion* (Birmingham: 1780), pp. 110–16.

of industrial activity until the 1780s, and most of that was conducted on a 'putting out' basis. Then the mines, blast furnaces and forges started to appear, established often enough by Birmingham entrepreneurs seeking to reposition their activities on or near to the canal. Aided by the enclosure of the parish, its population nearly doubled in the first two decades of the nineteenth century.[19]

The other dimension of the story of regional integration in the Black Country concerns the towns. Wolverhampton, Stourbridge, Walsall and Dudley were all urban centres of some antiquity whose local economies were well placed to take advantage of the opportunities materialising in the second half of the eighteenth century. Wolverhampton's profile of demographic growth was second only to that of Birmingham. In 1801 it was comfortably the second-largest urban centre in the district, having almost doubled in size since the middle of the century to attain around 12,500 inhabitants. Although the township retained an important market function throughout the period of interest to us, metal-working had been the mainstay of its economy since the 1740s, if not earlier. With a coal seam ten yards thick nearby, the opening of the Birmingham Canal was bound to have a huge impact. By 1802 no fewer than forty-two blast furnaces were in operation in, or close to Wolverhampton. 'The neighbourhood for many miles round is like a long straggling village',[20] advised a 1780 trade directory. The growth of Stourbridge on the southern perimeter of the Black Country was less spectacular, to be sure. But, like Wolverhampton, it had a long history – as a prosperous market town, as a centre of woollen cloth manufacture, and latterly as the principal site of the regional glass industry. Unlike any of the other towns mentioned so far, it also provided social sustenance for the local gentry, who were attracted to its race meetings.

Whilst Stourbridge expanded and prospered on the strength of demand for metal-wares (nails, edge-tools, chain, etc.) in common with other Black Country towns, it is glass manufacture which reveals most about the interlocking character of the West Midlands economy by the end of the eighteenth century, however. James Keir moved to the Stourbridge district around 1770 on quitting the army, and it was here as a partner in a glass-works that he launched himself on a new career as both manufacturer and industrial chemist. Having converted an old glass-house at Holloway End near Amblecote into a laboratory, he

[19] J. Stobart and B. Trinder, 'New towns of the industrial coalfields: Burslem and West Bromwich' in Stobart and Raven, *Towns, Regions and Industries*, pp. 123–7; also Trainor, *Black Country Elites*, p. 26.

[20] *The Birmingham, Wolverhampton, Walsall, Dudley, Bilston, and Willenhall Directory*, p. 72.

conducted experiments into the manufacture of lithage (red lead) and set about translating Macquer's *Dictionnaire de chimie*. His observations on the process of annealing in respect of vitreous materials would be communicated to the Royal Society and published in 1776. Until this date, the growth of the industry had been hampered by the lack of a canal link, however, for it was costly to bring in coals, potash and lead overland, and only the coarsest glass products could withstand trans-portation further afield. The cutting of a waterway linking Amblecote to the Staffordshire and Worcestershire canal at Stourton worked a trans-formation, therefore. Visitors to the district in the later 1770s and 1780s noted that the Stourbridge glass men were producing ornamental wares such as spiral-coloured wine glasses and opalescent scent bottles. They were also producing glass inserts for the Birmingham jewellery trade.[21]

Ringing Birmingham and the Black Country to the west and the north were the 'county' towns, that is to say, the long-established municipal and parliamentary boroughs, which were often county seats as well. Whilst it would be overly schematic to juxtapose dynamic industrial towns and stagnant 'county' towns as though industrialisation was a precondi-tion for urban expansion, the fact remains that places like Worcester, Lichfield, Stafford and even the more distant Shrewsbury had a gentler profile of growth in the eighteenth century. On the economic front Worcester probably had most to fear from the rise of Birmingham. Despite its advantageous position on the river Severn, the population of the town only increased by a little over a third across the century.[22] On the other hand, it remained an irresistible magnet for the cultured and the leisured. As the metals and minerals on which the industrial West Midlands depended travelled up-stream to Stourport and Bewdley, Worcester's population prospered from the traffic and spending power of the local gentry and pseudo-gentry. The town boasted all the leisure facilities customarily associated with the notion of a post-Restoration 'urban renaissance':[23] race meetings, concerts, exhibitions, lectures, music

[21] Court, *The Rise of the Midlands Industries*, p. 219; also D. R. Guttery, *From Broad Glass to Cut Crystal: a History of the Stourbridge Glass Industry* (London: Hill, 1956), pp. 83, 106.

[22] See D. Whitehead, 'Georgian Worcester' (MA dissertation, University of Birming-ham, 1976), p. 10; A. Dyer, 'Midlands', in P. Clark (ed.), *The Cambridge Urban History of Britain* (Cambridge: Cambridge University Press, 2000), ii, pp. 106–7; P. Borsay, *The English Urban Renaissance: Culture and Society in the Provincial Town, 1660–1770* (Oxford: Oxford University Press, 1989), p. 206.

[23] Borsay, *The English Urban Renaissance*.

festivals, coffee houses, public gardens and walks, not to forget the regular recreation of acrimonious parliamentary elections. Industrial activity was confined to the china-works, however.

The same may be said of Lichfield, which proudly rested on its laurels only to see the road network reconfigured to its detriment and the canal, and in due course the railway, pass it by. After mid century, long-distance movement by road was increasingly routed through Birmingham rather than Lichfield, and the town's small metal-goods and leather trades likewise relocated. By 1781 the population stood at little more than 3,800, having gained only 1,500 inhabitants since the Restoration.[24] Lichfield, like Worcester, concentrated instead on its status as an ecclesiastical capital and on its capacity to cater for the needs of the well-to-do. The town boasted a range of clubs and societies nurtured mostly by the families of the Anglican clergy, who formed a large component of the resident elite. Unsurprisingly, Dissent had no purchase whatsoever, although Dr Erasmus Darwin, one of England's discreet band of eighteenth-century free thinkers, lived in Lichfield, as did the poetess Anna Seward. James Watt, a man whose background was both solidly mercantile and nonconformist in matters religious (see Chapter 5), had no doubt that 'county' centres such as Worcester and Lichfield were fundamentally different in kind from Birmingham and the straggle of industrial towns and villages of the Black Country. When the natural philosopher Jean-André Deluc sought advice on boarding options for his daughter, Watt cautioned that it would be possible to learn 'common English civility' in Birmingham, but 'politeness must be learned in better company than this town affords'. Polite towns, he volunteered by way of explanation, were places where it would be possible to mix with 'idle' people such as clergymen, lawyers, old maids, widows and country gentlemen, and he directed his correspondent's attention to Worcester and Lichfield, 'both of which are Cathedral towns & have the consequent appendage of Drones etc.'.[25] Samuel Johnson, another denizen of Lichfield, would rebut this charge of idleness by claiming that his home town was full of philosophers: 'we work with our heads, and make the boobies of Birmingham work for us with their hands'.[26]

---

[24] H. Thorpe, *Lichfield: a Study of its Growth and Function* (n.p., n.d.), p. 49; L. Schwarz, 'On the Margins of Industrialisation: Lichfield', in Stobart and Raven (eds), *Towns, Regions and Industries*, pp. 176–86.

[25] BCL MS 3219/4/123 J. Watt snr to J.-A. Deluc, 26 June 1783.

[26] Thorpe, *Lichfield*, p. 53.

Birmingham

The 'miracle birth' of Birmingham should not be viewed purely in eighteenth-century terms as many accounts suggest. It is nonetheless true that only in the eighteenth century does it become possible to capture the town's development in any detail. Birmingham's gestation as a centre of metal-working must be traced back to the sixteenth century at least, for even in Tudor times it was not a village but a middling market town. By the 1670s this market town which had long echoed to the sound of forge hammers was beginning to approach in size the leading 'county' towns of the region. Thereafter, to be sure, an extraordinarily rapid increase in its population took place (see Figure 2.1), even if the precise demographic profile of the town at the start of the eighteenth century remains difficult to determine. William Hutton's[27] computation of 15,032 for 1700 is certainly too high, since C. W. Chalklin[28] found only about 11,400 in the town's principal parish around 1720. A baseline figure of between 7,000 and 8,000 seems more likely. If this estimate can be accepted Birmingham tripled in size during the first half of the century, and tripled again between 1750 and 1791, at which point its demographic expansion was more or less curtailed for a decade. By 1775 Birmingham appears to have become the third most populous town in England (after London and Bristol), its rate of growth exceeding all rivals. Sheffield, another metal-working town, evinced a similar trajectory, albeit from a lower base. Unlike Birmingham, however, Sheffield had a small and poorly integrated hinterland, and no canals before 1819. Manchester, the shock city of the nineteenth century, together with the port of Liverpool, would catch upon Birmingham and then surpass it around the turn of the century.

The trade directories and guide books describe the Birmingham of the third quarter of the eighteenth century as a settlement 'about two Miles in length (including the hamlet of Deritend and Bordsley)', which is 'pleasantly situated on the Side of a Hill forming nearly a half-Moon'.[29] Whilst not inexact, these statements scarcely capture the reality of a town which seems to have resembled a permanent building site from the 1750s onwards. Visitor evidence cannot be relied upon for population

---

[27] Hutton, *An History of Birmingham*, p. 69.

[28] C. W. Chalklin, *The Provincial Towns of Georgian England: a Study of the Building Process, 1740–1820* (London: Arnold, 1974), p. 22.

[29] *The New Birmingham Directory, and Gentleman and Tradesman's Compleat Memorandum Book: Containing a Brief Description of the Town of Birmingham* (Birmingham and London: Swinney, n.d. [1774]), p. 4.

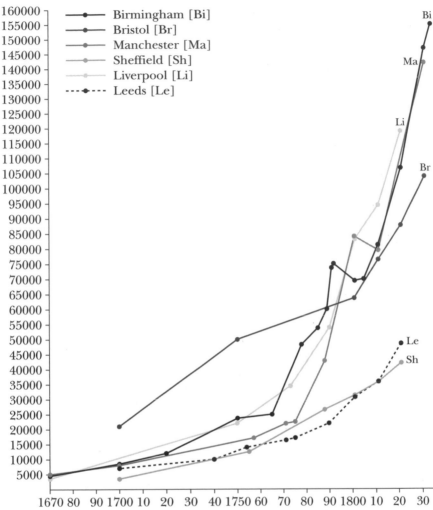

Sources: Census (www.histpop.org/ohpr); Hutton, *An History of Birmingham*; Dent, *Old and New Birmingham*; Langford, *A Century of Birmingham Life*; Beresford and Jones, *Leeds*; Chalklin, *The Provincial Towns*; Clark, *The Cambridge Urban History*; Stobart, *The First Industrial Region*.

2.1 Population growth in Birmingham and comparable
provincial towns, 1670–1820

estimates, but it is quite eloquent on the subject of the visual changes taking place in the town. And in any case, data generated for the purpose of Poor Rates assessment confirm the overall picture of dynamic urbanisation. Birmingham, we learn, consisted of 907 houses configured into fifteen streets laid out along the flank of a hill in 1660. The focal point was the River Rea (little more than a stream) and its crossing point at Deritend, thus aligning the town with the roads arriving from the south. Subsequent residential expansion would mainly take place on the higher ground of the plateau to the north. By 1700 the township embraced over 2,500 houses and twenty-eight streets, figures which had risen to 3,756 and fifty-one respectively by 1731. However, the first in a series of growth spurts which would transform the built environment began in the late 1740s, and by 1781 Birmingham comprised no fewer than 133 streets and 9,536 occupied dwelling houses.[30] Jabez Fisher, a Quaker from Philadelphia who visited during the summer of 1776, reported: 'half the town is new, and they continue to build with greater rapidity than ever'.[31] The onset of conflict in America may have cooled the speculative property market for a spell: the evidence is inconclusive. Matthew Boulton's own expansion at Soho faltered for a time as we shall see. However, the decade after 1781 proved to be the most prosperous in Birmingham's eighteenth-century history, whether measured qualitatively or in terms of demographic and urban growth. Capital for urban development within the private sector was easily raised, and landlords rushed to build street after street of low-rent dwellings for the migrating poor attracted by the town's booming workshops. Sometimes these houses were constructed on the courtyard pattern, which would become a typical feature of Birmingham's urbanisation in the nineteenth century. In the process, of course, open land and gardens became scarcer and the central areas of the town more tightly packed. In 1791 William Hutton calculated that the town contained 12,681 houses and 203 streets, of which 70 (and 3,745 houses) had been added over the previous decade.[32] It was noted, however, that only 1,300 of the 8,000 houses built during the previous thirty years (and only around 25 per cent of the town's total stock of housing) were rated for Poor Relief (see Figure 2.2).[33]

---

[30] See Hutton, *An History of Birmingham*, p. 69; Chalklin, *The Provincial Towns of Georgian England*, p. 229 and *passim*; R. K. Dent, *Old and New Birmingham: a History of the Town and its People*, 2 vols. (East Ardsley, Wakefield: The Scolar Press reprint, 1973), ii, p. 293; J. A. Langford, *A Century of Birmingham Life or a Chronicle of Local Events from 1741 to 1841*, 2 vols. (Birmingham: More & Co., 1870), i, pp. 15, 198, 443, 451.

[31] K. Morgan ed., *An American Quaker in the British Isles: the Travel Journal of Jabez Maud Fisher, 1775–1779*. Records of Social and Economic History, new series XVI. (Published for the British Academy by Oxford University Press, 1992), p. 254.

[32] Hutton, *An History of Birmingham*, p. 69.

[33] Dent, *Old and New Birmingham*, ii, p. 293.

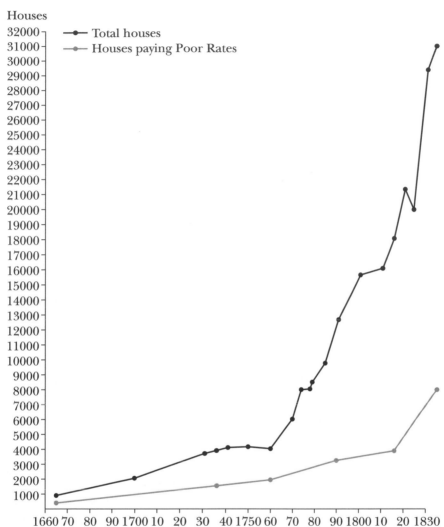

Houses

Sources: BCL 510639 Garbett–Lansdowne correspondence; CP/B Birmingham Rate Books, 1665, 1736, 1760; Hutton, *An History of Birmingham*; Dent, *Old and New Birmingham*; Langford, *A Century of Birmingham Life*; Underdown, 'Religious Opposition to Licensing'; Chalklin, *The Provincial Towns*.

2.2 Urbanisation in Birmingham in the eighteenth and early nineteenth centuries

This scenario of headlong expansion on all fronts would come to a halt in the early 1790s and 1800s, though. For reasons that we shall explore, the war with Revolutionary and Napoleonic France abruptly curtailed Birmingham's growth trajectory. Within a couple of months

of the outbreak of hostilities (February 1793) well-placed sources within
the town were claiming that 10,000 had been thrown out of work. Julius
Hardy, a substantial master buckle-maker, certainly laid off half his
work force and put the rest onto half time, for he confided as much
to his diary.[34] Yet it seems unlikely that 10,000 remained permanently
unemployed (many joined the army). Nevertheless, both Wedgwood and
Boulton, who were far better able to weather the commercial crisis, also
reported a down-turn consequent upon the war. The number of inmates
of the Birmingham workhouse increased by 75 per cent between the
summer of 1792 and the summer of 1793, and average weekly expenditure on outdoor relief by the Poor Law Guardians almost doubled.
The speculative building spree of the 1780s and early 1790s had probably outstripped demand by this date, in any case. Moreover, it had
resulted in a town of rather sombre appearance: ill-built houses of
dark red brick, unpaved or poorly cobbled streets, a dearth of civic and
monumental architecture, and everywhere smoke and coal dust. Adam
Walker, who passed through in the summer of 1791, referred charitably
to Birmingham's 'smoky majesty',[35] but most visitors and travellers were
a good deal less charitable about the atmospheric pollution. The Dutch
natural philosopher Martinus van Marum[36] travelled up from London
to visit Priestley in 1790 but found the heavily laden air so oppressive
that he abandoned plans to go to Soho and retreated from the town
with a hacking cough. By this date there were already some houses standing empty for want of tenants, and their number increased with the
onset of the war and the food scarcities of the later 1790s. According
to C. W. Chalklin[37] around 12 per cent of the town's 15,650 dwelling
houses were unoccupied by 1801, but a contemporary memorialist put
the figure much higher, at near enough 3,000, observing: 'this, I believe,
was the first decline Birmingham ever experienced'.[38]

The English agricultural writer Arthur Young visited Birmingham
several times in the 1760s and 1770s, and in 1791 labelled it 'the first
manufacturing town in the world'.[39] There can be no doubt that Birmingham had become the pre-eminent centre for the manufacture of metal

[34] BCL MS 218 diary of Julius Hardy, button maker of Birmingham, 1788–93.
[35] A. Walker, *Remarks Made in a Tour from London to the lakes of Westmoreland in the
Summer of M,DCC,XCI* (London, 1792), p. 16.
[36] See R. J. Forbes, E. Lefebvre and J. G. de Bruijn (eds), *Martinus van Marum: Life
and Work*, 6 vols (Haarlem: Tjeenk Willink & Zoon, 1969–76), iii, p. 63.
[37] Chalklin, *The Provincial Towns of Georgian England*, p. 278.
[38] See S. J. Pratt, *Harvest-Home: consisting of supplementary Gleanings, original Drama
and Poems, contributions of literary Friends and select republications*, 3 vols (London: Richard
Phillips, 1805), i, p. 309.
[39] See *Annals of Agriculture*, 16 (1791), 532.

goods by the century's end, nor that it was known as such throughout Europe and the Americas. It would keep this lead for much of the nineteenth century. In his preface to a handbook compiled in 1865, following the meeting of the British Association for the Advancement of Science in Birmingham, Samuel Timmins observed that 'within a radius of thirty miles of Birmingham nearly the whole of the hardware wants of the world are practically supplied'.[40]

Whilst the generous natural resource endowment and the precocious development of an integrated regional economy contributed much to this pre-eminence, allowance must be made, too, for the extraordinarily skilful, inventive and entrepreneurial site which was the West Midlands. Process innovation seems to have been the cornerstone of Birmingham's domination in domestic and international markets. Visitors commented repeatedly on how the town's manufacturers of ornamental metal wares were for ever on the look-out for cost savings through stratagems such as the division of labour. Samuel Garbett, who passed for an elder of the town, acknowledged this strength when he remarked to Lord Lansdowne in 1787 that 'our object is to excell in pretty appearances for little money – And in that respect we are wonderfully eminent'.[41] Even when compared with other domestic centres of metal goods production, the region outshone its rivals. The French metallurgist and inspector of mines Antoine-Gabriel Jars the younger[42] attributed Birmingham's superior labour productivity, when compared with that of Sheffield, to the lack of trade guilds and the greater flexibility of the work-force. Equally, British visitors to Paris and other capitals were struck by the routine and unenterprising nature of much craft activity on the Continent. Having profited from the Peace of Amiens (1802–3) to enquire into the processes of craft manufacture in the French capital, Richard Lovell Edgeworth noted that 'instead of the assemblage of artificers in manufactories, such as we see in Birmingham, each artisan in Paris, working out his own purposes in his own domicile, must in his time "play many parts", and among these many to which he is incompetent, either from want of skills, or want of practice; so that in fact, even supposing French artisans to be of equal ability and industry with English competitors, they are left at least a century behind, by thus being

[40] S. Timmins (ed.), *The Resources, Products, and Industrial History of Birmingham and the Midland Hardware District: a Series of Reports, collected by the Local Industries Committee of the British Association at Birmingham in 1865* (London: Hardwicke, 1866), p. viii.

[41] BCL 510639 Photostatic copies of letters from Samuel Garbett to Lord Lansdowne, 4 vols. 1766–1802, S. Garbett to Lord Lansdowne, Birmingham, 3 September 1787.

[42] J. Chevalier, 'La Mission de Gabriel Jars dans les mines et les usines britanniques en 1764', *Transactions of the Newcomen Society*, 26 (1947–48), 63.

precluded from all the miraculous advantages of the division of labour'.[43]

Product innovation or improvement – inventiveness – was the pendant to this singular discovery of how to mobilise the energies and skills of a work-force in a cost-effective manner. A former employee of the Patent Office, Richard Prosser,[44] assembled a remarkable record of patents granted to inhabitants of Birmingham between 1760 and 1850, the profile of which is recorded in Figure 2.3. With barely concealed pride, this son of Birmingham noted that Manchester (including Salford) lagged far behind the West Midlands town in the league table of technological prowess. Manchester, as previously mentioned, did not become a demographic rival to Birmingham until the final decade of the eighteenth century, and only after the mid-point of the nineteenth century, on this evidence, did it catch up with Birmingham as a centre of invention. Until this date no other provincial town could match Birmingham for artisanal skill and ingenuity, or so it would seem. Prosser claimed that it was two Midlanders, Lewis Paul and John Wyatt, who patented the first commercially viable roller spinning machine. It was subsequently taken up by Richard Arkwright and extensively employed in the cotton mills of the North-West. Matthew Boulton, who was a past master at tapping into other men's minds, took Wyatt into his own employ and also found work in the Soho Manufactory for his two sons. Patents were expensive to obtain and hard to defend, however, and, if anything, Prosser's evidence probably understates the scale of craft and trade inventiveness. Edward Thomason, another Soho graduate, invented, in rapid succession, a self-steering fire-ship; a one-sail windmill for pumping water from ponds; folding steps for carriages; an improved corkscrew; a sliding toasting-fork; a metal walking-cane incorporating a cigar lighter; and a dice-throwing machine.[45] Only the stow-away carriage steps and the improved corkscrew were patented, however, and only the latter proved to be profitable.

Another point on which visitors, and particularly overseas visitors, to Birmingham in the second half of the eighteenth century were generally agreed was the bustle of the place. The Göttingen *savant* Georg Christoph Lichtenberg, who left a memorable account of the division of labour he saw being practised at Soho in 1775, also commented

[43] *Memoirs of Richard Lovell Edgeworth Esq Begun by Himself, and Concluded by his Daughter Maria Edgeworth* (London: Bently, 3rd edn, 1844), pp. 404–6.

[44] R. B. Prosser, *Birmingham Inventors and Inventions being a Contribution to the Industrial History of Birmingham* (Birmingham, 1881).

[45] *Sir Edward Thomason's Memoirs during Half a Century*, 2 vols (London, 1845), i, pp. 3–4.

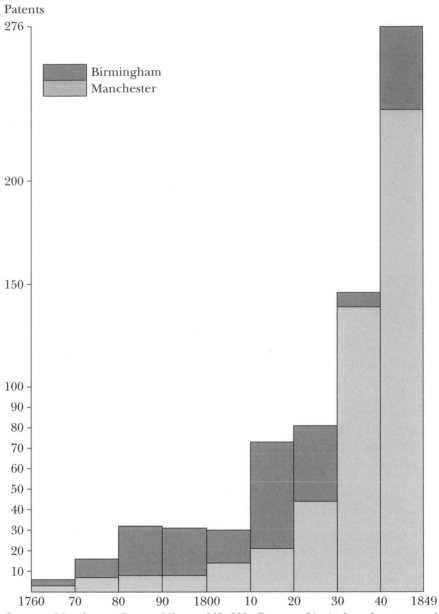

Patents

Sources: Manchester Patent Library MS 608; Prosser, *Birmingham Inventors and Inventions.*

2.3 Inventiveness as revealed by patent applications, 1760–1849

on the incessant 'hammering, pounding, rubbing and chiselling'[46] that greeted his ears and eyes on entering Birmingham. This assault on the senses prompted similar, if less favourable, remarks by John Bicknell,[47] a musicologist who passed through the town in the same year. But it was the accelerating speed of industrial life that drew comment from the 1780s onwards, as the frequency of communication by road and canal intensified. Chrétien de Malesherbes[48] was struck by the alacrity of ordinary work people as they sped about their daily tasks, and such observations became a diarists' commonplace thereafter. Only for a brief period during the small hours, according to Adolphe Blanqui, did the bustle of arriving and departing coaches and wagons cease, for the dominant obsession of Birmingham's inhabitants was 'la crainte de perdre du temps'.[49] Both Astolphe de Custine and Alexis de Tocqueville in the later 1820s and 1830s would echo this remark. For Custine 'the perpetual movement of crowds of work people'[50] numbered among the more disagreeable aspects of life in an industrial town, whereas de Tocqueville found only food for reflection in the sight of 'busy people and faces brown with smoke'.[51]

Quickness, and more especially quickness of response to the opportunities of the market-place, would in fact become the defining characteristic of Birmingham's formula for commercial success. In 1781 William Hutton remarked of the buckle – one of the town's staple products – that 'this offspring of fancy, like the clouds, is ever changing. The fashion of today is thrown into the casting pot tomorrow'.[52] Adaptability, innovation and speed (in getting to market) were harnessed together to produce an industrial version of the Enlightenment practice of 'emulation'. But speed and the cost advantage conferred by the division of labour underscored all other considerations. In his rather

[46] *Lichtenberg's Visits to England as Described in his Letters and Diaries.* Translated and annotated by Margaret L. Mare and W. H. Quarrell (Oxford: Clarendon Press, 1938), p. 99.

[47] 'BIRMINGHAM, A most noisy, unharmonious, smoaky town, where the harsh sound of the hammer and the anvil, together with the incessant clashing of pots, frying pans, and coppers, which was the only music I heard at my arrival, made me augur ill of my success at this place', J. Bicknell, *Musical Travels through England by Joel Collier* (London, 2nd edn, 1775), pp. 81–2.

[48] M. C. Jacob, *Scientific Culture and the Making of the Industrial West* (New York and Oxford: Oxford University Press, 1997), p. 7 and note 13.

[49] A. Blanqui, *Voyage d'un jeune français en Angleterre et en Ecosse pendant l'automne de 1823* (Paris, 1824), p. 81.

[50] Quoted in M. Letts, *As the Foreigner Saw Us* (London: Methuen, 1935), p. 123.

[51] J. P. Mayer (ed.), *A. de Tocqueville, Journeys to England and Ireland* (London: Faber, 1958), p. 94.

[52] Hutton, *An History of Birmingham*, p. 107.

self-congratulatory memoirs, Edward Thomason[53] describes several
speculations which earned him a great deal of money, thanks to the
dispatch with which he was able to turn out goods from his workshops.
He recounted how, on learning whilst traveling to Sheffield in May 1807
that Parliament had been dissolved, he sent by the same night's coach
an instruction to his engravers to prepare medal dies depicting the three
candidates who were to fight the vastly expensive and bitterly contested
Yorkshire election. Thousands of medallions were quickly struck and
drilled for ribbons so that they could be worn as a sign of allegiance.
All were sold to the campaign committees.

Birmingham's vocation as a centre for the manufacture of 'toys', that
is to say ornamental and fashion goods, was not pre-ordained. Rather,
it evolved in tandem with the expansion of the eighteenth-century
consumer economy. For perhaps the first three or four decades of the
century nails, utilitarian ironmongery and edge-tools remained the principal stock-in-trade of the town, as in times past. Only by mid century
did it become clear that unskilled and semi-skilled hardware manufacture
was moving to the outskirts of the town and into the Black Country.
In its place came buckle and button workshops, brass-founders, japanners, gunmakers and jewellers. These were the trades whose products
(buckles, buttons, watch-chains, snuff-boxes, papier-maché tea caddies,
ornamental brass fittings, pins, penknives, silver-plated wares, medallions, cut glass, etc.) were known collectively as 'toys'. Edmund Burke
had such products in mind in 1777 when he referred to Birmingham
as 'the great Toy Shop of Europe'.[54] Most of the merchants and manufacturers who became pre-eminent in the town during the latter part
of the eighteenth century or the early nineteenth century emanated
from this milieu. Henry Clay, japanner, whose workshops employed 300
at their peak, learned his trade as an apprentice of John Baskerville in
the 1740s. John Taylor began his career as a small-scale button-maker and
gilder before creating and then cornering the market for enamelled
snuff-boxes. In the process he built up a work-force which may have
reached 500 at its height, and would leave a considerable fortune on
his demise in 1775. Matthew Boulton, about whom more below, was
drawn from a similar background, and so was Edward Thomason. Later
on in life, Thomason recalled how his father's workshops could turn
out 1,000 pairs of buckles a day, or 6,000 a week, when working at full
stretch. Buckles were worn by men, women and children and were chiefly
made of white metal, to resemble silver. Depending on the vagaries of

---

[53] *Sir Edward Thomason's Memoirs*, i, p. 30.
[54] See Dent, *Old and New Birmingham*, ii, p. 258.

fashion, they might be as large as six inches by three and a half, remembered James Bisset in his commonplace book. But the domestic market for shoe buckles collapsed towards the century's end, owing to a shift in fashion towards slippers and laces.[55] Buttons, and particularly the showy but inexpensive gilded buttons, remained impervious to market fluctuations, by contrast. Between 1770 and 1788 the number of button manufacturers operating in the town more than doubled.

What drove Birmingham's industrial dynamo during these years? Economic historians have debated at length the role of internal and external factors, and at the macroscopic level at least there appears to be little agreement as to whether the emphasis should be placed on an expanding and captive market of domestic consumers, or on a speculative market made up of overseas customers. For a period largely devoid of reliable quantitative indicators, neither home demand nor overseas trade is easy to measure, to be sure. In the case of Birmingham, though, there is enough information available for us to get a sense of the direction of developments over time – but most of the evidence is qualitative and has to be taken at face value if our enquiry is to proceed. This methodological difficulty is increased by the fact that the town's manufacturers were intensely competitive, and therefore secretive about their trading activities. By the 1780s there had developed, too, a considerable sensitivity about estimating publicly the volume of overseas trade, for fear of provoking retaliatory action by foreign governments should the true state of affairs become widely known. Such nervousness in an age when the economic policies of many European states were being re-assessed is revealing in itself, of course.

During the first half of the eighteenth century the growth of Birmingham was almost certainly powered by domestic demand for its utilitarian hardwares. But this dynamic was already starting to change in the 1750s, if the testimony of John Taylor, the town's largest manufacturer, can be relied upon. In 1759 he informed a House of Commons committee that the metal 'toy' trade employed around 20,000 persons in Birmingham and its vicinity and put into the market-place wares to the value of £600,000 per annum. He went on to claim that over 80 per cent of these ornamental goods were exported, which seems excessive.[56] A little over fifty years later Thomas Attwood would testify

[55] On 10 May 1790 *Aris's Birmingham Gazette* contrasted 'the manly buckle' with 'that most ridiculous of all ridiculous fashions, the *effeminate* shoe string'. Quoted in Money, *Experience and Identity*, p. 262.

[56] E. Hopkins, *Birmingham: the First Manufacturing Town in the World, 1760–1840* (London: Weidenfeld & Nicolson, 1989), pp. 6, 16.

to Parliament in similar vein on the impact of the Orders-in-Council. However, his claim that Birmingham and district produced goods worth about two million pounds each year, of which 65 per cent by value were exported, seems entirely plausible.[57] We know that the town's merchants did an extensive and profitable trade with Portugal in the 1750s, because it was badly disrupted by the Lisbon earthquake of 1755, and in the mid-1760s Matthew Boulton remarked that 'more than half the letters we receive are wrote in the German language'.[58] Yet Eric Hopkins,[59] who has investigated the eighteenth-century history of the West Midlands in some depth, believes that Birmingham's growth in the third quarter of the century was still largely driven by the home market.

Be that as it may, a decisive adjustment of the town's industrial economy seems to have taken place in the 1780s. The leading manufacturers had already begun to concentrate on continental European markets from the mid-1770s – perhaps in response to the mounting dislocation of trade with the American colonies. John Fothergill, Boulton's first partner, had been promoting Soho wares throughout northern Europe since the late 1760s, in fact, and in 1776 he embarked on a trade mission to St Petersburg. Josiah Wedgwood, who kept a close eye on what Boulton was doing, also expanded into Europe. His partner, Thomas Bentley, made a sales trip to Paris in 1776, and by one calculation around 80 per cent of the output of Etruria was heading in the direction of European (mainly Dutch) markets by 1784.[60] Samuel Garbett, whose financial difficulties at the Carron ironworks in Scotland had not prevented him from running a successful precious-metal refining business in Birmingham, reckoned that his fellow manufacturers' success in penetrating European markets in the 1780s owed much to 'our Merchants resorting to every principal Town with their Patterns, & the Great Periodical fairs have been thereby reduced to insignificance for the sale of Manufactures'.[61] What he meant to say was that the principal 'toy' makers of the town had adopted the tactic of selling direct to shopkeepers via pattern books, cards or catalogues of goods, which were taken from town to town by travelling salesmen. By this route Birmingham metalwares made of brass and copper, in particular, became ubiquitous throughout Europe. Bourbon France seems to have constituted the most lucrative market

[57] E. Hopkins, 'The Birmingham economy during the Revolutionary and Napoleonic wars, 1793–1815', *Midland History*, 23 (1998), 111–20.
[58] Hopkins, *Birmingham: the First Manufacturing Town*, p. 15.
[59] *Ibid.*, pp. 15, 37, 74.
[60] Berg, *Luxury and Pleasure*, p. 143.
[61] BCL 510639 S. Garbett to Lord Lansdowne, Birmingham, 5 November 1789.

in these years, although entrepreneurs such as Matthew Boulton were extremely reluctant to discuss either the volume or the direction of the exports to the Continent lest the French government take steps to impede their commerce. All of the 'toy' manufacturers lived in fear of trade embargoes and taxes on raw materials. When the Habsburg Emperor promulgated an edict to restrict imported manufactured goods, its effects were felt immediately in Birmingham and, no doubt, in Sheffield and Manchester as well. John Scale, Boulton's factory manager, warned in the spring of 1785 that 'should Russia follow the steps of Denmark and Germany we may convert half of our Shops into Poor Houses'.[62] By the same token, news of a trade treaty such as that signed between Britain and France in September 1786 produced rejoicing. Birmingham's balladeers burst into song: 'And whilst mutual friendship and Harmony reign / Our Buttons we'll barter for Pipes of Champagne.'[63]

By 1790 at least a quarter of Birmingham's hardware output was heading in the direction of overseas markets – whether by official or unofficial routes. This fact helps to explain the shock felt by the regional economy when continental Europe, in particular, became inaccessible. The boom times of the 1780s continued until 1792, or so it would seem. This was certainly the impression gained by foreign visitors, and localised evidence provides confirmation. The button-maker Julius Hardy prospered in 1791, having sold 25 per cent more goods than the year before.[64] Yet by the autumn of 1792 the economic outlook had begun to deteriorate, and not just in the metalware towns. The descent of France into political revolution had generated commercial opportunities, not least for Matthew Boulton (see Chapter 6), but it had also caused turbulence in credit markets, and delayed remittances. A poor harvest in 1792 was depressing home demand, and war between France and the German powers (the Habsburgs and Prussia) was disrupting overland trade routes. From their very different vantage-points, both Julius Hardy and Josiah Wedgwood detected the change. The button-maker noticed that orders began to fall away in late September 1792, whilst the potter received reports of 105 commercial failures in the month of November 1792 alone.

In fact, the crisis that would arrest Birmingham's headlong growth only became fully apparent in April 1793, when Parliament was forced to intervene and authorise the issue of £5 million in exchequer bills to support leading merchant houses. France had declared war on Britain

---

[62] BCL MS 3782/12/72 J. Scale to M. Boulton, Soho, 9 April 1785.
[63] Langford, *A Century of Birmingham Life*, i, p. 329.
[64] BCL MS 218 diary of Julius Hardy, 1788–93.

on 1 February and within weeks the implications of the closure of much of the Continent to the products of Birmingham and the Black Country began to register. With a little over a quarter of the town's exports habitually directed towards France, many merchants found themselves overextended when remittances dried up. Garbett complained as early as 1 April that his sales of gold and silver to the gilding, plating and jewellery workshops had dropped by half. With well-founded doubts as to the viability of commercial intercourse during a time of war, all exports to France from Birmingham, Sheffield and Manchester abruptly ceased. The streets, he reported on 17 April, were filled with workmen and women who had been laid off. When even the Frankfurt Fair failed to generate orders, Hardy laid half his men off, too. According to Garbett, 3,000 unemployed males had enlisted in the army by the third week of April. 'The situation of Trade in this Town is frightful',[65] he reported that summer, adding that it would get much worse if a rupture with America were to take place as well.

Matthew Boulton coped with the credit crisis of 1793 rather better than most of his fellow manufacturers, thanks in no small measure to the strength and support of his London bankers. The lean years that followed, he was able to weather because of the diversification of his business and the buoyancy of the home market. The Cornish mines had partly recovered from the shock of the slump in copper and tin prices of 1787, and by the end of 1792 all of the Boulton & Watt pumping engines were back in operation once more. More important, demand for rotary-motion engines from the cotton-spinners of Manchester and Stockport was booming, not to mention the demand nearer to home from the colliery owners and iron-founders of the Black Country. In February 1791 James Watt[66] reported an order book of twenty, and a desperate shortage of skilled engine-erectors. It is true that the crisis of 1793 hit hard in the textile towns of the North-West as well, and several of Boulton & Watt's engine customers defaulted. But the cotton towns adjusted more quickly to the loss of overseas markets, as the demographic profile of Manchester serves to demonstrate. Birmingham town remained in the doldrums throughout the 1790s and even into the 1800s. The only local industry to positively flourish was the gun trade. The economic nadir was probably 1796–97, when the French ascendancy

[65] BCL 510639 S. Garbett to Lord Lansdowne, Birmingham, 28 August 1793.
[66] James Watt to Van Liender, Birmingham, 24 February 1791 in J. A. Verbruggen (ed.), *The Correspondence of Jan Daniel Huichelbos van Liender (1732–1809) with James Watt (1736–1819) and Boulton & Watt, supplemented by a few related Documents compiled and annotated by Jan A. Verbruggen* (privately printed, 2005), p. 228.

in Europe almost sealed off the Continent from British manufactured goods. Contemplating the stopping of remittances from France, the Netherlands, Italy and Spain in November 1796, Boulton expostulated to a correspondent that he had 'a thousand mouths, and more, to feed every week & whom I cannot request to fast till the war is over, without setting the example myself'.[67]

The years after 1806 seem to have witnessed a slow recovery, notwithstanding Napoleon's Continental Blockade. The town's manufacturers switched their attentions to the Americas, which had long been a steady market for nails, whips and fairly basic hardwares, and by 1811 it was reported that half of Birmingham's manufacturing output was being shipped across the Atlantic. Trade into northern Europe via Holland also held up remarkably well in the circumstances. In the meantime, new consumer-goods industries were developing on the strength of home demand. Louis Simond[68] described how the town's glass-works were turning out expertly cut flint-glass products for the neighbourhood's *nouveau riche* customers. These promising developments were sharply curtailed by the crisis over the Orders-in-Council, however. The determination of the British government to exercise control over neutral merchantmen sailing into French-dominated Europe produced a rift with the United States of America. The impact on Birmingham in 1811 was immediate, and little short of catastrophic. Many of the town's manufacturers joined forces to petition the government, and in June 1812 the Orders were repealed. But by this time the damage had already been done, for the confrontation with the United States turned into outright war, and another market was lost for the duration of the conflict.

Matthew Boulton and Soho

Surprisingly little is known about the backgrounds of most of the entrepreneurs (Taylor, Clay, Garbett, Simcox, etc.) whose energy helped to launch Birmingham on its eighteenth-century trajectory of headlong growth. Like the town itself, they seem to have emerged from the shadows fully formed. The same may be said of Matthew Boulton, although his emblematic status in the standard economic histories has ensured that he has received more attention than most of his industrial contemporaries. Even so, he too springs onto the stage fully formed:

---

[67] BCL MS 3782/12/4 [copy of] M. Boulton to E. G. Eckhardt, Soho, 7 November 1796.
[68] L. Simond, *Voyage d'un français en Angleterre pendant les années 1810 et 1811*, 2 vols (Paris, 1816), i, p. 128.

there is little mention of him in either public or private sources before about 1760. As Shena Mason,[69] who has done most to elucidate his early life, points out, the Boultons were a relatively well-connected family whose origins most probably lay in Lichfield. Matthew was the third of a least eight children born to a father who seems to have arrived in Birmingham during the second decade of the eighteenth century in order to serve an apprenticeship to a stamper and button-maker. In his *History of Birmingham*, Hutton insisted that his adoptive abode was a town of self-made men. But, if this is true, Boulton junior was not of this ilk. There was indisputably a great deal of 'self-making' and showmanship about Matthew Boulton, yet the resources to underpin his bid to become the country's greatest manufacturer flowed initially from family connections. Although we know very little about the button and buckle business established by his father at Snow Hill, close to the centre of town, the capital that enabled the son to contemplate building a brand-new, out-of-town factory almost certainly came from his marriage in 1749 to Mary Robinson, eldest daughter of a prosperous Lichfield mercer and owner of land. Since, on his wife's death in 1759, he married her sister, and since his brother-in-law died without issue, Boulton would eventually become heir to most of the assets of the Robinson family. In 1760, therefore, the thirty-two-year-old Matthew Boulton can be likened to one of the 'new species of gentlemen' identified by Dr Johnson, inasmuch as he 'straddled the increasingly blurred boundary between landed and mercantile fortunes'.[70]

In the absence of surviving documents or letters, it is impossible to know precisely what decided Matthew Boulton to lease thirteen acres of heathland in the parish of Handsworth, one and three-quarter miles to the north-west of Birmingham in 1761. But we may speculate that the deaths of his wife and of his father, in quick succession, gave pause for some personal reflection and consideration of the future direction of his business activities. The Birmingham trades were embarking on a period of rapid growth, and with his late wife's dowry secured by the remarriage, Boulton had the means to fund his ambitions. In fact, the unexpected death of Luke Robinson, his brother-in-law, left his second wife significantly better off – to the tune of £28,000, or so it would seem. Within a little over a year of taking the land, he also acquired John Fothergill for a partner, a man of roughly his own age although not possessed of the same entrepreneurial spirit. The resultant decision to build from scratch a new manufactory at a place known locally as

[69] Mason, *The Hardware Man's Daughter*, p. xiii.
[70] *Ibid.*, p. 1 and note 2.

'Soho' was Boulton's alone. It was to specialise in the production of Birmingham goods (hardware and toys), and draw its power from Hockley brook, which a previous tenant of the land had had canalised for industrial purposes. In taking over the lease Boulton also acquired a substantial dwelling house, although it was still to be decorated and made fit for habitation.

If retrospective evidence can be relied upon, Matthew Boulton did have a clear purpose from the outset – namely to set up the 'largest hardware Manufactory in the World'.[71] It was, as one historian puts it, his *folie de grandeur*, which is indeed how the timid Fothergill came to regard the undertaking when, in 1772–23, their partnership teetered on the edge of bankruptcy: 'you undertook the entire management of the factory, it was your desire, it was your delight'.[72] But these difficulties lay in the future: the 1760s were spent in the unalloyed fulfilment of Matthew Boulton's ambition. First the ground had to be cleared of a pre-existing rolling mill, whereupon, in 1762, an extensive industrial works would be laid out along the flank of Soho hill. Travellers approaching Birmingham from the direction of Wolverhampton would have noticed the façade of an imposing rectangular, three-storeyed building constructed in the Palladian style. Some 180 feet in length and 55 feet in height, it largely concealed from view four enclosed courtyards which were stepped into the hillside. The buildings were designed to accommodate workshops capable of employing up to 1,000 men, women and children, and the plans included provision for about twenty-eight workers' cottages in addition (see Figure 2.4). Fothergill, who had been installed in the dwelling house above the manufactory site, reported towards the end of 1765 that the premises were nearing completion: 'the buildings now begin to look so very sumptuous as to engage the attention of all ranks of people'.[73] But Jabez Fisher, who passed that way a decade or so later, expressed the commonest reaction on beholding Boulton's creation: 'the Front of this house is like the stately Palace of some Duke', and, he continued, 'within it is divided into hundreds of little apartments, all of which like Bee hives are crowded with the Sons of Industry. The whole Scene is a Theatre of Business, all conducted like one piece of Mechanism, men, Women and Children full of employment according to their Strength and Docility.'[74]

---

[71] Quoted in K. Quickenden, 'Boulton and Fothergill Silver: business plans and miscalculations', *Art History*, 3 (September 1980), 274 and note 5.

[72] Hopkins, *Birmingham: the First Manufacturing Town*, p. 87.

[73] Mason, *The Hardware Man's Daughter*, p. 8.

[74] Morgan, *An American Quaker in the British Isles*, p. 253.

2.4 The Soho Manufactory, 1798, engraved by J. Walker

2.5 The Soho Foundry, c. 1796, sketched by J. Phillp

It seems that Matthew Boulton intended to spend about £2,000 on his new factory, a not inconsiderable sum at that time. By the 1780s a utilitarian Arkwright-style cotton mill for 2,000 spindles, with no pretensions to grandeur, might cost £5,000. In fact, the Soho Manufactory came to fruition some £8,000 over budget, at a total cost of £10,000. Moreover, additional buildings were erected in subsequent years at a further cost of between £3,000 and £4,000. An on-site show gallery and tea room opened for visitors in 1772; in 1776 a new forging workshop was added; in 1781 a two-storey engine shop; in 1787 a mint; in the same year reverberatory and slag furnaces for smelting scrap copper; in 1793 a spring-latchet works; in 1795 a buckle-shop extension; and in 1797 a replacement mint building. By the 1780s guide-books and directories were referring to Soho as an industrial site of between 4,000 and 5,000 square yards, and in 1790 George Forster described it as a 'small town'[75] in its own right. There can be no doubt that Soho was a unique, indeed a 'wonderful', place. Not only was it the single largest factory site in Birmingham – a town scarcely noted for gigantic industrial enterprises to be sure – it was probably the biggest integrated factory in the country until large-scale cotton mills came into being (thanks in part to inventions pioneered at Soho) in the later 1790s. Josiah Wedgwood's contemporaneous Etruria was modest by comparison and seems to have employed a work-force of about 200. Arkwright's two mills at Cromford may have employed more, it is true.

However, the scale of the Soho operation was not the only thing that captured the imagination of visitors. Most were at least as impressed by the technology on display there. Even Wedgwood, who was no slouch in matters to do with machines, found something worthy of note or imitation each time he paid a call on Boulton. He visited the new factory in the spring of 1767 and immediately caught sight of a novel type of engine lathe with potential for his own works. Lord Shelburne, who had visited the year before, also took careful note of the machinery and how it was used. These work-bench machines were not necessarily of Boulton's construction, for he rented out shop space in the manufactory to many smaller masters. Yet he was a perfectly capable design engineer as well as a proficient metallurgist and industrial chemist, as we shall see in Chapter 4. Wedgwood seemed to realise intuitively that Boulton was a man of very different stamp from anything that the Birmingham toy trade had produced hitherto. Reporting to his partner Bentley on what was probably his first *in situ* encounter with

---

[75] G. Forster, *Voyage philosophique et pittoresque en Angleterre et en France fait en 1790 suivi d'un essai sur l'histoire des arts dans la Grande-Bretagne* (Paris: Buisson, an IV), p. 87.

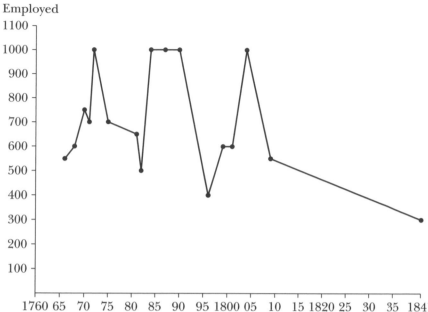

Employed

Sources: BCL MS 3147; MS 3219; MS 3782; Cornwall Record Office AD1583/2; Immer, 'The Development of Production Methods'; Dent, *Old and New Birmingham*; Hopkins, *Birmingham: the First Manufacturing Town*.

2.6 Labour force at the Soho Manufactory, c. 1760–1820

the Birmingham industrialist, he observed, 'there is a vast difference betwixt the Spirit of this Man & the Great Taylor, though both of them have behaved exceeding liberally to me in offering me every improvement they could furnish me with'.[76] He was back at Soho the following year and found Boulton experimenting with a new gold-embossing technique. After two days of intensive discussions, the pair seem to have agreed on a commercial collaboration 'betwixt the Pottery & Metal branches'[77] with the aim of exploiting the buying public's enthusiasm for metal-mounted vases in the Chinese style.

It is worth noting that Matthew Boulton's developing stature as a manufacturer and technologist pre-dated the arrival of James Watt on the scene and the formation in 1775 of the Boulton & Watt Company to manufacture the improved steam engine. Boulton had chosen the site for his new manufactory without any regard for future technological developments, which is scarcely surprising. Water to power a metal-rolling

[76] *Letters of Josiah Wedgwood*, i, pp. 142–3.
[77] *Ibid.*, i, p. 233.

mill was his most urgent need, but water was a commodity in which the elevated Birmingham plateau was signally deficient. Only after the Soho Manufactory had been built did the projectors of the Birmingham Canal Bill secure Parliamentary assent. There was talk from time to time of linking the Soho site to the new canal (about a mile distant at its closest point) by means of a cut, but Boulton seems to have taken the view that when the nature of his industrial activities demanded as much, he would move them to the canal rather than vice versa. For the first thirty years of its existence, Soho would specialise in ornately finished and high-value products whose commercialisation was not significantly hampered by the lack of immediate access to canal wharves. True, raw materials (cake copper, brass, pig iron, minerals) had still to be brought to the factory gate, and until the regional canal network was up and running, they had to be transported by overland wagon from Bewdley on the Severn, or from further afield.

Integrated engine manufacture was not carried out at the manufactory, since the first Watt steam engines were assembled *in situ*, that is to say wherever they were to be used. In 1781, however, a new engine court-yard was added to the complex of buildings at Soho in order to facilitate the machining of some of the smaller components, and gradually the manufactory, too, was equipped with steam power. By the 1790s visitors could see four of these great machines in operation. The first to be installed was the prototype engine brought down from Scotland by Watt in 1774, which was used to pump water over the twelve-foot wheel that powered Boulton's rolling mill. By the end of 1781 Watt had also managed to harness steam power to the factory's tilt or forge hammer. This engine would become the first to be capable of rotative motion when 'sun and planet' gear was attached to it the following year. No doubt this was the engine that the Russian engineer Lev Sabakin[78] managed to see in 1786. With the power needs of the factory continuing to increase, Boulton turned his attention next to the mechanisation of the polishing process, and in 1788 a double-acting 'sun and planet' engine was installed to drive the laps or polishing buffs. This was the engine that the Bavarian engineer Georg von Reichenbach sketched in 1791 (Figure 4.0). It would remain at Soho until the old factory began to be demolished in 1858, and is now on display in the London Science Museum. All of these steam engines were put to other uses as well: to water the lawns on either side of Soho House, to steam-heat the water

[78] A. G. Cross, '*By the Banks of the Thames*': Russians in Eighteenth-Century Britain (Newtonville: Oriental Research Partners, 1980), pp. 194–6.

for Matthew Boulton's bath, and to warm the counting house during the winter months.

The big turning-point in the story of the Soho undertakings occurred in the mid-1790s, when Matthew Boulton's business partnership with James Watt was remodelled to include their grown-up sons (the partnership with Fothergill had come to an end in 1782 on the latter's death), and a decision was taken to build a quite separate ironworks for heavy engineering. The Soho Foundry, as the new works was somewhat confusingly known, could not be anywhere else but on the canal, and in 1795 a location about a mile to the west of the old manufactory was acquired. The Soho Foundry is sometimes described as the first purpose-built steam-engine works in the world, which is not strictly accurate, since the Périer brothers[79] had erected something similar just outside Paris more than a decade earlier. Nevertheless, it was certainly the most extensive and innovative site of this kind, since the Périers' Chaillot works was heavily reliant on know how spirited out of Soho in the early 1780s and never seems to have managed to build up a technological knowledge base of its own. The partners poured money into the building of the foundry – confident that they would recoup their outlay from the sales of steam engines. James Watt junior, the inventor's son, was the driving force behind the engine business. He would systematise and standardise production, having taken care when planning the plant to ensure that everything needed would be either on site or easily accessible via the canal. By 1801 the so-called foundry comprised ten distinct engineering workshops, as well as a cylinder-casting pit and a boring mill. The Schaffhausen ironmaster Johann Conrad Fischer,[80] who visited Birmingham and the Black Country at the close of the Napoleonic Wars, also recorded the existence of a blast furnace and a (coal-) gas-generating plant. Matthew Boulton was approaching his seventies as the new foundry was taking shape. He had been appointed High Sheriff of Staffordshire and had had bearings prepared by the College of Arms. His social ascent from button-maker to baronet would surely have been realised, but for the failing eyesight of King George III, which forced the cancellation of his projected industrial tour to Birmingham in the summer of 1805.

The Soho Manufactory started off life as a 'toy' emporium – a place of manufacture of 'buttons, buckles, etwees, belt hooks, watch chains

[79] See J. Payen, *Capital et machine à vapeur au XVIIIe siècle: les frères Périer et l'introduction en France de la machine à vapeur de Watt* (Paris: Mouton, 1969).

[80] W. O. Henderson, *J. C. Fischer and his Diary of Industrial England, 1814–51* (London: Frank Cass, 1966), p. 68.

and trinkets, snuff-boxes, [buckle] chapes etc',[81] to quote from a regional trade directory printed in 1780. But Boulton had swiftly added other lines as part of his desire to participate in England's genteel, consumerist Enlightenment. Silversmithing, of which there was no tradition in Birmingham, was launched at Soho in 1765, following successful experiments to imitate what was generally known as 'Sheffield' plate, conducted a year or two earlier. Output of sterling silverwares peaked in 1776–77 before dropping back to negligible levels by 1782, although the plated-tableware business proved more successful and lasted much longer. Ormolu production (mercurial gilding onto brass or copper) at Soho began in earnest in 1768 and reached a climax about four years later. Like the silver business, ormolu craftsmanship was a specialist trade without a history in Birmingham or its district, and Boulton had to bring in skilled artisans from elsewhere. Wedgwood found thirty-five chasers employed in the factory during the winter of 1770–71.[82] The steep rise and slow decline of ormolu production at Soho speaks volumes about Boulton the entrepreneur – his proneness to sudden enthusiasms and reluctance to take costs into account when in pursuit of larger objectives. Wedgwood, too, pursued taste and ornament, but with a much firmer grip on the implications of luxury production for his core business than was ever exerted by his Birmingham contemporary. Jabez Fisher, the perspicacious young Quaker from Philadelphia, summed up Boulton during this buccaneering period of his life in a paragraph confided to his diary:

> He is a sensible, ingenious, and enterprizing Man, who plans and executes with equal Expedition, but like many other great men he has his hobby horse. He is scheming and changeable, ever some new Matter on the Anvil to divert his attention from the steady pursuit of some grand object. He is always inventing, and by the time he has brought his Scheme to perfection, some new affair offers itself. He deserts the old, follows the new, of which he is weary by the time he has arrived at it. This volatility prevents him from becoming very rich.[83]

The invention around 1778, in collaboration with one of his senior employees, of a device to copy paintings was Boulton's next hobby-horse, if we exclude the truly creative and remunerative partnership with James Watt. But neither ormolu nor 'mechanical' painting had proved themselves as serious commercial propositions by the mid-1780s. Fortunately, Soho continued to turn out its stock-in-trade 'toys'. With trade booming,

[81] *The Birmingham, Wolverhampton, Walsall, Dudley, Bilston, and Willenhall Directory*, p. xxxiii.
[82] *Letters of Josiah Wedgwood*, i, pp. 385–6.
[83] Morgan, *An American Quaker in the British Isles*, p. 255.

copper consumption at the works reached about four tons a week in the spring of 1787.[84] Another of Boulton's market speculations was the agreement with the Swiss inventor Aimé Argand in 1785 to produce his new, tubular-wick oil-lamp. Bedevilled by manufacturing problems and intractable disputes over copyright, it too lost money (see Chapter 4). The same may be said of the 'pneumatick machines' designed by James Watt in 1794 and marketed as a source of relief for consumptives and asthmatics. Apart from the steam-engine venture, which began at the manufactory in the 1770s and continued at the foundry for much of the next century, only Boulton's coining initiative seems certain to have turned a profit in the long run. Experiments with a view to the mechanisation of money production appear to have begun in 1786 – driven no doubt by the need to find markets for the quantities of copper being extracted from Cornish mines with the aid of Boulton & Watt steam pumps. Boulton began to erect a mint building on the Soho site the following year, and by the summer of 1789 he had one of his presses working tolerably well under steam power. Two further mints would be built, in 1797 and 1824 (the latter by Boulton's son). Only at the very end of the eighteenth century, however, did the mint venture move into profit. Between 1797 and 1806 around 4,200 tons of copper coins were struck at Soho.[85]

With the manufactory up and running, Matthew Boulton and Ann, his second wife, transferred their place of residence from the centre of Birmingham to the brick-built house that came with his land lease some time in 1766. It stood near the crest of Handsworth hill and obliquely overlooked the manufactory site situated about 200 yards below. After many alterations and embellishments, this dwelling came to resemble the Soho House that we know today (Figure 2.7). Lord and Lady Shelburne were among the first of many distinguished visitors to be entertained there, and her Ladyship noted in her diary: 'His house is a very pretty one about a mile out of town and his workshops newly built at the end of his garden where they take up a large piece of ground which he has named Soho Square. There, as in the morning we purchased some watch chains and trinkets at an amazing cheap price and drank tea afterwards at his house which is a very pleasant one'.[86] Subsequently, during the 1770s and 1780s, Soho House became one of

[84] Cornwall Record Office AD/1583/2 M. Boulton to T. Wilson, Soho, 6 May 1787.

[85] E. Roll, *An Early Experiment in Industrial Organisation being a History of the Firm Boulton & Watt, 1775–1805* (London: Longman, 1930), p. 135.

[86] M. B. Rowlands, *A History of Industrial Birmingham* (Birmingham: City of Birmingham Education Department, 1977), p. 18.

2.7 Soho House, contemporary photograph

the principal instruments of Matthew Boulton's self-invention as an
Enlightenment patron, entrepreneur and *savant*. In a letter written to
James Watt long before they became business partners, he described
his abode, in a revealing phrase, as 'l'hôtel de l'amitié sur Handsworth
Heath'.[87] This was more than a jest, for the improving function of social
intercourse was one of the key precepts of the continental Enlightenment. Over a fifty-year period of practised hospitality, Boulton invited
literally thousands of Soho visitors into his home. The tour 'circuit' that
developed would include a chance to inspect the landscaped Soho
gardens, an exploration of the workshops and, from 1772, a detour
through a sumptuous factory showroom. Decked out with glass-topped
display cases attended by liveried servants, Fisher thought it more
evocative of the splendour and pageantry of an 'Eastern Court'[88] than
a Birmingham 'toy' shop.

Yet Boulton was never entirely satisfied with his house. Although he
stuffed it full of the accoutrements of a man of science, it lacked grandeur
of scale. There was a library, of course, a fossilry and a laboratory (both
located in out-buildings), and an observatory in the grounds, but it
remained a domestic space of relatively modest proportions for someone of his ambition, and, moreover, a house which he had acquired

[87] BCL MS 3219/4/1 M. Boulton to J. Watt, Soho, 7 February 1769.
[88] Morgan, *An American Quaker in the British Isles*, p. 255.

rather than one that had been purpose built. In the later 1780s, there-fore, he began to entertain the idea of both enlarging his residence and giving it a more thoroughly neo-classical appearance. The plans drawn up by a number of architects and builders still survive, and have been reproduced by Shena Mason.[89] To judge from the architectural features common to each, Boulton wanted to make his house look more imposing to visitors, and all of a piece with his gravelled pathways and well-watered lawns. The building was to be adorned with a colonnaded portico and flanked on either side by single-storey wings. Interior space would be more rationally ordered, too, with specific rooms earmarked for 'Wet Chymistry, Dry Chymistry, Natural History, Botany-Green House, Astronomy',[90] according to one sketch. With more room for display, the library could be redesigned and filled with mechanical instruments (a barometer, thermometer, pyrometer, quadrant, optical and pneumatic apparatus and various types of clock were all mentioned in an earlier renovation scheme). None of these large-scale projects came to pass, however, and in 1798 the proprietor of Soho House contented himself with a relatively minor rearrangement of the external fabric. House improvement had ceased to preoccupy, and he turned his restless energies in the direction of the new mint installation instead.

In the thirty years following the visit of Lord and Lady Shelburne, Boulton's 'garden' became a park. No doubt its embellishment with conifer plantations, pools, walks and waterfalls provided some com-pensation for his inability to do much about the house. With the addition of a hermitage, a miniature temple to the goddess Flora, a small gothic tower, stone vases on plinths and two carved sphinxes, the gardens soon became part of the Soho 'experience'. For some visitors, indeed, the bucolic setting held greater interest than the manufactory itself. Giannantonio Selva,[91] the Italian architect who would go on to build the Fenice opera house in Venice, rhapsodised about Boulton's English garden. He was most impressed by the ingenious use of reflect-ing mirrors in the hermitage, which had the effect of transposing the ornamental waterfall draining the 'Shell Pool' from one side of the lake to the other. Boulton clearly hoped to turn his gardens into a miniature estate and he viewed with a somewhat jaundiced eye the urban and industrial development taking place around Soho, which he himself

[89] Mason, *The Hardware Man's Daughter*, pp. 105–9.

[90] *Ibid.*, p. 106.

[91] G. Zorzanello, 'Il diplomatico veneziano Simon Cavalli et le sua legazione in Inghilterra (1778–1782)', *Ateno Veneto*, 22 (1984), 239–40; *idem*, 'L'inedita correspon-denza del diplomatico veneziano Simon Cavelli con Matthew Boulton (1779–1786)', *Archivo Veneto*, 122 (1984), 45–8.

had done so much to encourage. In 1794 he profited from the enclosure of Handsworth common to buy another swathe of vacant land and set about altering the entrance to his property to ensure that it was more in keeping with the tree-lined driveway. 'Mr B is still going on with his improvements at a great expense', reported Anne Watt to her son Gregory, 'the grand entrance to his house is to go from the old appleman's stall where he has already placed a large bright green Gothick gate which cuts a most flaming dash.'[92] By the time of his death in 1809, the Soho park would extend to about fifty acres.

Culture and identity

The headlong urbanisation and industrialisation experienced by the West Midlands in the third and fourth quarters of the eighteenth century would not be conducive to social and cultural cohesion – at least not initially. Black Country villages which sprouted into towns in the space of a couple of decades scarcely had much chance of building up a stock of social capital, whilst pre-existing urban centres found their stock being diluted or depleted. In fast-growing places such as Wednesbury, Willenhall or West Bromwich it makes no sense to think in terms of a 'new leisure culture',[93] therefore; at any rate, not in the period covered by this study. Wednesbury in the 1790s had only one service-sector worker per 134 inhabitants, compared with Wolverhampton's 35.[94] But in Wolverhampton a trend towards social disaggregation was already under way as the town's active and enlightened mid-century elite were submerged by self-made men spawned by the booming metal-working economy. Like Birmingham, these were busy towns, not leisured towns, and ones in which members of the emergent commercial and industrial classes evinced little inclination towards civic-mindedness.

William Hutton[95] insisted stoutly that Birmingham was polite, if not genteel, but it is far from clear that many of the well-to-do would have agreed with him. However, the complication in any attempt to assess the cultural development of the town is the fact that – as in the case of Wolverhampton – it is not a linear story. Of Birmingham, yet living

[92] Mason, *The Hardware Man's Daughter*, p. 108.

[93] R. King, 'The sociability of the trades guilds of Newcastle and Durham, 1660–1750: the urban renaissance revisited', in H. Berry and J. Gregory (eds), *Creating and Consuming Culture in North-East England, 1660–1830* (Aldershot: Ashgate, 2004), p. 57.

[94] A. Hann, 'Industrialisation and the service economy', in Stobart and Raven (eds), *Towns, Regions and Industries*, p. 45.

[95] Berg, *Luxury and Pleasure*, p. 233.

outside Birmingham, for Matthew Boulton one mission in life seems to have been to avert the risk of a cultural melt-down in his native town. In 1777 he reported with some satisfaction that, whereas 'in the last century' his fellow citizens' favourite recreational activities had been 'bull-baitings, cock-fightings, boxing matches, and abominable drunkenness with all its train',[96] much progress had since been made towards more polite and civilised modes of behaviour. Yet the pell-mell expansion of the 1780s and the civil and religious turmoils of the 1790s (see Chapter 5) seem to have arrested and even reversed this so-called progress. In 1803 he remarked: 'When I reflect upon the Character, Dress & manners of the lowest Order of the working people of Birmingham & compare them with those of a similar Class that I remember nearly 70 years ago I am sorry to say that the present race have not improved in their Religion & Morals whatever they may have done in the Arts'.[97] The outstripping effects of population growth (on church accommodation and educational provision) and the vast increase in the number of houses and dram shops were the main causes of this state of affairs, he insisted.

It would be possible to interpret much, if not the whole, of Matthew Boulton's public career as an industrialist, scientist and paid-up member of the English provincial Enlightenment in terms of this tension. Were the meetings of the Lunar Society and the elaborate rituals of social intercourse practised at Soho all part of an unrequited mission to civilise? This is a question that we will need to explore in a more appropriate context. Suffice it to say, at this juncture, that Boulton was not alone in thinking that late eighteenth-century Birmingham was in danger of slipping out of control, that is to say out of the control of its still underdeveloped, uncivic-minded and denominationally fractured elite. James Watt's view of the matter has already been mentioned, and it is significant that in 1789 the leading citizens (including Boulton) gathered together to establish a Police Committee and to set up nightly patrols, because 'our streets abound with prostitutes & other disorderly persons who are a great nuisance to this Town and which ought effectually to be prevented'.[98] Watt's doubts about his adoptive abode only increased with time. After the anti-Priestley riots of 1791, he informed an old Glasgow friend, 'the town is principally composed of blackguards

[96] M. Boulton to Earl of Dartmouth, 22 March 1777, cited in Money, *Experience and Identity*, p. 90.

[97] BCL MS 3782/12/48 [copy of] M. Boulton to Spencer Madan, Soho, 29 January 1803.

[98] BCL 386813 Minute book of the Birmingham Police Committee, 1789–90, 19 November 1789.

of no property, as illiterate as horses & as debauched drunken & insolvent as any people used to be'.[99] The riots gave all property owners a nasty fright, and some exaggeration is only to be expected. Yet there is other evidence that the fragile social cohesion built up during the previous decades was weakening towards the century's end. In the summer of 1793 Samuel Garbett remarked on the changed temper of the town. The ban on bull-baiting, which had been observed for ten years past, had broken down: 'now we have had two days of Bull Baiting and such appearances of Disorder that it was dangerous to notice without proper force to suppress it'.[100]

Viewed from the perspective of a Garbett or a Boulton, the absence of 'proper force' was but a dimension of the institutional void from which Birmingham suffered. And that, in turn, was an aspect of the apparent cultural void, for it was axiomatic among educated members of the Enlightenment generation that good institutions possessed the capacity to civilise. Until the 1760s, Birmingham's apparatus of local government was rudimentary in the extreme. Even after a series of Improvement Acts were obtained which made possible the appointment of street commissioners, the town remained woefully under-equipped in the institutional sense. Only in 1838 did it secure municipal borough status, and not until the late 1820s were steps taken to begin the process of building a town hall. Until 1834, Town Meetings continued to be held in a furniture repository or in the open air. Needless to say, the magistrates were on their own when rioting broke out – unless the military could be summoned in time.

In the absence of borough records, it is difficult to form an accurate impression of the social structure of eighteenth-century Birmingham. But one thing is abundantly clear: the whole of what became the metal-working district of the West Midlands was an area of weak lordship and had long been so. The only local aristocrats whom Matthew Boulton conspicuously deferred to were William Legge, the Earl of Dartmouth, and his son Heneage. Under the heading 'Gentlemen's Seats', Hutton confirms that 'none of the nobility are near us, except William Legge, Earl of Dartmouth at Sandwell, four miles from Birmingham'.[101] The uppermost tier of the town's mercantile and professional middle classes was quite small still in the 1780s: perhaps fifty families, many of whom retired at night to country houses in surrounding villages, where the air was more breathable. They owned thirty-six private carriages between

99   BCL MS 3219/4/124 [copy of] J. Watt snr to Mr Hamilton, Heathfield, 24 July 1791.
100 BCL 510639 S. Garbett to Lord Lansdowne, Birmingham, 28 August 1793.
101 Hutton, *An History of Birmingham*, p. 410.

them. These men included John Taylor, son of the 'great' Taylor whose toy-manufacturing business had surpassed all others in the middle decades of the eighteenth century. By the 1780s, the Taylors resided in a mansion set in parkland at Bordesley, about half a mile from Birmingham, and they drew most of their profits from a bank established in 1765 in partnership with Sampson Lloyd II. The Lloyds were a Quaker family with roots in North Wales who had set up a slitting mill close to the river Rea in Digbeth, the industrial core of Birmingham, during the early part of the century. Since 1742 they had resided at 'Farm', an elegant house on the outskirts of the town.

William Hutton, too, was a migrant who had made good in the dynamic atmosphere of 1760s Birmingham. We learn from his compensation claim for losses sustained during the rioting of 1791 (see Chapter 5), that he had made a profitable living as a bookseller and stationer-printer, and in 1770 built himself a country house in the village of Saltley, two miles from town. One of his closest friends was William Ryland, wire-drawer, whose family ran a number of metal-goods businesses, including the pin manufactory inspected by Adam Smith in 1768. William's elder brother John purchased the house of John Baskerville, the japanner and printer, at Easy Hill just on the edge of town. Like Hutton's, it would be destroyed in the disturbances of 1791. The most prosperous of the gun manufacturers was undoubtedly Samuel Galton senior, who had come to Birmingham in the middle of the century. He lived next door to his workshops in Steelhouse Lane, but his son would move the family to a spacious country house at Duddesdon, a mile from town. The only non-manufacturing merchant to pass muster in this company was William Russell. A general wholesaler, he imported raw materials from as far afield as Sweden, and exported Birmingham goods to America and elsewhere. In fact 'Russells and Smith' of Paradise Street were the biggest firm engaged in the America trade in the 1780s. William Russell was a prominent Dissenter and became heavily involved in the campaign to secure the repeal of the Test and Corporation Acts, as we shall see. Whilst the firm's warehouse and counting house remained in the newly developed upper town, the family habitually lived in a comfortable rural residence at Showell Green on the south side.

The advantages of rural living as a means of escape from an increasingly polluted urban environment must have been obvious to all, but the drawbacks in terms of cultural conditioning only became apparent in the 1790s and 1800s, when internecine tensions burst forth. In the absence of 'natural' leaders, or any developed institutions of police, the physical absence of the town's most influential citizens left a space for the mischief-makers which the 'respectable' component of Birmingham's population could scarcely contain on their own. It is important to try and take the measure of this constituency, if only for the reason that such men and women would be the principal consumers of fashion and luxury articles and the principal imbibers of eighteenth-century scientific culture. Maxine Berg[102] has argued for a significant expansion of the middling classes over the course of the century, in terms both of numbers and of wealth. This expansion was particularly noticeable in provincial towns, she believes, where rising real incomes for those who were above the threshold of subsistence helped to fuel demand for an increasingly sophisticated range of ornamental and convenience goods. Birmingham, as we know, was a major centre of production, but with its expanding population and high-wage economy it was also a centre of consumption. If liability to pay Poor Rates can be taken as a rough guide to social status and the possession of a disposable income (see Figure 2.2), perhaps 29 per cent of the town's householders would have fallen within this middling category in 1777 – a figure close to that proposed by Berg.[103] But Birmingham's growth profile would dilute this constituency somewhat in the 1780s. The *Diary, or Woodfall's Register* informs us that by the end of 1790 the proportion of rated properties stood at no more than 25 per cent.[104] Such figures suggest considerable spending capacity, even if they can tell us nothing about the cultural inclinations of Birmingham's middle-class consumers. Yet it is worth noting in this connection the inventory of losses drawn up by William Hutton following the looting of his retail premises on High Street. Listed among the stock losses were over 300 glazed prints, 10,000 other prints, 100 plated figurines, 10 Derbyshire spar obelisks, 10 busts, 20,000 books, 100,000 reams of paper, 10,000 quills and 10,000 pens.[105]

A booming population replete with a monied middle class encouraged growing numbers of professional families to settle in the town. Between 1767 and 1788 resident physicians, surgeons and attorneys increased by 25 per cent.[106] Boulton's future soul-mate, Dr William Small, arrived in Birmingham in 1765 bearing a letter of introduction from Benjamin Franklin, and when he died at an unexpectedly early age some ten years later, the physician William Withering moved swiftly from Stafford to take his place. The fact that Small had made £500 a year from

[102] Berg, *Luxury and Pleasure*, pp. 205–12.
[103] *Ibid.*, p. 208.
[104] See Langford, *A Century of Birmingham Life*, i, p. 443.
[105] BCL MS 331068 Compensation claim: W. Hutton [1791].
[106] Hopkins, *Birmingham: the First Manufacturing Town*, p. 59.

his practice in the town, rising to £600 in the years immediately prior to his death, was no doubt a considerable incentive.[107] It is plausible to assume that men of this ilk spearheaded the demand for improvements to the town's cultural facilities. Prior to 1740 these were negligible – if we set aside the popular culture of the market-place and fair-ground of which Matthew Boulton so disapproved. Even in 1750, leisure and cultural facilities for the better-off were not well developed: easy access to print culture had only become feasible a few years earlier, with the founding of the *Birmingham Gazette* by Thomas Aris (another outsider), although there is some sparse evidence of the existence of an improvised circulating library as early as 1729. Not long after his arrival in the town, William Hutton would start to loan out books too, and the first recorded visit by an itinerant science lecturer took place at about this time as well.

The real cultural growth spurt started in the 1760s, as we might expect, and it took the form of a proliferation of clubs and societies. At the century's end Philipp Nemnich, a visitor from Hamburg, would record in his travel diary that 'the inhabitants of Birmingham are fonder of associations in clubs than almost any other place I know'.[108] Musical entertainment seems to have been one of the main instruments of middle-class cultural assertion; another was the theatre; and a third the growing enthusiasm for dilute and pre-packaged Newtonian science. By mid century musical activity in Birmingham had begun to rival that of Lichfield, the acknowledged cultural capital of the district – in terms of the quantity of what was available if not yet the quality. Even though Handel's *Messiah* was first heard in 1757, the town still lacked a permanent infrastructure on which to build a vibrant musical culture. This changed in the 1760s, however, with the founding of several musical and choral societies and the provision of 'polite' musical entertainment and concerts in venues such as the Vauxhall pleasure gardens located close by the town. Yet the most fruitful development in this area would be the founding, in 1768, of a music festival as part of an initiative to raise funds for the newly built General Hospital. The music festivals rapidly became a regular, triennial event, and one which epitomised the aspirations of the town's emergent middling classes as none other. What this new and still rather self-conscious elite lacked more than anything else, though, were physical spaces in which to meet and interact:

[107] See T. W. Peck and K. D. Wilkinson, *William Withering of Birmingham M. D., F. R. S., F. L. S.* (Baltimore: Williams and Wilkins, 1950), pp. 1–2.
[108] Cited in Chalklin, *The Provincial Towns of Georgian England*, p. 175 from *The Universal Register* (1802), p. 103.

squares, promenades and assembly rooms. The Duke of York had said as much when he visited the town in 1765. The construction of a public room attached to the York Hotel in 1772 brought some relief, but the problem would never be fully solved in the eighteenth century. By 1790 the festival repertoire could no longer be contained within St Philip's church, and had spilled over into the Royal Hotel assembly room and the New Street theatre. Nevertheless, a cultural practice which began in a spirit of Enlightenment emulation[109] had achieved the desired effect, inasmuch as it succeeded in reversing the flows between Lichfield and Birmingham. Anna Seward, whose poetry expresses some unease about the expansion of Lichfield's upstart industrial neighbour, would none-theless come to Birmingham for the musical entertainment the town could offer. So, too, would the aristocracy of the region, if only inter-mittently. The 1790 festival was patronised by the Earls of Aylesford and Warwick, Lord Dudley and Sir Robert Lawley, who was informally regarded as Birmingham's own MP.

The theatre was not a vehicle for polite intercourse engendering the same degree of cross-party support from Birmingham's well-to-do as did musical expression. Yet the campaign to equip the town with tasteful and potentially redemptive institutions in this sphere of cul-tural expression received consistent encouragement from manufacturers such as Matthew Boulton and John Taylor, and seems to have enjoyed wide support within the middling stratum of householders. As John Money[110] points out, informal street theatre in Birmingham had a long history, and the determination of at least some of the town's leading figures to differentiate what passed for popular entertainment from prac-tices and habits that the better-off considered to be more civilised, speaks volumes about bourgeois anxieties and pretensions in the tense decades of the 1770s and 1780s. Birmingham's first permanent and purpose-built playhouse opened in Moor Street in 1740 and it was followed, in 1752, by another in King Street, which was a more substantial venture and one rooted in the cultural model of the London theatre. Neither was licensed, and neither would monopolise performance-based spectacle in the town. Circus acts, acrobatics, puppet shows, satire, farce and tavern theatre continued to draw large audiences, notwithstanding the disapproval of self-appointed guardians such as Matthew Boulton.

In the 1760s the King Street theatre flourished on the patronage of 'respectable' citizens and eclipsed its rival which, ominously, was converted

---

[109] 'In other towns, whole oratories please / Shall we in gloomy silence spend our days?' Cited in Money, *Experience and Identity*, p. 84.
[110] *Ibid.*, chapter 4.

into a Methodist chapel. Indeed, John Wesley would preach against theatre as an undesirable social pastime when he visited Birmingham in 1764. However, the cultural battle over the theatre was only fully joined in the 1770s, when Matthew Boulton, John Fothergill, John Taylor junior, Dr William Small and a cross-section of the town's more substantial tradesmen and professionals stumped up funds for an entirely new playhouse. They then proceeded to petition Parliament in order to secure a licence. This New Street theatre opened its doors in time for the summer season of 1774, and it would become the principal cultural weapon of the town's 'improvers'. Designed by Samuel Wyatt, the architect who would submit plans to renovate Soho House a few years later, the very building was intended to be socially elevating and aspirational – particularly once a classical façade had been added in 1780. For Boulton, who appears to have been the driving force behind the venture, the New Street theatre would, if licensed, promote three highly desirable objectives. It would attract persons of fashion to the town and encourage them to prolong their stay and spend money. It would represent an alternative model of ('civilised') behaviour and, hopefully, discourage the 'barbarous amusements'[111] to which so many of his fellow citizens remained attached. Finally, a licensed theatre would perform an educative role – by helping industrious artisans to improve their skills in the graphic arts. Opponents of theatre in manufacturing towns often claimed that employers would substitute tickets to the playhouse for monetary wages, but Boulton insisted that he sent his Soho designers and painters to the play at his own expense, in order that they should learn to model from life. In the event, the Playhouse Bill of 1777 was lost. Boulton had counted on the patronage of the Earl of Dartmouth, among others. But Dartmouth was a zealous Methodist and declined to support the scheme. In the 1780s and 1790s the New Street playhouse (renamed the Theatre Royal in 1807) went from strength to strength, but it did not obtain a licence for another thirty years.

That Boulton should send his skilled craftsmen to the theatre for training in the graphic arts is revealing. It serves to remind us that Birmingham's mercantile classes were also seeking to institutionalise a commercial culture during these decades. In a town heavily reliant on the caprice of the market for fashion goods, industrial design was too important a matter to be left to chance. In Boulton's line of business, indeed, the need to copy and if possible surpass the styling sophistication of his European competitors was a constant preoccupation. This reasoning lay behind attempts to set up a drawing academy in the town

[111] *Ibid.*, p. 90.

in the 1750s in order to train modellers and engravers. Only towards the end of that decade did the initiative finally bear fruit, however. James Bisset, miniaturist, engraver, poet, publisher of trade directories and memorialist, would recount how he arrived in the town from Scotland and promptly enrolled in the drawing school. Numbered among his fellow students were the sons of middle-class professionals as well as the sons of manufacturers. At the age of sixteen or seventeen, he then apprenticed himself to a local japanner and spent the next two years painting flower designs on paper boxes and waiters at a rate of two gross per day. By this date – the mid-1770s – Boulton was making a determined effort to break into the market for high-status ornamental goods, and he had large numbers of designers and modellers in his employ. Yet there is little evidence to indicate that he recruited from the town's drawing schools. Many of his specialist gilders, chasers and engravers were bought in from abroad, and he may well have organised his own design training facilities at Soho.

The founding of a Commercial Committee can be construed as another sign of the increasing entrepreneurial sophistication of the town's merchants and manufacturers. Set up in 1783, this body institutionalised the experience gained in the late 1760s and early 1770s when the leading figures of the neighbourhood had campaigned, first for the cutting of a Trent to Mersey canal and then for an assay office to be established at Birmingham. Collaboration in matters to do with business did not come naturally to the town's manufacturers, as we have already noted. Yet the 1780s threw up a series of challenges that persuaded men like Garbett and Boulton of the advantages to be gained by putting industrial lobbying on a more formal footing. The successful campaign mounted by Birmingham's brass-founders to deter the government from lifting the ban on export of ingot-brass seems to have sown the germ of the idea, although the example set by Manchester's manufacturers counted for something too. Samuel Garbett, whom P. S. Bebbington has described as Birmingham's nearest equivalent to a public servant in this period, took over the chairmanship of the new body, which defined itself as 'a standing Committee for the purpose of watching over and conducting the public interest of this town and neighbourhood'.[112]

The remit of the Commercial Committee captures, if not the reality, then certainly the aspiration that Birmingham and the Black Country towns be acknowledged as possessing an identity of their own at the century's end. But an identity moulded around commercial interests

---

[112] P. S. Bebbington, 'Samuel Garbett, 1717–1803: a Birmingham Pioneer' (M. Comm dissertation, University of Birmingham, 1938), pp. 54–5.

was always likely to be a fragile construct. The Committee could usually secure majority support among the town's merchants and manufacturers when it was a question of opening up markets on the continent of Europe. In October 1786, for example, the news of the signing of a trade treaty with France was celebrated with a dinner attended by 100 trades-people. Indeed, the Birmingham Commercial Committee regarded the overcoming of obstacles to trade with France on terms favourable to the hardware and 'toy' industries as almost a personal triumph. But issues such as the export of machinery, or quality control, drew a more equivocal response. And Birmingham manufacturers did not necessarily practise what they preached when it was a question of the admission of strangers to their workshops. In 1786 the Committee announced a ban on such admissions – provoked, it seems, by fears of industrial espion-age and the enticement of workers. However, Matthew Boulton, to take only the best-known industrialist, never allowed the expressed views of the Commercial Committee to stand in his way when it suited him to behave differently. Refusing access to Soho clashed with his role as one of the chief purveyors of Industrial Enlightenment in the West Midlands. As for machinery and the highly sensitive question of the export of copper-rolling and cutting-out technology, he was deaf to the objections of his fellow townsmen when readying the shipment of an entire mint to St Petersburg in 1799–1800.[113] It comes as no surprise, therefore, to find that the Commercial Committee largely ceased func-tioning after the initial flurry of activity in the 1780s.

---

[113] BCL MS 3782/12/45 [copy of] M. Boulton to J. Smirnove, Soho, 23 April 1800.

3

The dissemination and validation of experimental science

Now that the regional setting of this study has been brought into sharper focus, it is possible to proceed with the investigation. If the arguments put forward by Joel Mokyr for an Industrial Enlightenment located in the interstice between the Scientific and the Industrial Revolutions are to be vindicated, a case must be made for a significant expansion in the production and diffusion of natural knowledge during the course of the eighteenth century. It will then be necessary to demonstrate the application of this knowledge to technological and industrial processes in specific contexts; or, as Mokyr puts it, to specify how 'communication between the *savants* and the *fabricants*'[1] actually took place. The present chapter tackles the first task, whereas its pendant, Chapter 4, will examine the porous interface between science and technology and attempt to identify the sites or locations in which the interaction occurred. Since the procedural shifts from knowledge, to 'know-how', to application are not easy to demarcate – even in a discrete context such as the West Midlands – certain themes will, of necessity, recur in both chapters. Mokyr's account of how useful knowledge was generated is very largely an a priori one. It is best employed, therefore, as an analytical tool for rendering transparent or 'legible' what was often a tacit or internalist process. Few, if any, of the documents on which this study is based mirror the neat distinction between 'propositional' and 'prescriptive' knowledge, and direct testimony as to how natural knowledge crossed the interface and was converted into a usable technique is rather sparse.

Instead, our main sources (epistolary correspondence, travel and visitor accounts) tend to lump everything together. Reportage on the latest experiments in natural philosophy sits cheek by jowl with advice

---

[1] Mokyr, *The Gifts of Athena*, p. 54.

regarding technological applications, marketing intelligence, or personal and family news. Yet this promiscuity, it will be suggested, gives us a far more vibrant sense of how the imagined 'Republic of Letters', in its late eighteenth-century incarnation, actually functioned in reality. Public and private spheres interpenetrated, and the Enlightenment quest for public knowledge would be pursued in tandem with information gathering for private pecuniary advantage, and even industrial espionage. In this respect the contemporaneous phrase, 'le commerce des lumières' comes closest to describing the cut and thrust of the knowledge economy that was taking shape in the second half of the eighteenth century. The present chapter will proceed therefore to examine this expanding corpus of experimental science at three different, albeit overlapping, levels. It will begin by exploring the burgeoning consumer market for pre-packaged Newtonian science in Birmingham. For as we noted in the preceding chapter, a taste for non-speculative scientific knowledge became one of the cultural hallmarks (along with music and theatre) of the town's nouveau riche elite. Until the 1790s, experimental science lectures offered safe consensual territory for cultural assertion – even more so, perhaps, than did music or theatre. This enthusiasm for science was not confined to Birmingham's middle class, however. In a town which took pride in its reputation for mechanical dexterity and ingenuity, demonstrations of the basic principles of Newtonian physics drew support from a broad constituency of willing and well-informed consumers.

The *savants* of the Lunar Society occupy a separate and superior tier in the discussion to follow. Although linked by multiple threads to the Birmingham market for dilute scientific knowledge, scientific spectacle and mechanical 'toys' or gadgets, they constituted a regional grouping with wider concerns and connections than the itinerant lecturers holding forth in the town's coffee houses and hotel back rooms. Since Lunar meetings were sometimes enlivened by visitors possessed of scientific credentials who had been drawn to the West Midlands on account of the region's prowess in mining and metal-working, it is important at this juncture to take stock of the Soho Manufactory as a node point in the circuits of scientific sociability and information exchange as well. However, Soho will feature principally in our exploration of the third and uppermost level at which natural knowledge and experimental data were disseminated. The leading members of the Lunar group – Darwin, Boulton, Keir, Watt, Priestley and perhaps Withering – all maintained an extensive and overlapping correspondence with Europe's elite of natural philosophers. Although James Keir and Joseph Priestley's papers have not survived, the epistolary correspondence of Matthew Boulton, James Watt and, to a lesser degree, Erasmus Darwin is both voluminous and highly specific. Not only does this corpus allow us to reconstruct the vascular system and to track the pulsations of natural knowledge throughout Europe in the latter decades of the eighteenth century, it also shines precious light into darker corners, such as the etiquette of information exchange in the age of the Enlightenment, the accreditation procedures operating among natural philosophers, and the complex question of the uneven 'take-up' or implementation of useful knowledge in different parts of Europe.

Science in the market-place

When the Milanese natural philosopher Count Marsilio Landriani[2] arrived in the town of Birmingham in September 1788, he was initially unimpressed by what was on offer. The bookshops, he noted, were full of novels, volumes of poetry and travel literature, not natural philosophy. Yet when he presented his letter of introduction at the gates of the Soho Manufactory he was immediately invited to dine, along with twelve other assorted foreigners. Dr Joseph Black, he learned, was staying with James Watt on a visit to the Midlands from Edinburgh, and if they did not meet over Boulton's dinner table, they were almost certainly honoured guests at the Lunar Society's monthly meeting two days later. Subsequently, Boulton took both of them on a tour of the mines and ironworks of Coalbrookdale. Most traveller accounts of eighteenth-century Birmingham are rather superficial, it has to be said. By contrast, accounts of the Soho 'experience', where visitors would find themselves rubbing shoulders with the like-minded, are richly textured. Yet we should resist the implication that the town and its district offered scant scientific fare in comparison with the drawing-rooms of the well-to-do. By the time of Landriani's visit, Birmingham was acknowledged to be one of the primary sites in the western world for the production of useful knowledge. Such knowledge did not flow spontaneously from the craftsman's work-bench.

The increasing commodification and consumption of scientific knowledge by the townspeople of Birmingham can be measured in various ways and at various levels. Although these levels or constituencies will be separated for descriptive purposes, it is worth bearing in mind Larry Stewart's[3] observation that the lines of demarcation between lecture

---

[2] See *Relazioni di Marsilio Landriani sui progressi delle manufatture in Europa alla fine dell Settocento a Cura di Mario Pessina. Introduzione di Aldo de Maddalena* (Milan: Edizioni Il Polifilo, 1981), p. 253.

[3] Jacob and Stewart, *Practical Matter*, p. 65.

audiences, consumers of scientific instruments and popular entertainment became increasingly fuzzy as the century wore on. The first recorded visit of an itinerant science lecturer to the town occurred in 1747, just a decade or so after the practice of public lecturing had become established. Unsurprisingly, the philosopher in question was Benjamin Martin (1704–82), one of the earliest practitioners of peripatetic knowledge dissemination. In the same decade he visited Bath, Shrewsbury, Chester and Coventry where, in 1742, he advertised 'A Course of Mechanical and Experimental Philosophy' – subject to the proviso that sufficient subscribers could be signed up. This is the course which he offered for a *second* time in Birmingham in the summer of 1747, which hints at an earlier visitation. Certainly, itinerant science lecturers were routinely touting for business in Derby by the 1730s, and it would be surprising if Birmingham were not one of their regular ports of call as well. Thereafter, both demand and entrepreneurship in this quarter expanded steadily. To judge from references in *Aris's Birmingham Gazette* and other sources, the town received at least four visitations in the 1760s, seven in the 1770s and fourteen in the 1780s.[4] By the latter decade the appetite for practical science demonstrations was such that fee-paying natural philosophy lectures had become monthly occurrences, to all intents and purposes. Birmingham was plainly a lucrative hunting-ground for the entrepreneurs of Newtonian science. Commenting on the difficulties that fellow physician Thomas Beddoes was facing at the century's end, William Withering acknowledged that it was much easier to drum up a paying audience for science lectures in Birmingham than it was in Bristol.[5]

Payment restricted access, of course, although the three guineas a head that Beddoes was proposing to charge would not have posed an insuperable barrier to artisan participation in Birmingham, in view of its high-wage economy. In good times John Taylor's snuff-box decorators could earn that much in a week or a fortnight. But the discipline of soliciting subscriptions in advance of launching a course of lectures did at least ensure that the customers received what they expected to receive. The evidence in this area is conclusive: Birmingham consumers wanted a straightforward introduction to Newtonian physics, a grounding in the mechanical sciences (hydraulics, hydrostatics, pneumatics) and, as the century advanced, a knowledge briefing in those fast-moving applied sciences most relevant to the manufacturing processes lying at the heart of the town's economy (chemistry, metallurgy, mineralogy).

[4] Money, *Experience and Identity*, pp. 130–1 and note 51.
[5] BCL 263547–48 W. Withering snr to W. Withering jnr, Edgbaston, 19 January 1798.

In 1761 and 1762, three or four years before Joseph Wright painted *The Orrery*, James Ferguson, the Newtonian populariser, passed through the Midlands towns, Derby and Birmingham included, offering a course of lectures on astronomy and the mechanical sciences. Although it now seems unlikely that Wright set out consciously to depict Ferguson demonstrating the universal law of gravitation, there can be no mistaking the didactic message of his painting. Ferguson, it is true, was not a natural philosopher or an inventor in his own right – unlike Adam Walker or John Warltire. Yet his tours in the 1760s and early 1770s did much to anchor a mechanical understanding of the physical world in the minds of those who attended his lectures and witnessed his demonstrations. Josiah Wedgwood welcomed him into his home and so did Matthew Boulton. When, in 1786, a Mr Burton tantalised his prospective Birmingham customers with a promise to include in his lectures an experimental proof of Newton's law of gravitation, it is likely that everyone who could read the newspapers would have grasped what was at stake.

Both Walker and Warltire were intimate with several members of the Lunar group. In fact they may have attended Lunar meetings when passing through the West Midlands. Dr Henry Moyes, the blind, touring philosopher, certainly did so, for we know that he became embroiled in a heated argument with the engineer John Smeaton at a meeting in Watt's house during the autumn of 1782. Walker was a protégé of Priestley, whose ideas he shared and propagated. When his lectures on astronomy employing an 'eidouranion' or transparent orrery became the talk of the town in the summer of 1781, Matthew Boulton invited him to dine at Soho House. Warltire was even better connected, having delivered private chemistry lessons at Etruria to Josiah Wedgwood's sons and Erasmus Darwin's eldest boy in 1779. Boulton had first got to know him three years earlier when he came to Birmingham to lecture on gases. No doubt he made the acquaintance of James Keir on this occasion, too. There is even a suggestion that Warltire may have joined Keir in a glass-making concern at about this time. By 1780 he appears to have been semi-resident in Birmingham and with a foot in both camps. As a public lecturer, he supplied the town with courses on metallurgy and mineralogy that were specifically attuned to the needs of local manufacturers, as well as instruction in scientific method and a grounding in mechanics derived from Newton. As a research chemist, he aided Priestley with his experiments on heat and the conversion of water into airs.[6]

---

[6] See N. G. Coley, 'John Warltire, 1738/9–1810: itinerant lecturer and chemist', *West Midlands Studies: a Journal of Industrial Archaeology and Business History*, 3 (1969), 31–44.

The natural philosophy lecture courses available to the people of Birmingham and surrounding towns in the 1780s not only increased in number but acquired a progressively utilitarian hue, then. There are, moreover, indications that visiting lecturers had a fairly precise understanding of the needs of individual markets and how best to cater for them. The 'polite' science purveyed in Lichfield or Worcester would not necessarily appeal to an audience composed partly of self-made men in Birmingham or Wolverhampton. Adam Walker seems to have led the way in this regard. His tour of 1781, replete with mechanical demonstrations of trade skills, both instructed and flattered the merchants and manufacturers of Birmingham. One of his subscribers was Samuel Galton junior, the Lunar associate, who had just taken over the family arms business (see Chapter 5). Having become the manager of a gun manufactory, he reasoned that it was time to educate himself in the sciences. A year or so later he installed a laboratory in his dwelling house where he conducted the prismatic colour experiments that would earn him election to the Royal Society in 1785. All itinerant lecturers understood the transfixing power that gadgets and models of machines could exert over audiences, of course. But as a wider and perhaps less sophisticated clientele demanded visual displays with more explicit relevance to trade and industry, so the number of 'props' increased. Whereas a kit-bag comprising an air pump, an electrical generator and an eudiometer might have sufficed in the 1760s and 1770s, the travelling salesmen of Newtonian science in the 1780s arrived loaded down with apparatus. Mr Pitt's second course of lectures, delivered in Birmingham in November 1784, covered optics, pneumatics, gravitation, pendulums and the expansion and cohesion of metals. His equipment included an orrery, a planetarium, a cometarium, globes, air pumps, condensers, telescopes, microscopes, prisms, magnets, pumps, a barometer, a thermometer, a hygrometer, a pyrometer and an electrical machine – that is to say, a baggage train weighing thirty hundredweight.[7]

The showy, almost theatrical, packaging enveloping itinerant-lecturer demonstrations in the 1780s cries out for closer investigation. It reflected, without a doubt, competitive pressures within a market-place pullulating with quacks, conjurors and entrepreneurs of the pseudo-sciences. As John Money[8] points out, the highly accredited Warltire was forced to delay the start of his lectures on metallurgy and mineralogy in April 1780 because the conjuror Herman Boaz was still in town –

---

[7] R. P. Sturges, 'The membership of the Derby Philosophical Society, 1783–1802', *Midland History*, 4 (1978), 215.

[8] Money, *Experience and Identity*, p. 131.

having transported from Lichfield his 'Grand Thaumaturgick Exhibition of Philosophical, Mathematical, Sterganographical, Sympathetical, Sciateroconatical and Magical Operations'. Of a similar stamp was Gustavus Kalterfelto, a Prussian showman whose performances blended electrical and chemical experiments with stunt science. His party piece consisted of the projection of fantastically magnified images of insects onto a screen with the aid of a solar microscope. Kalterfelto brought his show to Birmingham in 1792 and Boaz paid a return visit the following year – equipped now with what he called his 'Grand Hurlophysikon'. It is open to question, of course, whether such individuals contributed anything to the diffusion of Newtonian science as a body of public knowledge, for their stock-in-trade bordered on the occult and the alchemical. Their enduring popularity in a town and district which scarcely needed to be persuaded of the material benefits to be had from natural philosophy serves to remind us of the limits of the Enlightenment knowledge project.

If a simple enumeration of itinerant-lecturer visits to the towns of the West Midlands can be taken as a guide, a sea change occurred in the 1790s and early 1800s in any case. Whereas the market for science as shallow entertainment persisted, that for participatory experimental science as a form of self-improvement seems to have contracted for a time. The link between this development and the anti-Dissenter riots that broke out in the summer of 1791 is inescapable, and it will be explored further in Chapter 5. Dr Joseph Priestley had championed open-access experimental science and owed much of his renown and reputation to the proselytising efforts of the itinerant lecturers mentioned above. Yet his house, library and laboratory proved to be the principal targets of the rioters. But declining public support for the dissemination of scientific knowledge was a country-wide phenomenon of the 1790s, as many historians have noted. It cannot be explained by the impact of the events in Birmingham alone. Nonetheless, itinerant lecturers stopped coming to the town in large numbers, and the institutional fabric which men such as Priestley had put in place in the 1780s to provide a basic science education for ordinary working men crumbled. The few who did come narrowed the range of topics they covered, avoided the speculative and emphasised the utilitarian.

Two experimental fields which capture rather well the hybrid manner in which scientific knowledge was generated and disseminated in the second half of the eighteenth century are electricity and aerostatics or ballooning. Both were classic late-Enlightenment 'show' sciences, yet neither could have developed without a substantial input of natural knowledge, or a large measure of skill and ingenuity. In Birmingham and its district, all three ingredients could be found in ready supply from the 1760s onwards; that is to say *savants* capable of augmenting and interpreting the stock of knowledge, craftsmen capable of building the machines in question, and consumers willing to pay in order to behold demonstrations of the wonders of modern science. There is even some evidence to indicate that interested parties were also actively reflecting on the utilitarian applications of electricity and the possibilities for aerial navigation.

Although Dr Joseph Priestley had not yet taken up residence in Birmingham, his semi-popular book *History and Present State of Electricity*, published in 1767, gives some idea of the enthusiasm for electrical experimentation that had gripped the educated public through the preceding decade and a half. It was electricity which first kindled an interest in scientific experimentation in the mind of the twenty-nine-year-old Matthew Boulton. Perhaps the arrival of Dr Erasmus Darwin in Lichfield in 1756 stimulated his thoughts in this direction, but equally it could have been the course of lectures delivered in Birmingham in 1757 by Joseph Hornblower, who had promised to demonstrate the raising of water, the playing of tunes on bells and the shutting of doors – all by 'the surprising force of electricity'.[9] We know that Boulton owned the published accounts of Nollet's and Franklin's experiments, and had taken steps to acquire electrical apparatus. Benjamin Franklin visited Birmingham at least twice – in 1758 and 1760 – and on the latter occasion witnessed one of Boulton's home-made experiments demonstrating the non-conductivity of glass. By this time Franklin's discovery that lightning was a powerful form of electrical discharge was known and understood, and in 1765 the Birmingham inventor John Wyatt advertised in the local press, offering to install the discharge instruments (lightning conductors). James Watt would have one attached to the wall of his new house at Heathfield. It seems, too, that Priestley had grasped the practical implications of this rapidly developing field of science, for, as he tells us in his memoirs, he could not resist the temptation to indulge in a few investigations whilst writing his *History*. In March 1767 Josiah Wedgwood wrote to enquire whether he had carried out any further experiments relating to gilding by means of electricity.

With the power of electrical machines steadily increasing, the new science entered its show phase in the 1770s and 1780s. Like air pumps and barometers, the machines were often worked up as fine pieces of

---

[9] J. Money, 'Joseph Priestley in cultural context: philosophic spectacle, popular belief and popular politics in eighteenth-century Birmingham: part one', *Enlightenment and Dissent*, 7 (1988), 66.

drawing-room furniture, and in 1781 William Allen, 'the contriver and maker of the best electrical machines ever constructed',[10] was honoured with a benefit performance at the New Street theatre. Allen had also built the eidouranion used by Adam Walker. The Prussian traveller Karl Philipp Moritz, who passed through Birmingham the following year, noted that 'electricity happens at present to be the puppet show of the English. Whoever at all understands electricity is sure of being noticed and successful.'[11] Understanding electricity in terms of anything other than its effects was no straightforward matter, however. At the *savant* level, Darwin, Boulton and Priestley continued to express an interest in the new science and to transmit that interest to their Lunar colleagues, but on a rather episodic basis. By the spring of 1783 they were certainly familiar with the method of using an electric spark to explode dephlogisticated and inflammable airs – perhaps as a consequence of Alessandro Volta's visit to Birmingham the summer before. We know, too, that Boulton obtained one of Abraham Bennet's newly designed small-scale electro-meters or electric doublers, and carried out experiments using it – presumably in 1787 or thereabouts. Bennet was an Anglican cleric and future member of the Derby Philosophical Society who can probably be included in the Lunar diaspora. It would be interesting to know whether he collaborated with the Birmingham natural philosophers in person, but Boulton's jottings about these experiments are not dated. Certainly the Lunar group continued to use the power of electricity pragmatically, even if they left speculation as to its true nature to others. Reporting early in 1790 on their joint researches, Matthew Boulton informed his son that 'it was agreed at our last Lunar Meeting that Dr Priestley should hire a man to work a whole week at the electrical machine in the decom-posing of waters, the result of which I will inform you'.[12] This suggests that pneumatic chemistry remained the main focus of their concerns, although Luigi Galavani's announcement in 1792 that electricity derived from moist animal tissue did not pass unnoticed. By contrast, Volta's deduction and subsequent demonstration that a steady electrical cur-rent could be produced by a combination of different metals, produced a near instantaneous response even if no one could yet explain the chemical processes involved. In the spring of 1800 the news of the 'voltaic pile' was disseminated from northern Italy to the English Midlands in

---

[10] J. Money, 'Taverns, coffee houses and clubs: local politics and popular articulacy in the Birmingham area, in the age of the American Revolution', *Historical Journal*, 14 (1971), 20.
[11] *Travels of Carl Philipp Moritz in England in 1782* (London: Milford, 1924), p. 83.
[12] BCL MS 3782/12/57 M. Boulton to M. R. Boulton, Soho, 4 January 1790.

a matter of months. By May of that year it was being demonstrated in London and by August a battery had been built in Derby for William Strutt, one of the founder members of the Derby Philosophical Society. Darwin quickly added electric shock therapy to his medical repertoire, whilst Thomas Beddoes in Bristol introduced the apparatus to his Pneumatic Institution.

Unlike Volta's battery which opened up whole new fields of enquiry, the 'aerostatic machine' or air balloon was an invention with a short pedigree which rapidly stalled for want of technological development. Nevertheless, its early history can be said to have harnessed together the same combination of knowledge, know-how and public spectacle. The first large-scale experiments involving non-human ascent took place in southern France during the spring and summer of 1783. The Montgolfier brothers, who were the pioneers in this field, carried out trials with linen, silk and varnished-paper balloons filled with either hydrogen or hot air, and in June of that year succeeded in launching a globe some thirty-five feet in diameter which rose 6,000 feet above the town of Annonay. The news of this success quickly reached the ears of the Académie des Sciences in Paris and it triggered a frenzy of aero-nautical activity throughout Europe. The chemists Guyton de Morveau and Grossart de Virly took up the challenge on behalf of the Academy of Dijon; Klaproth and Achard launched balloons in Berlin, and Count Andreani carried out the first ascent in Italy from his estate near Milan. Volta, meanwhile, sniffed in a letter to the Portuguese *savant* Magellan that the French had no priority claim to the aerostatic machine, since Cavendish and Priestley had undertaken the theoretical groundwork in gaseous chemistry, whilst he had carried out similar experiments several years earlier. The merit of the Montgolfiers, he insisted, lay rather in knowing how to stitch and glue together an envelope of the requisite size.[13] Only James Watt seems to have remained unmoved at the news of man's ascent to the heavens: 'the whole world is full of these flying balls at present', he commented to Joseph Black in Edinburgh, 'I know very little more of them than you must have seen in the papers'.[14]

Watt's conviction that air balloons were mere gimmicks did not deter him from discussing the science lying behind the phenomenon, however. Nor would it prevent his partner Boulton, who was prone to sudden enthusiasms, from falling prey to 'ballonomania'.[15] Watt's letter to Black

---

[13] See J. de Carvalho, 'Correspondência científica dirigida a João Jacinto de Magalhães', *Revista da Faculdade de Ciências da Universidade de Coimbra*, 20 (1951), 183.

[14] BCL MS 3219/4/120 J. Watt snr to Dr Black, 25 September 1783.

[15] *Ibid.*, J. Watt snr to Dr Lind, Birmingham, 26 October 1784.

continued with the intelligence that 'Montgolfier has found a method to make inflammable air by burning wet straw so cheap that he can fill a ball of 30 feet dia.' for $\frac{1}{2}$ a crown'. But this was not yet public knowledge, or at least the 'secret'[16] had only been communicated to the Académie des Sciences, he confided. Within a year, however, Priestley hit upon a far superior method of fuelling balloons as an extension of his hydrogen 'gas' experiments, and this information was, in turn, reported back to France – probably through the medium of the Swiss inventor Aimé (or Ami) Argand (see Chapter 4). In a subsequent letter addressed to Dr James Lind, Watt acknowledged that he had not remained detached from balloon mania after all, and had even, briefly, considered the possibility of using copper in the construction of the envelope. As for fuel, he noted that 'the new process for obtaining inflammable air was found out by Mr Lavoisier who I presume took hint from Dr Priestley's late exp.' of making the steams of various substances pass through red hot tubes'.[17]

Employing Soho's skill in the thin rolling of copper was a non-starter, as Watt quickly came to realize. But Birmingham's japanners possessed a good deal of know-how in the area of paper glueing and varnish production which was relevant to the construction of aerostatic machines. Matthew Boulton was hampered in his desire to participate in the latest scientific craze by the necessity of spending many months of each year in Cornwall supervising the erection of the firm's mine engines, but in the summer of 1784 a small, varnished-paper balloon was launched from the grounds of the Soho Manufactory. The purpose of the exercise – at least for the natural philosophers who attended the launch – was to determine whether the growling of thunder represented successive detonations, or merely a series of echoes. To this end the envelope was filled with a mixture comprising two-thirds hydrogen and one-third 'common' air, and a lighted fuse was attached to the neck. Erasmus Darwin, however, had anticipated this first excursion of the West Midlands *savants* into the field of ballooning by using a launch to celebrate the founding of the Derby Philosophical Society. 'You heard we sent your society an air-balloon which was calculated to have fallen in your garden at Soho', he wrote to Boulton in January 1784, 'but the wicked wind carried to Sir Edward Littleton's [Teddesley Park]'.[18]

None of these experiments involved manned flights, though, and it was the sending of men aloft – whether volunteers or criminals – that

[16] *Ibid.*, J. Watt snr to Dr Black, 25 September 1783.

[17] *Ibid.*, J. Watt snr to Dr Lind, Birmingham, 26 October 1784.

[18] R. E. Schofield, *The Lunar Society of Birmingham: a Social History of Provincial Science and Industry in Eighteenth-Century England* (Oxford: Clarendon Press, 1963), p. 251.

turned aerostatics into a mass spectator sport. The first such ascent in Birmingham took place on 4 January 1785 after an elaborate build-up during which the show aspects of the new science were exploited to the full. The balloon employed seems to have been the one in which the inventor James Sadler had ascended from Oxford eleven months earlier. It was brought to the West Midlands and put on display in Birmingham's New Street theatre – admission one shilling. Mr Harper, the prospective aeronaut, then had the machine moved to its intended launch-pad, a tennis court in Coleshill Street, where the genteel public were milked in return for advantageous seats in a specially built spectators' gallery. The first attempt to launch ended in failure when the fuelling-up process broke down. A near riot ensued as non-fee-paying spectators converged on the platform and tried to pull it down, thereby endangering the balloon. A second attempt was made six days later, although the weather was far from favourable. This time the local *savants* were on hand to supervise the operation of the crude fuel-generation technology: Dr William Withering the Lunar associate, John Southern, a draughtsman from the Soho drawing department, and Aimé Argand, who passed for an expert, having been involved in the Montgolfiers' original ascents. After a near disaster at the launch, Harper stayed aloft for a couple of hours and travelled some fifty miles. But the landing (near Newcastle-under-Lyme) proved nearly as traumatic as the take-off. Priestley's atmospheric experiments were ruined when the balloon hit a tree and the bottles of air collected at different altitudes were smashed.

John Southern went on to draw up a report on his experiences and conclusions in the field of aerostatics. It combined theoretical calculations regarding canopy pressure and lift, with practical information on how best to construct the globe. Published as a *Treatise*[19] in 1785, the brochure represents an early example of the codification of local knowledge in a rapidly developing craft speciality. It complemented the scientific accounts of the first ballooning experiments published in French by Faujas de Saint-Fond[20] and in English by Tiberius Cavallo.[21] By this date, however, the first flush of enthusiasm was waning. French *savants* had been grappling with the problem of dirigibility since the spring of 1784, but with scant success. In Dijon, de Virly and his colleagues

---

[19] J. Southern, *A Treatise upon Aerostatic Machines containing Rules for calculating their Powers of Ascension* (Birmingham: Pearson and Rollason, 1785), pp. 1–63.

[20] B. Faujas de Saint-Fond, *Description des expériences de la machine aérostatique de MM. de Montgolfier* (Paris, 1784).

[21] T. Cavallo, *The History and Practice of Aerostation* (London: Dilly, 1785).

in the Academy had tried fitting their balloon gondola with a tiller and an oar. They had even shaped the canopy to give it a 'beak' in the hope of providing some sense of direction.[22] In London, likewise, similar experiments were in progress. Before returning across the Channel in December 1784, the Marquis de Bombelles noted that work was under way to equip Lunardi's balloon with 'ailes de fer'.[23] No doubt Southern's treatise found a local readership of some description, for the launching of fire balloons in the town would become a popular nuisance. Yet neither Boulton nor Watt, nor any other member of the Lunar group, persisted with this branch of experimental science beyond 1785, as far as we can tell. In Birmingham, at least, aerostatics remained confined to the realm of entertainment, alongside pyrotechnics. Darwin might speculate on the potential of flying machines in his didactic poem *The Botanic Garden* (1792),[24] but Boulton next launched a balloon in 1802 as part of the razzmatazz to celebrate the arrival of peace in Europe.

The Lunar group

The ten or a dozen individuals who formed the kernel of the Lunar Society maintained close and often supportive links with the science experimenters and promoters of the neighbourhood, as we have seen. They cannot be detached from Birmingham's booming market for useful knowledge in any neat and definitive way. After all, several of the members were West Midlands manufacturers in their own right. Yet the market-place in which they chose to operate was not, primarily, a mercantile and consumer-oriented one. When meeting as a club, they perceived themselves as gentlemen of the Enlightenment jointly engaged in the uninhibited acquisition and transmission of natural knowledge. As such, it seems more appropriate to view them as a small but influential cluster within the wider, pan-European community of late eighteenth-century natural philosophers. In the judgement of Margaret Jacob and Larry Stewart, this 'creative community'[25] of knowledge exchangers constituted the active ingredient in the catalytic reaction that launched and then sustained the industrialisation of the West. Joel Mokyr would not dissent from this verdict. Yet his depiction of the Lunar Society lacks

---

[22] See Carlid and Nordström, *Torbern Bergman's Foreign Correspondence*, p. 403.

[23] See J. Gury (ed.), *Marc de Bombelles: Journal de voyage en Grande Bretagne et en Irlande 1784* (Studies in Voltaire and the Eighteenth Century 269, Oxford: Voltaire Foundation, 1989), p. 306.

[24] See part one 'The Economy of Vegetation'.

[25] Jacob and Stewart, *Practical Matter*, p. 59.

the sensitivity which cultural historians of science have brought to the subject of knowlege diffusion. He sees the Society as more akin to a mart: 'a place where knowledge was exchanged, bought and sold in exchange for patronage. The buyers were industrialists such as Matthew Boulton and Josiah Wedgwood, the sellers natural philosophers such as Erasmus Darwin and Joseph Priestley.'[26]

This interpretation of the role and activities of the Lunar Society has a long pedigree. It can be found, for example, in the standard *History of Birmingham*, the first volume of which was published in 1952.[27] However, the most powerful and articulate statement of the Society's role was penned by Robert Schofield[28] in 1963. Schofield argued for a 'techno-logical' interpretation, insisting that he had simply followed the evid-ence trail which pointed unmistakably in the direction of a link with the Industrial Revolution. Describing its members as 'harbingers'[29] of another kind of society, he concluded that the Lunar Society 'can only be measured in terms of its impact on the Industrial Revolution'.[30] Indeed, he went so far as to describe the whole enterprise as a 'pilot project'[31] for what lay in store in the nineteenth century. Over the next decade this interpretation hardened into an orthodoxy. We find it em-bedded in the Warwickshire volume of *The Victoria History of the Counties of England* (1964);[32] in Francis Klingender's schematic *Art and the Indus-trial Revolution* (1968), where the Lunar Society is depicted as 'a kind of scientific general staff for the Industrial Revolution',[33] and even in some of A. E. Musson's[34] published work. Unsurprisingly, this orthodoxy was also relayed in books only tangentially concerned with science, tech-nology or industry. Marilyn Butler's biography of Maria Edgeworth describes the Lunar Society as 'a pioneer industrial research estab-lishment', although she acknowledges that 'only about half [*sic*] of the members were practising industrialists'.[35] Even today the interpretive

---

[26] Mokyr, *The Gifts of Athena*, p. 44 note 18; also Mokyr, 'The intellectual origins', 313.

[27] C. Gill, *History of Birmingham*. Volume 1: *Manor and Borough to 1865* (Oxford: Oxford University Press, 1952), p. 136.

[28] Schofield, *The Lunar Society of Birmingham*.

[29] *Ibid.*, p. 3.

[30] *Ibid.*, p. 419.

[31] *Ibid.*, p. 439.

[32] *A History of the County of Warwick*. Volume VII: *The City of Birmingham* (Oxford: Oxford University Press, 1964).

[33] F. D. Klingender, *Art and the Industrial Revolution* (New York: Kelley, 2nd edn, 1968), p. 34.

[34] See Musson and Robinson, *Science and Technology in the Industrial Revolution*, p. 142.

[35] M. Butler, *Maria Edgeworth: a Literary Biography* (Oxford: Clarendon Press, 1972), p. 34.

thread woven by Schofield in 1963 remains unbroken in the hands of some investigators. In a volume commemorating the bicentenary of the death of Erasmus Darwin, Desmond King-Hele writes that 'the Lunar men talked of many things, but most crucially about advances in science and technology, and how these might help industry'.[36]

The counter-argument adopts a broadly cultural approach to the Lunar Society and was first heard in the early 1980s, as part and parcel of the wholesale re-evaluation of history of science that was starting to take place in those years. If nothing else, it has the merit of seeking to place the Lunar group in a context they would have been conscious of (Enlightenment) rather than inserting them into one of which they could only have had the haziest apprehensions (Industrial Revolution). Although Eric Robinson,[37] a specialist whose researches on the Lunar Society were nearly contemporaneous with those of Schofield, had offered a more flexible and inclusive vision, it fell to Roy Porter[38] to formulate the most effective riposte, in an article that linked scientific activity to provincial culture rather than incipient industrialisation. He questioned the assumption that because late eighteenth-century science flourished in provincial urban settings such as Birmingham and Manchester, it must have had something to do with industrialisation, or, for that matter, the imperatives of Dissenter religion (see Chapter 5). Instead, the purpose of bodies such as the Lunar Society, he argued, might be better grasped by invoking the anxiety of provincial elites to bring a version of Enlightenment civility to their own doorstep. According to this scenario, therefore, the significance of scientific activity lay principally in the cultural 'added value' which it conferred on practitioners.

A corollary to this counter-argument must be that Schofield's judgement that the Lunar Society did not reflect the dominant characteristics of polite Augustan society, but 'another society'[39] in the making, is misplaced. Yet Arnold Thackray,[40] in an important article on the contemporaneous Manchester Literary and Philosophical Society, elaborated just this point. If the Manchester natural philosophers did not in any tangible way accelerate the process of industrialisation, then they

---

[36] C. U. M. Smith and R. Arnott (eds), *The Genius of Erasmus Darwin* (Aldershot: Ashgate, 2005), p. 17.

[37] See particularly E. Robinson, 'The Lunar Society: its membership and organisation', *Transactions of the Newcomen Society*, 35 (1962–63), 153–77.

[38] R. Porter, 'Science, provincial culture and public opinion in Enlightenment England', *British Journal for Eighteenth-Century Studies*, 3 (1980), 20–46.

[39] Schofield, *The Lunar Society of Birmingham*, p. 440.

[40] A. Thackray, 'Natural knowledge in cultural context: the Manchester model', *American Historical Review*, 79 (June 1974), 672–709.

certainly used science to build a distinctive identity for themselves as new men who did not easily fit within the hallowed categories of eighteenth-century society. So, they were still 'harbingers' even if they were no longer pioneers of the Industrial Revolution. Their conscious aim was, as Steven Shapin has put it, 'to redefine rather than to reject the values of politeness'.[41] But whether even this formulation can be accepted depends on who the natural philosophers were, and how they behaved. On the whole, researchers have not come up with much evidence that fits even the revised scenario. In Manchester it is far from clear that the membership of the Literary and Philosophical Society was drawn from an outsider class, and the same may be said of Darwin's infant Philosophical Society in Derby, most of whose members were professionals and Anglicans. As for the Lunar Society, John Money,[42] the historian who has carried out the most searching analysis of the social identity of eighteenth-century West Midlanders, remains unpersuaded. To annex science to a thrusting new elite risks underplaying its continuing relevance within the dominant or mainstream culture of Augustan England, he points out. He also questions whether Thackray's distinction between 'legitimising' pure science and 'marginalising' technical innovation is tenable in practice. How, then, should we depict the Lunar Society: along the lines suggested first by Robert Schofield, or as a 'conversation' group seeking to domesticate the Enlightenment in the less-than-auspicious context of the boom towns of the West Midlands?

Unlike Manchester's Literary and Philosophical Society, which was formally constituted in 1781, the Lunar Society remained an informal grouping from beginning to end. It had no premises, no presiding committee, no membership list, no rule book and no agenda. In the absence of minute books or any other official records, almost everything we know about the body is wrapped in conjecture, therefore. Few witness accounts of its proceedings have survived, and it left no legacy to speak of. Even the sons of the original Lunar men rarely made reference to the body, which strengthens our suspicion that it should be treated primarily as a generational phenomenon linked to the specific context of the Enlightenment. When James Watt junior came to update the biography of his father for the seventh edition of the *Encyclopaedia Britannica* in 1842, he made no reference whatsoever to the existence

---

[41] See R. Porter (ed.), *The Cambridge History of Science.* Volume 4: *Eighteenth-Century Science* (Cambridge: Cambridge University Press, 2003), p. 178.

[42] Money, 'Joseph Priestley in cultural context: philosophic spectacle, popular belief and popular politics in eighteenth-century Birmingham: part two', *Enlightenment and Dissent*, 8 (1989), 81–3; also Money, 'Taverns, coffee houses and clubs'.

of the Lunar Society. Only once virtually all who had had a link with the Society were in their graves was it rediscovered – by Samuel Smiles.[43] Yet the posthumous significance of the body which so few acknowledged, whether at the time or during the early decades of the nineteenth century, has been widely recognised in subsequent accounts. Werner Busch has described it as 'the most important private scientific association in eighteenth-century England'.[44]

The members were first and foremost personal friends, and the core group can be identified without difficulty.[45] They included Erasmus Darwin, who moved to Lichfield in order to practise medicine in 1756 and would be joined there by Richard Lovell Edgeworth and Thomas Day in 1765. By this date all three men already knew Matthew Boulton in Birmingham, as well as each other, and in that same year the friendship circle was extended by the arrival of Dr William Small from Virginia, bearing a letter of introduction to Boulton signed by Benjamin Franklin. Franklin, it will be recalled, had first met Boulton in Birmingham in 1758. Small set up a practice in the rapidly expanding West Midland metropolis and became the Boulton family's doctor. It was he who first established (epistolary) contact with James Watt up in Glasgow, and Richard Lovell Edgeworth later recalled that he had become acquainted with Small through the intermediary of one Captain Keir. After a decade in the army, James Keir had sold his commission and was casting around for an occupation when he renewed contact with Darwin, whom he had known as a student in Edinburgh. In 1770, or thereabouts, he moved to Stourbridge in the Black Country and established a glass-works – a business that would allow him to indulge his passion for chemistry. James Watt was the next to join the group – after much prompting from Small and Boulton. He arrived in Birmingham from Scotland in the late spring of 1774 and the following year entered into a partnership with Matthew Boulton to manufacture and market the improved steam engine. By this date Boulton would have been on familiar terms with senior members of the Galton family, whose arms foundry lay only a short distance from his father's original 'toy' works in Snow Hill. Samuel Galton junior came of age in 1774 and we know that he was trying to improve his knowledge of the sciences by 1776. It is probable that he became a Lunar associate towards the end of that decade. The final pieces in this

[43] S. Smiles, *Lives of the Engineers: the Steam-Engine, Boulton and Watt* (London: Murray, 1874), pp. 292–309.

[44] W. Busch, 'Joseph Wright of Derby: art, science, and the validity of artistic language', in Shea, *Science and the Visual Image in the Enlightenment*, p. 33.

[45] E. Darwin; M. Boulton; W. Small; R. L. Edgeworth; T. Day; J. Keir; W. Withering; J. Watt; S. Galton jnr; J. Priestley.

jigsaw of friendships and mutual interests fell into place in 1775, when Dr William Withering of Stafford moved to Birmingham in order to take over the practice vacated by Small, and in 1780, when Dr Joseph Priestley appeared on the scene as minister of religion to the New Meeting – one of Birmingham's two Presbyterian congregations.

By no means all of these gentlemen were regular attenders of Lunar meetings. Some remained in the district only a short time, whereas others – not mentioned above – were intermittent or spasmodic attenders. Neither Edgeworth nor Day settled permanently in Lichfield, whilst Darwin moved close to Derby following his remarriage in 1781. The Derby clock-maker, inventor and geologist John Whitehurst is often recorded as a 'lunatick',[46] but he left the Midlands for London in 1775. In any case, Derby was a long day's ride from Birmingham and its district. A more plausible case for membership can be made in respect of Robert Augustus Johnson, a well-connected Anglican clergyman residing in Kenilworth, about twenty miles from Birmingham. But Johnson was recruited late – in 1787 – and is unlikely to have attended meetings very frequently. Likewise Jonathan Stokes, who practised as a physician in Stourbridge and was, therefore, only an hour and a half distant from Birmingham. In a letter to the younger Linnaeus written in the summer of 1783 he reported that he had been invited to join the group, although it cannot have been for longer than three years or so, because in 1786 he moved to Shrewsbury. Josiah Wedgwood of Etruria, near Newcastle-under-Lyme, is sometimes described as a member of the Lunar Society as well. He was certainly on terms of friendship with most of those identified above, and was a fairly regular visitor to Soho, as we have seen. He seems to have had a standing invitation to attend meetings, too, if we may judge from a 1785 copy-letter surviving among James Watt's papers. However, the piecemeal record of *actual* meetings reveals no sign of Wedgwood's presence, although there is a suggestion that he would sometimes come over to join Darwin's discussion group in Lichfield in the 1760s. Given his location (even farther afield than Derby), then, Wedgwood should not be considered as anything more than a distant affiliate of the Lunar Society. All of these men regarded themselves as practising natural philosophers – whatever their day-to-day employment or source of income. In this connection it is worth noting that they would all secure election to the Royal Society too, save, that is, for Dr William Small and Dr Jonathan Stokes.

The list of occasional visitors welcomed to Lunar sessions is no less revealing. Such individuals would be invited to attend meetings as

---

[46] The term appears to have been coined by the butler of Samuel Galton jnr.

members' guests, either because they were passing through Birmingham
and its district, or because they had come to the West Midlands specifically in order to pay a call on Priestley, Watt, or Withering, or to visit
Boulton's showcase manufactory, or Keir's chemicals plant at Tipton.
Not all visitors were issued with an invitation, however. Since the Society
generally convened on those Sunday afternoons closest to a full moon
(from 1780 on Mondays in order to accommodate Priestley's ministry),
much depended on time of arrival and length of stay. Also, invitations
were only issued to the travelling intelligentsia of natural philosophers,
or to those such as Sir Joseph Banks – president of the Royal Society
– who occupied node points in the scientific knowledge networks of
the late Enlightenment. Of course, the two categories were often one
and the same. Joseph Banks, the well-connected Irish chemist Richard
Kirwan, Jean-André Deluc, the *émigré* Swiss physicist who served as Reader
to Queen Charlotte, Sir William Herschel, the Astronomer Royal, and
Dr Daniel Solander, the Swedish naturalist and one-time librarian to
Banks, all attended sessions. But so did Scots *savants* such as Joseph
Black and James Hutton, who had long-standing links with James Watt,
itinerant lecturers such as John Warltire, industrial chemists such as
George Fordyce and Alexander Blair, the radical philosopher-chemist
Thomas Cooper, and the independent-minded Anglican clergyman
Dr Samuel Parr. Many of these individuals, and most notably Kirwan and
Cooper, were also members of parallel bodies such as the Manchester
Literary and Philosophical Society, or the Chapter Coffee House Society
in London. Indeed, Banks and Kirwan both held regular science gather-
ings or 'conversations' of their own in their London town houses.

Foreign visitors tended to be invited solely on the strength of their
reputation in the sciences. But many were also house guests of Matthew
Boulton, and it is sometimes difficult to distinguish between polite
dinner-table gatherings at Soho House and scheduled Lunar meetings.
Reputation was not always an infallible guide to knowledge or competence, for James Watt welcomed the Duc de Chaulnes in 1783 on the
strength of a recommendation from ex-Lunar member John Whitehurst.
Chaulnes, he subsequently reported to Black, was a nice man, but no
great chemist. Yet such disappointments were comparatively rare, and
there can be no doubt that the presence of foreign visitors significantly
increased both the quantity and the velocity of knowledge dissemination across Europe in the 1770s and 1780s. The sources shedding light
on this 'commerce des lumières' are tantalisingly vague, as we shall see,
but contact between the Lunar group and the geologist Faujas de Saint-
Fond in 1784, the Dijon chemist Grossart de Virly, who had studied with
Torbern Bergman, in 1786, and Lamétherie, editor of the *Journal de*

physique, in 1788, seems to have been particularly fruitful. Likewise contact with the Dutch anatomist Petrus Camper (1785) and the Göttingen metallurgist and chemist Johann Göttling, who was enlisted into a month-long series of encounters and experiments supervised by Priestley towards the latter end of 1787. In the case of the visits of the King of Prussia's director of mines, Baron von Reden (1782), and the French military engineer Aimable Marie de Givry (1784), the exchange is likely to have been more one-sided. Neither Boulton the impresario of Soho, nor Boulton the whipper-in of the Lunar Society ever managed to resolve the tension between natural knowledge dissemination (a polite requirement) and 'know how' transfer (often a trade secret).

If the Lunar Society convened at roughly monthly intervals throughout the last quarter of the eighteenth century and into the new, up to 350 meetings could have taken place. But since the group remained fluid and failed to constitute itself as a formal literary and philosophical society, we shall never know in truth – even approximately – how many times the members gathered at each other's houses. Researchers disagree, moreover, on when the Society first took shape and when its monthly meetings finally petered out. Even though Darwin evoked 'your Birmingham philosophers'[47] in a letter to Boulton written at the very end of 1765, Robert Schofield[48] is not persuaded that a definable society or club existed by this date. He opts instead for the year 1775, and finds no record of any Lunar meetings after 1794. Yet Samuel Smiles[49] clearly believed that the Society could be traced back to the mid-1760s, and Eric Robinson,[50] who had access to the Watt papers, which were then in private ownership – unlike Schofield – finds evidence of meetings dating back to 1772 and perhaps even earlier. The geologist James Hutton, who accompanied James Watt from Scotland to Birmingham in the spring of 1774, certainly encountered some kind of functioning philosophical society centring on Boulton and Soho at that time, for he acknowledged the fact in a letter to Watt.[51] As for a terminal date, 1794 cannot be accepted for there is now ample evidence to indicate fairly regular meetings into 1802, the year in which Darwin died and Boulton became physically incapacitated and virtually house-bound, and even beyond. Kirwan certainly attended a meeting at Soho House in

---

[47] See D. King-Hele (ed.), *The Letters of Erasmus Darwin* (Cambridge: Cambridge University Press, 1981), p. 16; also the editor's expanded and revised *The Collected Letters of Erasmus Darwin* (Cambridge: Cambridge University Press, 2007), p. 67 note 6.

[48] Schofield, *The Lunar Society of Birmingham*, pp. 141–5.

[49] Smiles, *Lives of the Engineers*, p. 293.

[50] Robinson, 'The Lunar Society: its membership and organisation', p. 156.

[51] BCL MS 3219/4/78 J. Hutton to J. Watt snr, n.d. [docketed late 1774].

1795; Banks one held at Duddesdon – Samuel Galton junior's residence – in the summer of 1797; and Herschel one held at Soho in the summer of 1801. In all probability the Society had become extinct by the end of 1804. It was definitely non-functioning by 1813, for in that year a ballot was held among surviving members (Watt, Galton and Keir) to dispose of jointly purchased library books.

As a result of the researches undertaken in the course of this study, it has proved possible to identify, or deduce, the occurrence of about 130 meetings of the Lunar Society. The chronological distribution of these meetings is presented in Figure 3.0. Although the members expected to convene at roughly monthly intervals, there appear to have been periods of prolonged inactivity, owing to the absence of key players, pressures of work or, in some cases, the interruption of events. Boulton seems to have initiated a renewal of activity in the second half of 1775 and early 1776, perhaps, as Schofield speculates, in response to the shock of the death of William Small. He certainly had it in mind to give the meetings a more official character henceforward, for he informed both James Keir and James Watt as much. The fact that we hear no more of rules and regulations after the gathering at Soho House on 3 March

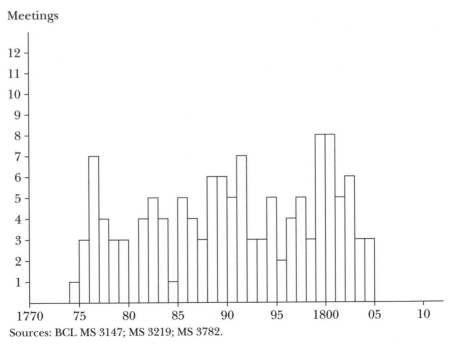

Sources: BCL MS 3147; MS 3219; MS 3782.

3.0 Frequency of (known) meetings of the Lunar Society, c. 1770–1810

1776 suggests that the members vetoed the idea of becoming a formally constituted literary and philosophical society. Nevertheless, a system of sessional subscriptions appears to have been introduced, presumably in order to defray the costs of experiments and the purchase of books. The next we hear of waning commitment is in 1786 and 1787, when Boulton and Watt were overwhelmed with business and obliged to travel incessantly. Watt told his eldest son in the summer of 1786 that the weight of the steam-engine orders was such that he had been obliged to halt his 'philosophical pursuits'.[52] Political events on the continent of Europe could also cause disruption. Although revolutions accelerated the flow of refugees across the Channel and enhanced word-of-mouth transmission of news, they tended to interrupt more measured *savant* discourse and inject tensions where none had previously existed. Jan Daniël Huichelbos van Liender,[53] a Dutch Patriot who quit his homeland in 1788 following the Prussian invasion, became a regular at Lunar meetings during the autumn of 1789, before moving on to Paris. It is thanks to his correspondence that we learn that meetings thinned out again in the spring and summer of 1790.

The data presented above are gleanings deriving for the most part from references in letters and diaries. They cannot provide an accurate profile of the frequency of Lunar meetings. Given the absence of minute books or any other type of official documentation, it could scarcely be otherwise. Nevertheless, if we combine this evidence, such as it is, with information from other sources and turn our attention to the question of what was discussed during Lunar sessions, one conclusion does emerge clearly: the early 1780s constituted the most intellectually fertile period of the Society's existence. No doubt the arrival in Birmingham of substantial philosophical reinforcement in the shape of Dr Joseph Priestley provides part of the explanation. Priestley more than compensated for the loss of Darwin, and he was probably responsible for nudging the Society away from a preoccupation with gadgets and contrivances and towards the study of heat, combustion and 'airs'. However, it should also be remembered that the 1780s was a decade in which the volume and speed of knowledge exchange – in all its forms – increased sharply. Finally, the decade witnessed startling advances in the realm of chemistry which produced much ground for discussion. Indeed, a far from negligible portion of this experimental work was carried out, or replicated, by the Lunar philosophers themselves. It seems no accident, therefore, that the Society began purchasing science periodicals for common use

---

[52] BCL MS 3219/4/123 J. Watt snr to J. Watt jnr, n.p., 13 August 1786.
[53] See Verbruggen, *The Correspondence of van Liender*, p. 211.

in the 1780s. Orders were generally placed through the foreign-book importer and seller J. C. de Boffe in London, although in December 1783 Watt asked Jean-Hyacinthe Magellan to order for the Society a run of Rozier's *Journal d'observations sur la physique* and the *Mémoires de l'Académie de Dijon* from Paris.

In general we may conclude that the Lunar gentlemen used their leisurely working dinners to explore topics in the fields of physics, chemistry, mineralogy, metallurgy, optics and education (then perceived as an experimental science *à la Rousseau*). Some idea of what precisely was discussed, or demonstrated, during these prolonged 'conversations' can be obtained from Table 3.0. It has been compiled on the basis of primary evidence, or inference, rather than in accordance with historians' claims regarding the subject matter of Lunar meetings. For all their proximity to the industrial pulse of the West Midlands, it will be noticed at once that natural knowledge, not technology, chiefly engaged their attentions. None of the foreigners who came to hear of the existence of the Lunar Society, or who were invited to attend its sessions, seems to have drawn the conclusion that its *raison d'être* was primarily industrial. On the contrary, the well-travelled and inquisitive J.-H. Magellan supposed that the affiliates must be alchemists who laboured by the light of the moon: 'are you working in the silver-philosophical stone?'[54] he asked Watt in 1783. The more prosaic truth is that the Lunar Society held wide-ranging discussions on topics of

Table 3.0 *Activities of the Lunar Society (with approximate dates)*

Date	Activity
1771	Erasmus Darwin's speaking automaton
Spring 1775	Experiments on time pieces
Early 1776	Experiments to determine the nature of heat
April 1779	Optimum design for a horizontal windmill
Summer 1779	Improvements to Erasmus Darwin's letter-copying machine
January 1781	Carl Scheele's research into heat transfer
January 1781	Chemical composition of inks
February–March 1781	Repetition of James Watt's kettle experiments
April 1781	Joseph Priestley's experiments igniting a mixture of inflammable air and common air with an electric spark

[54] BCL MS3147/3/509 J.-H. Magellan to J. Watt snr, 22 March 1783.

Table 3.0 (*cont'd*)

Date	Activity
July 1781	Chemical analysis of white spar
Early 1782	Experiments to determine the composition of water or steam
October 1782	James Smeaton's experiments with circular motion from steam engines
December 1782	Joseph Priestley's experiments on chalk
February–May 1783	Water to air experiments of Joseph Priestley and James Watt
November 1783	Richard Kirwan's communication of the discovery of Prussian blue by Carle Scheele
November 1783	Decimal weights and measures
December 1783	James Watt's experiments with boiling water under pressure
November 1784	Joseph Priestley's experiments on the decomposition of water
December 1784	Hot-air and hydrogen balloon experiments
Winter and Spring 1785	Experiments with the distillation of the spirit of nitre
September 1785	Richard Kirwan's communication of a new gas (phosphine)
June 1786	The theory and practice of the education of children
January 1788	Replication of the water experiments of Antoine Lavoisier and others
April 1789	Latin inscriptions for Matthew Boulton's George III recovery medallion
May 1789	Analysis of a black substance sent by the Rev. Bretland
December 1789–January 1790	Decomposition of water with the aid of an electrical machine
Summer 1790	Replication of the Amsterdam experiments of Paets van Troostwijk and Deiman on the analysis and synthesis of water
February 1791	Joseph Priestley's experiment to demonstrate that water and nitrous acid consist of the same elements
1796	A humorous piece about the phlogiston debate, composed by William Withering
August 1797	Resistance to heat and cold of Lisbon lamp glass
February 1804	The electric meridian; the composition of platina

Sources: BCL MS 3147; MS 3219; MS 3782.

interest to its members *as natural philosophers.* It carried out experiments – particularly when meeting at Fairhill or Soho, since Priestley and Boulton possessed the best-equipped laboratories. These experiments could be path breaking: Priestley and Watt's work on the decomposition of water in 1782–83 is a case in point. But, equally, they carried out many experiments to test and verify the findings of others. And no less important, they acted as a kind of relay station for the dissemination of natural knowledge. In this respect, the Lunar Society was little different from scores of vehicles of the Scientific Enlightenment which could be found all over Europe by the 1770s and 1780s.

It seems unlikely that the members of the Lunar Society conceived their primary purpose as being to augment the stock of useful knowledge, then. The notion of economically useful knowledge is a time-bound concept in any case and, as such, more suited to the industrial climate of the early nineteenth century than to the mind-set of the 1770s and 1780s. John Money[55] points out that the 'utility' of knowledge for someone of Priestley's stamp had more to do with the revelation of divine intent than the Victorian obsession with material progress. When Darwin founded a clone of the Lunar Society in Derby in 1783, he used a revealing analogy when recommending the new creation to the good offices of his old friend in Birmingham: 'Perhaps like the free-mason societies, we may sometime make your society a visit.'[56] If the Lunar associates perceived themselves as something akin to a masonic fraternity, it should come as no surprise if they generally chose to leave their mundane, mercantile preoccupations at home when banding together in their monthly quests for enlightenment.

The international network

Some sense of the role of Birmingham and its district in the distribution network for natural knowledge and experimental data emerges from our attempt to analyse the activities of the Lunar Society. But the real hub of international exchange, as it impinged upon the West Midlands in the second half of the eighteenth century, was the Soho Manufactory. Over the forty-year period during which Matthew Boulton remained in effective control, it was a magnet for literally thousands of home and overseas visitors. The correspondence generated by these visitors, together with the numerous published accounts of their tours, provides

---

[55] Money, 'Joseph Priestley in cultural context: part two', 81–2 and note 108.
[56] King-Hele, *The Letters of Erasmus Darwin*, p. 128.

a means of exposing to view the working mechanisms of the putative Industrial Enlightenment which few other sources can match. Not only can we track the movement of knowledge around Europe, including the movement of know-how (the subject of Chapter 4), we can also explore fruitfully the codes of civility applying to knowledge transmission and the manner in which trust between contracting parties was negotiated.

It is possible to identify securely nearly 1,100 of the men and women (mostly the former) who applied to visit the Soho Manufactory – perhaps a quarter of the total visitor flow. This figure excludes dependents and servants. A little over half of the named individuals (54%) were visitors from overseas – either leisured travellers bent upon an excursion through the British Isles, or else semi-official agents commissioned by institutions or governments to carry out a 'technological' Grand Tour. However, the ratio of home to overseas visitors did not remain constant over time, for reasons that will need to be explained, and nor, for that matter, did the types of visitor. As for country of origin, France – the leading scientific knowledge-generating state of the eighteenth century – dispatched scores of open-minded tourists across the Channel, whereas Spain, whose Enlightenment was of recent date and shallowly rooted, sent just a handful. Matthew Boulton initially welcomed visitors to his manufactory, notwithstanding intermittent worries about the 'kidnapping' of useful knowledge (industrial espionage), but towards the end of his life he grew to dread the summer-season influx of carriages pulling up at his factory gates. In 1805 he informed Johanna Schopenhauer that 'Nichts ist unerträglicher als ein Haus zu besitzen, das eine Sehenswurdigkeit ist'[57] – a rich comment, she confided, from a man who used to take boundless delight and satisfaction in showing visitors around Soho.

Visitor flows tended to mirror the state of international relations, although war remained a matter principally for governments rather than peoples until the 1790s and did not automatically curtail movement across borders. Nevertheless, applications to view the Soho Manufactory from overseas travellers plummeted with the onset of the American War which, by 1780, had entangled Britain with France, Spain and the Dutch Republic as well as with her North American colonies. The signing of a peace settlement in Paris in 1783 produced a sharp recovery, to the extent that the flow of travellers from abroad began to parallel the growth

---

[57] 'Nothing can be more unbearable than to own a house that is a tourist attraction', see W. von Kroker, *Wege zur Verbreitung technologischer Kenntnisse zwischen England und Deutschland in der zweiten Hälfte des 18 Jahrhunderts* (Berlin: Duncker & Humbolt, 1971), p. 95.

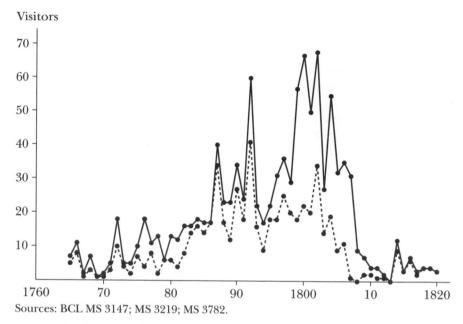

Sources: BCL MS 3147; MS 3219; MS 3782.

3.1 Total recorded visitor flows to the Soho Manufactory, 1765–1820
(dotted line indicates foreign visitors)

profile of home-based tourism once more. Horace Walpole reported 'swarms' of French visitors to Strawberry Hill, and Boulton was besieged by French academicians and royal engineers (Lesage, Prony, Coulomb, Perronet, Cachin, Givry, Wendel etc.) on a hunt for knowledge that would help to rebuild the sinews of the Bourbon state. The same thing happened in 1801–3 (peace interlude of Amiens), and again in 1814. 'Foreigners are coming here in shoals', reported James Watt junior in August 1814, 'first a Spanish admiral & hydrographer Don Saxpp [*sic*] de Espinoza; next a Polish Count & magnate Sierakowski & today Mr Fischer, Director of the iron mines in the canton of Schaffhausen.'[58] The French *polytechniciens* and engineers, Dupin, Hachette, Cécile and Martin, were not far behind – arriving in 1816 and 1819. After the collapse of the Peace of Amiens in the spring of 1803 and the resumption of the struggle against French domination in Europe, Britain had become isolated and virtually cut off from the Continent, as Figure 3.1 makes plain. Hence the influx of visitors following the final defeat of Napoleon and the reopening of land borders and sea lanes.

[58] BCL MS 3219/4/35 J. Watt jnr to J. Watt snr, Soho, 27 August 1814.

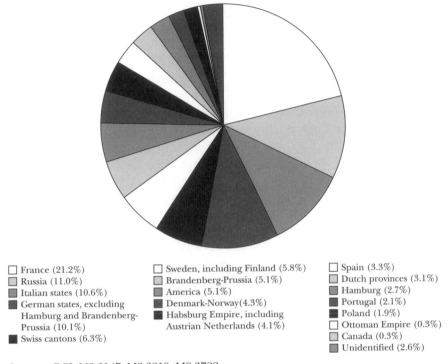

□ France (21.2%)
■ Russia (11.0%)
■ Italian states (10.6%)
■ German states, excluding
   Hamburg and Brandenberg-
   Prussia (10.1%)
■ Swiss cantons (6.3%)

□ Sweden, including Finland (5.8%)
■ Brandenberg-Prussia (5.1%)
■ America (5.1%)
■ Denmark-Norway(4.3%)
■ Habsburg Empire, including
   Austrian Netherlands (4.1%)

□ Spain (3.3%)
□ Dutch provinces (3.1%)
■ Hamburg (2.7%)
■ Portugal (2.1%)
■ Poland (1.9%)
□ Ottoman Empire (0.3%)
□ Canada (0.3%)
■ Unidentified (2.6%)

Sources: BCL MS 3147; MS 3219; MS 3782.

3.2 Foreign visitors to the Soho Manufactory by origin, 1765–1820

Knowledge transmission via interpersonal contact was also affected by more localised factors. The launch of Soho as a visitor venue where 'genius and the arts preside'[59] was greatly facilitated by Matthew Boulton's decision to go into ormolu production and the opening of a show gallery and tea room in 1772. The substantial influx of Russians owed everything to the liberal policies pursued by Catherine on her accession to the imperial throne (reaffirmation of Peter III's Manifesto of 1762 granting freedom to travel to the nobility and gentry; trade treaty of 1766, etc.). Princess Ekaterina Dashkova, the future Director of the St Petersburg Academy of Sciences, was able to acquaint herself with the west European Enlightenment and visit Soho as a direct result of Catherine's lifting the travel embargo. As for the Swedish visitors to Birmingham and Coalbrookdale (Angerstein, Ferrner, Robsahm, Broling,

[59] J. Bisset, *A Poetic Survey Round Birmingham With Brief Description of the Different Manufactories of the Place* (Birmingham: The Author, 1800).

Svedenstierna, Edelcrantz, etc.), they were mainly technologists sent out to Britain after mid century by the powerful Ironmasters' Association (*Jernkontoret*). A similar observation could be made in respect of the many visitors hailing from the territories controlled by the King of Prussia. Friedrich Anton von Heynitz,[60] the man responsible in 1766 for the establishment of the Freiberg Mining School in Saxony before transferring to the service of Prussia, had been powerfully influenced by several technological tours of England undertaken since the mid-1770s. As Minister of State and Head of Prussia's Department of Mines, he dispatched a succession of highly inquisitive gentlemen (Bückling, Eversmann, his nephew Friedrich Wilhelm von Reden, the Baron Heinrich Friedrich Carl vom Stein, etc.) to Soho in the 1780s.

The etiquette of person-to-person knowledge transmission followed a predictable pattern which was grounded in the unwritten rules of eighteenth-century civility. Whether Boulton's interlocutors requested permission to visit the works as sight-seeing tourists or as philosophers in pursuit of useful knowledge, gentlemanly good manners demanded that they present a letter of introduction. Such recommendations might be drafted in advance for the bearer and presented physically (usually by a servant dispatched from a Birmingham inn or hotel), or they might be sent in the post direct to Soho in anticipation of the arrival of the person to whom they related. The astronomer Jérôme Lalande[61] disembarked in London, just as peace was being concluded after the Seven Years' War (1756–63), with over forty letters of introduction in his pocket, and the Hamburger Philipp Andreas Nemnich[62] claimed that he had set out on his second tour of England in 1805–6 equipped with nearly 1,200 supporting letters, not to mention a sheaf of questionnaires. In conditions where the contracting parties were not personally known to one another, letters of introduction circulated like a form of moral currency, therefore. They signalled a presumption of social parity and gentlemanly trustworthiness – this latter an important consideration for Boulton, since Soho, like the Ravenhead plate-glass-works near St Helens or the Carron iron-foundry in Scotland, tended to attract spies and other emissaries who exploited the Enlightenment's commitment to commodified public knowledge up to and even beyond the limits of social acceptability.

---

[60] See W. Weber, *Innovationen im frühindustriellen deutschen Bergbau und Hüttenwesen: Friedrich Anton von Heynitz* (Göttingen: Vandenhoeck & Ruprecht, 1976).

[61] Lalande, *Journal d'un voyage en Angleterre 1763*, p. 12.

[62] See O. Viennet, *Une Enquête économique dans la France Impériale. Le voyage du Hambourgeois Philippe-André Nemnich, 1809* (Paris, 1947), p. iii.

Provided that the preconditions of civility had been satisfied, it was very nearly impossible for a gentlemanly manufacturer with a substantial claim to *savant* status, such as Matthew Boulton, to refuse hospitality to a visitor – no matter how awkward or inconvenient the arrival of the putative guest might be. Yet Boulton expected something in return, for otherwise the knowledge flow was apt to be one sided. The invitation to 'dinner', whether issued to a travelling natural philosopher or to a title-bearing tourist, was an encoded invitation to converse, an art in which he excelled and which he expected others to show a comparable commitment to. But if the late eighteenth century was pre-eminently a 'discussing age',[63] it is important not to lose sight of the transactional character of Boulton's hospitality. As Felicity Heal[64] has noted, the aristocratic honour code of courtesy developed a commercial, even a utilitarian, edge to it in the course of the eighteenth century. Many a time the Soho House dinner table proved a source of valuable intelligence, but it could also descend into linguistic pandemonium. Of one occasion in the spring of 1781, when six foreigners were assembled for dinner, Boulton afterwards remarked ruefully: 'our house has been like that of Babel, by bad English, French, Italian, German and bad translations'.[65] Yet he consoled himself with the thought that such occasions were unavoidable if the firm of Boulton & Fothergill wished to keep up their trade connections.

Letters of recommendation were liable to devaluation, however, like any other currency. The more they were used and the more dilute the link between the issuer and bearer, the less credibility they carried. As president of the Royal Society, Sir Joseph Banks was constantly assailed by visiting gentlemen and scientific luminaries for letters attesting to their status and professional capacities, and in 1778 he discussed the problems this posed with Matthew Boulton during one of the latter's London visits. Ambassador Vorontsov of Russia faced a similar problem and his secretary would explain apologetically to Boulton that His Excellency could not refuse to oblige noblemen who were connected to the Emperor. The immediate consequence of this devaluation was a growing scepticism among those to whom recommendations were addressed. This, in turn, provoked an ever greater compensatory effort on the part of writers to give their missives enhanced persuasive power.

[63] A. Herman, *The Scottish Enlightenment. The Scots' Invention of the Modern World* (London: Fourth Estate, 2001), p. 263.
[64] F. Heal, *Hospitality in Early Modern England* (Oxford: Oxford University Press, 1990), pp. 392–400.
[65] BCL MS 3147/3/5 M. Boulton to J. Watt snr, 26 June 1781.

The laconic, almost condescending letter of introduction of the 1760s and 1770s was partly superseded by recommendations offering reassurance, or seeking to forestall objections. Thus Benjamin Vaughan, the Unitarian merchant and natural philosopher, wrote in May 1793 on behalf of Messrs Andreani (the aeronaut) and Pisani (formerly Venetian ambassador to France) stating, 'their manners are such as of themselves to give assurance that they travel only for their own instruction & amusement & will not violate any confidence reposed in them'.[66] By 1803, though, even this might have raised sceptical eyebrows. A Mr Browne petitioned Boulton on behalf of a middle-class couple, Mr and Mrs Solly, who wished to view Soho 'though not with the eye of a manufacturer or [a] man of science'.[67]

Travel was the most direct way of getting and passing on knowledge, then. And in an age largely innocent of printed technical literature, it was virtually the only means of securing control of know-how. Yet Matthew Boulton, James Watt and their Lunar brethren all maintained extensive and overlapping science networks based on communication by letter. Whilst some of this letter writing was speculative (Alessandro Volta's self-introduction to Priestley in 1772 is a case in point),[68] much was based on personal contact. Nearly all of the members of the Lunar group travelled to the continent of Europe and epistolary relationships were sometimes rooted in contacts made years previously. When Gregory Watt set off on a version of the Grand Tour in 1801, his older half-brother James equipped him with a list of natural philosophers to call upon whom he had met during his own educational travels some fifteen years earlier (Berthollet and Prony in Paris; Karsten in Berlin; Werner in Freiberg; Göttling in Jena, etc.). But the reverse might apply, too. Having made contact with Priestley by letter, Volta took care to consolidate the link by paying a call on him in Birmingham in 1782. Correspondence networks during the high decades of the Enlightenment were extraordinarily wide-ranging and, as far as we can judge, extraordinarily efficient in conveying information around the western world. Only in the dark years after 1806 (see Chapter 6) did the Republic of Letters largely break down.

Much of the documentation which enables us to draw these conclusions is fully accessible. Over 20,000 items of Boulton and Watt correspondence are available for scrutiny, although it is the letters exchanged with approximately 100 natural philosophers or self-styled

---

[66] BCL MS 3782/12/49 B. Vaughan to M. Boulton, London, 11 May 1793.
[67] *Ibid.*, J. H. Browne to M. Boulton, n.p., 9 June 1803.
[68] Pancaldi, *Volta: Science and Culture in the Age of the Enlightenment*, pp. 150–1.

savants which are of greatest relevance. This material can be extended and contextualised further by reference to the Banks correspondence (over 6,000 letters survive), the Linnaeus correspondence (a corpus of 5,500 letters and 600 correspondents), the Marc-Auguste Pictet correspondence (3,000 letters and around 400 correspondents), not to mention the smaller and only partially intact holdings of Magellan (700 letters), Darwin (460 letters), Priestley, van Liender, etc.[69] Such is the volume of material, indeed, that it invites some consideration of networking as a sociological concept. The first point worth making is that letter writing, by the second half of the eighteenth century, had become a highly fluid and non-formulaic genre of communication. Individuals expressed themselves uninhibitedly (women as well as men) and, in the case of *savants*, often worked out their thoughts on paper. It follows that writers did not confine their thoughts, either, although the correspondence of a Boulton or a Watt is perhaps an extreme example of this promiscuity of subject matter. Lorraine Daston's[70] characterisation of the Scientific Enlightenment as a gigantic echo chamber in which ideas and information ping-ponged back and forth is amply confirmed on the evidence of the sources referred to above, therefore. When the dissemination of scientific knowledge is analysed from a well-documented networking perspective we are reminded, too, that there was nothing random or passive about the process. Sites of calculation, such as Birmingham, did not take shape by accident, for network building was a purposeful exercise even if the consequential intersections and overlaps were largely unpredictable in their ramifications.

The community of scientific knowledge disseminators of the second half of the eighteenth century comprised actors, emulators, bit-part players, journalists and a substantial cohort of consumers, then. But as Peter Dear remarks in a slightly different context, it was not 'a homogeneous thought-collective'.[71] The linkages between these individuals were contingent, often indirect and unstructured, or only loosely structured. Embedded at the heart of the Industrial Enlightenment we can find no clearly articulated system of beliefs, but rather a proselytising desire to diffuse non-dogmatic experimental knowledge, with the question of how that knowledge was to be applied left open ended – left

---

[69] See Bibliography: primary manuscript and printed sources.

[70] L. Daston, 'Afterword: the ethos of the Enlightenment', in W. Clark, J. Golinski and S. Schaffer (eds), *The Sciences in Enlightened Europe* (Chicago: Chicago University Press, 1999), p. 498.

[71] P. Dear, 'Cultural history of science: an overview with reflections', *Science, Technology and Human Values*, 20 (1995), 157.

in many instances, indeed, for another generation to determine. Maybe, as D. S. Lux and H. J. Cook[72] have argued, it is in the nature of networks to facilitate information transmission. The argument, which they take from Mark Granovetter,[73] that knowledge will percolate more easily and reach a greater number of people if filtered through weak social bonds rather than strong, certainly makes sense of what we can observe in the case of the Lunar group, or its larger international extension, the Soho network. After all, much of the scientific knowledge being purveyed was in fact 'news', rather than 'discoveries' or 'inventions'. Perhaps an *a contrario* proof of the viability of the 'weak links' theory can be found in the area of tacit knowledge, however. For tacit knowledge, and particularly know-how, was less susceptible to communication at a distance and, as a constituent of technology, more likely to be bonded together and therefore constrained in the manner described by Lux and Cook. Yet the fact that 'weak links' theory appears to fit with the evidence as we have uncovered it does not actually explain why this should be so. Here the concept of 'nodes' is helpful, for, as Jane Everett[74] points out, an exchange of letters between two individuals mobilises at least two networks. This is another way of saying that networked knowledge moves effortlessly between groups and, in the case of nodal figures (or locations), may spill out in many different, unplanned directions more or less simultaneously.

The case for viewing Birmingham and the urbanising and industrialising West Midlands as a physical node point in the circuits of late eighteenth-century scientific sociability scarcely requires further demonstration. Yet it is worth emphasising the close cognitive link between the region's natural philosophers and manufacturers and their counterparts in Lowland Scotland. Although Boulton & Watt would develop strong commercial relationships with Manchester and its satellites in the North-West from the late 1780s, this was not a channel along which a great deal of scientific information flowed. If we exclude the case of Thomas Cooper, Birmingham's philosophers had only intermittent contact with the luminaries of Manchester's Literary and Philosophical Society. Glasgow and, more especially, Edinburgh were universally acknowledged centres of calculation, by contrast. The Prussian traveller

---

[72] D. S. Lux and H. J. Cook, 'Closed circuits or open networks? Communicating at a distance during the Scientific Revolution', *History of Science*, 36 (1998), 179–211.

[73] M. Granovetter, 'The strength of weak ties', *American Journal of Sociology*, 78 (1973), 1360–80.

[74] J. Everett, 'Réseaux épistolaires: le cas du Québec dans les années trente', in B. Melançon (ed.), *Penser par lettre. Actes du colloque d'Azay-le-Ferron, mai 1997* (Québec: Fides, 1998), p. 128.

Johann Wilhelm von Archenholz opined that 'more true learning is to be found in Edinburgh than in Oxford and Cambridge taken together',[75] and most of his contemporaries of the 1780s would have concurred. Under the dynamic leadership of its Principal, William Robertson, the University of Edinburgh became a veritable power station for scientific knowledge generation during the period covered by this study. Many members of the Lunar group had close and enduring contacts with this energy source, as we have already had occasion to remark.

Another node which emerges clearly when we come to trace out the knowledge network in its international dimension is the Freiberg *Bergsakademie*. Founded as part of the Saxon state's bid to recover from the trauma of the Seven Years' War, this mining school shaped a whole generation of European mineralogists and mining engineers. The hands-on training pioneered at Freiberg once Abraham Gottlob Werner had taken up the chair of mining there in 1775 will be considered in Chapter 4. Suffice it to say at this stage that Freiberg – under Werner – became a source and distribution centre for mineralogical knowledge, as well as a magnet for manufacturers who wished their sons to be educated in both the theoretical and the practical branches of earth science. Watt's eldest son was sent to study there in 1786 and Boulton entertained similar plans in respect of Matthew Robinson, for in the summer of 1789 he asked Priestley to supply a letter of introduction to Werner. In the event, his son seems to have been packed off for a stint at Wiegleb's school in Langensalza instead. Werner's 'neptunist' views on the origins of the earth's crust were debated hotly in both Birmingham and Edinburgh (not least by James Hutton), and the intellectual interplay between the three centres was undoubtedly stimulated by the regular to-ing and fro-ing of visitors. The young Alexander von Humboldt passed through Birmingham on a summer tour in the year prior to the start of his studies at Freiberg, and so did William Maclure, who would become Gregory Watt's continental travel companion but is better known as the pioneer of American geology. Less well known is Charles Hatchett (1766–1847), whose day-by-day diary records his wanderings from Berlin, where he met Klaproth, to Freiberg (August 1791), and on to Edinburgh, where he found opinion divided as to the merits of Werner's and Hutton's theories. Hatchett would tour Etruria, Coalbrookdale and Soho in the company of the Neopolitan mineralogist André Savaresi, who had also studied at Freiberg.

[75] Cited in P. E. Matheson, *German Visitors to England, 1770–1795*, The Taylorian Lecture (Oxford: Clarendon Press, 1930), p. 23.

When we come to look for nodal figures whose position astride the network intersection points facilitated the process of knowledge diffusion, several names suggest themselves. Science journalists such as Lorenz Crell[76] and Marc-Auguste Pictet[77] clearly played an important role. Although Crell's *Chemische Annalen* had few English subscribers and none in the West Midlands, this enterprising Helmstedt professor-turned-journal editor did his utmost to connect up the German and the British chemical communities. He promoted Richard Kirwan's phlogistonian views and, in 1790, offered to publish in the *Annalen* James Watt junior's early papers – probably in hopes of establishing a conduit to the Lunar group. This he seems never to have succeeded in doing, for Boulton, at least, had other sources of information on developments in the German-speaking lands, in the shape of Rudolf Erich Raspe[78] (mineralogy) and Franz Xaver Swediaur (chemistry). The liberal-minded Genevan Calvinist M.-A. Pictet had more success, by contrast. His science was Baconian and utilitarian in approach and, by the time the *Bibliothèque britannique* was launched in 1796, he and his brother had built close ties of friendship among both British and French natural philosophers. In the case of James Watt, these went back to 1785, when Pictet had welcomed James junior to Geneva and allowed him to attend his lectures at the Academy. Boulton seems to have encountered Pictet for the first time in 1787, when he showed him around Soho. Both brothers translated copious amounts of English-language material for their journal, and on a wide range of topics. In 1798 and 1799 they even serialised a translation of Edgeworth's *Practical Education*. Marc-Auguste Pictet would pay a fifth and probably final visit to Britain in 1819, for we know that he called on the elderly Watt just two months before his death.

Much less is known about Franz Xaver Swediaur[79] (1748–1824), and to this day no biography of the man exists. Yet the frequency with which his name appears in correspondence runs and in the science and medical literature of the late eighteenth century, leaves no doubt that he played a pivotal role in the circulation of pure and useful knowledge

[76] See K. Hufbauer, *The Formation of the German Chemical Community, 1720–1795* (Berkeley: University of California Press, 1982), pp. 62–82.

[77] *Marc-Auguste Pictet, 1752–1825. Correspondance: sciences et techniques*, 3 vols. (Geneva: Slatkine, 1996–2000).

[78] For R. E. Raspe, see *Singular Travels, Campaigns and Adventures of Baron Munchausen* (London: Cresset, 1948).

[79] On Swediaur, see BCL MS 3782/12/91 and B. Linder and W. A. Smeaton, 'Schwediauer, Bentham and Beddoes: translators of Bergman and Scheele', *Annals of Science*, 24 (1968), 259–73.

around Europe. Equipped with a medical degree from Vienna, Swediaur migrated to London in the 1770s where he set about building a correspondence network that would include Banks, Crawford and Kirwan as well as five members of the Lunar group. At some point he moved to Edinburgh and proceeded to ingratiate himself with the natural philosophers of the University, for Black later described him as 'a great Projector & pryer into Secrets'.[80] Presumably this was a reference to the unsuccessful attempt to establish an artificial alkali works at Prestonpans on the Firth of Forth. For present purposes, however, the labour he undertook to translate Bergman and Scheele into English, and Scheele into French, is the more relevant. That and the time he spent carrying out experiments with Lavoisier and Macquer in Paris during the autumn of 1782. When, precisely, he first met the members of the Lunar group in Birmingham is hard to determine. However, he informed Bergman of Keir's successful experiments to produce a new compound metal in 1780, and even sent him a sample. Moreover, in a letter to William Withering in 1788, he stated that he had been keeping continental correspondents up-to-date with developments in the natural sciences in the British Isles for the previous ten years.[81] When revolution beckoned in France, he relocated to Paris and became an enthusiast for *liberté*. Boulton would employ him as his eyes and ears when bidding for a contract to strike the new revolutionary coinage in 1791–92 (see Chapter 6).

The nodal role of João Jacinto de Magalhães[82] (Jean-Hyacinthe Magellan), the Portuguese *savant*, by contrast, is much better known. A multi-linguist and dabbler, like Swediaur, he made it his business to get to know everybody in the Republic of Letters. By providing services which might include a little industrial intelligence gathering as well as procuring books or the placing of orders for scientific instruments, he built up an extensive network of correspondence – and obligation – from his base of operations in London. His contact with the Lunar group probably dated from the early 1770s. We know that he came to Birmingham around 1775 in order to visit Watt, with the French *savant* Chastenet de Puységur in tow. In all probability he had received reports of the improved steam engine and wanted to take a look for himself.

---

[80] See J. Golinski, *Science as Public Culture: Chemistry and Enlightenment in Britain, 1760–1820* (Cambridge: Cambridge University Press, 1992), p. 40.

[81] BCL MS 3782/21/transcripts F. X. Swediaur to W. Withering, Port Seton, 4 November 1788.

[82] See Carvalho, 'Correspondência científica dirigida a João Jacinto de Magalhães'; also M. Villas-Boas, *Jacinto de Magalhães. Um empreendedor científico na Europa do século XVIII* (Aveiro: Fundação João Jacinto Magalhães, 2000), pp. 72–6; and BCL MS 3147/3/509.

He chaperoned Volta in 1782 during the West Midlands part of his tour as well. But even before these dates, Magellan was performing a crucial role in diffusing the new chemistry of gases. When Priestley's *Directions for Impregnating Water with Fixed Air* appeared in 1772, Magellan procured a copy of the pamphlet and sent it to the French *intendant de commerce*, Trudaine de Montigny. Within months a translation had appeared in the pages of Rozier's *Observations sur la physique* which caught the attention of Lavoisier and others. Joseph Priestley would travel to Paris in person two years later, bringing with him more momentous news, of course. Nevertheless, R. W. Home credits Magellan with being 'the principal channel by which the French learned of the work of Black, Cavendish, Priestley and others on gases'.[83]

In 1802 the Italian natural philosopher Giuseppe Gazzeri observed that 'la chimie a plus avancé dans les dix dernières années que dans les dix siècles précédents'.[84] It is true that the startling progress made in the field of chemistry – and particularly pneumatic chemistry – provides the best illustration of the process of pure knowledge dissemination during these decades. The combustion experiments carried out quite independently by Priestley and the Swedish apothecary Carl Scheele which resulted in the isolation of 'dephlogisticated air' / 'fire air' (that is, oxygen) are a case in point. Priestley stumbled on the existence of 'dephlogisticated air' between 1772 and 1774, and casually reported the fact to Lavoisier and his colleagues by word of mouth whilst visiting the French capital in the entourage of the Earl of Shelburne. The following year, in 1775, he published his discovery in the second volume of *Experiments and Observations on different Kinds of Air*. Scheele's experiments identifying what he called 'fire air' occurred earlier, however. Whilst these findings, too, were reported verbally, publication of his *Chemische Abhandlung von der Luft und dem Feuer* only occurred in 1777. Swediaur translated this important text into French in 1777, whilst Johann Reinhold Forster produced an early English version in 1780. It was duly noticed by the Lunar group in January 1781.

The so-called 'water controversy' of the 1780s provides a further powerful illustration of how networks functioned within the parameters set by the knowledge highways connecting Birmingham, London and Paris. Joseph Priestley had reported that an explosion of common air and inflammable air left a 'dew', as early as 1781, but attached no significance to the observation. Whether he and Warltire, who was assisting him in

[83] R. W. Home, 'Volta's English connections', in F. Belvilacqua and L. Fregonese, *Nuovo Voltiana. Studies in Volta and his Times.* Volume One (Milan: Hoepli, 2000), p. 125.

[84] Cited in *Marc-Auguste Pictet, 1752–1825. Correspondance: sciences et techniques*, i, p. xiv.

his experiments, understood the deposit to be a product of the explosion is unclear, but unlikely. Nonetheless, the finding must have been discussed at Lunar meetings, for James Watt informed Jean-André Deluc at the very end of 1782 that Priestley had made 'a most surprising discovery which seems to confirm my theory of water's undergoing some very remarkable change at the point where all its latent heat would be changed into sensible heat'.[85] This and other experiments he had witnessed led him to the conclusion: 'I now believe air is generated from water'.[86] Henry Cavendish, meanwhile, had been carrying out similar investigations in London and reported his findings to Priestley, who passed them on to Watt – through the medium of the Lunar Society no doubt. Yet even when Cavendish used an electric spark to explode dephlogisticated and inflammable airs and detected the deposit of a quantity of water of an equal weight, he seems not to have drawn clearcut theoretical conclusions from the experiment. Instead it fell to Watt to venture the hypothesis, in April 1783, that water was not an element but a compound of dephlogisticated and inflammable airs. Thanks to Charles Blagden, however, the news of these primordial findings then jumped networks, so to speak. Having assisted Cavendish in his investigations, Blagden transmitted the results of the British water-to-air experiments to Lavoisier and the French chemists whilst on a visit to Paris in June 1783. Lavoisier, Laplace and Meusnier swiftly replicated the research and by the end of the year were able to insert a report in the *Observations sur la physique* confirming the findings. Having been the first to enunciate the hypothesis, James Watt was surprised and not a little put out when two more powerful and more famous chemists (Cavendish and Lavoisier) claimed it as their own, particularly after Blagden's role in the transmission came to light. But the *amour propre* of the various parties to the discovery that water is a compound of oxygen and hydrogen did not prevent them from continuing to collaborate. Cavendish and Blagden came on a visit to Soho in the summer of 1785, whilst Watt and Boulton would be entertained by Lavoisier and La Place in Paris during the winter of 1786–87.

The water experiments of 1781–84 seem now to lead inexorably towards an obvious conclusion.[87] But this is not how the matter appeared at the time. During the summer of 1783 the Dijon chemist

[85] BCL MS 3219/4/122 J. Watt to Mr Deluc, Birmingham, 13 December 1782.
[86] *Ibid.*
[87] For a recent account of the phases of the 'water controversy', see D. P. Miller, *Discovering Water: James Watt, Henry Cavendish and the Nineteenth-Century 'Water Controversy'* (Aldershot: Ashgate, 2004).

Guyton de Morveau wrote sceptically to Bergman: 'vous avez sans doute oui parler de l'expérience par laquelle M. Priestley pensoit avoir converti l'eau en l'air. M. Kirwan m'en écrivit en me priant de la répéter, je reconnus très bien que c'étoit l'air qui avoit pénétré dans la cornue qui l'avoit trompé'.[88] Trust waited upon accreditation, then, which in turn depended upon the validating opinion of experts expressed through the organs of reputable institutions. Hence Lavoisier's anxiety to replicate the experiment in an authoritative setting, and to publish his findings in a properly 'written-up' manner. Likewise Watt's concern to have his hypothesis communicated formally to the Royal Society (by Priestley, since he himself was not yet a Fellow). Natural philosophers who failed, or refused, to communicate their findings in an officially sanctioned manner threatened to undermine the whole edifice of the Republic of Letters, which could scarcely function without a large degree of 'system trust'.[89] Indeed, non-communication risked breaching the unwritten rules of civility. In this connection it is significant that Watt should urge his old mentor, Joseph Black, to publish his own discoveries on heat in the same missive in which he stated his hypothesis that water must be a compound.[90] Watt, it should be said, was not alone in feeling that Black's casual attitude to natural knowledge diffusion was potentially discourteous. In a letter to Volta, Magellan contrasted the behaviour of Kirwan and Black as natural philosophers. Whereas Kirwan merited praise for submitting a steady flow of communications to the Royal Society, Black was criticised for his failure to recognise that he had a duty to communicate ('le grand paresseux Black, qui malgré son grande [sic] savoir et profondes connaissances n'a jamais la bonté de laisser connoître au Public par écrit ce qu'il découvre ou qu'il avance'.)[91]

Yet James Watt's own perception of his treatment at the hands of Lavoisier and Cavendish indicates that the theory and the practice of gentlemanly science did not always match up. In a fairly restrained letter to Jean-André Deluc recounting how his theory had come to be noised in Paris, he remarked of Lavoisier: 'You see from the above that it is possible for a philosophe to be disingenuous'.[92] However, when his full report on the composition of water was finally read before the Fellows

---

[88] See Carlid and Nordström, *Torbern Bergman's Foreign Correspondence*, p. 133.

[89] The concept belongs to the sociologist Niklas Luhmann, see T. Broman, 'The Habermasian public sphere and "Science *in* the Enlightenment"', *History of Science*, 36 (1998) 123–49.

[90] BCL MS 3219/4/123 J. Watt snr to Dr Black, Birmingham, 21 April 1783.

[91] See Carvalho, 'Correspondência científica dirigida a João Jacinto de Magalhães', pp. 184–5.

[92] BCL MS 3219/4/123 J. Watt snr to J.-A. Deluc, Birmingham, 30 December 1783.

of the Royal Society in April–May 1784 and greeted with applause, he dispatched a much less restrained letter to a non-natural-philosopher correspondent – the Quaker manufacturer Joseph Fry. 'Soon after I wrote my first paper on the subject', he remarked, 'Dr Blagden explained my theory to Mr Lavoisier at Paris, and soon after that Mr Lavoisier invented it himself and read a paper on the subject to the Royal Academy of Sciences. Since that Mr Cavendish has read a paper to the Royal Society on the same idea, without making the least mention of me – The one is a French financier & the other a member of the illustrious house of Cavendish worth above £100,000 & and does not spend £1,000 p^r y^r. Rich men may do mean actions'.[93] International *savants*, we may conclude, were all in favour of knowledge dissemination, but apparently only after priority rights had been fairly attributed. But when knowledge became 'useful' – indeed, capable of supporting a technology, different rules were apt to apply. Both James Watt and Matthew Boulton understood this practice because they were manufacturers as well as *savants*. So, for that matter, did James Keir and Josiah Wedgwood. Their interlocutors within the Republic of Letters could find the distinction hard to grasp, however, for they were not, generally speaking, '*savant-fabricants*'. Some of the confusions that arose as a consequence will form part of our exploration of the interface between science and technology in the chapter to follow.

---

[93] *Ibid.*, J. Watt snr to J. Fry, n.p., 15 May 1784.

4

The science and
technology interface

In 1839 the British Association for the Advancement of Science held its annual gathering in Birmingham. Although no one could have anticipated that the meeting would be held amid the clamour of a Chartist agitation, the choice of venue was deliberate and highly evocative. Where better to celebrate the huge extension to the nation's natural knowledge base that had taken place over the previous sixty years? Where better to drive home the message that science and industrialisation marched hand in hand? In the event, the meeting was somewhat soured by a festering dispute pitting the claims of Henry Cavendish against those of James Watt as the prime discoverer of the compound nature of water. Local hero notwithstanding, Watt did not measure up in the eyes of the scientific establishment.[1] His alleged lack of credibility as a 'scientist' – a term newly minted in the 1830s – begs questions which are central to this chapter. What was the role of the natural philosopher supposed to be? Could he be both a generator and an applier of useful knowledge? Or was the applier another species altogether, and never the twain should meet?

The accelerating rate of knowledge production in the second half of the eighteenth century scarcely requires further demonstration. It was remarked upon by contemporaries, not least by James Keir, and has been widely noted by historians subsequently. No less significant was the extent of diffusion. On the evidence of the West Midlands, the 'taste for science'[2] knew few bounds in the 1780s, and travellers who visited Birmingham, the Black Country and the Severn Gorge ironworks were in no doubt that it was linked intimately to the mechanisation of

---

[1] See Miller, *Discovering Water*, chapter 1.
[2] See above p. 1.

industry. Our focus switches to the process of application, therefore; that is to say, the manner in which bodies of useful knowledge were generated and fashioned into effective technologies. Even researchers who admit the connection between science and technology (some do not) find it difficult to be explicit about this process – hence the room for a case-study enquiry. The Industrial Enlightenment thesis outlined briefly in Chapter 1 must be our starting point. If nothing else, this plausible conceptualisation will help to pinpoint the issues that require particular scrutiny.

When making the argument for the Industrial Enlightenment as a stepping-stone on the road to modernity, historians of science have pointed, above all else, to cultural shifts: the escape from an Aristotleian world-view, the adoption of Baconian experimental methodology, and the growth in the West of societies and polities which attached pre-eminent value to scientific enquiry. Joel Mokyr,[3] who readily acknowledges his debt to the cultural historians of science, has intellectualised this vision, but the thrust remains more or less the same – as indeed do the difficulties inherent in carrying out the investigation. The task demands a probing of the complex dialectic linking science to technology, for it is his conviction that the Industrial Revolution must ultimately be explained in terms of intellectual developments which triggered – in localised settings – a surge of creative technological activity. Specifically he envisages a scenario in which the store of useful information available within a given society attains a level sufficient to trigger a cycle of renewal (the feedback loop between 'what' and 'how' knowledge). This, in turn, brings into being the optimum conditions for a step change in technology. The phenomenon of Industrial Enlightenment can be understood, therefore, as a context possessing the potential to gestate an Industrial Revolution.

However, since our study is not directly concerned with the aetiology of the Industrial Revolution, the focus in this chapter will be directed towards the facilitating conditions. In common with others, Joel Mokyr[4] draws attention to the decline in the cost of accessing useful knowledge across the century, and the evidence (rather patchy, in our view) of the inscription of craft 'know-how' in dictionary compilations such as the *Enclyclopédie*. The percolation of an understanding of Newtonian mechanics – albeit dilute – must also be accounted a factor in the calculating spirit of the age. It seems plausible, after all, that technological

---

[3] Mokyr, *The Gifts of Athena*, pp. 30 note 1, 39–40.
[4] *Ibid.*, pp. 67–70; also Mokyr, 'The intellectual origins of modern economic Growth'.

progress presupposed at least some understanding of *why* things worked as well as *how* they worked. Here lies the key, for, as Mokyr would doubtless acknowledge, it is not sufficient to demonstrate that a handful of pioneering individuals proved themselves capable of construing useful knowledge in a technologically creative way. If the Industrial Enlightenment thesis is to carry real conviction, we need to be satisfied that the calculating spirit penetrated into the productive layers of society. It is in this context that the specifics of the knowledge-conversion process become particularly relevant; that is to say, the process which Mokyr visualises as *savants* communicating with *fabricants*.[5] But we need to go deeper, if possible. Useful knowledge exchange, we may conjecture from the sparse evidence of artisanal scientific societies,[6] embraced sections of the work-force as well. At Soho, for instance, it would be unwise to assume that only the partners in the business were adepts of natural philosophy. Several of the firm's engine erectors had a grounding in the principles of Newtonian mechanics, and it highly unlikely that the skilled craftsmen of the Foundry, or the foremen of the Soho Mint, would have been able to perform their duties without access to theoretical knowledge as well.

This chapter will begin, therefore, with a discussion of some of the issues that require clarification before a proper investigation of the merits of Mokyr's argument in favour of an Industrial Enlightenment can be mounted. The case for a significant expansion of the natural knowledge base during the second half of the eighteenth century having already been outlined, it will then proceed to a linked examination of the purveyors and consumers of useful knowledge and the mechanisms of exchange that facilitated the gestation of productive technologies. Since the objection is sometimes raised that it is difficult to document direct connections between scientific theory and industrial practice, case-study evidence will be presented, too. The case studies involve the West Midlands cast of *savants* and *fabricants* and are drawn from the rapidly evolving fields of late eighteenth-century metallurgical chemistry and physics. The vexing problem of scientific 'cultures', which receives inadequate coverage in Mokyr's analysis, will also be addressed – within a comparative frame of reference. Finally, the chapter will explore that other interface: the physical transfer of technology – in all its forms – via the movement of men and machines.

[5] Mokyr, *The Gifts of Athena*, p. 54.

[6] L. Stewart and P. Weindling, 'Philosophical threads: natural philosophy and public experiment among the weavers of Spitalfields', *British Journal for the History of Science*, 28 (1995), 37–62.

Debates

The distinction between science and technology should not be considered a given. Historians of science tend nowadays to question the idea that sharply etched boundaries can be drawn around both theoretical knowledge and hands-on practice, and the same is true of economic historians. But it was not always thus. Even the terms in which the debate has been conducted are scarcely problem free. Whilst 'science' has a long pedigree and was understood by the West Midlands philosophers to signify a body of natural knowledge that was acquired by study, the word 'technology' is a relative newcomer to the English language, inasmuch as it was borrowed from the German in the late eighteenth century. In German usage 'technologie' implied a description of crafts and trades according to their procedural characteristics, but the term belonged with the body of Cameralist thought and was devised for the use of bureaucrats rather than those actually involved in craft activity.[7] In English, though, it quickly shed this latter connotation to become the study of know-how and, increasingly, the study of the processes and machines embodying that know-how. Yet even in the late eighteenth century it was hard to keep these two concepts entirely separate. 'Science' might embrace knowledge derived experimentally, which presupposed a degree of artisanal skill as well as cognitive activity, whereas E. A. W. Zimmermann in his 1787 survey of current affairs in Europe introduced 'technology' as 'a new branch of scientific knowledge' consisting of 'the theory of trades and mechanical arts'.[8]

We need to be careful how we juxtapose the 'sciences' and the 'arts', then. In the period covered by this study they were not diametrically opposed. Yet there have been two trends in the historiographical literature that assert the divergent view. Until the 1970s economic historians tended to belittle the role played by scientific knowledge in the transition to mechanised industry. For economists, indeed, science, like entrepreneurship, was deemed an exogenous factor – presumably because it was not amenable to quantification. Only Simon Kuznets[9] appeared willing to grant the accumulation of useful knowledge a role in economic development. It is worth pointing out that in his early work Joel Mokyr shared the general reluctance to allow any seepage of science into the process of industrialisation. In this regard a comparison

[7] See J. Beckmann, *Anleitung zur Technologie* (Göttingen, 1777).

[8] E. A. W. Zimmermann, *A Political Survey of the Present State of Europe* (London, 1787).

[9] Musson, *Science, Technology, and Economic Growth*, pp. 13–16.

of his study of *Industrialisation in the Low Countries* (1976) with *The Gifts of Athena*, where Kuznets' views are warmly endorsed, is instructive.[10] It was the painstaking researches of A. E. Musson and Eric Robinson, referred to in Chapter 1, which challenged and in due course undermined this consensus – with a little help from the cultural historians of science. Even if the precise nature of the technical literacy that developed in manufacturing and artisanal milieux in Britain during the second half of the eighteenth century still needs to be clarified, it is no longer tenable simply to argue that inventors were little more than practical tinkerers, or that the Industrial Revolution was largely the product of uneducated empiricism.

The second strand of revisionist thinking on the subject of the science–technology interface is of more immediate relevance, however, because it focuses specifically on the attributes of technology rather than the much broader question of the causes of the Industrial Revolution. Technology has long been regarded as the poor relation of science. Denied integrity, it has often been described – rather dismissively – as 'applied science'. Alternatively, it is granted free-standing status on a par with science, but the causal sequence is reversed. Thus, some economic historians argue that science owes more to technology than technology has ever owed to science.[11] The challenge to the traditional notion that technology was little more than science applied developed most vigorously in the 1980s as a by-product of the shift in scholars' interests away from outcomes and towards the practice of scientific enquiry. It is a fallacy, we are told, to suppose that 'technology is the direct translation of scientific knowledge',[12] as though natural philosophers or scientists generated new knowledge experimentally or deductively and then just handed it on to technologists or craftsmen who put it to work. Apart from anything else, this would imply that every new technological development was rooted in an antecedent scientific advance. Scientists, no less than technologists, functioned within specific cultural contexts – always assuming for the moment that the two species can be clearly demarcated. Given the present state of research, therefore, it seems safer to posit a symbiotic relationship, that is to say, one which blurs the conventional distinctions. Indeed, we might do better if we were to acknowledge that

[10] Mokyr, *The Gifts of Athena*, pp. 2–3, 117, 297; also Chapter 1 above.

[11] See for example, D. Landes, *The Unbound Prometheus: Technological Change and Industrial Development in Western Europe from 1750 to the Present* (Cambridge: Cambridge University Press, 1969), pp. 61, 104, 113–14.

[12] K. Alder, *Engineering the Revolution: Arms, Enlightenment, and the Making of Modern France* (Princeton: Princeton University Press, 1997), p. 87.

'science' has long been a portmanteau word and think instead in terms of 'science-as-knowledge' and 'science-as-practice'.[13]

The value of this approach will become apparent when we discuss the role of oral and tacit know-how. This knowledge field sits a little uneasily within Mokyr's schematisation. The cultural approach to scientific knowledge also invites us to examine closely the various languages or narrative strategies employed by natural philosophers when rendering account of their activities. Viewed from this angle, scientific methodology – one of the pillars of the Industrial Enlightenment – looks far less neutral and objective than we might suppose. On learning of the French chemists' proposed nomenclature reform, Richard Kirwan accused Lavoisier of succumbing to the 'Cartesian itch',[14] by which he meant deducing reality from abstractions rather than facts. For a Priestley, a Watt or a Keir, only experiment, repeated relentlessly if need be, could be relied upon to sort facts from opinions. Experiments, moreover, should be recorded in sober and accessible language. James Keir was not alone when he expostulated: 'I wish M. Berthollet and his associates would relate their facts in plain prose, that all men might understand them, and reserve their poetry of the new nomenclature for their theoretical commentaries on the facts.'[15] Whatever we may think of Keir's complacent belief that facts would speak for themselves, this approach had indeed the merit that it was understandable. It created a conceptual bridge facilitating communication and exchange between philosophers and practitioners. The very language of scientific enquiry and demonstration must therefore be accounted a factor in the knowledge-conversion process underpinning the Industrial Enlightenment.

As our examination of the different science cultures of the late eighteenth century will make plain, these linguistic preconditions for convergence were much less evident across the Channel, however. Even in Bourbon France, which was equipped with most, if not all, of the raw material for an Industrial Enlightenment, knowledge communication (and therefore conversion) encountered obstacles, and they were by no means only of a linguistic nature. In view of the tensions within the chemical community by the 1780s, it is not too surprising that the West Midlands philosophers should treat the claims of Lavoisier and

[13] A. Pickering (ed.), *Science as Practice and Culture* (Chicago: Chicago University Press, 1992), p. vii.
[14] M. Beretta, 'The grammar of matter: chemical nomenclature during the XVIII century', in R. Chartier and P. Corsi (eds), *Sciences et langues en Europe* (Paris: EHESS, 1996), p. 124.
[15] R. E. Schofield (ed.), *A Scientific Biography of Joseph Priestley, 1733–1804: Selected Scientific Correspondence* (Cambridge, Mass: MIT Press, 1966), p. 252.

the Arsenal group with a degree of scepticism. But engineers-turned-*académiciens* such as Charles-Augustin Coulomb were also to experience difficulty in finding a linguistic idiom which expressed their research findings as precisely as possible whilst at the same time conveying them as potentially useful knowledge. Coulomb's grasp of mechanical processes and his understanding of the physics of heat were considerable; after all he had travelled to England in 1787 and had had the opportunity to assess *in situ* Watt's latest improvements to steam-power technology. Yet the *mémoires* or narrative accounts of his experiments disclose conflicting objectives: a desire for exactness consistent with the preferred methodology of the Academy of Sciences alongside a desire to communicate his findings to craftsmen in a language they could readily understand. For all the public rhetoric of symbiosis between science and the mechanical arts in the 1770s and 1780s, Christian Licoppe[16] wonders whether French *académiciens* were not in fact retreating from the user interface in these years, as their pursuit of mathematical precision undercut their commitment to utility. Communication between *savants* and *fabricants* which initially perplexed Joel Mokyr must be tackled as a problem existing at several levels, therefore. The most effective communicators, as we shall see, were those who were fluent in both languages.

Savants and fabricants

The straightforward answer to the question 'How was useful knowledge generated and applied?' must be that the generators, carriers and appliers were very often one and the same. But this is less an answer than a hypothesis in need of empirical support. The purpose of this section, therefore, is to elucidate the process at the level of individuals and individual technologies in the setting of the West Midlands. Lest it be suggested that men such as Boulton, Watt and Keir who combined *savant* and *fabricant* functions in their own personal career paths were exceptional and untypical of the English Enlightenment, some attention will also be paid to individuals whose philosophical and manufacturing activities were not Midlands based. Where it seems helpful in order to clarify the argument, counter-examples will be discussed as well. Nevertheless, it must be accepted at the outset that the 'counting of heads' approach cannot make the case for an Industrial Enlightenment on its

---

[16] C. Licoppe, *La Formation de la pratique scientifique: le discours de l'expérience en France et en Angleterre, 1630–1820* (Paris: La Découverte, 1996), pp. 260–9.

own. The measure of the phenomenon must ultimately lie in the diffusion of Newtonian science outside the parlours and laboratories of well-to-do merchants and manufacturers; in other words, in the expansion of technical literacy at the level of the skilled and semi-skilled workforce. Here the evidence is much more meagre, but still indicative.

We already know a good deal about Matthew Boulton's scientific pretensions. Less is known, however, about his accomplishments in the field of natural philosophy or technology, where inference will have to serve as our guide. Unlike fellow *savant-fabricants* (Watt, Keir, Roebuck, etc.), he was not university trained or influenced; nor did he enjoy the benefits of an education in one of the Dissenting academies. In fact he left school at the age of fourteen and seems to have been largely self-taught. Self-taught and well taught, it appears, for his correspondence reveals a man in possession of a high degree of literacy and endowed with ample powers of calculation. To judge again from his correspondence and some piecemeal information about his library at Soho, he was also widely read – particularly in natural philosophy. Although not fluent in French, he liked to own both the standard scientific treatises and works of a more topical interest. In 1772 he tried, unsuccessfully it would seem, to acquire a copy of Diderot's *Encyclopédie*, and in the 1780s he took steps to obtain Jacques Necker's publications on the political economy of France. Boulton's lack of formal education would not have marked him out among his contemporaries, of course. On the contrary, a sampling of nearly 500 applied scientists and engineers born in Britain between 1700 and 1850 reveals that only 28 per cent studied at university – usually a Scottish institution.[17]

There can be no doubt, however, that the man was an inveterate experimentalist, and a theoretically informed one at that. His early dabblings in electricity have already been mentioned, also his enthusiasm for ballooning, in both its spectacular and knowledge-enhancing dimensions. With the move to Soho came the opportunity to build a laboratory and develop an interest in chemistry – particularly the chemistry of metals – that sustained him throughout his life. His earliest steam-engine experiments (conducted with William Small rather than James Watt) provided the spur, but as the Lunar group began to coalesce, the range of his philosophical enquiries expanded and acquired a speculative bent as well. Joseph Priestley acknowledged as much when referring to Boulton as 'a friend of *science* as well as a great promoter of the *arts*'[18]

[17] See J. Mokyr (ed.), *The British Industrial Revolution* (Boulder: Westview Press, 2nd edn 1999), p. 37.

[18] BCL MS 3782/12/24 J. Priestley to M. Boulton, Calne, 22 October 1775.

in a letter written from Calne five years before he would come and take up residence in Birmingham. As a measure of his esteem, he announced that Boulton would shortly receive a copy of the second volume of *Experiments and Observations on different Kinds of Air*. Although overshadowed nowadays by his illustrious Scottish partner, it was not always thus. Contemporaries, and contemporary visitors to Soho in particular, tended to attribute the credit for the research and development of the improved steam engine fairly evenly. Matthew Boulton would be elected to the Royal Society in November 1785, in the same promotion as James Watt and another member of the Lunar group, Dr William Withering. In these years he was also accounted a member of Kirwan's Coffee House Philosophical Society, which met fortnightly in London, although his attendance must have been infrequent; and a member of the Smeatonian Society of Civil Engineers, which gathered for convivial dinners in various taverns of the capital. It is less certain that he supported that other late-century monument to the diffusion of knowledge, the Royal Institution. Yet he seems to have been elected to it, notwithstanding, and in May 1800 was solicited to strike its admission tokens.[19]

If Matthew Boulton is to be granted emblematic status as one of the new breed of manufacturing scientists of the late Enlightenment, it is important to emphasise, too, that he was an accomplished technologist. In an undated letter draft which seems to have been written in the early 1780s, when the fortunes of the Boulton & Watt partnership were wholly dependent on the health of the Cornish copper and tin mines, he likened himself to a man who might easily have adopted the life-style of a gentleman of leisure. But instead, 'I rather chose to be of the class wch Le Baron Montisque [Montesquieu] describes as the constant contributors to the purze of the commonwealth rather than of another class which he says are always takeing out of it without contributing any thing towards it.'[20] Josiah Wedgwood, another manufacturer who knew the value of experimentally derived knowledge, was sufficiently impressed with Boulton's 'hands-on' skills to remark of Soho's ormolu wares that 'he prepares the gold himself, & lays it on without the loss of a grain'.[21] Despite much effort, gilding technology was an area in which Matthew Boulton never managed to equal the skill of French craftsmen, however. Nevertheless, his own efforts were recognised years later when Priestley

---

[19] See M. Berman, *Social Change and Scientific Organization, The Royal Institution, 1799–844* (London: Heinemann, 1978), pp. 75–7; S. C. Brown, *Benjamin Thompson Count Rumford* (Cambridge, Mass: MIT Press, 1979), pp. 228–9; also BCL MS 3782/12/45 F. Hanmacher to M. Boulton, London, 5 May 1800.

[20] BCL MS 3782/12/55 [draft of] M. Boulton, n.d.

[21] *Letters of Josiah Wedgwood*, i, pp. 142–3, J. Wedgwood to T. Bentley, 15 March 1768.

disclaimed a gilding innovation that had been attributed to him. It was, he told a correspondent, a technique perfected by the proprietor of Soho long before he arrived in Birmingham.

From time to time Boulton's friends made the suggestion that he write down an account of his improvements. This he seems never to have done, or at least, nothing intended for circulation has survived. William Small urged him to draw up a report on his steam-technology experiments in 1773 and there is a suggestion that Boulton may have entertained the idea. Much later on in life he certainly prepared a Rumford-style treatise on 'the principles & means of constructing Houses so as to make them dry, warm, healthy & comfortable',[22] only to destroy it subsequently. No doubt this would have included advice on double glazing, steam heating and chimney flue design, for by the end of the century Soho House could boast most of these amenities, not to mention a steam-warmed bath tub and a water closet. The major technological improvements and innovations of his later years concerned steam-driven coining machinery, however, but the cognitive detail of this pioneering venture largely escapes us. In 1802 Boulton told a government official that he had brought his coining mill to the level at which it now performed by a process of 'reasoning [. . .] confirmed by experience'.[23] It would be interesting to know how far the design work was Boulton's, and how far that of his foremen and superintending engineers. Rather than write treatises or manuals, he seems to have preferred to rehearse his achievements in letters to men of influence. When, in 1794, Lord Lansdowne sought advice on a banal matter of domestic heating, Boulton treated him to a missive in reply which contained the following justification:

> Mr Watt & myself have been persuing a constant series of Exp^{ts} upon Fire, Water & Steam for 30 years past & were the first persons who discovere^d & determin^d the relative bulk of steam to that of the water contained in it. 2dly we determin^d the absolute & latent heat contained in it. 3dly we were the first who ascertained its elastick force under different degrees of heat [. . .] These things were unknown even to philosophers until we ascertained them and at present are not commonly known. Upon the foundation of this knowledge we have made many important improvements on steam engines.[24]

[22] BCL MS 3782/12/39 [copy of] M. Boulton to Lord Lansdowne, Soho, 1 December 1794.
[23] BCL MS 3782/12/47 [draft of] M. Boulton to H. Herisse, September 1802.
[24] BCL MS 3782/12/39 [copy of] M. Boulton to Lord Lansdowne, n.p., 12 November 1794.

In 1820 the Prime Minister, Lord Liverpool, spoke publicly of Boulton, Watt and Arkwright as men to whom 'England was indebted for its present greatness'.[25] Recognition of Matthew Boulton's achievements, albeit posthumous, was probably reaching a peak by this time. It would be followed by a rapid eclipse. Not so the reputation of James Watt, however, which was about to be subjected to extravagant praise. Any attempt to assess Watt's role as a *savant-fabricant* must overcome the adulation heaped upon him as the personification of the Industrial Revolution. It started with the launch in 1824 of the public subscription for the commemorative monument which now stands in Westminster Abbey. In subsequent decades it was relayed by the 'water controversy', mentioned briefly at the start of this chapter. With Watt describing himself as an 'engineer' and insisting that he be labelled as such whenever his name appeared in print (not even 'Esq'.[26]), and with his son James insisting that the inscription on the Chantrey monument read 'Philosopher, mechanician & Civil Engineer',[27] it is not easy to separate the man from the myth.

Perhaps the testimony of visitors to Soho, Harper Hill and Heathfield (Watt's residences) is the best place to begin, since it can scarcely be suspected of *ex post facto* bias. Whether agents of governments or philosophical tourists travelling for their own pleasure, foreign visitors were unanimously of the opinion that James Watt possessed an immense store of practical knowledge and skill. However, they tended to add the observation that this knowledge was theoretically grounded. Two examples will suffice. The Russian engineer Nicolai Korsakov, who had the good fortune to arrive at Soho during the summer of 1776 when the partners were keen to make themselves accessible, jotted down the specifications of Watt's improved steam engine in his travel journal with the remark: 'à son grand Génie d'invention il a joint des connaissances profondes de chymie et de Physique'.[28] The Italian natural philosopher Count Marsilio Landriani arrived a dozen years later, when conditions were no longer quite so favourable to unfettered industrial tourism. However, his visit happened to coincide with the presence of Dr Joseph Black – a house guest of the Watts – and he seems to have been hospitably

[25] C. MacLeod, 'James Watt, heroic invention and the idea of the Industrial Revolution', in M. Berg and K. Bruland (eds), *Technological Revolutions in Europe: Historical Perspectives* (Cheltenham: Elgar, 1998), p. 103.
[26] BCL MS 3219/4/124 J. Watt snr to Dr Beddoes, Birmingham, 2 March 1795.
[27] Miller, *Discovering Water*, p. 100; *idem*, ' "Puffing Jamie": the commercial and ideological importance of being a "Philosopher" in the case of the reputation of James Watt (1736–1819)', *History of Science*, 38 (2000), 1–24.
[28] See A. Cross, *'By the Banks of the Thames'*, p. 181.

received by the Birmingham philosophical community. James Watt, he noted, had not made as many important discoveries as had Priestley. Nevertheless, his practical knowledge of the crafts, and particularly the mechanical crafts, was encyclopaedic and had theoretical knowledge linked to it ('egli ha una profonda cognizione di tutte le arti da quelle dipendenti ed unisce alle cognizioni teoriche molta pratica').[29]

This should come as no surprise. After all, we know that he had read the Dutch Newtonian s'Gravesende's *Mathematical Elements of Physics* as a young man and came under the direct influence of the Glasgow and Edinburgh-based natural philosophers, in common with so many of the West Midlands science experimenters and practitioners (Darwin, Keir, Roebuck, Reynolds, Stokes etc.). Whether his conclusions regarding latent heat were drawn independently of those of Black, as Boulton subsequently claimed, may be a matter for legitimate debate, but it can scarcely be maintained any longer that he was simply a clever mechanic who happened to stumble on truths of a wider import. There may have been such engineers in eighteenth-century England, but Watt was not one of them. As David Miller[30] points out, his early kettle experiments of 1765 can just as plausibly be interpreted to be chemical enquiries into the composition of water as meaningful experiments to determine the useful properties of steam. The view of Watt propounded many years ago by A. E. Musson in association with Eric Robinson[31] seems closest to the mark, therefore. They depicted him as a man who was, without question, indebted to the scientific and technical knowledge of his day, but who was perfectly capable of conducting experiments out of sheer intellectual curiosity. That said, when industrial applications for his experimental knowledge became apparent, he was quick to use his skills to overcome the problems inherent in product development. In short, there can be little doubt that Watt was keenly aware of the importance of interlocking knowledge at the user interface. The engineering business, he commented to his wife in 1785, 'is now in general in the hands of very illiterate people. The world seeming to think that science and genius are not necessary in it, but that self-conceit, ignorance, impudence & a little experience may very well supply their place. Consequently men of real knowledge & abilities not being paid as they deserve have deserted the calling.'[32] This seems an unduly gloomy assessment, but the remark

[29] *Relazioni di Marsilio Landriani*, p. 250.

[30] D. P. Miller, 'True myths: James Watt's kettle, his condenser, and his chemistry', *History of Science*, 42 (2004), 352.

[31] See Musson and Robinson, *Science and Technology in the Industrial Revolution*, pp. 79–80; also Musson, *Science, Technology, and Economic Growth*, p. 62.

[32] BCL MS 3219/4/123 J. Watt snr to A. Watt, Birmingham, 31 October 1785.

effectively reveals Watt's own perception, and that of informed contemporaries, that he at least occupied a position astride the crafts and the sciences.

Joel Mokyr's emphasis on feedback is perfectly exemplified in the case of the improved steam engine, for not only did natural knowledge go into its construction, but significant advances in the science of thermodynamics would be derived from it. Stress engineering also benefited, as Watt and his erectors anxiously calculated the loads on the timber beams used in the construction of the early reciprocating engines. The beam of the first of the engines to be installed at the Albion corn mill in London was found to bend by $5/8^{\text{ths}}$ of an inch.[33] Yet James Watt's contributions to the Industrial Enlightenment were not confined to steam technology. In common with nearly all members of the Lunar circle, he followed closely the debates taking place within the fast-moving field of chemistry and corresponded or collaborated with many of the prime movers. The knowledge gleaned thereby was usually put to work in one form or another. Thus we find him engaged in (abortive) attempts between 1766–69 to apply a process suggested by Black for the manufacture of soda from sea salt and lime; and in protracted experiments on the composition of inks, between 1779 and 1782, in order to find the best medium for his letter-copying press. The early experiments on inks involved James Keir, who would become a business partner when the press went into production. Watt also designed a furnace that would consume its own smoke. Pollution had already become an issue, for the smoke from the engines was poisoning the plantations in Matthew Boulton's gardens. It was trialed successfully at Soho in the autumn of 1785 and quickly incorporated into the design for the Albion Mill engines in London. Four years later, we learn from the preserved press copies of Watt's correspondence, he would be experimenting with varnishes (a major article of consumption in Birmingham). Two years after that his attention had turned to the production of artificial marble, or alabaster – if we may judge from a copy letter to Black. Yet whilst all these technologies were in the making, Watt still found time to participate in the chemical nomenclature debate. In a letter to James Hutton, the Edinburgh savant, he criticized some of the French symbols and enclosed a set of characters of his own devising.[34]

James Keir was another Scot who came to the West Midlands through ties of friendship, and in order to build a fortune for himself. His interest in chemistry as both a theoretical and a practical discipline

[33] BCL MS 3219/4/267A J. Watt snr to A. Watt, 4 February 1787.
[34] BCL MS 3219/4/123 J. Watt snr to Dr J. Hutton, Birmingham, 14 October 1788.

had been kindled at Edinburgh rather than Glasgow, but it remained dormant until he quit the army in 1768. In all likelihood he would have known something of Watt's interests and activities through mutual friends (Darwin and Small), although he seems only to have moved to Stourbridge around 1770, after a sojourn in Ireland as a house guest of R. L. Edgeworth. His contributions to natural philosophy have already been mentioned and so it is only necessary to highlight the techno-logical prowess of this archetypal *savant-fabricant*. Keir's first foray into artificial alkali production overlapped with Watt's in 1769 before either man had moved to the West Midlands. The business was potentially extremely lucrative, for at this time alkalis were used extensively in glass making, soap manufacture and bleaching, and could only be obtained from vegetable ash. Keir's correspondence with Macquer and his sub-sequent translation of the French chemist's *Dictionary* probably stemmed from his efforts to find a solution to the problem of alkali manufacture which did not involve the use of common salt, a commodity which was heavily taxed in both countries. In the event Keir only made progress, in collaboration with Watt and the other Lunar chemists, towards the end of the following decade whilst in residence at Soho as Boulton's general manager. The big chemical works which he then proceeded to set up at Tipton got round the problem of salt by employing the cheap and freely available waste products of nitric and sulphuric acid manufacture instead. By 1785 the plant was booming and turning out large quantities of white lead (used by the Staffordshire potters) and red lead (used by the flint-glass makers of Stourbridge), as well as sodium carbonate. The alkali was mostly used on site for soap making, and it was on soap that Keir was eventually able to consolidate his fortune.

His simultaneous venture into metal alloys proved far less satisfactory by contrast. The aim was to produce metal nails and bolts which could be employed in the copper sheathing of ships without risk of galvanic action. At a time when most navies and even merchant fleets were resort-ing to coppering, the prize for a technology that actually worked was enormous. Keir's efforts were noised around Europe: Swediaur reported that the metal could be forged like iron but not welded, and he sent a specimen to Torbern Bergman for analysis.[35] Unfortunately trials at a Navy yard showed the alloy not to be fit for purpose, and by 1783 the technology had been more or less withdrawn. Keir's metal was used for sash-window frames in several of Birmingham's finer houses and business premises, but that was all. By the time that Landriani turned up in Birmingham (1788) the gossip among natural philosophers had

---

[35] Carlid and Nordström, *Torbern Bergman's Foreign Correspondence*, p. 327.

switched to Keir's new *Dictionary of Chemistry*, the first (and only) part of which was published locally the following year. However, he had not abandoned the taste for wide-ranging experimentation, particularly now that the family's finances were secured. Landriani saw his 'lampada idrostatica' [hydrostatic lamp], which was intended to remedy one of the acknowledged defects of Argand's otherwise brilliant oil lamp. We know, too, that he perfected a method of retrieving the silver from plated scrap metal, which must have been a by-product of his alkali experiments. In 1791 James Watt reported to a correspondent that Keir had found that 'a mixture of oil of vitriol & nitre will dissolve silver without dissolving copper which affords an easy manner of separating the silver from the copper of the scraps or parings of plated metal manufactured here'.[36]

Were men like Boulton, Watt and Keir just shooting stars in a late eighteenth-century firmament of unenlightened artisan empiricism? It seems unlikely. If we set off in search of *savant-fabricants*, that is to say, individuals who sat astride the science–technology interface, they turn out to have been quite numerous. Margaret Jacob and Larry Stewart[37] have drawn attention to the claims of the textile manufacturers James M'Connel and John Kennedy in Manchester and Benjamin Gott in Leeds, but in Manchester alone the species was almost as thick on the ground as in the West Midlands. The case of Charles Taylor, whose multifaceted interests earned him election in 1799 to the secretaryship of the Society of Arts, has already been mentioned, and A. E. Musson has pointed to other candidates. The cotton-spinner George Augustus Lee, who was a close friend of James Watt junior and a regular visitor to Soho, is an obvious example. He commissioned Watt junior to buy him the first volume of Gaspard de Prony's *Nouvelle architecture hydraulique* when the latter travelled to Paris in the spring of 1792, and probably made use of theoretical knowledge gleaned from this and other French texts in the steam-indicator experiments which he embarked on in 1793. Together with a partner, Nathaniel Philips, Lee erected a seven-storey mill at Salford in 1799–1801 which the Soho engineer, William Murdoch, would fit out with gas lighting. Johann Fischer, the Schaffhausen ironmaster, paid a visit in 1814 and described him as 'an expert in many branches of knowledge',[38] as well as a singular entrepreneur. Another of Watt junior's Manchester comrades was Thomas Cooper. Cooper's remarkable career

---

[36] BCL MS 3219/4/124 J. Watt snr to M. G. G. ten Haaf, Director of the Batavian Society, Birmingham, 27 January 1791.

[37] Jacob and Stewart, *Practical Matter*, pp. 127–38.

[38] Henderson, *J. C. Fischer and his Diary*, p. 143.

will be evoked in Chapter 6, but when Watt first met him in late 1787 or 1788 he was active in both the Literary and Philosophical Society and the London Chapter Coffee House group. His industrial experience derived from a partnership in a Bolton firm of calico printers and dyers to which he brought Berthollet's new bleaching process. He subsequently pioneered an improved method of obtaining oxymuriatic acid. Later sources record that he would go on to acquire an encyclopaedic knowledge of chemistry-based manufacturing processes.[39]

Josiah Wedgwood at Etruria, William Strutt the Derby industrialist and innovator, and the Bradford ironmaster and mineralogist Joseph Dawson fit the bill too. Wedgwood and Strutt would be elected to the Royal Society (in 1783 and 1817 respectively), and Strutt appears to have been the first in the district to build a voltaic pile. Of greater interest in the context of this study, however, are William Reynolds and John Roebuck. Both men can be treated as outliers of the West Midlands regional diaspora of natural philosophers, and both had multiple connections to its mining and metal-working industries. William Reynolds was the son of the Darbys' long-standing manager-cum-partner at Coalbrookdale, Richard Reynolds. A Quaker, he nonetheless studied under Black at Edinburgh, and like so many of his pupils developed an unquenchable thirst for experimental knowledge. Having taken over the ironworks at Ketley, he built a laboratory, dabbled in electricity and initiated an extensive correspondence with philosophers such as Black and Priestley and fellow *savant-fabricants*. The link with Watt and Boulton seems to have been established when he ordered one of Soho's first pumping engines in 1777, followed by a rotative engine for forge work in 1783. His would be the driving force behind the iron bridge that spanned the Severn at Coalbrookdale in 1781, and the inclined plane at Ketley for the transportation of canal barges to river level, which first came into use in 1788. John Roebuck is chiefly remembered for his role in the founding of Carron ironworks near Falkirk, and rightly so. But after an apprenticeship in scientific knowledge at both Edinburgh and Leiden universities, he settled in Birmingham with the intention of pursuing a medical career. In the event, the industrial rather than the medical applications of chemistry proved to be his overriding interest. The 1740s saw Roebuck and his partner, Samuel Garbett, make a series of technological improvements in the refining and recovery of precious metals. The most important breakthrough, however, was the 'lead chamber' process which facilitated the large-scale production of sulphuric

---

[39] D. Malone, *The Public Life of Thomas Cooper, 1783–1839* (Columbia: South Carolina University Press, 1961), p. 6.

acid. Oil of vitriol was used extensively in the Birmingham metal trades, and also in Scotland, where the linen-bleaching industry provided an expanding market. Accordingly, in 1749 the partners opened a second vitriol works at Prestonpans in the Lothians.

Scientifically informed manufacturers seem to have been an integral part of the English Enlightenment, then, particularly in those enterprises reliant on properly industrial technology. In this connection, Donald Cardwell[40] was surely right to question the once-prevalent view that eighteenth-century engineers could not have had much knowledge of mathematics and only a primitive understanding of the mechanical sciences. But a category that expands to include everybody loses its power to explain anything. Not all manufacturers were *savant-fabricants*. Samuel Garbett is a case in point. Although it can be argued that he was the driving force behind the commercial success of the Carron ironworks during its early years, there is little evidence that he showed an interest in science, whether in its polite or utilitarian versions. His formal education seems to have been quite basic, it is true, but so was Matthew Boulton's. Despite being united with Boulton by ties of friendship over a course of fifty years, he never sought admission to the Lunar group. Neither Richard Arkwright, the pioneer of new carding and spinning technologies, nor John 'iron-mad' Wilkinson showed an interest in science for its own sake, either. After a Nonconformist elementary education, Wilkinson was apprenticed to a merchant in Liverpool. Thereafter he learned on the job in his father's ironworks at Bersham. Samuel Skey, a one-time partner of Keir in the Holloway End glass-house concern is another example. Although he would establish a successful chemical works of his own near Bewdley, with the help of a workman who transferred Roebuck's lead-chamber technology, there are few signs of independent scientific literacy in any of his undertakings.

At the sub-entrepreneurial level the picture is no less mixed. The English Industrial Enlightenment gestated some impressively qualified craftsmen, mechanics and superintending engineers. But it is no less true that a number of the great technological advances of the period owed little or nothing to the application of scientific knowledge. By the time of Boulton's death in 1809, Soho's more skilled employees tended to be viewed as a race apart. In reply to a query about training, James Watt senior once observed that 'most of our Engineers who have not been regularly bred to the theoretical or practical part of the business, have been bred to analogous ones, such as millwrights, architects, surveyors

---

[40] D. S. L. Cardwell, 'Science, technology and industry', in Rousseau and Porter (eds), *The Ferment of Knowledge*, p. 479.

etc. from which having almost all the previous learning it is easy to step to the other otherwise it must be uphill work'.[41] Training on the job, whether at Soho or on contract work, produced some impressively qualified mechanics and engine erectors who sometimes went on to become engineers and entrepreneurs in their own right. The case of John Southern has already been mentioned in connection with ballooning, but John Rennie, Peter Ewart and William Murdoch are the obvious examples. Rennie learned his science first (at the knee of Black and Robison in Edinburgh) before tackling millwork in London on behalf of Boulton & Watt, whereas Ewart was home grown. He built the water-wheel that drove the improved rolling mill at Soho, as well as some of the early mint machinery. In the autumn of 1789 he signalled his desire to pass the winter in Edinburgh in order to improve his knowledge of mathematics under the guidance of Professor John Robison, although it is unclear whether he actually travelled to Scotland. Nevertheless, he would eventually leave Soho to become an engine erector in Stockport. In due course, he became an engineer and a manufacturer in his own right. Murdoch, by contrast, worked for the firm all his life. Having refused a partnership, he remained a salaried employee. Johann Fischer met him in 1814, already aware of his pioneering role in the industrial application of gas lighting, but was impressed to discover him 'a very competent metallurgist'[42] as well.

Steam-engine erectors were peripatetic by definition and they seem to have occupied an intermediate niche in the hierarchy of scientific-knowledge bearers. All possessed a basic competence in mechanics, of course, but the job did not provide an automatic spring-board to *savant-fabricant* status. Murdoch's brother James was an engine erector and a spendthrift drunkard – a condition all too frequently associated with itinerant employment. On the other hand, the Creighton brothers, as described by Jennifer Tann,[43] were avid consumers of contemporary scientific literature, with a preference for the physical and mathematical sciences. Henry, the principal superintending engineer, possessed a library of over 200 volumes. Among them featured Emmerson's *The Principles of Mechanics* (1754), eighteen volumes of *Philosophical Transactions of the Royal Society* and several of the *Repertory of Arts and Manufactures* (1794 onwards). Yet for every theoretically informed mechanic or jobbing engineer, there were – even in industrialising England – many more

[41] BCL MS 3219/4/124 J. Watt snr to P. Wilson, Birmingham, 27 August 1794.

[42] Henderson, *J. C. Fischer and his Diary*, p. 132.

[43] J. Tann, 'Two knights of pandemonium: a worm's eye view of Boulton, Watt & Co', *History of Technology*, 20 (1998), 47–72.

experimentalists whose inventions and micro-improvements were based on little more than unlettered wisdom and skill. Some of these individuals beat a path to the gates of Soho in the hope of selling their ideas and thereby avoiding the development costs. Most were sent away, and with good reason. But in 1784 Black wrote from Edinburgh to recommend a Henry Cort of Gosport. 'He is a plain English man without science but by dint of natural ingenuity and a turn for experiment has made such a Discovery in the art of making tough iron, as will undoubtedly give this island the monopoly of that business.'[44] Cort had already tried to interest the proprietors of the Carron in his process – presumably because the works had difficulty producing anything other than pig-iron. The response of Boulton & Watt is not recorded.

To judge from Fischer's richly informative travel journals, the entrepreneurs and manufacturers of the Industrial Enlightenment were somewhat removed from the later Victorian stereotype. He depicts a public-spirited class of men who were well informed, well travelled on the continent of Europe and comfortably housed, in keeping with the latest standards of taste and consumer culture. Their technical and managerial abilities placed them ahead of their European counterparts – more than a generation ahead, in the view of Margaret Jacob.[45] Whilst this lead would not long endure, it is worth pausing for a moment to consider how a cosmopolitan generation, fashioned in the values of the Enlightenment, absorbed the knowledge and skills to master a world that was now held to be eminently intelligible. Travel was indeed hugely important, and nearly all of the members of the Lunar group indulged in the activity – repeatedly. It spread ideas, as we have seen, and provided a means of acquiring information not readily available at home. In the expectation that the societal structures they had known would continue indefinitely, both Watt and Boulton invested considerable sums in sending their sons abroad in order to extend their education. Although Matthew Boulton allowed his son to reside in Paris for a time, this was not intended to be the start of a Grand Tour under another name. Both partners envisaged travel primarily as a means of imbibing useful knowledge. 'A knowledge of Mechanicks, mathematicks, Chymistry, Mechanical Arts & Commerce, join'd to the Character of an Honest Man is what I am very anxious you should possess',[46] Boulton advised Matthew junior in the summer of 1789. By this date Matt had been sent on to Germany, which Midlands manufacturers were agreed was the only place in Europe that could offer a practical science education in some ways

[44] BCL MS 3219/4/123 Copy letter of J. Black to J. Watt snr, 28 May 1784.
[45] Jacob, *Scientific Culture and the Making of the Industrial West*, p. 133.
[46] BCL MS 3782/12/57 M. Boulton to M. R. Boulton, Soho, 3 August 1789.

superior to what was available in Great Britain. Three years earlier, James Watt junior had taken the same route after a less-than-successful sojourn in Geneva. His father laid down precisely the programme of studies that he was to follow, adding a note to his Lutheran clergyman tutor that 'he should be taught to confine himself to the *Utile*'.[47]

The intended terminus for these tours was the Saxon *Bergsakademie*. Whilst Rachel Laudan[48] pours cold water on the notion that mining schools such as the one at Freiberg provided a technical education of use to geologists and mining engineers, a whole generation of industrial entrepreneurs, not to mention government officials, begged to differ. We know that the Freiberg school taught pure mathematics, mechanics, mineralogy, metallurgical chemistry, surveying, assaying, technical drawing and much else besides. We know, too, that it was patronised by the sons of Cornish and Derbyshire mine owners, as well as the eldest son of James Watt. When Hatchett paid a visit in 1791, he reported an encounter with two English students, 'Messrs Weaver and Barker in their Miners' dresses'.[49] Thomas Barker was the son of a Bakewell lead merchant who had previously learned his German as a boarder with the same Thuringian clergyman as the Boulton and Watt offspring, whereas Thomas Weaver would go on to translate Werner's writings into English and work as a minerals inspector in Ireland. James Watt junior looked back on his two years spent in Germany with affection, having acquired far more useful knowledge there than in Geneva. He lodged in Freiberg with Ludwig Kabisch, who was in charge of the School's mineral collections, and the pair went on prospecting trips together. In the meantime he improved his grasp of mathematics under the direction of Johann Charpentier, of whom his father had a high opinion. He is also known to have attended the experimental lectures of Christlieb Gellert, the Professor of Metallurgy and Chemistry, and those of his one-time pupil Johann Klotzsch. Gellert was a particular authority on smelting and had introduced to Freiberg Born's amalgamation process for extracting silver.

Metals, heat and combustion

Contemporaries were in no doubt that scientific method had a role to play in the perfecting of technology. Nor was there much disagreement

---

[47] BCL MS 3219/4/123 J. Watt snr to Mr Reinhard, Birmingham, 15 February 1786.

[48] Laudan, *From Mineralogy to Geology*, pp. 54–5.

[49] See A. Raistrick (ed.), *The Hatchett Diary: a Tour through the Counties of England and Scotland in 1796 Visiting their Mines and Manufactories* (Truro: Bradford Barton, 1967), p. 10.

that the British led the field in the conversion of knowledge into know-how, for a time at least. Yet when researchers have tried to specify the precise causal sequences involved, difficulties have arisen. As a result some economic historians and even some historians of science, such as Robert Fox, remain sceptical.[50] Chemistry would be the obvious field to investigate in this connection. After all, in the closing decades of the eighteenth century startling advances were made in the manufacture of alkalis, soaps and bleaching agents. But this field is now well covered, and besides it would be hard to argue that these developments were *not* theoretically informed. Keir's alkali experiments have already been mentioned, and it is worth noting that the elder James Watt had both the opportunity and the incentive to connect up the science and the practice of bleaching. He witnessed Berthollet's bleaching demonstration whilst in Paris during the winter of 1786–87, remaining in direct communication with him thereafter, and his father-in-law, James McGrigor, was a prominent Glasgow linen merchant and bleacher. Rather than look at textiles, which played no role in the Industrial Enlightenment of the West Midlands, this section will examine instead the question of metals. The story is less clear cut, probably for the reason that a properly scientific understanding of the properties of metals seems only to have caught up with the forensic skills of West Midlands metal-workers towards the very end of the century.

Birmingham constituted one of the biggest metal markets in the country in the eighteenth century – as we might expect. With the retreat of domestic-hardware manufacture into the Black Country, demand focused instead on copper, brass and blister-steel, which were all used in the button, buckle and ornamental goods industries. Copper came from the Cornish and Anglesey mines, chiefly by way of the Swansea smelters and Bristol merchants. By 1786 around 1,500 tons of the metal were being shipped to Birmingham each year, and with the commercial boom of the late 1780s under way, this figure may have risen to 2,000 tons per annum by 1792. But a large proportion of the copper destined for Birmingham was converted into brass, whether en route or in the town's own brass-houses. Of the 1,000 tons of brass being consumed in the 1780s, perhaps 650 tons were derived from the consignments of copper cake. In other words, if we assume that brass consumption moved in tandem with copper consumption, it can be estimated that, at the height of the fancy-metalwares boom, Birmingham's workshops

[50] See M. Berg and K. Bruland (eds), *Technological Revolutions in Europe: Historical Perspectives* (Cheltenham: Elgar, 1998), pp. 8, 86–7.

were using about 2,400 tons of copper and brass a year.[51] Blister-steel was employed, above all, in the button and toy trade, and since it was principally made from Swedish bar-iron, this is the commodity that we need to quantify. However, the iron trade never generated the controversy that beset the copper trade from the 1780s onwards, with the result that the sources are much less eloquent. All we can call upon are Swedish visitors' accounts, and they tell us that Birmingham and the area to its south-west (the Stour valley in particular) constituted the most import-ant steel-making region after Sheffield in the first half of the eighteenth century. In 1720 Birmingham's three or four steel-houses took 200 tons of Oregrund iron, and in the 1730s this figure rose slightly to about 220 tons per annum. Small though this figure seems, it represented 74 per cent of all the high-grade, forgeable Swedish bar-iron imported into Britain at that time. However, in the 1730s Russian bar-iron began to make an appearance. Sampson Lloyd's slitting mill in Digbeth, which catered principally for the nailing trade, began to put in large orders for this lower-priced commodity.[52]

The main manufacturer of blister-steel in Birmingham during the early part of the century was John Kettle, of whom little is known. Matthew Boulton did not appear on the scene until the 1750s. The Swedish traveller Reinhold Angerstein reported the existence of a cementation furnace using Oregrund iron at Snow Hill in 1754, which was probably Boulton's, or rather his father's. It would have made steel of sufficient quality for his run-of-the-mill button business. Another visitor to Birming-ham, in 1770, described a steel-house or furnace that can definitely be attributed to Boulton. It had a capacity of eight tons and the account, although brief, gives the impression that its owner already possessed considerable metallurgical know-how: 'in the same bar, even of Swedish iron, there is often two different kinds of metal a white and a grayer kind. The white Mr Bolton finds to his purpose to have chizzled out and have separated from the other. The science of knowing the different

---

[51] This figure is based on J. R. Harris, *The Copper King: a Biography of Thomas Williams of Llanidan* (Liverpool: Liverpool University Press, 1964), pp. 93, 118–26, 132–3; H. Hamilton, *The English Brass and Copper Industries to 1800* (London: Longman, 1926), pp. 220, 229, 333; Cornwall Record Office AD 1583/1–12 Boulton & Watt and Thomas Wilson Correspondence, M. Boulton to T. Wilson, Soho, 3 November 1786.

[52] See C. Evans, O. Jackson and G. Rydén, 'Baltic iron and the British iron industry in the eighteenth century', *Economic History Review*, 55:4 (2002), 656–8; also M. Ågren (ed.), *Iron-Making Societies: Early Industrial Development in Sweden and Russia, 1600–1900* (New York: Berghahn, 1998, reprinted 2003), p. 5; S. Lloyd, *The Lloyds of Birmingham with some Account of the Founding of Lloyds Bank* (Birmingham: Cornish Bros, 1907), pp. 22–5.

natures and properties of iron, is not to be acquired in a day.'[53] This seems
a plausible conclusion to draw, for we know that Matthew Boulton was
cognisant of the advantages of the crucible process of steel-making from
its very earliest days. He was already doing business with Benjamin
Huntsman in Sheffield in 1757, and in one letter saluted his endeavours
in characteristic fashion: 'I hope the philosophic spirit still laboureth
within thee and may soon bring forth fruit useful to mankind but more
particularly so to thy selfe.'[54]

At Soho, crucible steel was used primarily to manufacture the very
best quality steel buttons. It was also needed for button and coining
dies, and for the rollers that pressed together silver and copper plate.
We know that Boulton consumed about four tons of cake copper per
week in 1787, but that was before the move into industrial coining. But
copper, like steel, came in different grades and with different properties, depending on where it was mined and how it had been smelted.
The coining technology perfected so laboriously at Soho presupposed
heavy-duty rolling and the material had to be 'tough', whereas the
copper employed in silver plating needed to be highly refined and therefore ductile and free from flaws. Anglesey copper from the Parys mine
proved ideal for this purpose, but of no use for coining until it had been
remelted, cast into ingots, and then hot- and cold-rolled. Brass had to
be made fit for purpose, too. Founders catering for the button and 'toy'
trades sought to make a malleable brass that was golden in colour,
whereas steam-cocks and industrial fittings required a highly resistant
material. Common brass consisted of copper and zinc in a ratio of two
to one, but Birmingham's founders quickly discovered that the metal
could be given a wide range of properties by varying the blend and
adding tin, lead or iron.

The complex business of preparing metal for stamping undoubtedly
spurred on Matthew Boulton's technological efforts in this area, not
least because copper and steel were apt to behave quite differently. He
experimented constantly and gleaned what he could from the 'ping-
pong' of metallurgical information exchange within the Republic of
Letters. However, it was the preparation of steel for dies and die-sinking
in connection with the coining operation which really stretched his
resources. With a regal coining contract seemingly imminent, we find
him in regular correspondence with Huntsman on this subject in 1789–
90. He asked the Sheffield steel-maker to send him cast metal cut to

[53] K. C. Barraclough, *Steelmaking before Bessemer*, 2 vols (London: The Metals Society,
1984), i, pp. 220–1.

[54] *Ibid.*, i, p. 3 note 12.

size which originated from the very best Swedish forges, so that he could experiment with different ways of forging the dies. The choice, it appears, lay between engraving the metal in its longitudinal section or on its flattened end; that is to say, across the grain.[55] However, dies used for coining called upon skills and processes of another order from those employed for striking medals and tokens. They had to be capable of withstanding one very hard blow, whereas 'the striking of medals', he informed a correspondent, 'required many blows & as many anneal-ings'.[56] Boulton, as we noted earlier, was a skilled technologist in his own right, for in another letter dating from the summer of 1791 he reported that he had just hardened and tempered a (medal) die 'with my own hand'.[57]

It would appear, then, that the 'science' of metallurgy as practised in Birmingham was expressed above all in the rolling and annealing of metals, although it is clear that local manufacturers possessed considerable expertise in the area of alloys, refining and recovery as well. Boulton was immensely proud of his rolling capacity and heavily dependent on Huntsman for the supply of cast-steel rollers in various sizes. At one point he had three mills in operation at Soho – all activated by water – and they were a regular tourist attraction. Barthélemy Faujas de Saint-Fond waxed lyrical about these 'lamineries'[58] when he visited in 1784. Until Watt had adapted his engine to produce rotative power, however, there was no prospect of driving the heavy-duty copper-rolling mill by steam. Yet this seems to have happened once Boulton had got his mint up and running. Extolling the Soho coining 'apparatus' as the best in Europe, a correspondent of Thomas Jefferson reported: 'the whole machine is moved by an improvd steam Engine which rolls the Copper, for half-pence finer than copper has before been rolld for the purpose of money – It works the Coupoirs or screw press's, for cutting the particular peices of copper, & coins both the faces *& edges* of the money at the same time'.[59]

None of the aforesaid adds up to a conclusive case for a theoretical knowledge input into the everyday business of metal-working, of course.

[55] *Ibid.*, ii, p.18.
[56] BCL MS 3782/12/50 [copy of] M. Boulton to Sir H. Englefield, Birmingham, 18 December 1805.
[57] BCL MS 3782/12/36 [copy of] M. Boulton to C. Dumergue, Soho, 10 August 1791.
[58] B. Faujas de Saint-Fond, *Voyages en Angleterre, en Ecosse et aux Iles Hébrides*, 2 vols (Paris: Jansen, 1797), ii, p. 396.
[59] See R. H. Elias and E. D. Finch (eds), *Letters of Thomas Attwood Digges, 1742–1821* (Columbia: University of South Carolina Press, 1982), p. 443, T. Digges to T. Jefferson, Birmingham, 10 March 1793.

K. C. Barraclough, who has written the most comprehensive account of eighteenth-century steel-making in Britain, cautions that perfectly satisfactory steel was being produced long before anyone understood the structure of metals. It was being made by virtue of a combination of 'innate genius, care, patience, and close observation of trial and error methods'.[60] The contributors to a comparative study of iron-making in Sweden and Russia concur. The capacity of the Russian forge-masters to turn out high-grade iron and steel without the least scientific knowledge 'amazes the metallurgists of a later industrial era'.[61] But if smelting, cementation, and perhaps annealing and tempering, were activities largely dependent on oral knowledge and manual skill, the manufacture of metal alloys seems to have called for a more explicit theoretical grasp of the processes involved, not to mention a measure of entrepreneurial flair for finding market outlets. James Keir's efforts in this area were certainly informed by a full understanding of the metallurgy of his day and so, we suspect, were William Murdoch's. The Swiss ironmaster Johann Fischer, who was one of the first to make crucible-cast steel on the Continent, recalled a dinner-table conversation on the composition of metals in ancient times when he visited Soho in 1814. Murdoch was summoned to participate when Fischer produced from his pocket a sample of a 'yellow steel' [apparently an alloy of copper and steel][62] he had contrived at Schaffhausen. Yet Matthew Boulton was no slouch in this department, either. The experimental habits of a lifetime were poured into his quest to produce tough and flawless copper strip. No less energy was directed towards the challenge of producing steel dies that would not crack. With France descending into revolution, he warned in 1791 that the abundant supplies of monastic bell-metal coming on to the market would not be suitable for coining. The metal lacked sufficient ductility to be rolled, presumably because of its tin content, and would crack the dies and matrices – as indeed happened.[63] As for steel, one wonders whether he read Réaumur's *L'Art de convertir le fer forgé en acier* (1722), which constituted holy writ for French cementation steel-makers until near the end of the eighteenth century. It seems likely, because he had a copy of the first edition in his library and appears to have believed that sulphurous particles were the critical ingredient taken up during the conversion of iron into steel – just like everybody

[60] Barraclough, *Steelmaking before Bessemer*, i, p. 7.
[61] Ågren, *Iron-making Societies*, p. 283.
[62] Henderson, *J. C. Fischer and his Diary*, p. 132.
[63] See R. Trogan and P. Sorel, *Augustin Dupré, 1748–1833: graveur-général des Monnaies de France* (Paris: Paris Musées, n.d. [2000]), pp. 31–2; also BCL MS 3782/12/39 M. Boulton to J. Lugo, Soho, 24 June 1794.

else of his generation. But he emphatically did not follow Réaumur in supposing that any locally produced iron would serve the purpose. Engravers working on commission for him in Paris were sent out supplies of Swedish die-steel from his Birmingham warehouse.

Our second close-quarters examination of the connections between scientific theory and industrial practice takes us into the realm of eighteenth-century physics, in this case heat, light and combustion. It provides additional persuasive evidence of the way in which the Industrial Enlightenment facilitated the conversion of formal knowledge into a recognisably useful body of instructional data which could then be taken up and applied. The example also has the merit of demonstrating that the phenomenon of *savant-fabricant* was not confined to the English provinces, even if that was where it most obviously flourished. Finally, the example takes us directly into a world catering for the values of the fashion-conscious consumer whose vanity was flattered by ownership of objects in which scientific ingenuity was conspicuously embedded.

James Watt and Matthew Boulton first met Aimé Argand in the late winter of 1784. This was the Argand whose involvement almost a year later in the first manned balloon ascent from Birmingham was mentioned in Chapter 3. Watt acknowledged the meeting in a letter to Jean-André Deluc, observing, 'I found that Gentleman very ingenious, too much so to be made a confidant in mechanical matters of business.'[64] Argand's path to Soho is so evocative of the career of the *savant*-turned-*fabricant* that it is worth retracing the stages. The son of a Genevan watch-maker, he received an initial grounding in natural philosophy thanks to Horace-Bénédict de Saussure, the incumbent of the Chair of Philosophy at the *Académie* (university) there. Saussure then launched Argand into the more theoretically driven world of the French Academy of Sciences with letters of introduction to Lavoisier and Fourcroy. Arriving in Paris in 1775, Argand appears to have found employment either as a laboratory assistant to the Arsenal chemists, or else in a teaching capacity, although his activities whilst in the French capital are not well documented. He certainly moved within the ambit of the Academy and, in 1776, presented a paper on the supposedly electrical origins of hailstones. We know, too, that he was in contact with Jean-Baptiste Meusnier, one of the most mechanically literate of the *académiciens*, and there is a possibility that during these years he was already making contributions to the science of distillation. These indications, when combined with the more plentiful information about his subsequent career, suggest

---

[64] BCL MS 3219/4/123 J. Watt snr to J.-A. Deluc, n.p., 22 February 1784.

strongly that Argand's theoretical understanding of pneumatic chemistry and the physics of heat was built up whilst in Paris.

His first venture into manufacturing occurred in 1780, when he secured the financial support of the Estates of Languedoc in Montpellier to set up a brandy distillery incorporating his improvements to still technology. Jean-Antoine Chaptal, who moved in similar circles and would himself make notable contributions to industrial chemistry in the 1780s, seems to have been involved in the experimental testing of Argand's enhanced process. Whilst in Languedoc Argand also encountered the Montgolfier brothers, who were clearly men after his own heart. They ran the family paper-making business at Annonay on scientific lines, and divided their time between experimental philosophy and industry. After the successful balloon launches of 1783, Joseph Montgolfier would be elected a corresponding member of the Académie des Sciences. Argand's long association with the brothers probably arose from a pooling of technological knowledge, for in running efficiently his distillery operation he had had to overcome problems of lighting and heat loss.

The solution to the night-time running of the stills was an improved oil lamp which would provide a far greater illumination than candle-light, burn without smoke, and do so for long intervals without the need for refuelling. Once fully developed, this tubular-wick cylinder lamp proceeded to work a quiet revolution in both domestic and industrial lighting. Not until the advent of gas lighting would it be supplanted. Aimé Argand did not invent the oil lamp, of course, but he pioneered two innovations which would be integral to the design of all subsequent models. The first was the idea of a tubular wick held between concentric tubes which allowed air to enter at the base and play upon both sides of the flame. The second was the chimney or funnel, which enhanced the draught and drew off the heated gases from the burner. As early as 1780 Argand had prototypes of his lamp made up and put to use in his very first distillery, although it is unclear whether the design for the chimney was settled at this stage. Argand seems initially to have trialed a number of metal flue designs, following consultations with Meusnier. The solution of the tight-fitting glass chimney waited upon improvements in glass-house technology, since no one in France appeared able to make flint glass of a quality that could withstand the highly concentrated heat of the burner. This improvement only became feasible early in 1784 when a London firm of instrument makers devised a shatter-proof chimney.

There can be little doubt that Argand's improved lamp was the product of scientific thinking rather than improvisation, or tinkering. Whilst he hailed from an 'ingenious' craft background, his exposure to, and probable participation in, the advances taking place in chemistry and physics in Paris during the late 1770s underscored his own practical work on distillation, lighting and propellants for aerostatic machines. The need on several occasions to defend his innovations against patent infringers fully reveals the extent to which his technological practice was theoretically informed. So, too, does the relative ease with which he was accepted by the natural philosophy communities on either side of the Channel. The plagiarists he had to deal with in Paris simply copied the lamp and then advertised it for sale in pseudo-scientific language, claiming a smokeless flame of a brightness comparable to the burning of substances in dephlogisticated air. When challenged, however, they more or less conceded that the conception of the lamp was Argand's alone. If they had been spurred to copy the device, it was because the inventor himself had insisted that it 'was based on principles of physics' and that 'problems of physics could be solved by known laws'.[65] Further corroborative evidence of the lamp's intellectual provenance came to light when Argand sought to take legal action against English patent infringers. Joseph Montgolfier and several other friends came over from France to serve as expert witnesses, and the day before the hearing in the Court of Common Pleas a case conference was organised so that the prosecuting counsel could concert with the witnesses and Argand could rehearse with the barristers 'the philosophical part of the lamp'.[66]

We may surmise, then, that Aimé Argand did not take the road to Birmingham in 1784 purely in order to pay courtesy calls on the West Midlands philosophers. He had a product to develop, manufacture and market; a product, moreover, with a potential for sale either as a consumer durable or as a scientific instrument. Although Deluc's letter was not explicit on this point and referred chiefly to the attainments of his *protégé* as a natural philosopher, it is clear that Boulton was the object and, more especially, Soho the place where further research and development as well as manufacturing could be carried out. In the event, the research and development benefited more from the Soho milieu than did the manufacturing. Both Keir and Watt set about finding remedies for some of the defects in Argand's design. The 'hydrostatic' version of the lamp has already been mentioned, and James Watt sought to obviate the need for the oil reservoir to be placed above the burner by experimenting with various types of miniature forcing pump. The

<hr />

[65] See J. J. Wolfe, *Brandy, Balloons and Lamps: Ami Argand, 1750–1803* (Carbondale: Southern Illinois University Press, 1999), p. 49.

[66] *Ibid.*, p. 67.

earliest attempts to manufacture the lamp for the consumer market in 1784–85 were not a success, however. Boulton was absent from Soho for long periods, and his skilled tin-smiths were mostly engaged on more pressing work. The few that were made were either earmarked for scientific experiments, or given away to important personages – and even they often proved defective. The fact that the lamps could be seen brilliantly illuminating shop windows merely stoked up demand and complicated matters further. In the summer season of 1785 they were used at the Birmingham theatre for the first time, and in September of that year Watt wrote to tell Boulton, who was still in Cornwall, that 'several shops in Birmingham have got the new lamps and cut a good appearance'.[67] Pearson and Rollason, the printers, were not only displaying the lamps, they had had new window sashes made of Keir's alloy installed as well.

It was in this context that the challenge to Argand's copyright arose. In the absence of a regular supply of saleable lamps from Soho, forgers on both sides of the Channel made a killing. In Paris, where the Swiss inventor's priority claim was most vigorously contested, poor-quality copies had been in the shops since the spring of 1784. In fact the Comédie Française had employed about forty of the lamps for the first performance of Beaumarchais's *Marriage of Figaro* on 27 April. It seems unlikely, therefore, that Aimé Argand ever made much money out of his improved lamp design. As for Boulton, he lost money by his involvement in the venture. But science undoubtedly gained thereby, for Argand was ultimately more of a *savant* than he was a *fabricant*. His long periods of enforced residence in London and in Birmingham made a great deal of technical know-how about aerostatics available to the English natural philosophers. As for the cylinder lamp, experimentalists all over Europe quickly acknowledged its worth. When it was demonstrated at the Académie des Sciences in Paris in November 1784, *académiciens* hastened to place orders. Significantly, they assumed that the London instrument maker Jesse Ramsden would build them. James Watt and Joseph Priestley took steps to obtain specimens for experimental purposes as well. After his setbacks in the English courts, Argand returned to France, but he continued both to improve the effectiveness of his lamp for domestic lighting, and to carry out heat and combustion investigations with it. In October 1786 he wrote a long epistle to Jean-André Deluc in which he described his experiments and recounted how he had been comparing Watt and Priestley's theories as to what happened to air in the flame of the lamp with those of Lavoisier.[68]

[67] BCL MS 3782/12/79 J. Watt snr to M. Boulton, Chacewater, 20 September 1785.
[68] Wolfe, *Brandy, Balloons and Lamps*, p. 97.

Cultures of science

It is significant that Argand should have travelled to England in order to realise the economic potential of his lamp technology. On arrival he was feted as the natural philosopher who had been involved in the Montgolfier ascents, and thanks to Deluc secured easy access both to the royal family at Windsor and to the Royal Society. Like so many continental visitors of the 1780s, he was staggered at the affluence of London and the evidence of industrial ingenuity on display in shop windows. As far as manufacturing was concerned, however, he was advised to proceed forthwith to the West Midlands. Although the French government had been given the opportunity to evaluate the cylinder lamp, it displayed far greater interest in Argand's still technology. Free-trade negotiations with Britain were impending, and brandy distilling offered a better prospect of economic pay-back than did domestic or industrial lighting. Louis XVI would eventually come up with a generous subsidy to set up a lamp factory on French soil at Versoix in the Pays de Gex, but its commercial viability was precarious from the outset. Nearly all of the materials used at the plant had to be imported from Britain.

In England inventors approached philosophers and industrial entrepreneurs, whereas in France they approached governments – or so it would seem.[69] This difference should help us to explore the complex question of the uneven take-up of useful knowledge in different parts of Europe. Joel Mokyr observes that 'useful knowledge could only become economically significant if it was shared, and access was shaped by institutions, attitudes and communications technology'.[70] After all, it is feedback, in his model, as much as the overall quantum of knowledge available that allows him to identify the Industrial Enlightenment as a discrete phenomenon. Nothing in our case study of the West Midlands invites a different conclusion. Nevertheless, the fact remains that Mokyr tends to buttress his arguments with data drawn from the nineteenth and twentieth centuries which lend weight to the view that cultural barriers were not all that important in the final analysis. Integration is his theme and, in the long run, 'useful knowledge flowed across boundaries to blend these difference [*sic*] sufficiently to create a more-or-less coherent "Western useful knowledge"'.[71] Yet when we compare the situation in England, or the West Midlands, with that prevailing on the continent of Europe in the more confined time-frame of the second

[69] In this connection see J. Horn, *The Path Not Taken: French Industrialization in the Age of Revolution, 1750–1830* (Cambridge, Mass: MIT Press, 2006).
[70] Mokyr, *The Gifts of Athena*, p. 288.
[71] *Ibid.*, p. 289.

half of the eighteenth century, the picture is much less clear cut. On the contrary, the balance of the evidence provides support for the science historians who maintain that very real obstacles inhibited the permeation of useful knowledge.

If we look no further than France, it is possible to identify several important factors which discouraged interaction across the science–technology interface. Unlike England, Bourbon France never developed a free-flow market for scientific knowledge. Innovators consequently approached central government or regional equivalents such as the Estates of Languedoc for backing. It followed, therefore, that the diffusion of instructional data regarding a new technology was considered to be the job of government. In England, by contrast, the state did not play an educative role in either the science or the technology arena. Indeed, Sir Joseph Banks would take pride in the fact that the Royal Society, unlike continental academies, was *not* beholden to institutions of government.[72] English Newtonians had little choice but to build their bridges elsewhere, therefore – in the direction of entrepreneurs and industrialists. For all the precocity of its Enlightenment, both literary and scientific, France remained a compartmentalised society. Before 1789 knowledge circulated, but in sealed packages. The Académie des Sciences had few contacts with regional natural philosophy nodes, and in any case tended to adopt a policing attitude towards knowledge. It disliked rivals, as Roger Hahn[73] has demonstrated, and it successively torpedoed attempts to set up bodies that might have brought *philosophes* and artisans into closer contact with one another. As noted at the start of this chapter, the majority of *académiciens* remained ambivalent about *utilité* in any case. Moreover, men like Réaumur or Coulomb who did accept the need to reach out, found it difficult to hit upon an all-purpose language of communication. In the absence of social and institutional structures that facilitated interpersonal contact, the Industrial Enlightenment in France was always going to be a lopsided affair.

Deprived of avenues for communication or feedback, talented mechanics such as the Périer brothers, who pioneered the construction of the improved steam engine in France, were left marooned. Meanwhile, the few genuine *savant-fabricants* gestated within the bosom of the *ancien régime* were, like Chaptal or the Montgolfiers, often formed in

---

[72] See J. Gascoigne, *Science in the Service of Empire: Joseph Banks, the British State and the Uses of Science in the Age of Revolution* (Cambridge: Cambridge University Press, 1998), p. 31.

[73] R. Hahn, *The Anatomy of a Scientific Institution: the Paris Academy of Sciences, 1660–1803* (Berkeley: University of California Press, 1971), pp. 108–11.

the provinces. The Périers obtained their industrial know-how almost entirely from England, and more especially from Birmingham, the Black Country and Coalbrookdale. The engine manufactory which they built at Chaillot on the outskirts of Paris was state-of-the-art in consequence. For all their doubts about the brothers' commercial integrity, Watt and Boulton could not help but be impressed with the premises when they visited Paris in 1786–87. But the plant proved incapable of evolution for, in Mokyr's terms, the technology had been separated from its propositional knowledge base. Whilst Watt and his Soho engineers would continue to develop the engine, the Périers found it difficult to do more than reproduce the technology they had been supplied with, or which had been obtained by espionage in the 1780s.[74] English travellers to France in the years before the Revolution could be forgiven if they experienced some bafflement, then. They found themselves in a country whose knowledge-generating capacity appeared second to none; a country where science was granted far more public recognition than had ever been the case in Britain, as Sir Charles Blagden was moved to observe.[75] Yet its natural philosophers were curiously detached from the everyday business of putting knowledge to work. In his Paris diary of 1786–87 Matthew Boulton made a long list of the various instructional facilities and lecture courses on offer in the French capital, only to add the quizzical comment, 'Science too much cultivated & the practice too little.'[76]

It is difficult to generalise about the science culture of the German-speaking lands as compared with England. Nonetheless, certain facts stand out. One of the most obvious is the huge knock-on effect of institutional difference. In Prussia, Saxony and the Habsburg territories mining and smelting were crown monopolies, with the result that the science–technology configuration was almost entirely determined by the state. Whilst private-enterprise industrial activity was not unknown, it was taken for granted that the administration would set the direction and the pace and everyone else would follow. German visitors to the West Midlands, even more than French visitors, were constantly surprised by the extent of *laissez-faire*, the absence of guild regulation and the willingness of private individuals to risk large sums on industrial ventures. On the other hand, this situation allowed precious little room for ambiguity on the subject of 'useful' knowledge. Most German states

[74] See Payen, *Capital et machine à vapeur*, pp. 175, 244.
[75] Gascoigne, *Science in the Service of Empire*, p. 153.
[76] BCL MS 3782/12/108/49 M. Boulton: diaries and notebooks, 1786–7; also M. R. Lynn, *Popular Science and Public Opinion in Eighteenth-Century France* (Manchester: Manchester University Press, 2006), pp. 8–9.

espoused the gospel of utility in the guise of cameralism. And states with a mission to aggrandise (Prussia), or to recover from war (Saxony), or backwardness (Bavaria) were in the van of the drive to augment fiscal yield. It is significant in this context that the mining school at Freiberg was founded as part of the Saxon Elector's effort to reverse the devastating effects of the Seven Years' War on his country. Similar schools were set up in Schemnitz in Lower Hungary, in Berlin, and at Clausthal in the Electorate of Hanover.

In Bavaria the employment by Elector Carl Theodor of Sir Benjamin Thompson (from 1792 Count Rumford) as his adjutant-general briefly invigorated the science culture of this impoverished and clericalised country. It was he who sent the talented engineer Joseph von Baader to Soho in 1791 – ostensibly to order a pumping engine for the Mannheim city reservoir, but in reality to conduct a spying mission. All the German cameralists were convinced that direct technology transfer was the best way forward. After mid-century English and Scottish industrial premises were besieged by questionnaire-wielding German utilitarians seeking to prise away the secrets of the 'wealth of nations'. They were at pains to organise a reverse flow of technological knowledge as well, being among the foremost recruiters of British entrepreneurs, industrialists and craftsmen to work abroad. In this regard the Prussian example is instructive, for it illustrates well the purposeful attempt to create a scientifically informed technological culture from the top down.

Once the Treaty of Berlin had added Silesia to Prussia's territories in 1743, the preconditions for state-directed industrial growth were almost all in place. Frederick II acquired, in the most literal sense, substantial coal and ore deposits. Over the decades that followed an entirely new culture of technology sprouted in the region as Silesia developed to become Prussia's Black Country. This was unquestionably state-sponsored scientific and industrial endeavour – if only for the reason that regalian law granted to the monarch the right to mine anywhere within his realm, regardless of the property title of the surface owner. Similar controls had once applied to tin mining in Cornwall, but had been renounced in the late seventeenth century. The Prussian government thus took the lead in mineral extraction and smelting, or else conceded its mining rights to others in return for a tithe. This tithe generated significant sums for the Prussian treasury, thereby increasing the incentive to manage the coal-field and the ore mines according to the best technological practices available. The two men on whom Frederick devolved the task were Freiherr Friedrich Anton von Heynitz and Friedrich Wilhelm von Reden. As previously noted, Heynitz had been the driving force behind the Freiberg *Bergsakademie* before entering Prussian service in 1777, and his nephew Reden would succeed him at the helm of the Prussian Mines Department. Over a span of nearly twenty-five years they would oversee the Prussian state's policy on science and technology, whilst superintending the expansion of mining and metal-working in Silesia on which it was largely based.

Having been put in charge of the Silesian Oberbergamt in 1779, Reden energetically set about implementing the cameralist agenda. He sought to maximise the production of minerals that were habitually brought in from abroad; to import knowledge and know-how; and to ensure that best practice was introduced to state mines and foundries in the hope that it be filtered down to independent mining contractors and ironmasters by a process of emulation. We know most about his efforts to acquire the necessary technology because he travelled widely in Europe (as did Heynitz), and regularly visited the West Midlands and Coalbrookdale. In fact several generations of the Reden family became personal friends of the Watts as well as the Wilkinsons. James Watt briefly considered sending his eldest son to Clausthal in order to complete his technical education under Reden's direction. As for William Wilkinson, he was persuaded in 1788 to travel to Silesia and provide *in situ* technical advice. Since Silesian coal appeared to be unsuited to modern coke-fired smelting, Reden faced a constant problem of fuel supply. Wilkinson's advice was sought on blast furnace design and with his help lead ore was successfully reduced, using coke, at the Friedrichsgrube works. Further trials of coke smelting followed, this time at the iron foundries in Gleiwitz (1794–96) and Königshutte (1800–2), both of which were fiscal works. But by this date the heroic epoch of state-led technological advance was drawing to a close in Prussia. Reden left Silesia in 1802, having brought the improved steam-engine technology to the region, having thereby reinvigorated the mining of lead (a regalian mineral), and having had some success with coke smelting. There were by this date even some signs of emulation, as private furnace-owners prepared to follow the lead.[77] Four years later, however, it was the state which failed in its self-appointed mission. After the battle of Jena Prussia became a dependency of the French and the industrial development of Silesia ground to a temporary halt.

Although it has been suggested that Sweden was never able to sustain a home-grown version of the European Enlightenment,[78] there can

---

[77] For the preceding paragraphs, see N. J. G. Pounds, *The Upper Silesian Industrial Region* (Bloomington: Indiana University Publications, 1958).

[78] See T. Frängsmyr, *A la recherche des Lumières: une perspective suédoise* (Pessac: Presses universitaires de Bordeaux, 1999).

be no doubt that the country gave birth to a highly specific science culture in the decades between 1730 and 1780. The frequency with which the names Bergman, Cronstedt, Linnaeus, Scheele and Wilcke crop up in the correspondence of the West Midlands network of natural philosophers is ample testimony to the fact. On examination, however, this culture more closely resembles the *dirigiste* German pattern than the market-orientated model so characteristic of Hanoverian England. For all the wishful thinking of politicians and bureaucrats, Sweden was primarily a producer of raw materials; its manufacturing base was tiny. In the humiliating aftermath of the collapse of its Baltic empire (1697–1718), science was embraced as a creed of national recovery. 'Patriotic' science became both a gospel of economic renewal and a cultural value in its own right. If science was to be harnessed to military ambitions in Prussia, in Sweden it would serve to efface the memory of military disaster. The emergence in the Riksdag of a new political party with a clear mercantilist agenda lent substance to this vision, and it resulted in the founding, in 1739, of the Royal Swedish Academy of Sciences.

The Academy promoted science with an experimental and utilitarian emphasis, and did so within an unusual ideological consensus embracing the aristocracy, politicians, bureaucrats and the Lutheran church. New chairs in physics and chemistry were established at Uppsala University and old professorships in Latin verse and oriental languages discontinued. In its heyday the Academy tried hard to bridge the science–technology interface. It published works in the vernacular, and blended articles on pure science topics with useful information on technological processes. By continental European standards, the Swedish body assembled an extraordinary mix of science professionals, amateurs and practitioners (engineers, architects, surveyors) as well. But, as the Riksdag's power ebbed in the 1760s and 1770s in the face of a resurgent monarchy, the membership of the Academy gradually became more exclusive. Technically trained individuals dwindled from nearly 30 per cent at the first election in 1739 to around 15 per cent by the century's end.

However, the culture of science during the Swedish Age of Freedom was not as facilitating as these remarks would seem to imply. Academicians disputed the thrust of utilitarianism, with some insisting that agriculture should be the priority, whilst others argued for state aid to be given to handicrafts or manufacturing. None of these options automatically presupposed a move in the direction of technological development as understood in England, though. When the ironmaster and founder member of the Academy Jonas Alströmer secured the support of his colleagues for assistance to be given to manufacturing industry, the differing interpretations of utility came out into the open. Whereas everyone could agree that a knowledge of mechanics would be useful to manufacturers, the idea that machine technology might save on labour was completely alien to the mercantilist way of thinking. The purpose of manufacturing, according to most advocates of 'patriotic' science, was to support the industries that were intrinsic to Sweden (farming, mining) and thereby to expand the population. In this connection it is worth recalling the difficulties encountered in his homeland by the English-trained engineer Mårten Triewald[79] earlier in the century. With the aid of Alströmer, who had passed through the West Midlands on several occasions in the 1710s, he contrived to bring over to Sweden Newcomen's new 'fire engine', with a view to installing it at the Dannemore iron-ore mines. Indeed, Linnaeus[80] saw it in operation in 1729 and noted that its reciprocal motion shook the whole superstructure of the mine. Although the technology performed reasonably well, it was soon abandoned, however. Running and maintenance costs proved to be higher than anticipated and the social cost was simply not acceptable. The engine jeopardised the livelihoods of those who were reliant for their daily bread on the traditional methods of draining the mines and raising the ore. In this instance, then, the cultural barrier proved insuperable; the immediate product of Mokyr's feedback process was a consensus that steam-power technology was not suited to Sweden's domestic conditions.

Denmark-Norway was another small kingdom on the periphery of Europe. Yet it too experienced a number of dramatic changes, starting in the middle decades of the eighteenth century. One of these was the institutionalisation of a science policy which in some ways resembled that practised from Stockholm, or Uppsala. In Denmark, however, the drive to exploit new technology appears to have been embedded in a reformist economic doctrine that was much less resistant to machine-based industrialisation and the social implications carried in its wake. Two of the most active ferreters of new technology were actually Swedes who transferred to Danish service on discovering that their own government was not particularly keen to patronise modern factory industry. One was Charles Axel Nordberg, who visited Birmingham and Manchester repeatedly between 1760 and 1791, and the other, rather better known, individual was Jøns Mathias Ljungberg. He left for Copenhagen

---

[79] S. Lindqvist, *Technology on Trial: the Introduction of Steam Power Technology into Sweden, 1715–1736* (Stockholm: Almqvist & Wiksell, 1984).

[80] http://linnaeus.c18.net/letters, C. Linnaeus to K. Stobaeus, Uppsala, 4 July 1729.

in 1778 when the Swedish Chamber of Commerce showed little interest in the fruits of his forays abroad. Ljungberg would settle in Birmingham for a time, where his information-gathering activities were tolerated with reasonably good grace. But when, in the summer of 1789, he tried to leave the country with packing cases filled with tools, machine models, technical drawings and even clay samples, there was indignation throughout the West Midlands.[81] Dan Christensen, whose researches have done most to clarify our understanding of the science–technology interface in Denmark-Norway, stresses that there developed after 1750 'a close cognitive link'[82] between natural knowledge and technological applications. It developed, of course, because science professionals became deeply involved in the modernisation project. As in Sweden, though, the trajectory of the sciences remained vulnerable to political and institutional shifts. When Hans Christian Oersted succeeded Thomas Bugge as secretary of the Royal Danish Academy of Sciences in 1815, collaboration between natural philosophers and mechanics began to ebb.

The difficulties encountered by Triewald and Alströmer in seeking to domesticate industrial technology which had been conceived elsewhere are mirrored in the experiences of Dutch entrepreneurs. Yet the paradox is greater because the Dutch provinces conformed more closely to the model of scientific activity prevailing in England than to the 'command economy' format adopted in Prussia. Political decision taking was decentralised, the creative community of experimental philosophers was quite large and well organised, and scientific knowledge developed in a market-driven environment. Indeed, the Dutch natural philosophers had been among the first to espouse Newtonian science, and Dutch universities and schools had led the way in providing instruction in modern physics and mechanics. It is true that this lead was lost after the middle of the century, but Alessandro Volta, who visited the United Provinces in 1782 in the company of Jean-Hyacinthe Magellan, was struck by the deep penetration of matters scientific even among amateurs. After England, he viewed it as the most enlightened and civilised country in Europe. However, this civilisation had been built on commerce rather than mechanised industry. If we set to one side traditional hydraulic engineering, Dutch elites seem to have confined their interest in labour-saving machines and alternative power technologies to the exhibits in the collections of the Teyler Museum in Haarlem.

Only when a handful of creative individuals grouped in the Batavian Society of Experimental Philosophy began to meet in Rotterdam and

---

[81] BCL MS 3219/4/124 J. Watt snr to J. Watt jnr, 11 October 1789.
[82] Christensen, *Det Moderne Projekt*, p. 813.

to agitate a reform agenda did the huge inertial weight of opinion opposed to change become apparent. This culture of resistance in a country which might reasonably have participated in the late eighteenth-century Industrial Enlightenment perplexes historians. However, it is possible to shed some light on the phenomenon if we take steam technology as an emblematic case, and look at the arguments that were voiced for and against its adoption. The patriots of the Batavian Society initially viewed the steam engine as natural philosophers, that is to say, as an invention worth more for its curiosity value than for any practical benefit it might bestow. However, they were willing to put it to the test and petitioned the municipal authorities of Rotterdam for permission to erect an engine in order to see whether it would be capable of flushing the canals.[83] In the meantime James Watt introduced his improved version and the secretary of the Society, J. D. Huichelbos van Liender, wrote to him with the suggestion that he participate in the Society's prize essay competition on the subject of the utility of steam engines for polder drainage. Watt was absent from Birmingham, but Boulton replied memorably on his behalf: 'As Mr Watt & I are engaged in the Fire-Engine as a business or profession, we do not enter ourselves as candidates for honorary awards, neither do we engage in any discussions upon theory or principles.'[84]

The reprimand was a little undeserved, for van Liender, at least, had a businessman's view of utility. In addition to being a natural philosopher and secretary to the Batavian Society, he was a merchant, a white-lead manufacturer and a keen amateur engineer: a *savant-fabricant*, in fact. But in a land where conventional wisdom decreed that wind- and water-mills constituted the only secure and reliable pumping technology, winning support for an alternative proved to be an uphill struggle. Watt acknowledged as much in an impatient remark to Jean-André Deluc, who had raised the subject of the applications of steam power in Holland: 'I fear that the whole dutch nation have to [*sic*] great an aversion to novelties ever to come into so salutary a scheme as you propose.'[85] Nevertheless, van Liender persisted and in the summer of 1787 a trial Boulton & Watt engine was erected on the Blijdorp polder in the province of Holland. Although it proved capable in October of that year of reducing the water level to seven inches below summer levels in just a few hours of pumping, the conservative and Orangist polder authorities were determined not to be impressed. Three weeks later,

[83] Verbruggen, *The Correspondence of van Liender*, pp. 12–13.
[84] *Ibid.*, p. 110.
[85] BCL MS 3219/4/123 J. Watt snr to J.-A. Deluc, Birmingham, 18 May 1783.

however, heavy rains flooded the polder to nine and a half inches above summer levels and a lack of wind rendered the windmill inoperative. The polder authorities had little choice but to ask for the engine to be restarted.[86]

Attitudes did not swiftly change, though. After all, wind power was free, if irregular, and since the Republic had no coal mines fuel for the engine had to be imported. Moreover, the demonstration at Blijdorp coincided with the outbreak of civil strife between the Patriots and the Orangists, followed by a Prussian intervention to restore the Stadholder. Van Liender and his colleagues in the Batavian Society were mostly fervent Patriots and their opponents were quick to dub the steam engine a Patriot contraption. In view of the political situation, van Liender decided that it would be prudent to withdraw from the country for a time. In a letter to James Watt penned early in 1788 he reported on the performance of the Blijdorp engine, adding: 'Were public circumstances in another turn, than they now are, the Steam Engine would undoubtedly take footing in this country, but by being a work of Patriots it is quite condemned and abhored.'[87] This was an optimistic assessment. When the Board of Directors of the Batavian Society assembled to demonstrate the power of the engine to Prince Willem, the Stadholder, and his family in October 1790, awkward questions were asked as to why the machine had not been brought into more general use. A diplomatic answer seemed to be called for, and the visitors were politely reminded of 'how difficult it was to start anything new in our Country, however useful it might be'.[88] In fact, steam-power technology would not be domesticated in the Netherlands until the middle of the next century.

Even in core regions of western Europe, it seems that useful knowledge did not flow with the ease and speed that Joel Mokyr implies, then – at any rate not in the second half of the eighteenth and the early nineteenth centuries. In Italy and the Iberian Peninsula, by contrast, science cultures may actually have been caught in a spiral of decline. Evidence of a linkage to industry in these parts of Europe is sparse in the extreme. Eighteenth-century Italy boasted a dozen capitals and at least a dozen centres in which natural philosophers habitually gathered, but there existed no connected scientific community. Volta, who practised in a secondary centre, felt his isolation keenly. Insofar as scientific activity was institutionalised, it tended to be subject to aristocratic patronage and play a decorative role. Adam Walker, the itinerant lecturer who

---

[86] Verbruggen, *The Correspondence of van Liender*, pp. 26–7.
[87] *Ibid.*, p. 201.
[88] *Ibid.*, p. 28.

collaborated with Priestley, would expostulate: 'They are wretched mechanics in Italy, never saw a clock with a minute hand to it, in the whole country.'[89] This fits with the experience of Boulton & Watt. In 1788 the firm supplied an engine to the King of the Two Sicilies – a fact revealing in itself – and it was installed at a royal palace near Capua. The erector sent to do the job reported that none of the ancillary parts could be made locally since no iron was cast in the kingdom. In a semi-literate hand he described the Neapolitans as 'a ignorant sett of piple' who 'kow nothing of machinery of no sort'.[90] James Watt junior, who passed that way in 1793, agreed: the local mechanics could make absolutely no sense of how the engine functioned.

Technology transfer

In 1776 an unemployed Cornish millwright named Thomas Dudley travelled up to the West Midlands in search of work. Whilst visiting Soho he heard about Mr Watt's improved pumping engine, which had just been put into operation at the Bloomfield Colliery in Tipton. Having inspected the engine, he described the fuel saving it had achieved in a letter to friends. Thomas Wilson, the newly appointed manager of a copper and tin mine near Chacewater, got hold of this information. His deep-shaft mine had been experiencing drainage problems. By September 1777 the first of Boulton & Watt's engines in Cornwall was up and running.[91] More often than not, this is the story of how technology transfer took place. In this instance the transfer was successful because the mine adventurers of Cornwall were already familiar with the operation of (atmospheric) steam engines; because they could call upon a great deal of embedded skill; and because James Watt came down to Cornwall to supervise the erection personally. Within a year, two more Soho-designed engines were sucking water out of mines in the district.

Skill and know-how often feature as quantities that can be taken for granted in the technology-transfer equation. If not directly portable like scientific data-sets or hardware, it is assumed either that they were swiftly codified by virtue of the very process of industrialisation, or that their

---

[89] Pancaldi, *Volta: Science and Culture in the Age of the Enlightenment*, p. 68.

[90] BCL MS 3782/12/34 M. Logan to M. Boulton, 27 April 1789.

[91] Cornwall Record Office AD 1583/11 An account of the state of the principal mines of Cornwall; also R. L. Hills, *James Watt. Volume 2: The Years of Turmoil, 1775–1785* (Ashbourne: Landmark, 2005), pp. 96–7.

stubborn non-transmissibility was not sufficient on its own to prevent a technology from being successfully implemented. Joel Mokyr's splitting and lumping of knowledge in a bid to create analytical categories out of which to build his Industrial Enlightenment thesis incurs this objection. Whilst at pains to emphasise that 'propositional' knowledge should be understood to embrace more than scientific laws and phenomena, he overfills the category so that it also includes informal practical knowledge, intuitive understanding of mechanical processes and folk wisdoms – in other words, tacit and orally transmitted knowledge. These additions are described elsewhere in his book as a 'master catalog',[92] or repository of all the techniques that have been found to work. But if skill and know-how can be likened to a set of effective techniques, it is not at all clear why they should be bracketed with 'propositional' rather than 'prescriptive' knowledge. In fact, Mokyr places techniques alongside other forms of instructional 'how' knowledge as well.[93]

This fundamental ambiguity perhaps explains why *The Gifts of Athena* never comes fully to grips with the issue of tacit knowledge. Its role is mentioned repeatedly and the significant findings in this area of the economic historian J. R. Harris[94] are duly noted, yet the reader is left with the impression that a closer analysis of skill and hard-to-define ways of knowing might deflect from the main argument.[95] There is, for instance, a tension on the subject of the codification of tacit knowledge, that is to say, the process by which it is rendered legible and accessible to others as well as the bearers. Joel Mokyr's eighteenth-century 'knowledge revolution'[96] is predicated on the speedy inscription of the 'tacit' and the 'oral'. Indeed, the Industrial Enlightenment can be considered the phenomenon that brought this process (as well as others) to a conclusion. Yet, as the argument proceeds beyond the period of the classical Industrial Revolution, the author readily concedes that the process was far from complete even at the dawn of the twenty-first century. It could perhaps be argued that the hurdle posed by tacit knowledge was steadily reduced in the course of the eighteenth century by focusing not on codification or classification,[97] but on an expansion of the pool of technologically literate individuals. To give an apposite example,

[92] Mokyr, *The Gifts of Athena*, p. 36.

[93] *Ibid.*, p. 10.

[94] J. R. Harris, *Industrial Espionage and Technology Transfer: Britain and France in the Eighteenth Century* (Aldershot: Ashgate, 1998).

[95] Mokyr returns to this question in 'The intellectual origins of modern economic growth', pp. 298–310.

[96] Mokyr, *The Gifts of Athena*, p. 56.

[97] See C. C. Gillispie, 'The natural history of industry', *Isis*, 48 (1957), 398–407.

every time Boulton & Watt lost a millwright-turned-engine erector to a competitor they would have found it necessary to train a replacement, thereby adding to the constituency of the mechanically literate and skilled. But this is a hypothesis in need of investigation.

The role of Europe's elites in person-to-person transfer of technological knowledge is fairly well understood, even if we do not yet have a synoptic view of the phenomenon. Several historians have documented the very extensive contacts between Britain and Scandinavia in the second half of the eighteenth century, and J. R. Harris has explored the commerce in useful knowledge between Britain and France.[98] Less is known about transactions involving Germany, the north and central Italian states and Russia, by contrast. Nevertheless, it will be evident from this and the previous chapter that governments were heavily involved in the process. As the rhetoric of utility became all pervasive in the later 1780s, Europe's travelling intelligentsia adroitly secured the patronage of officialdom in return for undertaking to include a technological dimension in their tourism. The Austrian administration of Lombardy helped both Volta and Landriani to defray the costs of their tours, and Leopold, Grand Duke of Tuscany, behaved similarly. In Prussia the technological Grand Tour became an object in itself, of course. The reports submitted by those travelling wholly or partly on government business are a major source of information on the operation of technology transfer. Indeed, they occasionally yield information about the domestic industries of Great Britain that cannot be found in any other source. Yet some specialists doubt whether travel, or journeys of investigation, played as big a role in this area as is often supposed.[99] It is true that natural philosophy – science – travelled far better than technology in the majority of cases because it was less dependent on context. This being the case, we might do better to concentrate on the reverse flow of knowledge and expertise; that is, the 'taking out' rather than 'bringing back'.

Despite all the prying, not to say spying, missions mounted by the Prussian government in the late 1770s and 1780s, the evidence clearly indicates that the Upper Silesian mines and foundries only began to

---

[98] See M. W. Flinn, 'The travel diaries of Swedish engineers of the eighteenth century as sources of technological history', *Transactions of the Newcomen Society*, 31 (1957–58), 95–108; Linqvist, *Technology on Trial*; K. Bruland (ed.), *Technology Transfer and Scandinavian Industrialisation* (New York: Berg, 1991); Christensen, *Det Moderne Projekt*; Harris, *Industrial Espionage and Technology Transfer*.

[99] For instance Ralf Blanken, 'The diffusion of coke smelting and puddling in Germany, 1796–1860', in C. Evans and G. Rydén (eds), *The Industrial Revolution in Iron: the Impact of British Coal Technology in Nineteenth-Century Europe* (Aldershot: Ashgate, 2005), p. 55.

make significant progress once British *fabricants* had agreed to go out as consultants and help solve technological problems on the spot. The case of William Wilkinson has been mentioned, but he had been preceded by Samuel Homfray of the Pennydarren ironworks in 1786, and he would be followed by John Baildon, who brought expertise from the Carron in 1794. Baildon successfully introduced Cort's puddling process to the region, albeit not until the 1820s. Manufacturers who could be persuaded to travel long distances and reside in foreign lands for protracted periods of time were far and few between, however. The real key to technology transfer was the migrant skilled worker. It is impossible to estimate with any degree of accuracy how many British craftsmen had been recruited to work on the Continent by 1792–93 (the date at which warfare between European states interrupted the flow), but anecdotal evidence suggests that they must have numbered several thousands. In 1801–3, when peace intervened, there was a further outflow, and in 1825, when statute law was amended to actually permit artisan emigration, another exodus occurred. Henry Maudslay the machine- and tool-maker reported that skilled workers from England 'have gone in flocks'[100] to the Continent. When Catherine of Russia opened up her country to colonists in 1762–63, around 30,000 arrived from all parts of Europe over the next fifteen years or so. Ambassador Vorontsov tried to dispatch a party of 200 from London in 1763, in ignorance or defiance of the law, and in 1784 a group of 139 skilled workers arrived in St Petersburg from Scotland.[101] Such was the alarm among manufacturers by the mid-1780s, in fact, that they prodded the government into reissuing the sections of the George I statute of 1719 proscribing the enticement of artificers and the export of tools. James Watt, who had himself briefly considered taking his skills to Russia in 1775, believed the French government to be the principal source of enticement activity.

Machines without men to erect, maintain and repair them were, generally speaking, quite useless, as J. R. Harris has noted.[102] All of the parties engaged upon knowledge transfer in the latter part of the eighteenth century were agreed on this point. As early as 1752 the head of the French Bureau de Commerce, Daniel-Charles Trudaine de Montigny, sagely observed that 'the arts never pass by writing from one country

---

[100] See W. O. Henderson, *Britain and Industrial Europe, 1750–1870: Studies in British Influence on the Industrial Revolution in Western Europe* (Liverpool: Liverpool University Press, 1954), p. 122.

[101] A. Cross, *By the Banks of the Neva: Chapters from the Lives and Careers of the British in Eighteenth-Century Russia* (Cambridge: Cambridge University Press, 1997), p. 240.

[102] Harris, *Industrial Espionage and Technology Transfer*, p. 441.

to another, eye and practice can alone train men in these activities'.[103] The tacit-knowledge deficit which inevitably arose when machines were extracted from one cultural context and inserted into another is well illustrated by the case of the Prussian mines councillor Carl Friedrich Bückling. Under instructions from Heynitz, Bückling and another official of the state mining administration visited Soho in 1779 with the ostensible purpose of purchasing four of the newly improved steam engines. Although trained at the Freiberg mining school, Bückling seems to have had no hands-on knowledge of steam technology, and Watt welcomed him to his home primarily as a natural philosopher. He even took the party on a tour of inspection of the pumping engine which the firm had recently erected on the Birmingham Canal. On his return to Prussia, Bückling attempted to build a copy of Watt's engine at a pit near Hettstedt in the Mansfeld district. All he had to rely on was information gleaned from Watt and drawings made illicitly at Soho, and in the absence of skilled metal-workers or engineers the engine failed to perform when first stroked (in the presence of Minister Heynitz) in 1785. The following year Bückling returned to England in order to resume his know-how-gathering activities – to the intense irritation of Boulton & Watt, it should be said. He bought a cast-iron cylinder from Samuel Homfray's Pennydarren works and arranged for it to be shipped out. But even four years later – in 1789 – the engine was still not capable of adequate work. Only when a British engineer by the name of Richards came to the rescue and carried out a complete rebuild did the Hettstedt engine finally pass muster. In the meantime, however, Boulton & Watt had begun a criminal prosecution against Bückling, on discovering that he had attempted to recruit one of their trained erectors from the Cornish mines.[104]

The Hettstedt engine was the first to be built in the German-speaking lands, and the venture was hampered chiefly by the lack of an indigenous casting and boring technology. Yet it would be wrong

[103] J. R. Harris, 'The diffusion of English metallurgical methods to eighteenth-century France', *French History*, 2 (1988), 40.

[104] On the activities of Carl Friedrich Bückling, see BCL MS 3219/4/123 J. Watt snr to J.-A. Deluc, Birmingham, 1 July 1786; J. Watt snr to J. Watt jnr, Birmingham, 13 August 1786; also L. von Mackensen, 'The introduction of English steam engine and metallurgical technology into Germany during the Industrial Revolution prior to 1850', in *L'Acquisition des techniques par les pays non-initiateurs. Pont-à-Mousson, 28 juin – 5 juillet 1970* (Paris: CNRS, 1973), pp. 429–53; *'Der Curieuse Passagier': Deutsche Englandreisende des achzehnten Jahrhunderts als Vermittler kultureller und technologischer Anregungen. Colloquium der Arbeitsstelle 18. Jahrhundert Gesamthochschule Wuppertal Universität Münster. Münster vom 11.-12. Dezember 1980* (Heidelberg, 1983), pp. 65–6; Kroker, *Wege zur Verbreitung technologischer Kentnisse zwischen England und Deutschland*, pp. 154–5.

to imply that a knowledge deficit could not be made good, or even that a native-born engineering competence could not be built up from scratch. By 1800 Bückling's efforts and those of his chief collaborator, Friedrich Wilhelm Holtzhausen, were beginning to pay dividends in Prussian Silesia. The Malapane foundry had begun to turn out reasonably sound cylinders, and the Watt engine was being extensively and successfully copied throughout the region. Meanwhile, in the Ruhr an artisan cabinet-maker with no prior experience of metal-working, Franz Dinnendahl, managed to construct an atmospheric steam engine without ever having heard of Boulton & Watt, or even seen a cylinder-boring machine. 'It was', as he put it in his autobiography, 'a weighty undertaking, especially since in those parts there was not even a smith competent to make a proper screw, let alone other parts of the engine such as valve gear, piston rods and boiler-work, or who understood drilling and turning.'[105] On the strength of this success he went on to copy Watt's improved steam technology successfully in 1803–4. The skill deficit could be overcome, then, particularly in the case of large undertakings that were in receipt of state patronage.

More often than not, though, it is the passing comments of overseas visitors that capture best the yawning gulf that had opened in the machine and tool industries by the end of the century. In the light of his tour through Birmingham, the Black Country and the Severn valley, Marsilio Landriani[106] remarked on the robustness and smoothness of operation of the machinery he had inspected. The tilt-hammers powered by steam in Coalbrookdale struck regular blows, unlike the jerky, water-driven contraptions he was familiar with in Lombardy. Johann Fischer,[107] for his part, was struck by the superior quality of the hand tools which English workmen used. At Soho he was lost in admiration as he watched smiths carrying out the task of making a chisel.

The rudimentary technical literature of the late eighteenth century was quite incapable of spanning this gap. Whilst the French and the Swedes published mining journals and treatises and M.-A. Pictet's *Bibliothèque britannique* carried regular digests of the latest useful knowledge, nothing comparable emanated from the shores of the British Isles. Both James Watt and Matthew Boulton were subscribers to the French *Journal des Mines*, yet they were chary about producing any technical literature that

[105] Cited in F. Klemm, *A History of Western Technology* (London: Allen & Unwin, 1959), p. 271; see also H. Behrens, *Mechanikus Franz Dinnendahl (1775–1826), Erbauer der ersten Dampfmaschinen an der Ruhr: Leben und Wirken aus zeitgenössischen Quellen* (Cologne: Rheinisch-Westfälischen Wirtschaftsarchiv, 1970).

[106] *Relazioni di Marsilio Landriani*, pp. 254–5.

[107] Henderson, *J. C. Fischer and his Diary*, p. 132.

described the processes and innovations pioneered at Soho. They were even reluctant to produce models of the improved steam engine, as we have seen. Apart from patent applications, the only occasion on which the firm seems to have supplied detailed engineering drawings to a third party was when the French government requested that they tender for the rebuilding of the Marly Waterworks in 1786. It is true, of course, that infiltrators and industrial spies were forever seeking out a means of compiling their own freelance blue-prints, and from time to time they succeeded in their endeavours. A rare extant example of such literature is the drawing of the Soho 'lap' engine (Watt's double-acting steam engine with rotary drive) which Georg von Reichenbach, the talented young mechanic sent over from Bavaria with Joseph von Baader, was able to make in 1791 (see Figure 4.0). The difficulties and frustrations confronting the would-be industrial spy are recorded by Reichenbach in heart-felt detail alongside his note-book sketch of the engine.[108]

Soho's know-how remained tacit, localised and elusive for the most part, then. The best way of getting hold of it was to bribe or entice the firm's specialist employees (gilders, modellers, engravers, engine erectors, etc.), and it does appear that some of the hurdles impeding useful knowledge circulation were diminished in this way. The itinerant engine erectors were particularly susceptible to enticement and the partners found that they were largely powerless in the face of this challenge from competitors, or would-be competitors. James Smallman, who had been erecting an engine at Mijdrecht in the Dutch province of Utrecht, disappeared without trace in the summer of 1794 following his recall to Birmingham. Strangely, enquiries revealed that a box of maps he had been transporting for James Watt junior had nonetheless made its way safely from Rotterdam to the customs house in London. Yet neither Boulton & Watt nor Smallman's wife could shed any light on his whereabouts. In all probability he had been waylaid in transit by the

---

[108] '. . . I left my inn to go to Soho but unluckily I lost my way for four hours as I could not ask anybody the way; when I at last found it and went to my right quarter I was truly perturbed at my unfortunate position regarding learning anything and at having been separated from all my friends – but I endeavoured as speedily as possible to reconcile myself to this unpleasant position; and I soon observed it had its advantageous side, for I was able by giving a few small tips to obtain the opportunity, despite the secrecy of Herrn Watt and Boulton, thoroughly to study the mechanism of the fire – or steam engine. I worked at my drawings for six weeks, for I had to maintain secrecy not only against Boulton but also against all the workers who were there. For this reason, this work cost me indescribable labour, for not only could I ask no questions of anybody but also might not for fear of arousing suspicion . . .' See W. von Dyck *Georg von Reichenbach.* (Deutsches Museum Lebensbeschreibungen und Urkunden, Munich, 1912); translation taken from Klemm, *A History of Western Technology*, p. 260.

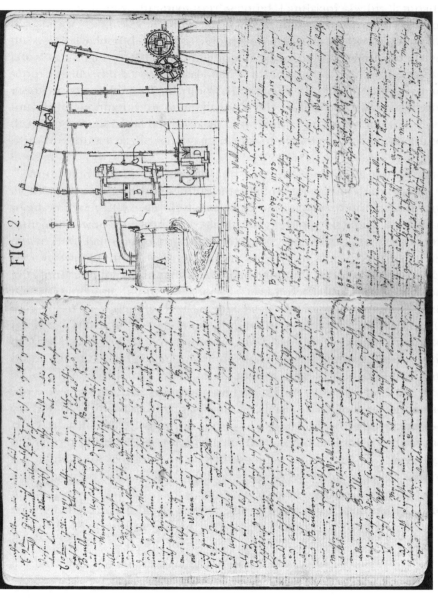

4.0 Soho Lap Engine, 1791, sketched by G. von Reichenbach

American entrepreneur and steam-boat pioneer Nicholas Roosevelt, for in 1802 one of Matthew Boulton's correspondents reported that a individual named Smallman was employed in a steam-engine manufactory built close to the Schuyler mine in New Jersey at a place dubbed 'Soho'.[109] The American plant had also provided work for another ex-employee of Boulton & Watt by the name of John Hewitt.

In view of the acknowledged difficulties inherent in transmitting tacit knowledge, it is a little surprising that individual natural philosophers and individual governments should devote so much energy to spying. Industrial espionage presented *savant-fabricants* such as Boulton, Watt and Wedgwood with something of a dilemma. Keenly aware that their industrial premises had become the target of knowledge 'kidnappers', they nonetheless found it hard to navigate a straight course between their duties as enlightened patrons of the Republic of Letters and their commercial self-interest as men in possession of leading-edge technologies. Only in the 1820s, when European governments finally abandoned all remaining shreds of mercantilist thinking in the technological domain, was this tension smoothed away. In answer to the stock argument that improved weaponry must always be kept secret, Henri-Joseph Paixhans, the French artillery officer who perfected the explosive shell, would point out in 1822 that the British government felt no compunction about publishing its nautical charts. Secrecy, he submitted, militated against knowledge diffusion and without diffusion, emulation – that is to say improvement – could not take place.[110]

Matthew Boulton felt the embarrassment of dealing with visitors whom he guessed had been sent as spies more acutely than did James Watt, if only because he took his responsibilities as an enlightened host more seriously than did his partner. 'We have had many philosophical & mechanical robbers', he reported to his son, 'who have come here under false names and pretences, but they have all failed in making good machines upon returning to their own countries.'[111] Nevertheless, the behaviour of a man such as Bückling urged caution. He had assumed a noble title in order to win Watt's trust and had then proceeded to bribe workmen in charge of the engines at Soho: two unpardonable breaches of Enlightenment civility. Consequently, when another Prussian

[109] BCL MS 3782/12/47 J. Tustin to M. Boulton, Canaan, in Connecticut, 23 August 1802; also Verbruggen, *The Correspondence of van Liender*, pp. 284–93.

[110] See P. Bret, 'Genèse et légitimation patrimoniale d'une invention: les archives de l'Artillerie à l'origine d'une innovation cruciale dans la Marine au XIXe siècle', in L. Hilaire-Pérez and A.-F. Garçon (eds), *Les Chemins de la nouveauté: innover, inventer au regard de l'histoire* (Paris: Editions CTHS, 2003), pp. 385–410.

[111] BCL MS 3782/12/57 M. Boulton to M. R. Boulton, Soho, 26 October 1789.

emissary hove into view – albeit one with impeccable noble credentials – no room could be left for any misunderstanding. Like Bückling, Baron Heinrich Friedrich Carl vom Stein set off for England with the full authority of the Prussian government attaching to his mission. He had been placed in overall charge of the mines of Westphalia in 1784, a couple of years earlier. James Watt expressed disquiet at his approach in a letter to his partner: 'I have told the Baron that we must consider his or his draughtsman's going into or making any drawings of our engines, as an end to any treaty with us.'[112] When Boulton eventually agreed to a visit to Soho by Stein and his party, he was no less explicit whilst at the same time striving to reconcile his two roles as Enlightenment patriarch and captain of industry: 'If I can promote your views as a Natural Philosopher, as a Mineralogist or as a Gentleman I shall be happy, But as a Mechanick & as an Engineer you must pardon me if I throw obstructions in your way.'[113] Baron Stein's imperious manner did not endear him to English industrialists, nor did his assumption that data collection on behalf of sovereigns was somehow different from private enterprise snooping. Factory gates were closed to him all over the West Midlands, and his party fared little better in Cornwall. He subsequently described his 1786–87 mission to England as a 'velorenes Jahr'.[114]

Did it matter if spies succeeded in carrying off potentially useful knowledge? Eric Roll[115] has argued that by the 1780s the firm's technological lead was so great that it had nothing to fear from competitors. Moreover, Boulton's remark to his son, quoted above, reveals an awareness that 'tacit' knowledge did not travel well even if he does not actually use the phrase. On the other hand, the partners plainly worried about the breaches of confidentiality. The behaviour of men like Bückling, Stein and Ljungberg offended against more than simply the honour code of the Enlightenment. Domestic competition in the steam-engine business would become quite intense, in fact. Even so-called friends, such as the ironmaster John Wilkinson, were not above pirating Watt's enhanced steam technology, and the firm's engine erectors were bound in their Articles of Agreement not to divulge or disclose 'any Secret, Art or Mystery whatsoever relative to the Business'.[116] As for overseas

---

[112] BCL MS 3782/12/79 J. Watt snr to M. Boulton, London, 9 March 1787.

[113] J. Tann (ed.) *The Selected Papers of Boulton & Watt.* Volume 1: *The Engine Partnership* (Cambridge, Mass: MIT Press, 1981), p. 163.

[114] Kroker, *Wege zur Verbreitung technologischer Kentnisse zwischen England und Deutschland,* p. 93; also G. S. Stanton, *On and Off the Campus* (Minnesota: University of Minnesota Press, 1938), pp. 162–202.

[115] E. Roll, *An Early Experiment in Industrial Organisation,* p. 66.

[116] Cornwall Record Office AD 1583/6 Articles of Agreement between J. Varley, engine erector, and Boulton & Watt, 4 August 1790.

installation work, the partners always feared that their technical know-how would leak beyond the contracting parties, and with some justification. It was for this reason that Boulton & Watt sought the protection of 'exclusive privileges' when dealing with various emissaries of the French, Dutch, Prussian and Spanish authorities. The Dutch natural philosopher van Liender, who acted as a middleman for the engine commissioned by the Estates of Utrecht for the Mijdrecht lake, was reminded that he should only pass on information about the installation on a need-to-know basis – so that nobody was able to 'carry our knowledge elsewhere'.[117] In the event, the leakage of skill came not from the Patriots of the Batavian Society, whose inability to overcome the cultural and political inertia of the Dutch old order has already been highlighted. Rather, it occurred as a consequence of the migration of one of Soho's most trusted and capable employees – the engine erector James Smallman.

Yet if we leave to one side the problematic question of performance, it is not difficult to find instances of formal know-how transfer via espionage. The birth of the Danish textile industry is attributed by Dan Christensen[118] almost entirely to the snooping activities in England of Charles-Axel Nordberg and Jøns Mathias Ljungberg, and both the Venetian and the French authorities were kept informed of the onward march of Watt's steam technology by the same route. The news of his early experiments to adapt the engine to produce rotary motion first reached Venice by way of the architect Gianantonio Selva,[119] who visited Soho and its park during the summer of 1781. Not until the autumn of that year would Watt patent his alternatives to the crank, and the first rotative engine was not built at Soho until 1783. The technology involved in the production of the first double-acting engine was more closely guarded, however. Neither Boulton nor Watt saw any reason to mention it when invited to Paris for talks with ministers in the winter of 1786–87. The conduit by which this improvement made its way to France some two years later is known, however. A peripatetic natural philosopher of Spanish extraction, Augustin de Betancourt y Molina,[120] turned up in Birmingham in 1788 on a mission to collect models of hydraulic machinery for his immediate employer – the Spanish Crown.

[117] Verbruggen, *Correspondence of van Liender*, pp. 29, 208.

[118] Cited in K. Bruland, 'Skills, learning and the international diffusion of technology: a perspective on Scandinavian industrialisation', in Berg and Bruland, *Technological Revolutions in Europe*, pp. 176–7.

[119] See Zorzanello, 'Il diplomatico veneziano Simon Cavalli et le sua legazione in Inghilterra', 246.

[120] See Payen, *Capital et machine à vapeur au XVIIIe siècle*, pp. 157–63.

Boulton greeted him civilly, but refused to show anything other than the button and plated-goods workshops. In consequence, Betancourt obtained access to Albion Mill in London instead, where he was able to deduce that the millstones were powered by a new type of engine from the evidence of two columns of steam and the visible fact that the beam was no longer connected to the piston by a chain. This intelligence was swiftly converted into a working model of the double-acting engine which was doubtless intended for the *cabinet des machines* in Madrid. It was also communicated to the Académie des Sciences in Paris and probably to the Périers as well.[121] When Gaspard de Prony had the effrontery to lay claim to the invention in his *Nouvelle architecture hydraulique* (1790–6), Matthew Boulton exploded with indignation and labelled Betancourt a thief. Unlike natural knowledge, technology retained something of the cloak of secrecy that had surrounded the arts and crafts in the seventeenth century, then. But when it leaked, the all-too-familiar squabbles over priority followed hard on the heels of blame.

[121] J. Muirhead, *The Life of James Watt with Selections from his Correspondence* (New York: Appleton, 1859), 216.

5

Industry,
Enlightenment and Dissent

The overview of eighteenth-century Europe's uneven science cultures which brought the argument in the last chapter to a close begs an obvious question which now needs to be tackled. How should we construe the relationship between science and religion? Voltaire's 'Ecrasez-l'infâme'[1] offers a point of departure, but it only requires a moment's reflection to realise that his impatient condemnation of intolerant Roman Catholicism as a barrier to human progress leads nowhere. Many of the advances registered in Europe during the sixteenth and seventeenth centuries were nurtured by religious belief, and the eighteenth century would be little different in this respect. Dissenters of various sorts were legion, but non-believers and non-believing natural philosophers remained quite rare. In the absence of a master narrative which would enable us to chart the social impact of religion over time, therefore, it makes better sense to divide the question into parts – the parts most likely to further our understanding of the phenomenon of Industrial Enlightenment. Did Protestant Nonconformity facilitate a palpable expansion of scientific knowledge? Were Dissenters disproportionately numerous among the entrepreneurs and industrialists of the second half of the eighteenth century? Finally, is it possible to identify a characteristically Dissenter dimension of the provincial English Enlightenment?

The focus is placed on the Protestant Dissenters, in particular, for good historical and historiographical reasons. Contemporaries were keenly aware of the role of Nonconformity in Georgian England, and the Dissenters themselves sedulously cultivated myths about their contributions to scientific knowledge and the industrial economy which historians have mostly endorsed rather uncritically. One version of the

---

[1] Literally, 'Crush the infamous one', i.e. persecuting religion.

'myth of origins' of Birmingham that we shall need to consider states that the town's industrial vocation stemmed from its refuge status for ejected clergy and persecuted Dissenters following the passing of the Five-Mile Act in 1665. The Quakers and their historians have been particularly active in this regard, and by the time Industrial Enlightenment was giving way to full-blown Industrial Revolution, the supposed affinity of Nonconformists for trade, industry and experimental science had become something of a mantra. 'The various dissenting denominations derive their chief strength from the trading and manufacturing classes', *The Eclectic Review* observed flatly in 1857.[2]

Whilst this was probably true, it is far from certain that the reverse obtained, as a casual reading of the statement might lead us to expect. Even in the cities of mid-Victorian England, most entrepreneurs and industrialists would have subscribed to the Church of England – if they subscribed to any church. The more so a century earlier, when the Evangelical Revival had scarcely begun, and Dissenting congregations bespoke perhaps six per cent of the population at large. Our enquiry cannot afford to concentrate on the Dissenters in isolation, therefore. If those who refused to subscribe to the doctrines of the Established Church developed a special affinity for science and industry, we shall need to explain why this was less the case among Anglicans – or Churchmen as they were more commonly labelled in the eighteenth century. And if it should prove hard to make such a distinction on theological grounds, we will need to abandon it, or seek out alternative variables. Birmingham's denominational history should enable this exercise to be carried out. When anatomised from a religious point of view, its profile in the eighteenth and the early nineteenth centuries seems not unlike that of any other large centre of trade and industry. The constellation of West Midlands mining and metal-working towns emerges neither as a stronghold of religious Nonconformity, nor indeed as a region in which Dissent was notably weak. But two circumstances lend added interest to the enquiry: the presence in Birmingham and the Black Country of an active and entrepreneurial constituency of natural philosophers, and the late-century collapse of civil order, linked indissolubly to the name of Dr Joseph Priestley. The Lunar Society, together with the Philosophical Institution which superseded it, provides an obvious platform from which to mount an investigation of experimental science and industrial innovation in denominational terms, whereas the Church and King riots of 1791 cast a harsh light on the persistence of sectarian allegiances and the ultimate failure of the town's bourgeoisie

---

[2] Quoted in E. Isichei, *Victorian Quakers* (Oxford: Oxford University Press, 1970), p. 166.

to agree on a partly secularised version of the Enlightenment. The shock of the riots not only damaged a regional variant built in part from the raw materials of Rational Dissent, it helped to trigger a rerouting of the Enlightenment in a more conservative and socially controlled direction throughout the country at large.

A Protestant ethic?

The partial retreat from class-bound explanations of human motivation has encouraged social historians to take a fresh look at the role of religious beliefs. Nowhere is this shift more apparent than in the interpretation of the 1791 riots, as we shall see. But historians of science have altered their angle of vision somewhat as well. The cultural approach to natural knowledge generation and use necessarily entails a consideration of the role of religion, whether as an autonomous variable or in conjunction with other factors. John Brooke's[3] nuanced and historically sensitive survey of the shifting boundaries between science and religion is especially valuable in this respect. In place of the conflict model long favoured by presentist writers on scientific topics, we are reminded of the overlaps and interpenetration which render attempts to keep the two provinces sharply demarcated – if not actually in conflict – an ultimately fruitless exercise. As should be apparent by now, Hanoverian England's natural philosophers were an eclectic breed who cannot simply be equated with the scientists of the modern world. They were men who rebelled at the notion of compartmentalised knowledge, and the questions raised by religious knowledge were by no means the least of their concerns. Yet when we turn for assistance to the social scientists, in hopes of a general theory that might make sense of the multiple points at which religion and science came into contact, the response is scarcely encouraging. The problems attaching to the sweeping formulations of a Max Weber[4] or a Robert Merton[5] are held to diminish significantly their explanatory value. Much of the evidence which undermines these attempts at synthesis derives from the researches of historians, of course. But this places social and cultural historians in a paradoxical position, for it is from their ranks that the support for a causal link between

[3] J. H. Brooke, *Science and Religion: some Historical Perspectives* (Cambridge: Cambridge University Press, 1991).

[4] M. Weber, *The Protestant Ethic and the Spirit of Capitalism.* Translated by T. Parsons (London: Allen & Unwin, 1930).

[5] R. K. Merton, *Science, Technology and Society in Seventeenth-Century England* (originally published in *Osiris*, 4 (1938), 360–632) (New York: Harper, 1970).

certain types of religious belief or behaviour and the experimental sciences now tends to come.[6] Since the Protestant sects seem also to have provided a favourable context for capitalist enterprise and expressions of civic republicanism, it would be unwise to dismiss the general-order explanations formulated by social theorists out of hand. Perhaps, as Margaret Jacob and Matthew Kadane have put it, Weber was 'onto something'[7] after all.

In a long essay published at the start of the twentieth century, Max Weber argued that the theology of Calvinistic Protestantism in the early seventeenth century generated a particular outlook in the minds of believers which proved extraordinarily conducive to capitalist economic endeavour. The principal denominators of this ascetic mentality, according to Weber, were diligence in the pursuit of one's calling, the efficient and constructive use of time, and self-restraint in the immediate satisfaction of material needs. Thus equipped, it was not difficult to comprehend why some Protestants should have become capitalist entrepreneurs, he submitted. Although the proposition that Protestantism thereby caused capitalism does not belong to Weber, many critics have pointed to examples of manifestly capitalist behaviour that antedated the Reformation, whilst others have argued that he misconstrued the thrust of Calvin's theology. Of greater interest for present purposes, however, is R. H. Tawney's[8] reaction. He did not dispute a link between capitalism and the more rationalistic formulations of post-Reformation religious belief, but hypothesised a reversal of the causal sequence. Maybe the newly minted Protestants took over the ethics of the capitalists rather than vice versa. On the subject of science Weber had little to say, although it is clear that he viewed the spirit of capitalism as also facilitating the expansion of experimental natural philosophy and the accumulation of technologically useful knowledge of the type which powers Joel Mokyr's Industrial Enlightenment. It is less certain, however, that Mokyr would accept the large claims which Weber made for the role of religion in kick-starting this process. 'On the whole', he observes, 'religion was at least as much a source of resistance as one of inspiration for inventors and innovators.'[9]

---

[6] See, for instance, C. Webster, *The Great Instauration: Science, Medicine and Reform, 1626–1660* (London: Duckworth, 1975); M. C. Jacob and M. Kadane, 'Missing, now found in the eighteenth century: Weber's Protestant capitalist', *American Historical Review*, 108 (2003), 20–49; C. A. Bayly, *The Birth of the Modern World, 1780–1914* (Oxford: Blackwell, 2004); P. Wood (ed.), *Science and Dissent in England, 1688–1945* (Aldershot: Ashgate, 2004), pp. 1–18.

[7] Jacob and Kadane, 'Missing, now found', 20.

[8] R. H. Tawney, *Religion and the Rise of Capitalism: a Historical Study*. Holland Memorial Lectures, 1922 (London: Murray, 1926), pp. 113, 212 and note 32.

[9] Mokyr, *The Gifts of Athena*, p. 249.

The debt which Robert Merton's thesis owes to Weber's *The Protestant Ethic and the Spirit of Capitalism* will be obvious. Indeed, it seems likely that the doctoral dissertation which saw light of day in 1938 in the shape of a monograph entitled *Science, Technology and Society in Seventeenth-Century England* was inspired by Weber's essay. It had been translated into English several years earlier by Merton's colleague at Harvard, Talcott Parsons. Merton focused his attention on the English Puritans of the second half of the seventeenth century rather than on the salvation-imperilled faithful of the continental reformers during the first half, and he set out the argument for regarding Puritanism as one of the principal vectors of the rise of experimental natural philosophy in Restoration England. Weber had noted in passing the probability of a causal connection between the efflorescence of science and the Puritan version of Protestant Christianity, but had not fleshed out the link in a systematic fashion. Unlike Weber, Merton placed less stress on properly religious motivation – that is to say, on the individual's preoccupation with salvation as the driver of behaviour – and rather more on a wider set of beliefs and cultural reflexes that can be taken as hallmarks of the Puritan way of living. At a time when the contextualisation of scientific enquiry was in its infancy and the sociology of scientific knowledge virtually non-existent, this was a novelty in itself. But Merton carefully modulated his argument in two other ways as well. He took care to emphasise that he was not positing an association of experimental science with Puritanism to the exclusion of other explanatory factors. Indeed, he explicitly acknowledged that such factors could override the socio-religious on occasion. And secondly, he allowed that the impact of Puritanism on science might occur at one remove – as the 'largely unwitting'[10] knock-on effect of Puritan cultural values.

This last refinement was introduced as his doctoral dissertation was being revised and prepared for publication. It makes room for the long-term and quite possibly unintended consequences of Puritan asceticism, and some might argue that it stretches the causal thrust of his thesis to breaking point. If distant correlations are to be substituted for tightly causal sequences, it becomes rather difficult to see how Merton's hypothesis can be put to the test. However, the proposition has attracted plenty of critics who express reservations or objections on more empirical grounds. Identifying Puritans and the mixed bag of Dissenters coming after them who possessed scientific credentials or a propensity for experimental activity is no straightforward matter, and historians have

[10] I. Bernard Cohen (ed.), *Puritanism and the Rise of Modern Science: the Merton Thesis* (New Brunswick: Rutgers University Press, 1990), p. 2; Wood, *Science and Dissent*, p. 1.

disputed Merton's claim that the early Fellows of the Royal Society evinced a clear Puritan bias. Whether it is the theology or the spirit of Puritanism which is at stake, there is a dearth of direct, motivational evidence which records the process by which religious Nonconformists were turned into budding scientists or early modern capitalists, too. Margaret Jacob and Matthew Kadane[11] instance the case of Joseph Ryder, the Leeds merchant-draper, who left behind a detailed spiritual diary, remarking that he might have been scripted for the part of Weber's early capitalist, and we shall have occasion to mention a similar document compiled by the Birmingham button manufacturer Julius Hardy. But these are rare sources that cannot be expected to testify to the validity of Weber or Merton's conclusions on their own. In any case, Hardy was a Methodist equipped with well-tuned capitalist instincts but no discernible commitment to utilitarian science.

The obvious difficulty which R. H. Tawney first raised with respect to Weber's *The Protestant Ethic* also applies to the Merton thesis. Did Puritanism encompass a penchant for science in the specific context of Interregnum England? Or, on the contrary, is it more likely that practitioners of natural philosophy adopted the spiritual and moral precepts associated with Puritanism because these values appeared more consistent with experimental and observational activities aimed at unlocking the secrets of nature? Merton allowed for both possibilities, which secures further the connection between religion and science but does little to unravel the conundrum of causality. It would help, of course, if we had more biographical information about those who dabbled in natural philosophy in the late seventeenth and the eighteenth centuries, for then the mix of motivations and intentions could be teased apart – assuming always that intentionality was not 'deflected'.[12] But the prosopographical approach to our problem is not currently feasible. And even if it were, there is a risk that it would inject not clarity but additional layers of complexity. All theories rely to some extent on plausible generalisation, after all, and both Weber and Merton indulge in the procedure of lumping in order to generate useful categories for analytical purposes. Yet all religious Nonconformists were not of one mind and nor, for that matter, were all adherents of the established church – be they Roman Catholic, Reformed or Anglican. A candid observation by Dr Joseph Priestley is relevant here, if only because it contains a frequently overlooked truth. 'Dissenters as such', he noted, 'have nothing

[11] Jacob and Kadane, 'Missing, now found', 26.
[12] See L. Daston, 'Are you having fun today?' *London Review of Books*, 23 September 2004, p. 31.

in common but a dissent from the established church; and it by no means follows that they, therefore, agree in anything else.'[13] In Robert Merton's case there is also the possibility that the line of demarcation is being drawn in the wrong place. For Margaret Jacob[14] the bridge between reformist religion and science was provided by Latitudinarian Anglicans rather than Puritans. Thus, clergymen of the Established Church emerge among the prime movers in the domestication of Newtonian physics. Whatever the fundamental strength of this argument, it does help to make sense of the finding that in the 1660s the Royal Society contained more Anglican and Royalist science enthusiasts than Puritan.[15]

In view of the sharp disagreements over the spiritual or practical value attaching to scientific activity – to look no further than the ranks of Protestant Nonconformity – it is scarcely surprising that John Heilbron should feel moved to call for an 'ecumenical'[16] Merton thesis. The alternative is to confine its scope to groups such as the Quakers and the Unitarians, who appear more likely to fit the remit. Otherwise we must content ourselves with 'correlations' between ascetic Protestantism, science and capitalist industry, where the causal links are far from proven, and perhaps not even susceptible of proof. However, Michael Watts, who has written the standard history of the Protestant Dissenters, briskly dismisses even this *faute de mieux* proposition. 'One does not need to invoke an elaborate theory of the connection between "the Protestant ethic and the spirit of capitalism,"' he exclaims, 'to explain the evolution of Baptist tradesmen and Quaker ironmongers into Baptist merchants and Quaker ironmasters in a period when the country's trade was increasing and Parliament was removing monopolistic restrictions from commerce and industry'.[17] Perhaps not; yet the questions raised by cultural historians in more recent times regarding the take-up of science in the eighteenth century and its repackaging as an Enlightenment discourse extend far beyond the issues discussed by Weber and Merton. Equivalent questions arise in respect of the science input to industrial technology,

[13] J. Priestley, *A Free Address to Protestant Dissenters, as Such* (London: G. Pearch, 1769), p. iv.

[14] M. C. Jacob, *The Newtonians and the English Revolution, 1689–1720* (Ithaca: Cornell University Press, 1976); also J. R. Jacob and M. C. Jacob, 'The Anglican origins of modern science: the metaphysical foundations of the Whig constitution', *Isis*, 71 (1980), 251–67.

[15] See L. Mulligan, 'Civil War politics, religion and the Royal Society', *Past and Present*, 59 (1973), 92–116.

[16] Cited in S. Widmalm, 'Instituting science in Sweden', in R. Porter and M. Teich (eds), *The Scientific Revolution in National Context* (Cambridge: Cambridge University Press, 1992), p. 256.

[17] M. R. Watts, *The Dissenters.* Volume 1: *From the Reformation to the French Revolution* (Oxford: Oxford University Press, 1978), p. 361.

as we have seen. It is, after all, a matter of some relevance to know whether the active ingredient of the Industrial Enlightenment – the *savant-fabricants* – were Dissenters, Anglicans or a mutant species of Deists who found all forms of revealed religion rather distasteful. First of all, though, we need to establish some basic parameters for our enquiry: who were the Dissenters and where could they be found?

Joseph Priestley's trenchant observation of 1771 provides a starting-point, for at that date the Protestant Dissenting community of England and Wales was made up of Presbyterians, Baptists, Independents (also known as Congregationalist), Quakers and Methodists. The first three denominations were sometimes referred to as Old Dissent, although the Society of Friends (Quakers) might equally lodge a claim to this description since they, too, could trace their origins to the Puritan sects of the Civil War and Interregnum decades. During Priestley's lifetime the Presbyterians were slowly fragmenting into Trinitarians and Anti-Trinitarians – the latter eventually adopting the label Unitarians. As for the Methodists, they did not, strictly speaking, become Dissenters until the death of their founder John Wesley in 1791 triggered a definitive breach with the established Church of England. Nevertheless, they viewed themselves as a species of Dissenter and were increasingly treated as such by others. In 1689, when the penal laws against Old Dissenters and Quakers were put into abeyance, it is thought that these groups numbered collectively between 5 and 10 per cent of the population at large. For much of the succeeding century their growth trajectory remained flat and may even have dipped. By 1773 only nine English counties could muster a Dissenter strength of 5 per cent or more – largely, it appears, because of departures from the ranks of the Presbyterians and the Quakers, for Baptist and Congregationalist numbers held steady. The trend was only reversed towards the end of the eighteenth century, when New Dissent (essentially Methodism) and the Evangelical Revival gave birth to the mass phenomenon of Protestant Nonconformity, which was captured in snap-shot some half-century later by the religious census of 1851.

The counties intersecting the Black Country cannot be regarded as strongholds of Dissent, any more than can the town of Birmingham before the clergy ejectments of 1662. The only systematic study of early Nonconformity in this region hazards an overall figure of 5 per cent for the Dissenting population, albeit one with significant local variations.[18] This chimes with the estimates for the early eighteenth century provided

[18] A. G. Cumberland, 'Protestant Nonconformity in the Black Country, 1662–1851' (MA dissertation, University of Birmingham, 1951), pp. 32–3.

by Michael Watts, which are based on the Evans List of Dissenting Congregations and Ministers (1715–29).[19] Warwickshire's tally of Dissenters is said to have numbered 100,510 (6.59 per cent of the total population), that of Staffordshire 112,560 (4.46 per cent) and Worcestershire 101,420 (5.40 per cent). In every case the Presbyterians formed the best-endowed congregations, both numerically and institutionally. They therefore had most to lose as a spirit of quiescence pervaded the ranks following the suspension of the penal laws and the securing of the Hanoverian succession. Congregationalism gnawed at their strength in several localities, following doctrinal disputes. In fact, Birmingham's first Congregational meeting came into being as a result of a secession in 1747. But it is likely that Presbyterianism lost more adherents to the secularising spirit of the age. Of all the Dissenting affiliations they were perhaps the least well equipped to withstand the intellectual blandishments of the Enlightenment. The Quakers also declined in numbers, but for reasons more akin to their status as an exclusive and inward-looking sect. For a Quaker, marrying out entailed 'disownment' – a practice that was systematically enforced until the middle decades of the nineteenth century. As a result the Society of Friends dwindled from around 60,000 effectives in 1680 to 20,000 in 1800, and perhaps as few as 16,000 by the start of Queen Victoria's reign. In sharp contrast, Methodist preachers were able to report a pattern of almost uninterrupted growth from the 1770s. The number of Methodist hearers almost quadrupled (to 109,961) during the last three decades of the eighteenth century, thereby retrieving almost at a stroke the fortunes of the Dissenting interest across the country.

The spatial distribution of West Midlands Dissenters conforms closely to what we might expect. There existed long-established congregations in Birmingham and the older urban centres of the Black Country (Wolverhampton, Walsall, Dudley, Stourbridge, etc.), and pockets often of a more recent vintage located in the industrialising villages of the district. These latter were often linked to the passage of charismatic itinerant preachers. In the mining settlement of Netherton, close to Dudley, for instance, there was a well-rooted Baptist meeting of 300 souls, and in nearby Sedgley over 15 per cent of the population were reported as dissenting from the Established Church at the start of the eighteenth century. The doctrinal fluidity of the Presbyterian congregations was evident throughout the district, as in the nearby metropolis. The Presbyterian chapels in Walsall, Tipton, Coseley, Oldbury and Kingswood all became progressively Unitarian in outlook as the century advanced.

[19] Watts, *The Dissenters*, i, Appendix, Table XII.

In fact the rural chapel of Kingswood, beyond Kings Norton, would pay dearly for its pro-Priestley orientation during the riots of 1791. At West Bromwich, on the other hand, the Congregationalists took control of a long-standing Presbyterian congregation and no Unitarian meeting developed in this locality.

The biggest concentration of Dissenters outside Birmingham could be found in Wolverhampton, however. In 1780 a trades directory claimed that one third of the inhabitants attended meeting houses – chiefly Presbyterian. Even if the writer intended to lump Methodist hearers with Dissenters proper, this seems implausible. It would mean that the nonconforming population rose from around 400 to something approaching 4,000 in little over a century. Nonetheless, the town certainly acquired a reputation for pugnacious sectarianism. John Wesley frequently found himself on the receiving end of crowd violence in the vicinity of Wednesbury and Wolverhampton, and labelled the latter 'this furious town'.[20] Quakerism had almost died out in Wolverhampton by this date, and since the other partners in Old Dissent seem not to have recruited widely until the end of the century, it is likely that the chief source of the tensions lay in a triangle of antagonisms pitting Anglicans, Methodists and anti-Trinitarian Presbyterians against one another. Because their numbers were so low, Quakers were rarely in the forefront of such quarrels, although their visibly increasing affluence excited attention and negative comment, as we shall see. The only Quaker meetings in the Black Country to have withstood the attrition of the century were those in Dudley and Stourbridge. Birmingham's sixty-odd Quaker families held their own, demographically speaking, but no more. They managed to increase their numbers from 285 to 320 between 1789 and 1806, notwithstanding sixty individual disownments, but still constituted under 0.5 per cent of total households.[21] In Bristol, by contrast, they represented a little over 1.0 per cent of the population and in Manchester 0.7 per cent.[22]

It is difficult to settle on an estimate of the size of Birmingham's Dissenting interest overall, for reasons that will by now be obvious.

[20] Cited in J. Smith, 'Industrialisation and social change: Wolverhampton transformed, 1700–1840', in J. Stobart and N. Raven (eds), *Towns, Regions and Industries: Urban and Industrial Change in the Midlands, c. 1700–1840*, (Manchester: Manchester University Press, Press, 2005), p. 142.

[21] Archives of the Birmingham Meeting, Bull Street, Birmingham register of members, 1789–1807.

[22] See R. T. Vann and D. Eversley, *Friends in Life and Death: the British and Irish Quakers in the Demographic Transition, 1650–1900* (Cambridge: Cambridge University Press, 1992), p. 72; D. H. Pratt, *English Quakers and the First Industrial Revolution* (New York: Garland, 1985), pp. 57–8.

Table 5.0 *Birmingham's Protestant Dissenters (households), 1751–1820*

Denomination	1751–55	1771–80	1791–1800	1811–20
Old Meeting (Presbyterian)	240?	213?	82	100?
New Meeting (Presbyterian)	240	213	138	180
Quakers	43	65	62	66
Baptists	50?	132	197	405
Congregationalists	40?	50?	100?	160?
Methodists	10?	160	224	300?
Total	623	833	803	1211
As percentage of all Birmingham households	14.9	11.6	6.1	7.3

Sources: Archives of the Birmingham Meeting; Bushrod, 'The history of unitarianism'; Money, 'Science, technology and dissent'; Ram, 'Influences on patterns of belief'; *A History of the County of Warwick*; Chalklin, *The Provincial Towns*; Pratt, *English Quakers*.

Population figures for the town before 1720 or thereabouts are either non-existent or unreliable, the boundaries of what passed for the Dissenting community shifted significantly during the final quarter of the century, and we lack even the most rudimentary attendance data for several meeting houses – most notably the Carrs Lane Congregational chapel. The fact that the original building, which could hold about 450 worshippers, was demolished and rebuilt in 1801 suggests, however, a congregation in excess of 100 families and one experiencing rapid growth. After 1820 the demographic structure of Nonconformity within the city becomes easier to piece together, but it can tell us little about the sectarian profile of the eighteenth century, or any shifts in allegiances that may have occurred as a consequence of the riots. The data presented in Table 5.0 should be treated with caution, therefore. In some instances (the Old Meeting; the Baptists; the Congregationalists) the figures represent not much more than informed guess-work.

One thing seems reasonably clear, however. Birmingham began its drive for growth in the eighteenth century with a hard core of Protestant Dissenters in its midst. Whether they represented a legacy community descended directly from the Puritan sects of the Civil War and Interregnum years, or a recent influx consequent upon the ejectments and the Five-Mile Act is hard to determine precisely. In all probability the nucleus whose presence we can first detect in the 1680s consisted of both. Most were Presbyterians, although this is not to say very much at a time when theological differences among the bulk of the Dissenters were poorly defined. However, Birmingham's Presbyterians would start

to metamorphose in the 1740s and would eventually give birth to an influential body of Rational Dissenters. Contemporaries were in agreement
that Unitarian beliefs were unusually well represented in Birmingham
and Dr Joseph Priestley, who took charge of the New Meeting in 1780,
regarded it as the most liberal-minded congregation in the country. In
common with other manufacturing towns, the Dissenters' strength did
not lie in numbers, though. In fact their proportional numerical presence declined across the century as Birmingham's population boom was
repeatedly fuelled by in-migration from the surrounding, and overwhelmingly Church-dominated, countryside. Even the meteoric growth
of the Baptists and Methodists would scarcely alter this profile before
1820. The heyday of Nonconformity in Birmingham had yet to come.

The Dissenters play an important role in the 'free town' myth of
Birmingham's origins and rise to industrial supremacy. Galvanised by
the 1865 meeting of the British Association for the Advancement of
Science in Birmingham, Samuel Timmins compiled a hand-book guide
to local industries in which he celebrated the long-standing absence of
guild and union restraints on trade, the mobility afforded by a largely
unapprenticed work-force, and the lack of corporate supervision of the
town (before 1838). 'Heretics of all sorts', he continued in a rare display
of municipal pride and amnesia, 'were welcomed and undisturbed.'[23]
This 'free trade–free religion' refrain soon hardened into an orthodoxy
repeated endlessly, and one from which even the Birmingham historian
Eric Hopkins finds it difficult to escape.[24] The truth of the matter is
that the origins of the town's industrial vocation are as poorly understood as are most other aspects of its early modern history. We know
that Birmingham supported Parliament during the Civil War and can
conjecture that the Puritan sects put down roots at about this time.
George Fox certainly visited in 1655 and it is probable that small gatherings of Friends existed from this date. They erected a meeting house
in Bull Street, close to the centre of town, in 1703. The researches of
David Wykes[25] have shed a little more light on these poorly documented
decades, and it does indeed appear that the clergy ejectments of 1662
reinforced the strength of the Nonconformists. Many years later, one
of the refugee ministers recounted how Birmingham became 'an *asylum,*
a Place of Refuge to nine of us, and two more who lived near your

[23] Timmins, *The Resources, Products, and Industrial History of Birmingham and the Midland
Hardware District*, p. 211.
[24] See Hopkins, *Birmingham: the First Manufacturing Town*, pp. 4–5, 93, 100–1, 137–8.
[25] D. L. Wykes, 'James II's Religious Indulgence of 1687 and the early organisation
of dissent: the building of the first Nonconformist meeting-house in Birmingham', *Midland
History*, 16 (1991), 86–102.

Town'.[26] It is perhaps significant, too, that the final decades of the seventeenth century witnessed the introduction of several new industrial trades to Birmingham.

Whether the restrictions of the Five-Mile Act passed in 1665 played a particular role in bolstering the Dissenter presence in Birmingham is debatable. It is true that, as neither a municipal nor a parliamentary borough, the town was exempt from its provisions. But the Act applied to nonconforming ministers, not lay Dissenters. If the latter gravitated in droves to the up-and-coming West Midlands town, it seems more likely that they were drawn by commercial opportunity. Sampson Lloyd, a Quaker, may well have moved from North Wales to Birmingham in the belief that he would thereby escape religious harassment, but he also established a prosperous ironmongery business and together with his sons would build a slitting mill in Digbeth to supply the local nailing trade. Whatever the forces in play, there can be no doubt that a vigorous and confident Presbyterian community existed in the town by the 1680s for, as Wykes[27] points out, they were willing to risk erecting a building for public worship two years before the so-called Toleration Act of 1689. Interestingly, the subscribers were all substantial tradesmen. Until this date the various Dissenter species had met in private houses, and the Presbyterians continued to support an off-shoot meeting in rented accommodation in Deritend, whilst also making use of their purpose-built premises in Phillip Street. When, in 1732, the Deritend meeting moved in turn to its own chapel in Moor Street, the two congregations became known as the Old Meeting and the New Meeting respectively. Although no membership records for the Old Meeting have survived, it must have been prospering around the turn of the century, notwithstanding worries over the Hanoverian succession. An assistant minister was taken on in 1700 and the original 1687 meeting house was enlarged six years later.

Yet this progress was thrown into question by the bitter party strife at the close of Queen Anne's reign. In 1709–10, following Henry Sacheverell's incendiary sermons against Dissenters and the Whigs' support for toleration, unrest broke out in Birmingham and the Black Country. Crowds tore down a meeting house in Walsall, and in Birmingham the celebrations to mark the coronation of George I were marred by collective assaults on the houses of prominent Presbyterians. Far more serious disturbances ensued several months later as a response to the Jacobite uprising, however. In July 1715 roaming crowds attacked

[26] *Ibid.*, p. 87.
[27] *Ibid.*, pp. 90–3.

premises where Dissenters worshipped in Coseley, Pensett, Oldbury, Stourbridge and West Bromwich. The Dudley town 'mob' toured the streets shouting 'Down with the Roundheads' and 'For High Church and Dr Sacheverell'.[28] This rekindled Birmingham's anti-Dissenter prejudices. Indeed, the High Sheriff of Warwickshire complained that the rioters were drawing recruits from 'the side of Staffordshire next Birmingham'.[29] For ten days the populace remained in control of the town, threatening Presbyterians' houses with destruction by fire. The Old Meeting was completely destroyed and the same fate would have befallen the nearby Deritend meeting had the landlord of the building not reached a compromise with the rioters. Since he was not a Presbyterian, they targeted its contents instead. Many of the features of this crowd violence against Dissenters would reappear in 1791 during the riots aimed at Dr Joseph Priestley.

Nonconformity and Enlightenment

The efforts of Birmingham's intelligentsia to replicate a provincial variant of the pan-European Enlightenment were rooted in increasing affluence, the pursuit of 'polite' leisure activities, and perhaps also the desire to draw a line of social demarcation between themselves and a potentially unruly population who appeared woefully deficient in urban culture. The challenge facing the elite and some of the initiatives taken to address it were outlined in Chapter 2. Now we need to examine those who sought to lead the town – and who partially lost control of it in the 1790s – in close up. The Dissenters must be our starting point, for it is apparent that they played a role in Birmingham and the wider West Midlands economy that was not in proportion to their numerical strength. Whether this role originated in their Calvinistic belief system, as Weber and Merton variously suggest, is a legitimate question and one worth considering in the context of our case-study evidence. However, it is subordinate to the larger task, which is to capture the composite and non-denominational character of the Enlightenment culture that was taking shape in Birmingham by the 1770s.

There is plentiful evidence to suggest that the Dissenters numbered many wealthy and high-status individuals in their ranks. William Hutton, the local chronicler, remarked that 'the proverbial expression, as rich as a Jew is not altogether verified in Birmingham but perhaps time is

---

[28] Cumberland, 'Protestant Nonconformity in the Black Country', p. 40.
[29] *Ibid.*

transferring it to the Quakers'.[30] Hutton seems to have joined the Congregationalist Carrs Lane chapel on his arrival in Birmingham in 1750, but by the end of the 1780s his wealth and cultural inclinations, not to mention family pressures, were pulling him in the direction of Dr Priestley's New Meeting. He was not alone in his expression of unease at the visible well-being of the Bull Street Friends; Julius Hardy, the Methodist button manufacturer, referred privately to Quakers as driven by 'self-interest'[31] – presumably because of a perceived discrepancy between their wealth and their social activism. But the Quakers were in all other respects a rather self-effacing group: most comments about wealth and influence, whether favourable or unfavourable, would have been directed at the Presbyterians. When probing the Dissenter population, however, it is important not to lose sight of the fact that large numbers of wealthy and influential individuals could be found in the town's swelling ranks of Church attenders as well. The key question is one of *relative* strength. Did the Dissenters possess wealth and influence disproportionate to their numbers? And did they disproportionately dominate certain sectors of the local economy? The answer to both questions is a qualified 'yes'.

The qualifications are necessary for two reasons. Unlike Birmingham, the denominational landscape of the Black Country is poorly mapped and it would be hazardous to generalise about the economic and occupational character of Dissent in this still semi-urbanised district at the end of the eighteenth century. Piecemeal evidence suggests that Black Country Dissent drew its biggest battalions from the lowest stratum of the working class – the unskilled nailers and their like. However, R. H. Trainor's[32] longitudinal analysis of nineteenth-century political elites reveals a picture in which the strength of the Established Church was rivalled by Nonconformity in the towns of West Bromwich, Dudley and Bilston. The second qualification is related to the first, for it is evident – even in the Black Country – that the term Dissenter, or Nonconformist, brackets together a wide spectrum of individuals both wealthy and impoverished, powerful and powerless. Well-to-do Unitarians played a prominent role in public life in West Bromwich and Dudley which was out of all proportion to their numbers in the nineteenth century. So too, it seems, did the Congregationalists, whereas the Baptists scarcely made their presence felt. There are some parallels here with the better-documented situation in Birmingham.

[30] Hutton, *An History of Birmingham*, p. 192.
[31] BCL MS 218 diary of Julius Hardy, 1 March 1790.
[32] Trainor, *Black Country Elites*, pp. 112–19, and table 3.7.

Although a 'counting of households' approach has provided a rough measure of the Dissenter presence in Birmingham, together with the trend over time, it is not obvious how this information might be recast so as to tell us something about the economic roles performed by Dissenters, or why they congregated in certain occupations and professions. The qualitative evidence provides some clues, of course, but it is mostly biographical or anecdotal, and will not serve to make a case on its own. One way of proceeding, however, is to adopt the technique employed by R. W. Ram,[33] which measures the contributions of several of the Dissenting sects against entries recorded in trades directories. The method is not exempt from reproach because it begs the question of how the trades directories were compiled in the first place. Nevertheless, it produces the reasonably clear answer that the Birmingham Dissenters were indeed disproportionately wealthy and disproportionately engaged in trade and industry. This is a generalisation, however. When Ram filters his data by denomination, it becomes obvious that the well-to-do manufacturers were chiefly to be found among the Presbyterians and the Quakers – proportionately speaking – and least likely to be found among the Baptists. For instance, he finds that 37 per cent of the members of the New Meeting congregation were engaged in manufacturing in 1751–55 (42 per cent in 1781–85; 46 per cent in 1811–15) compared with 0.5 per cent in the professions (1.0 per cent in 1781–55; 3 per cent in 1811–15). In the case of the Quakers, the bias towards industrial activity was even more pronounced in the second half of the eighteenth century, and they were well established in the town's merchanting and banking sectors as well. The Baptist householders of the Cannon Street chapel congregated at the lower end of the socio-economic hierarchy, by contrast. When, eventually, they started to enter the manufacturing sector (in the 1780s), it was as small-scale craftsmen with little capital who often worked alone. Since their only professional men were the chapel incumbents and there were few Baptist shopkeepers and even fewer merchants, we must conclude that the denomination recruited overwhelmingly from among Birmingham's wage-earning population.

In the absence of membership lists for the Old Meeting, Ram's New Meeting data must stand proxy for the generality of Presbyterians. As for the Congregationalists, it is likely that their socio-economic station

---

[33] R. W. Ram, 'Influences on the patterns of belief and social action among Birmingham dissenters between 1750 and 1870', in A. Bryman (ed.), *Religion in the Birmingham Area: Essays in the Sociology of Religion* (University of Birmingham Institute for the Study of Worship and Religious Architecture, n.d. [1975]), pp. 29–44.

placed them closer to the Presbyterians than to the Baptists. After all, they had seceded from the former in protest at the retreat from Trinitarian orthodoxy. The Methodists, all sources agree, recruited heavily from the unskilled and semi-skilled labour force. Julius Hardy, who employed between thirty and forty journeymen in 1789, would have passed for a man of real substance in the Cherry Street chapel. Should we therefore conclude with Michael Watts that 'within those manufacturing and commercial communities in which Non-conformity thrived, Dissenters were not distinguished by occupation or social status from the population at large'?[34] Evidently not: Birmingham can be compared with Bristol, where the Dissenters also tended to occupy a higher position on the socio-economic scale than their Anglican counterparts. Indeed, there were close trading, family and denominational links between the two towns, as we shall see. Although the Quakers totalled only 1 per cent of the population, or thereabouts, a third of the ironmasters of the town were Friends, as were a third of tanners, a quarter of soap-boilers and nearly a fifth of distillers. In marked contrast to Birmingham, the Bristol Quakers were largely represented in the professions at the century's end as well, with 10 per cent of physicians and surgeons adhering to the sect.[35] None of this sheds any light on what impelled Dissenters towards becoming so heavily involved in trade and industry, whether in Birmingham or Bristol, however. This is the question which needs to be considered next.

The non-Weberian answer must be that towns do not make Dissenting industrialists; they suck them in from elsewhere and reward them with economic opportunities which then tend to dissolve specific religious convictions. Broadly speaking, this is the process that we can see operating in Birmingham from the middle decades of the eighteenth century: a convergence in which the wealthy and increasingly cultured regrouped around the concept of 'rational' religion. The process would only be halted and put into reverse when a series of events subverted the rapprochement from the mid-1780s onwards. An alternative argument might be that the Dissenters became successful manufacturers and businessmen because they were excluded from other avenues of social advancement and cultural assertion. However, there are good grounds for supposing that this was not the case in eighteenth-century Birmingham, or Bristol. Even in Manchester it now seems less likely that Dissenter members of the Literary and Philosophical Society espoused science as a culturally acceptable activity in order to overcome their

---

[34] Watts, *The Dissenters*, i, p. 354.
[35] Vann and Eversley, *Friends in Life and Death*, p. 73.

supposedly marginal status.[36] The Quakers of Birmingham, the Black Country and Coalbrookdale may represent an exception, however, for they constituted something of a subculture within the ranks of Protestant Dissent. If only for organisational reasons, they did not participate fully in the general regrouping of the elite around a common set of spiritual and cultural values. Whilst it is not possible to demonstrate a causal link between their theology or religious practices and their migration towards heavy industry, wholesale commerce or banking, it does seem that their moral outlook and the precepts of the Meetings informed the manner in which they conducted themselves in business.

The injunction against marrying out and the pervasive discipline of the Monthly Meeting certainly facilitated the creation of impressive Quaker dynasties – particularly in those industries involving a large financial outlay, with all its attendant risks. In a context of unlimited liability in business the raising of capital among co-religionaries was often the safest option, and the Meetings provided a ready-made network for the purpose. It is perhaps no accident, therefore, that Quakers should have owned or controlled between a half and three-quarters of the ironworks in England and Wales at the start of the eighteenth century.[37] The fact that property law did not grant them absolutely secure possession until 1722, owing to their refusal to swear oaths, only emphasised the need to adopt business practices that minimised risk. However, it is the enduring personal asceticism and its reinforcement by the peer pressure of the Meeting which really marks out the eighteenth-century Quaker, even among his fellow Dissenters. The Friends made no distinction between business behaviour and the rules governing their religious life, and the Meetings routinely reminded members of the importance of regular book-keeping, punctual debt repayment and the duty of mutual assistance. They also inveighed against time wasting, sloth, gambling, commercial impropriety and the worst sin of all – bankruptcy. Defaulting on business undertakings usually resulted in expulsion. Many of these behavioural norms applied to members of the other Dissenting denominations, of course, and, no doubt, to Churchmen as well. What seems to have distinguished Quaker businessmen and professionals, however, was the perception among non-Quaker contemporaries that they did indeed conduct their daily lives on a higher moral plane. Barthélemy Faujas de Saint-Fond[38] was hugely impressed with the Quaker physician

---

[36] See Chapter 3, pp. 84–5.

[37] J. Walvin, *The Quakers: Money and Morals* (London: Murray, 1997), p. 105; also Rowlands, *Masters and Men in the West Midland Metalware Trades before the Industrial Revolution* (Manchester: Manchester University Press, 1975), pp. 111–14.

[38] B. Faujas de Saint-Fond, *Travels in England, Scotland, and the Hebrides*, 2 vols (London: Ridgway, 1799), ii, pp. 35–8, 115–23.

and naturalist, John Lettsom, on meeting him over dinner; and another late-century visitor to England, Horace-Bénédict de Saussure, would record that Friends 'never charge more for their goods than they are worth'. However, he noted that the younger generation of Quakers appeared less willing to accept the sacrifices that other-worldliness entailed, for they 'have a hankering to wear buttons on their sleeves like other young men'.[39]

Unsurprisingly, Birmingham's Quakers had close links with a network of iron-founders and merchants stretching westwards towards Wales, and to Bristol and beyond in the South West. Indeed, many of the families had migrated to the town in the late seventeenth century or the early decades of the eighteenth century – drawn thither by marriage alliances, by commercial considerations, or for protection. The Lloyds hailed originally from Dolobron in Merionethshire, the Galtons from Bristol and Somerset and the Fidoes from Wednesbury. The Darbys and Reynoldses, whose ironworks and mining interests in and around the Severn River gorge provide the best-documented example of a Quaker industrial dynasty,[40] also had multiple connections with Birmingham. Abraham Darby I was apprenticed by his father to a Birmingham ironmonger – also a Quaker – before settling into a career as an iron-founder in Coalbrookdale. The firm manufactured a wide range of domestic ironwares, together with the iron-framed screw presses used by the Birmingham metal-stamping trades. Its Quaker ethos was reflected in the large number of Friends who had found employment in the 'Dale Company', and in the reluctance of Abraham I to make weapons of war. His son, Abraham II, built a meeting house for the Quaker element of the work-force, although when the War of the Austrian Succession broke out (1740–48) he retracted his father's policy on armaments production. The Lloyds have already been mentioned in several contexts. Sampson Lloyd's slitting mill in Digbeth was supplied with Russian bar-iron by the Bristol merchant Graffin Prankard, also a Friend, and the business maintained close links with Richard Reynolds, the Quaker patriarch of Ketley, as well. On the other hand, the move into banking in 1765 required a rather different entrepreneurial approach. In forming a partnership with John Taylor, the Presbyterian toy manufacturer, the

[39] See R. Bayne-Powell, *Travellers in Eighteenth-Century England* (London: Murray, 1951), p. 160; also E. Jones, *Les Voyageurs français en Angleterre de 1815 à 1830* (Paris, 1930), p. 217 and note 6.

[40] A. Raistrick, *Dynasty of Iron Founders: the Darbys and Coalbrookdale* (London: Longman, 1953); *idem., Quakers in Science and Industry being an Account of the Quaker Contributions to Science and Industry during the 17th and 18th Centuries* (Newton Abbott: David and Charles, 1968), chapter 4.

Lloyds joined together two networks. By 1775 the bank had 277 individual and business customers, of whom only 40 were Quakers.[41]

The Galtons deserve closer scrutiny, if only for the reason that Samuel Galton junior would become one of the longest-serving members of the Lunar Society. His career will provide a point of entry into the relationship between Nonconformity and activity in the sciences. The family's mercantile and industrial pursuits also shed some light on the manner in which Quakers responded when conflicts between business and conscience arose. The first Galton to appear in Birmingham arrived from Bristol in order to conclude a matrimonial alliance with the Farmers – a family of Quaker ironmongers who had branched out into gun-making. When the Farmers suffered heavy losses as a result of the Lisbon earthquake, Samuel Galton (senior) came to the fore as the dominant partner in the firm, and in the 1760s and 1770s the gun-manufacturing side of the business went from strength to strength. Although Samuel was a convinced Friend and proceeded to marry his son (Samuel junior) to a female descendant of Robert Barclay, the 'Apologist', there is some evidence – even at this stage – that he was conscious that arms manufacture scarcely befitted a Quaker – the more so perhaps as gun-making in Birmingham was closely tied to the fortunes of the slave trade. Still, if we can judge by the behaviour of the Darbys, this was a matter which tended to be left to individual consciences.

Not so by the late 1780s, however. The evils of slaving were now firmly in the spot-light, for the Birmingham Quakers had joined forces with several prominent Presbyterians and Churchmen in order to campaign for government action to end Britain's involvement in the slave trade. Moreover, a continental war appeared to be in the offing. In 1790 the Yearly Meeting sent out an epistle instructing that 'none among us, whose principle is peace, be employed to prepare the means of war',[42] and although the message was not formally adopted by the Birmingham Monthly Meeting, it was plain to all that Galton father and son were in an anomalous position as the biggest gunsmiths in town and the only Quakers. Despite mounting unease inside the Bull Street community, however, no formal action was taken until 1795, when a Monthly Meeting at Tamworth appointed 'visitors' to remonstrate with the family. Samuel Galton senior chose this moment to retire, although he seems to have left his capital in the business, which would not have satisfied tender

[41] R. S. Sayers, *Lloyd's Bank in the History of English Banking* (Oxford: Clarendon Press, 1957), pp. 9–10.

[42] See B. D. Smith, 'The Galtons of Birmingham: Quaker gun merchants and bankers, 1702–1831', *Business History*, 9 (1967), 144.

consciences. But the son mounted a spirited defence of his conduct, pointing out that he had not chosen the occupation of gunsmith, having received it as an inheritance from his father and grandfather, and that for seventy years the Society had remained undisturbed by arms making in the town. Lest his auditors should suppose that the case admitted of no ambiguity, he further pointed out that the making of weapons implied no endorsement of war, any more than the brewing of beer signalled an endorsement of intemperance. In any case, everybody contributes to warfare by virtue of the payment of taxes to the state, he continued and, in a jibe nicely tailored to the growing epicureanism of the town's wealthy Dissenters, he asked whether sugar consumption should be curtailed on the ground that it helped to sustain the slave trade.[43] Samuel Galton was disowned, notwithstanding, although he continued to attend the Birmingham Meeting and only slowly reduced his involvement in the complex of arms workshops around Steelhouse Lane. The episode of the 'visitors' must have rankled, though. When his own youngest son, Howard, married out (to a daughter of Joseph Strutt of Derby) in 1819, he advised him not to accept a visitation from the Friends.[44]

The science credentials of the Quakers have been thoroughly reexamined by Geoffrey Cantor.[45] His work navigates between the broadbrush approach of Robert Merton and the abundant, if piecemeal, evidence of individual biographies. Although his investigation of the impact of reformed Protestantism in this area tends to roam, making it difficult to identify the contributions of specific generations, he corrects a number of exaggerated claims that have been made in respect of Dissenter and, more especially, Quaker involvement in science. Evangelicalism among Nonconformists, for instance, is shown not to have been intrinsically opposed to the speculative sciences. John Wesley had little time for natural philosophy that lacked experimental foundations, it is true, perhaps because mathematised Newtonian science enjoyed the backing of Deists. But he read the *Transactions of the Royal Society* and showed a sustained interest in electricity. After a visit to Matthew Boulton's manufacturing emporium at Soho, he responded in a manner that was equivocal at best: 'if faith and love dwell here, then there may be happiness too. Otherwise all these beautiful things are as unsatisfactory as straws and feathers.'[46] No doubt he was happier

[43] *Ibid.*, 146.

[44] BCL MS 3101/C/D/10/9 S. Galton jnr to J. H. Galton, 5 December 1819.

[45] G. Cantor, *Quakers, Jews, and Science: Religious Responses to Modernity and the Sciences in Britain, 1650–1900* (Oxford: Oxford University Press, 2005).

[46] See W. R. Ward and R. P. Heitzenrater (eds), *The Works of John Wesley*, 24 vols (Nashville: Abingdon Press, 1988–2003), xxiii, p. 256.

reading 'Dr Witherings *Treatise on Foxglove*'[47] as he tells us on the occasion of a subsequent passage through Birmingham. However, Quakers too were unmoved by Newtonianism – or so Cantor concludes. If the quietist generation made a characteristic contribution to natural knowledge, it lay more in the area of observational sciences such as botany. Nature study fitted in well with eighteenth-century Quakers' illuminist theology, and it helped, furthermore, to inculcate practical skills of immediate benefit to the community.

What we know of Samuel Galton junior's scientific attainments and interests mirrors this assessment, at least in part. He did not receive a Quaker education as such, for schools of this type scarcely existed in the 1750s and 1760s. Instead, he attended a number of Dissenting institutions, including the Academy at Warrington. Whilst there he may have received a grounding in the sciences, but researchers now question whether Nonconformist establishments offered a curriculum which was very much different from that of their Anglican counterparts.[48] In any case, neither Priestley nor Dr John Aikin would have taught the young Galton at Warrington. Evidence from later on in his life indicates that he was a highly proficient classical scholar as well as a fluent French speaker, which hints at home tuition, as befitted the son of an affluent Quaker. Like so many of his peers in the Lunar Society, Galton was probably self-educated in natural philosophy. His bent for the observational sciences – botany and ornithology in particular – is well attested, for he compiled from Linnaeus and the Enlightenment authors a book on bird life for the instruction of his children, and would become an early member of the Linnean Society. However, a daughter and a grand-daughter both recalled that he was a practised experimentalist with a strong interest in the exact sciences, too. Indeed, it was work in optics carried out in his home laboratory that secured his election to the Royal Society in 1785.

On balance it seems more likely that Galton's scientific interests were nurtured in the context of the Lunar Society than in the context of the Bull Street Meeting. As Joseph Priestley would ruefully observe, the Society was a place where cultured men met, conversed and learned from one another irrespective of religious orientation. Allowing that his own personal religious convictions lay completely beyond the pale, he wrote to his erstwhile colleagues in the months before his departure for America: 'you know that neither politics nor religion were ever the

---

[47] *Ibid.*, p. 387.
[48] Wood, *Science and Dissent in England*, p. 2.

subject of our conversation. Philosophy engrosses us wholly.'[49] Indeed, when we turn to examine the Lunar Society from a denominational perspective, the difficulty of sustaining an articulation between religion (whether as 'theology' or 'temperament') and the practice of experimental philosophy becomes quite obvious. Matthew Boulton, James Keir and William Withering were all Churchmen, though of a distinctly temperate hue, and Robert Augustus Johnson was a practising Anglican clergyman. Erasmus Darwin, by contrast, can only be described as a closet free-thinker, whilst James Watt was a (lapsed) Scots Presbyterian, Galton a Quaker and Priestley a Unitarian and denier of the divinity of Jesus Christ. The same point holds in respect of our *savant-fabricants*, albeit to a lesser degree. In effect, therefore, the Lunar Society functioned as a discursive space lying beyond conventional socio-religious frontiers. Whether consciously or subconsciously, it provided a model and an example of how the convergence of an elite around the liberal values of the Enlightenment might operate.

The objection most frequently cited against such a process of social regrouping is that provincial urban society in England was deeply fissured. Sectarian animosities ensured that those who could not, or would not, conform to the doctrines of the Established Church were excluded from influence and positions of trust. Indeed, prominent Dissenters would exploit this argument themselves when renewing the campaign to remove the Test and Corporation Acts from the statute book in the late 1780s. Yet the reality of exclusion has been questioned by James Bradley[50] and a number of other historians, and their scepticism is fully confirmed by the example of Birmingham. An unincorporated borough, Birmingham relied principally on manorial officials for local policing, whilst the bulk of the town's commercial litigation passed through a small-claims tribunal known as the Court of Requests, which had been set up in 1752. The most important manorial agent was the Low Bailiff, for he summoned the Court Leet – the body which nominated the town's officers for the following year. Ever since the early eighteenth century, custom and practice had decreed that a Dissenter would normally be chosen to serve as Low Bailiff, and a Churchman as High Bailiff. And indeed, from 1733 until 1838 – the date of Birmingham's incorporation – there were only twenty-seven years in which a member of one or other of the two Presbyterian meetings was not

[49] Rutt, *Life and Correspondence of Joseph Priestley*, ii, p. 211.

[50] J. E. Bradley, *Religion, Revolution and English Radicalism. Nonconformity in Eighteenth-Century Politics and Society* (Cambridge: Cambridge University Press, 1990); also J. Seed, 'Gentlemen dissenters: the social and political meanings of Rational dissent in the 1770s and 1780s', *Historical Journal*, 28 (1985), 299–325.

holding this public office.[51] The Quakers, it should be noted, adopted a much lower political profile, especially before mid century. Dissenters were also well represented – that is to say, numerically over-represented – in the ranks of the Street Commissioners. According to R. W. Ram's statistics, the New Meeting supplied twelve of the original fifty commissioners appointed in 1769, and Bull Street three.[52] A similar situation appears to have obtained in the Court of Requests, perhaps unsurprisingly in view of the property-owning qualification attaching to membership. Finally, two of the wealthiest Presbyterians – John Taylor the toy manufacturer and William Russell the wholesale merchant – managed to sit as County Justices by virtue of the country houses they owned in Warwickshire and Worcestershire.

How the Dissenters secured this sizeable role in the governance of Birmingham is scarcely relevant. Presumably occasional conformity was widely practised with the willing complicity of the Anglican majority, for the formal barriers to Nonconformist office holding were not removed until 1828. In a populous and potentially unruly town it must have made sense to have had all of the most substantial inhabitants involved in the task of social control, albeit that a number of them were, strictly speaking, second-class citizens. Even in 1789, at a time when cooperation within the elite was breaking down, the town's Police Committee for the repression of prostitution and nocturnal disorder was entirely bipartisan in composition. Ostensibly, therefore, Burke's 'grand Toyshop' entered a long period of intra-elite harmony and collaboration once the damage wrought at the end of Queen Anne's reign had been repaired. Everyone settled down to the business of making money, to the exploration of common ground rather than the reheating of disagreements that had been a source of division in the past, and to the task of equipping the town with cultural institutions appropriate to its growing demographic and economic stature. Mutual tolerance, reason, rational religion, confidence in the possibility of human betterment and a commitment to modernity were the watchwords of the endeavour. It is in this sense, then, that we can say that the cultural substructures of the Industrial Enlightenment were being put in place during the third quarter of the eighteenth century. The Enlightenment in the making was not specifically Dissenter or Anglican, but a fusion of the two. Not until the final

---

[51] See E. Bushrod, 'The History of Unitarianism in Birmingham from the Middle of the Eighteenth Century to 1893' (MA dissertation, University of Birmingham, 1954), p. 221; also W. H. Ryland (ed.), *Reminiscences of Thomas Henry Ryland* (Birmingham: The Midland Counties Herald Limited, 1904), p. 3.

[52] Ram, 'Influences on the patterns of belief', p. 33.

decade of the century would it dawn on the political establishment that there was anything to fear from the exercise of reason.

The religious sentiments of Matthew Boulton and James Watt are worth trying to pinpoint at this juncture. The partners hailed from rather different backgrounds, yet they ended up subscribing to the same secularised, almost deistical conception of the Almighty. Both are said to have worshipped at St Paul's, the Birmingham church closest to Handsworth, but if they did so few traces of their attendance have survived. References to matters spiritual in their correspondence are extremely rare. In 1775 or 1776 Boulton reported (to Watt) that he had launched a chapel subscription for his Soho work-force, and with a significant sum already raised, announced 'we will begin our Temple & dedicate it to one God, for thou shalt have no other'.[53] Yet there is scant evidence of a building ever having been erected. His attitude to death reveals a brisk, no-nonsense approach which appears to have been commonplace among the Lunar group. When an old family friend transmitted the news of the death of her mother, Boulton replied with an admonition not to indulge in excessive mourning – 'a sin instead of a virtue'.[54] James Watt seems to have taken on the coloration of his immediate environment in matters of faith. As a young man he travelled everywhere with his Bible, but on moving to Birmingham all formal connections with Presbyterianism were severed. However, dispiriting months spent overseeing the erection of engines in the depths of Cornwall appear to have reactivated his Dissenter reflexes. Writing from Chacewater, Anne Watt warned Mrs Boulton that the county was in the grip of the evangelicals: 'take care Mr Bolton's principals are well fixt before you trust him here, poor Mr Watt is turned Ana Baptist & duely attends their meetings, he is indeed and goes to Chapel most devoutly'.[55] Yet once back in Birmingham his detached and normally unemotional attitude towards organised religion gained the upper hand once more. Young Jimmy was scolded for the unguarded use of the cliché 'God's providence' in a letter home to his parents. 'The proper phrase is *providentially*, luckily or happily', he was told; 'remember Horace's rule whenever you introduce a Deity "dignus sit vindice nodus [*sic*]"'.[56] In fact it seems that Watt had ceased altogether to think of himself as a Dissenter by the 1790s. Only when threatened with the prospect

---

[53] BCL MS 3219/4/66 M. Boulton to J. Watt snr n.d. [March 1775].

[54] BCL MS 3782/12/50 M. Boulton to Miss M. Linwood, June 1805.

[55] Mason, *The Hardware Man's Daughter*, p. 37.

[56] BCL MS 3219/4/123 J. Watt snr to J. Watt jnr, 13 July 1784. ('Nec deus intersit, nisi dignus vindice nodus', Horace, *Ars Poetica*, verse 131).

of inclusion on the Staffordshire shrievalty list did he invoke – with evident reluctance – the argument that he could not in conscience take the sacrament according to the Church of England.[57] According to his only surviving child – the same Jimmy who had been ticked off for taking God's name in vain – he contemplated his approaching death with the calm tranquillity of a philosopher arising from a mind at peace with itself and with the world.[58]

The Birmingham Presbyterians, meanwhile, were becoming increasingly worldly. Although Watt retained a life-long distaste for self-indulgence, or any pandering to the senses, even as he lost his religious faith, Priestley's Unitarians were busily reconfiguring God in their own image as rational, integrated with mankind and benevolent. By justifying the accumulation of wealth and the enjoyment of its by-products, the philosophy of Rational Dissent both sanctioned and anointed Birmingham's consumerist Enlightenment. Few signs of the ascetic Puritan heritage remained by the 1770s and 1780s, for the Dissenters counted themselves among the town's principal consumers. John Taylor, the most successful 'toy' manufacturer before Matthew Boulton appeared on the scene, died in Bath having virtually completed the transition to Dissenting country gentleman. He started to buy land in the 1750s, and by the end of that decade had an income from rural rents amounting to £1,290 a year. In 1764 he consecrated his migration from the pungent varnishing and enamelling workshops of Crooked Lane by purchasing Moseley Hall, the gentry seat of the Grevises. Indeed, by the 1780s, the Presbyterians seem to have completely lost the inhibitions they once felt about worldly pleasures – card-playing, dancing, attendance at the playhouse, the races, etc. After the low point of 1773, when an alliance of Quakers, evangelical Anglicans and Methodists opposed the granting of a licence, Birmingham's New Street theatre had built up a seasonal turnover of £300 a week by the late 1780s.[59] The most prominent Dissenters, moreover, had taken to aping the gentry habit of attending the races. With the crisis over the Test and Corporation Acts repeal bill brewing, Samuel Garbett informed Lord Lansdowne that he would have the opportunity to meet William Russell – Birmingham's prime mover in the affair – at the races in Warwick. Lest any doubts remain about the epicurean dimension of Rational Dissent, one has

57 BCL MS 3219/4/119 J. Watt snr to Sir J. Banks, Birmingham, 15 November 1803; *idem.* to *idem.*, 16 January 1804

58 BCL MS 3219/6/70 J. Watt jnr to B. Delessert, 9 September 1819.

59 See W. Hutton, *Court of Requests: their Nature, Utility, and Powers Described with a variety of Cases, determined in that of Birmingham* (Birmingham: Pearson and Rollason, 1787), p. 250.

only to consult the compensation claims lodged by the victims of the 1791 riots. The Nonconformist bourgeoisie lived well, and indistinguishably from their Anglican peers. Wine cellars were ample (Priestley's contained sixteen dozen Fontiniac [*sic*] and five dozen claret, as well as Madeira, old port and Cape wines[60]), and drawing rooms replete with mahogany furniture. William Hutton would declare the loss of a dozen gilded Argand lamps with chains and pulleys from his several properties.[61]

The Quakers participated less whole-heartedly in Birmingham's Enlightenment, as will be apparent by now. This was not because they were excluded, but because they excluded themselves. Of all the Protestant Dissenter groups, they alone still tried to practise a culture of apartness in the second half of the eighteenth century. One might question their personal asceticism, for the Galton family's cellars were filled with fine beverages, too. Nevertheless, their style of living – whilst certainly opulent – showed more restraint. As late as 1827 the drawing room of Samuel Galton junior's fine neo-classical villa at Duddesdon was completely unadorned. There were no pictures on the walls nor pier-glass mirror above the fire-place.[62] Samuel's father, it should be remembered, had played a leading role in the campaign against the theatre licence – one of the key moments in the acculturation of eighteenth-century Birmingham. To his dying day he was always driven to Meeting in a four-horse carriage, as was the custom, wearing a muff and clogs. Perhaps this was what offended Julius Hardy, the Methodist button manufacturer: the mixture of visible wealth and self-abasing humility. But there appears to have been another spur to his criticism of Quaker 'self-interest'. From the 1770s the Friends mixed their rather measured contributions to the collective life of the town with an extreme touchiness on the subject of public rejoicings. No doubt the conflicts of conscience and commerce engendered by the American War played on their sensitivities, for James Bisset recounts how he organised an impromptu civic celebration to mark Admiral Rodney's victory over the Comte de Grasse at the Battle of the Saints (1782), only for it to degenerate into stone-throwing when the Quakers refused to light up their windows.[63] We know, too, that the Friends were distinctly unenthusiastic when a subscription was set on foot for a monument to Nelson

[60] BCL Church of the Messiah 238 MS 399801 'Inventory of the House and Goods of Dr Joseph Priestley which were destroyed during the Birmingham Riots of 1791'.
[61] BCL MS 331068 Compensation claim: W. Hutton [1791].
[62] A. Moilliet (ed.), *Elizabeth Anne Galton (1808–1906): a Well-Connected Gentlewoman* (Hartford, Léonie Press, 2003), p. 3 figure.
[63] BCL MS 263924 J. Bisset, commonplace book, folio 70.

after the battle of Trafalgar (1805). They would have preferred the monies raised to have been diverted towards the building of a new Public Dispensary in the town.

It is unlikely that Birmingham's small Quaker community were unique in their hesitant embrace of modernity. Industrial Enlightenment left little room for religious subcultures, and many of the reflexes depicted here have also been documented by Richard Allen[64] in his study of the Friends of Newcastle-on-Tyne. The problem facing Dissenters of this ilk by the end of the century was that their desire to shrink from society ran exactly counter to their need to participate in it. The dilemma was neatly summarised by John Howard junior, son of a London Quaker tinsmith, who went to Switzerland to help Aimé Argand manage his Versoix lamp manufactory. On setting out for home he wrote to forewarn his father that his travels had not been conducive to upholding the practices of the faith, 'so impossible is it to associate with a people without adopting to a certain degree their habits, fashion and modes of living'.[65] Both his Quaker dress and mode of address had fallen by the wayside, but he promised to mend his ways on arriving back in London, lest his younger brothers and the Meeting be scandalised.

Marginalisation by riot

The event which would eclipse this version of the Enlightenment in Birmingham and the West Midlands was the extensive rioting of the summer of 1791. It dealt a severe blow to the carefully confected collaboration of the town's freshly minted elite; it thinned and weakened the ranks of the Presbyterians, and it nudged the whole enterprise of natural philosophy in a safer, more utilitarian direction, as we have already noted. However, the event of the riots cannot be understood in isolation. By the time the ill-fated dinner to mark the second anniversary of the fall of the Bastille occurred, the zenith of intra-elite collaboration had passed. And, by the same token, subsequent developments on which the riots had no direct bearing would prove hugely influential in setting the town on a fresh course. The French Wars and the economic dislocation and distress they caused are also part of the story of the retreat from the Enlightenment.

[64] R. C. Allen, 'An alternative community in North-East England: Quakers, morals and popular culture in the long eighteenth century', in H. Berry and J. Gregory (eds), *Creating and Consuming Culture in North-East England, 1660–1830* (Aldershot: Ashgate, 2004), pp. 98–119.
[65] See Wolfe, *Brandy, Balloons, and Lamps*, p. 121.

The high-water mark of cooperation among the town's well-to-do seems to have been reached in the early 1780s. Campaigning to found and build a General Hospital (1765–79) had pulled all strands of the elite together, and in the first edition of his *History of Birmingham* (1781) William Hutton judged it appropriate to congratulate his fellow citizens: 'I have frequently beheld with pleasure, the churchman, the presbyterian, and the quaker uniting in their efforts, like brethren, to carry on a work of utility.'[66] Was the turning-point therefore the appearance in Birmingham of Dr Joseph Priestley with an invitation to take over the pulpit of the New Meeting? John Money[67] thinks not, believing the town's trajectory to have been set by the time of his arrival, and Priestley would doubtless have concurred. He later recalled that he had been on friendly terms initially with several of the Anglican clergy, including Edward Burn and Spencer Madan, who would become his most redoubtable local opponents. No doubt, but the fact remains that his quickness of opinion and tendency to rush into print soon turned him into a source of irritation, and not just to Anglicans. The live-and-let-live cordiality between St Martin's and the two Presbyterian meetings which in the 1760s and 1770s had extended to consultation over the dates of charity sermons, no longer applied by 1785. The breakdown thereafter was not sudden, but piecemeal and it was probably not complete until the early months of 1790.

Priestley's first encounters with the local clergy seem to have occurred in the context of the anti-slave trade agitation and it is true that cooperation under this head persisted well into 1788, even though several of the town's biggest merchants and manufacturers pointedly refused to join in the crusade. But by this date several disputes had broken out and compromised the atmosphere of entente. The first occurred in the committee of subscribers which managed Birmingham's principal proprietary library – an institution founded by Dissenters in the main, but enjoying the support of the Established Church. Characteristically, Priestley considered the library to be ripe for development as an instrument for the furtherance of human progress from the very first moment of his arrival in Birmingham. Initially all went well, but an incident occurred in 1785 which raised hackles and resulted in competitive, that is to say denominational, voting for the committee. A decision to stock Priestley's *History of the Corruptions of Christianity* (1782), in which

[66] Hutton, *An History of Birmingham to the End of the Year 1780* (Birmingham: Rollason, 1781), p. 109.

[67] J. Money, 'Science, technology and dissent in English provincial culture: from Newtonian transformation to agnostic incarnation', in P. Wood (ed.), *Science and Dissent in England, 1688–1945* (Aldershot: Ashgate, 2000), p. 87.

he claimed to have had no hand, further exacerbated the situation and by the end of 1787 the body of subscribers was irretrievably divided on party lines.[68] Julius Hardy noted as much two years later when called upon to participate in the annual ballot of subscribers to renew the committee. A liberal Methodist with leanings in the direction of Dr Priestley's New Meeting, he voted for a slate comprising two Unitarians, two Quakers, two highly reputable Churchmen (Samuel Garbett and George Simcox), and the Soho engineer James Watt.[69]

There are signs that the provision of Sunday schooling had become a bone of contention, too. This was an initiative in which the clergy of the Established Church had taken the lead and, by 1788, 1,800 Birmingham children were enrolled in Sunday classes. The original scheme drawn up in 1784 presupposed that children under instruction would attend the town's two Anglican parish churches or chapels, however. When, in 1786, Dissenter demurrals were brushed to one side, the New Meeting resolved to make alternative arrangements. The outcome was a Unitarian Sunday school, which came into being in 1787, aiming to provide a non-sectarian and secular-minded type of instruction. But by this date the decision by prominent Dissenters to launch a fresh campaign for the repeal of the seventeenth-century legislation excluding Non-conformists from office-holding was completely altering the political landscape. Birmingham's Dissenters were not excluded from local government, or even from the magistrate's bench, as we have seen. On the contrary, an unenlightened Anglican clergyman or lay person who found cause for concern at the onward march of Rational Dissent could have been forgiven for supposing that the Nonconformists enjoyed the upper hand. Why, then, did the Dissenters suddenly work themselves into a rhetorical lather over discrimination? The answer, it seems, falls into two parts. Since they had tasted the fruits of office, those restraints that served to underline the shortcomings of the Toleration Act appeared all the more irksome. However, it is far from established whether, in a town such as Birmingham in which the disparate elements of the manufacturing bourgeoisie had learned to work together under the common banner of enlightened civility, the bulk of Dissenters actually thought the issue of repeal worth fighting for. James Watt, who had ceased to think of himself as a Dissenter, clearly regarded Priestley in a rather equivocal light outside the confines of the Lunar Society, and in this he was not alone.

[68] See C. Parish, *History of the Birmingham Library: an Eighteenth-Century Proprietary Library as described in the Annals of the Birmingham Library, 1779–1799* (London: The Library Association, 1966), pp. 1–23.
[69] BCL MS 218 diary of J. Hardy, 3 December 1789.

The prime mover in the Birmingham campaign was the Unitarian merchant William Russell. Although possessed of considerable manufacturing interests overseas, he did not form part of the coterie of West Midlands industrialists and experimental philosophers. His commitment to the Enlightenment was rooted in theology and of a piece with his previous conduct as a domestic opponent of the American War and his subsequent endorsement of the French Revolution (see Chapter 6). Joseph Priestley would describe Russell as his 'second' in the New Meeting, and it is probable that Russell's wealth, influence and undeviating religious convictions were the main reasons why the doctor chose to settle in Birmingham in the first place. With a whole string of offices of trust to his name, Russell was no outsider. Moreover, he was known beyond the West Midlands and in the corridors of government. In fact he seems to have been one of the leading players in the national repeal movement as well. Early in 1787 we find him busily engaged in the recruiting of a Dissenter committee to spearhead the campaign, and in bankrolling its regional propaganda initiatives. He would go on to pick up the bills for the printing in Birmingham of Gilbert Wakefield's *Address* and Priestley's *Familiar Letters.*[70] Some sense of the extent to which the repeal venture depended on the energy of a few can be gleaned from his correspondence, however. Whilst wishing for success, the London Unitarian Thomas Jeffrys declined nomination to the committee, observing, 'but if we continue dissenters; perhaps it might have been as well for us (individually) to have remained under the old laws: as many Troubles are avoided by continuing in a private station'.[71]

Buoyed by the confidence of a Priestley and the lobbying skills of a Russell, the Birmingham Dissenters seem to have supposed that with a few short blasts of the trumpet the walls of Jericho would crumble. And perhaps with good reason, for Samuel Garbett, an enlightened Anglican, later expressed the puzzlement of many when remarking to Lord Lansdowne, 'it is astonishing that such a frivolous object of Contest is allowed for Priests & Bigots to raise Riots upon'.[72] In the event, a protracted three-year struggle ensued, which served to catalyse those other niggling sources of tension in the town. The doctor's prominence throughout 1788 in another moral crusade – that of anti-slavery – probably did the campaign to repeal the Test and Corporation Acts no favours, even though this initiative largely transcended the sectarian divide. The

[70] British Library Add. MSS 44998 William Russell papers, vol. 7, accounts, 1768–1813.
[71] BCL MS 661782 Russell family of Moseley, T. Jeffrys to W. Russell, London, 17 February 1787.
[72] BCL 510639 S. Garbett to Lord Lansdowne, Birmingham, 5 August 1791.

narrowness of the vote when a second motion for repeal was put to Parliament (and lost) in May 1789 served only to galvanise those on both sides of the argument, which the Anglican clergy now concluded had become a battle for the defence of the Establishment itself. That winter Priestley and Russell were indefatigable in their efforts to organise Dissenters, but so were Spencer Madan, the rector of St Philip's, and the Rev. Burn of St Mary's for the opposition. Inevitably, Priestley's misreported 'train of gunpowder'[73] remark was peddled once more. However, the doctor scarcely helped the campaign by repeating it in a polemical exchange with Edward Burn, and by making an explicit connection to the events in France. The town's pulpits became the new platforms for political oratory, with 'Gunpowder Joe' offering assurances that his aims were peaceful and his arguments expressed in no more than 'an ironical and rather pleasant manner',[74] whereas Spencer Madan charged the Presbyterians with setting out deliberately to republicanise the state. Early in the New Year an attempt was made to break into Priestley's house and, as the appointed time for the vote in Parliament drew near, he informed the Rev. Theophilus Lindsey: 'the spirit of party here is astonishing. Mr Russell says measures are taken to ring the bells & illuminate the town, on the expected event of Tuesday next; and, in that case, we apprehend that the mob will be instigated to do mischief. We think to apply to Mr Garbett, Mr Boulton, and a few others, to prevent it.'[75] Sure enough, in March 1790 a third motion to repeal the Test and Corporation Acts was lost – this time resoundingly. The business now seemed over. Symbolically, the Rev. Burn took over the chair of the Birmingham Library committee as the Dissenter members withdrew.

The convulsion that gripped the town some sixteen months later has received a great deal of attention from researchers, but in the context of this chapter we need only concentrate on the causes and the consequences. In a thorough investigation of the fortnight of rioting in July 1791, Barrie Rose[76] comes to the conclusion that the cause was latent class antagonism, made actual by the coming together of ancient sectarian prejudices and political frustrations of more recent date. There can be no doubt that all of these ingredients, plus some others, went into the making of the riots. However, we would prioritise the reawakening of religious tensions as the main causal factor, and one which

[73] S. Andrews, *Unitarian Radicalism: Political Rhetoric, 1770–1814* (Basingstoke: Palgrave, 2003), pp. 80–1.

[74] Parish, *History of the Birmingham Library*, p. 26.

[75] Rutt, *Life and Correspondence of Joseph Priestley*, ii, p. 54.

[76] R. B. Rose, 'The Priestley Riots of 1791', *Past and Present*, 18 (1960), 68–88.

might easily have resulted in a wholesale attack on the rich by the poor, had military force not arrived to forestall it. Despite its pell-mell growth and obvious lack of socio-economic cohesion, Birmingham was not a pathologically riot-prone town. After the unquestionably serious – and sectarian – disturbances of 1714–15, there had only been inter- mittent, and minor, crowd interventions in the ensuing decades (against Wesleyans in 1751; Quakers in 1759; food shortages in 1762–63, 1766, etc.). After 1791 it was a different matter, for it would take at least a decade before the rupture within the elite mended to the extent that the degree of cooperation practised in the 1760s, 1770s and early 1780s became feasible once more. This line of argument places a heavy bur- den on the actors involved in the break-down of relations between 1785 and 1790, of course, and on Priestley and Russell in particular. The challenge they mounted overturned a consensus that everyone had grown used to in the town – notwithstanding its anomalous character. After the failure of Fox's motion, William Russell requested an interview with William Pitt, the Prime Minister, and found him every bit as hostile as Henry Dundas, the Home Secretary. The government, he was told, found it difficult to know how to satisfy the Unitarians, for they were 'a dif- ferent set of persons from the old [i.e. quietist] Dissenters and did not know what they wanted'.[77] Priestley, meanwhile, was writing to Lindsey within days of the vote to report that the High Churchmen of Birming- ham were now adopting a more conciliatory stance. However, he had absolutely no intention of conceding ground.

On the afternoon of 14 July 1791 a mixed group of about eighty Dissenters and Churchmen gathered at a Birmingham hotel in order to mark in convivial fashion the second anniversary of the start of the French Revolution. James Keir presided but neither Priestley nor Russell attended, there having been rumours in the town for several days that the dinner would occasion some rowdiness. In the event, the stone throwing quickly degenerated into a wholesale assault on Dissenter property in which the houses and places of worship of the Presbyterians were particularly singled out. Both the New and the Old Meeting build- ings were gutted and largely demolished, as were the out-of-town houses of Priestley at Fairhill, Russell at Showell Green, Taylor at Bordesley and Moseley, and Ryland on Easy Hill (the former Baskerville residence). William Hutton, the historian, lost both his stationer's shop in High Street and his villa in Washwood Heath, and George Humphry's dwell- ing in Sparkbrook was ransacked. Several other Dissenter properties were visited and threatened, but not pillaged or burned, notably those

---

[77] Andrews, *Unitarian Radicalism*, p. 122.

of John Coates, the minister of the Old Meeting, Joseph Jukes, and the Quaker gun manufacturer Samuel Galton junior. The only non-Dissenter dwelling that appears to have been targeted by one of several roaming 'mobs' was Edgbaston Hall. It was tenanted by the lukewarm Anglican and Lunar philosopher Dr William Withering. Most of these assaults took place on the south side of town. To the north and in the parish of Handsworth there was widespread alarm but little actual damage. James Watt at Heathfield had clothing and valuables packed up in readiness for a quick getaway, and Samuel Garbett moved his account books to a place of safety. At Soho, meanwhile, Matthew Boulton made sure of the loyalty of his work-force in case of an invasion, but acknowledged privately that his house might still fall victim should the rioting continue.

Clearly the town's Presbyterians-cum-Unitarians were the principal object of attention, whether because of pent-up resentment of their institutional dominance, indignation at their theology, or because the crowds were directed by malevolent magistrates and Anglican clerics. It is interesting, however, to note the equivocations of the rioters in respect of the other Dissenters. The Friends' Meeting House in Bull Street was not assaulted, even though a number of Quakers' homes had been damaged as recently as 1789 (on account of their failure to participate in the illumination to mark the King's recovery). The Swedenborgians, who had opened their first chapel only weeks earlier, were targeted for molestation because of their association with Priestley, but their minister saved the building in the nick of time by distributing the previous day's collection plate. Even so, a fire bomb would be hurled into the chapel the following year. As for the Wesleyans, the rioters seemed unable to make up their minds whether they were true or false brethren. Julius Hardy identified strongly with the Presbyterians in their campaign to remove civil disabilities, we know, and he was destined to take up a position in the secessionist camp. Other Wesleyans felt quite differently, and a contemporary Methodist source recounted that 'One part of the mob were for destroying our chapels, but the other part opposed them and prevailed *because we were Church People.*'[78] As a consequence the various Wesleyan chapels, together with that of the Lady Huntingdon connection, survived unscathed. Only in 1813 would one of their places of worship suffer crowd violence.

Outside Birmingham the rioting produced a ripple of fear throughout the district, widespread acts of intimidation and sporadic assaults on property. A Baptist meeting house in the village of Kings Heath

[78] G. Robson, 'Religion and Irreligion in Birmingham and the Black Country' (PhD dissertation, University of Birmingham, 1998), p. 67.

was ransacked, and the Presbyterian chapel at Kingswood burned down, together with the parsonage. Towards the west, the example of Birmingham triggered crowd violence in Wolverhampton, Wednesbury, Dudley and Stourbridge. A meeting house in Wolverhampton was only saved by a last-minute intervention, and something of the sort preserved a Dissenter chapel from destruction in Wednesbury. Even to the east, which was not normally a zone much influenced by events in the West Midlands, the Coventry 'mob' put itself on stand-by in case the arrival of troops should fail to contain the activities of the rioters operating out of Birmingham and the Black Country towns. In the aftermath of the anti-Priestley disturbances, 'the terror spread through the country, and base people threatened our meetings at Coventry', recorded the Baptist preacher George Burder; 'a mob waited every night at ten o'clock to hear the news from Birmingham, and it seemed only to want a leader to begin the work of destruction among us'.[79] He was the more alarmed in that it was rumoured that Dr Priestley had taken refuge in his house: 'we had our plate and writings packed up, to be ready for departure on the first alarm'.[80]

The 1791 riots in Birmingham called Dr Joseph Priestley's bluff. They also exposed the fissure which had opened since 1787 between militant Unitarianism and those whom Priestley labelled the religious 'quietists'.[81] Yet, with the possible exception of the Methodists, all members of the broad Dissenter family suffered marginalisation in the decade that followed. Priestley left the town immediately and Russell would prudently withdraw for a time as well. It is likely that other Dissenters' households removed from Birmingham, too, for the numbers attending Presbyterian services in makeshift facilities after the summer of 1791 plunged (see Table 5.0). It is true that, within a matter of weeks of his explusion, Priestley promised to return, if only to say farewell to his congregation, but moderate Anglicans such as Keir and 'quietist' Dissenters such as Taylor and the Rylands beseeched him to do no such thing. James Watt felt so cross about what had happened that he could not even bring himself to write a letter of commiseration to his erstwhile Lunar colleague until about four months after the conflagration. The Dissenters were weakened by economic boycotts as well, for James

---

[79] A. Argent, 'The founding of the London Missionary Society and the West Midlands', in A. P. F. Sell (ed.), *Nonconformists and the West Midlands of England* (Keele: Keele University Press, 1996), p. 23.

[80] *Ibid.*

[81] D. L. Wykes, ' "A finished monster of the true Birmingham breed": Birmingham Unitarians and the 1791 Priestley Riots', in A. P. F. Sell (ed.), *Protestant Nonconformists and the West Midlands of England*, p. 52.

Bisset[82] observed in his commonplace book that High Churchmen were withdrawing their custom from shops and businesses owned by Non-conformists. Attempts of a similar nature were made to undermine the Unitarians of Stourbridge.

However, it was probably the institutional backlash which hurt most. For a campaign to remove vestigial barriers to civil equality actually resulted in a substantial disempowerment of Dissenters at the local level. A year after the riots, they lost control of the office of Low Bailiff. Then, at the Warwick and Worcester Assizes, their relative weakness was underlined again, as the judicial machine failed to deliver them either justice or adequate financial redress for the damage to their property. The opportune death of the Steward of the Court Leet (a Dissenter) a short time after the riots enabled the High Church party, with the support of the Lord of the Manor of Birmingham, to overturn the custom and practice of close on a century, with the result that in 1792 an Anglican banker was confirmed in office as Low Bailiff. Meanwhile, a packed jury ensured that few of the rioters would ever be brought to book. Samuel Garbett reported to Lord Lansdowne that 'consider-able sums of money were expended by Country Gentlemen to prevent the sufferers obtaining reasonable compensation for their losses and to defend the Rioters'.[83]

The Dissenters were not alone in concluding that the riots signalled the start of an eclipse. The victory won by Birmingham's High Churchmen in 1791 proved to be a pyrrhic one though, for the town became less and less governable for the rest of the decade. Condoning collective violence when aimed at one's religious and political opponents set an unfortunate precedent. The riots also undermined the modus vivendi between liberal-minded Anglicans and the more quiescent of the Non-conformists on which Birmingham's polite and rational Enlightenment had been erected. Matthew Boulton epitomised this rapprochement and in the aftermath of the disturbances would remark, somewhat melodra-matically, 'I live peaceably & securely amidst the Flames, Rapin, plunder, anarchy & confusion of these Unitarians, Trinitarians, predestinarians & tarians of all sorts.'[84] Nevertheless, he too had sensed his vulnerability and, when the September full moon fell due, decided to absent himself from the Lunar meeting and to quietly make known the fact. The venue was Samuel Galton junior's house at Barr, four miles out of town, and the rumour had gone abroad that Priestley would be attending.

---

[82] BCL MS 263924 J. Bisset, commonplace book, folio 104.
[83] BCL 510639 S. Garbett to Lord Lansdowne, Birmingham, 7 November 1792.
[84] BCL MS 3782/12/36 [copy of] M. Boulton to C. Dumergue, Soho, 10 August 1791.

Matthew Boulton's carefully cultivated middle-of-the-road stance in religion and politics offered no protection from the vagaries of the industrial economy, though. Only months after the anti-Priestley disturbances, Birmingham workmen were again on a mobile footing, owing to the escalating price of cake copper. In response to spiralling raw material prices, white-metal button manufacturers sought to safeguard their profit margins by cutting back journeymen's piecework rates. Boulton became a target because he was suspected of having cornered the market for copper in order to supply his coining presses. It is true that the metal had traded at £70 per ton in 1787, whereas in November 1791 it touched £105. Early in the New Year Samuel Garbett predicted a break-down in law and order, noting that even trade disputes were now carrying a tincture of sectarianism. He started to withdraw from public life in disgust at the erosion of popular deference since the riots. Boulton's complacency since the successful quelling of the disturbances had taken a knock, too. In several letters to the firm's Cornwall agent in February 1792, he reported that workmen were mustering in the streets of Birmingham to the beat of a drum and with cockades in their hatbands. All envious eyes were turning towards Soho and 'I accordingly expect a Riotous visit from them'.[85] In the event, the detonation was delayed until May and was largely contained by the troops now billeted in the town. The Dissenters' compensation claims had been scheduled for a hearing at the Warwick and Worcester Assizes that spring and this time the authorities were well prepared. On 21 May Boulton informed another correspondent that 'several thousand persons assembled in a riotous manner last night and gutted six houses in different parts of town'.[86] Soho was no longer a target, however. Instead, the soldiery had been drawn up in St Philip's churchyard in readiness to defend the elegant residences of the wealthy.

Sporadic outbreaks of disorder continued through the summer and into the autumn. Most of the incidents can be linked to the ripple effects of the 1791 disturbances, for neither food shortages nor serious trade dislocation were yet visible on the horizon. In late August the populace delighted in its new sense of freedom by gathering to hurl stones as the well-to-do indulged in polite leisure activity at the Vauxhall pleasure gardens. In December a gang of youths clothing themselves in King and Country patriotism tried to renew the pressure on the Dissenters. Cash ransoms were extorted from the Taylors and the Humphrys – both

[85] Cornwall Record Office AD1583/5 Watt & Boulton to T. Wilson, Birmingham, 11 February 1792; M. Boulton to T. Wilson, Soho, 15 February 1792.

[86] BCL MS 3782/12/9 M. Boulton to Bourdieu & Co., 21 May 1792.

families which had suffered badly in the riots – causing them to flee
the town. In the absence of resident magistrates, Garbett worried about
what would happen when the troops were finally withdrawn, whilst James
Watt thought that he could detect a politicisation of urban animosities
as the French revolutionaries' language of natural rights began to sup-
plant that of Rational Dissent. In a town whose rank and file would
remain steadfastly Church and King throughout the 1790s, the epithet
'Presbyterian' was starting to be replaced by that of 'Jacobin'.[87] Nevertheless, the riotous behaviour of the second half of the decade seems
mainly to have been a protest against economic conditions. 'Partial insur-
rections',[88] as a local commentator described them, occurred in 1795
and 1800, and on both occasions the magistrates were prevailed upon to
read the Riot Act. Distress caused by high corn prices and the collapse
of the shoe-buckle trade were the root causes, but the repression was
counter-balanced by a concerted effort from within the town's elite to
organise soup kitchens.

Exactly when the rifts engendered in the late 1780s were finally healed
is hard to determine exactly. The chapter opened by the 1791 riots was
officially closed in the autumn of 1793, when the Constables began
the business of recovering the monies paid in compensation to the
Dissenters by means of a special rate levied on all householders –
but even this caused street disturbances. James Keir ended up paying
£37 6s.10½d. as the price of his attendance at the infamous dinner.[89]
According to the barrister John Morfitt, writing at the very end of 1802,
the 'coldness generated by mutual suspicion'[90] had eased only very
recently when the town's bourgeoisie joined forces to promote a
theatrical entertainment for the benefit of both the Anglican and the
Nonconformist charity schools. Perhaps it was this atmosphere of *détente*,
if not reconciliation, that prompted a group of Dissenters in late 1804
to contemplate erecting a monument or tablet to the memory of
Dr Joseph Priestley, who had died an exile in America earlier that year.
Significantly, the Low Church Anglican and occasional attender of Lunar
Society meetings, the Rev. Dr Samuel Parr, was invited to pen a suitable epitaph. In a letter to Jeremy Bentham he commented on the fruits
of his labours as follows: 'I believe, that my clerical Brethren will not
be very much dissatisfied – my great object was to avoid all Sectarian,

---

[87] BCL MS 3219/6/7 J. Watt jnr to J. Priestley jnr, Soho, 1 July 1794.
[88] See Pratt, *Harvest-Home*, i, p. 283.
[89] Guttery, *From Broad Glass to Cut Crystal*, p. 113.
[90] Pratt, *Harvest-Home*, i, p. 282.

Unitarian, democratical, jargon.'[91] Yet perhaps they were still more than a little dissatisfied, for the monument or tablet – it is not clear which was intended – never saw the light of day. Maybe the sense of hurt had not entirely disappeared after all.

Enough has been said to indicate that the riots of 1791 substantially curtailed Birmingham's cultural experiment with Enlightenment. This experiment had enlisted both Anglican and Dissenter members of the town's elite behind a banner of Latitudinarian religion, polite learning and rational recreation. It was wrecked by a recrudescence of unbridled enthusiasm – on both sides. Yet Industrial Enlightenment continued unabated, with natural philosophy now increasingly channelled towards the economically useful and the uncontentious. Whether science in the form of popular philosophic spectacle had any direct bearing on the patterning of the riots is difficult to judge. Commentators such as Edmund Burke and Edward Gibbon, who dubbed the Birmingham outrages an object lesson in why natural philosophy should be kept beyond the reach of the masses, knew very little about the internal dynamics of the events in question. Nevertheless, it is certain that the riots gave seekers after natural knowledge considerable pause for thought, and ensured that experimental science would come to rest on rather different foundations in the town during the years to follow. Several commentators,[92] indeed, have remarked on the fact that Birmingham's pure science capability seems to have declined after the 1800s, this despite the fact that its reputation for creativity and inventiveness in the industrial arts persisted undiminished. Whether the early prowess in science and industry had much to do with the religious configuration of the town is the question with which we began this chapter. Yet it has to be conceded that it is extremely hard to demonstrate the kind of causal links which a Weber or a Merton hypothesised. The moral outlook of the Quakers certainly informed their conduct as industrial entrepreneurs, and the unusually tight organisation of the eighteenth-century Friends may also have contributed to their startling success in business. Priestley's science owed a great deal to his Unitarian faith, too. But it is far from proven that he was drawn to a career in experimental natural philosophy because of his religious beliefs. The

[91] See J. H. Burns (ed.), *The Collected Works of Jeremy Bentham: Correspondence*, 11 vols (London, Athlone Press, 1968–2000), vii, p. 297.

[92] See I. Inkster and J. B. Morrell (eds), *Metropolis and Province: Science in British Culture, 1780–1850* (London: Hutchinson, 1983); Money, 'Joseph Priestley in cultural context: part two', 81.

time and the place would also bring forth outstanding Anglican experimentalists and industrialists. Although a number of *savant-fabricants* of
the West Midlands were in fact Dissenters, it seems reasonable to conclude, nevertheless, that they were not a breed fashioned from the very
fabric of religious Nonconformity.

6

The Republic of Letters
in disarray

It will be evident that by the time of the anti-Priestley riots the probability that religion, politics and natural philosophy could be kept
in separate compartments was rapidly diminishing. That the violence
should have been triggered by a dinner to celebrate the French Revolution was no fortuitous event. In the aftermath of the disturbances a
mocking poem[1] would circulate in Birmingham condemning Priestley's
pneumatic chemistry as a vehicle for atheistic materialism. James Watt,
meanwhile, decided to travel to the philosophers' meeting immediately
following the riots with loaded pistols in his greatcoat pockets. In quitting England for exile in America, Priestley expressed his confidence
that a republic must, of necessity, be more favourable to the sciences
than a monarchy. But others were less sanguine. Early in 1792, as Europe
teetered on the brink of another continent-wide conflict, the British
Foreign Secretary, Lord Grenville,[2] gave warning that a new type of warfare was in the making. Entire social orders and systems of government
were now at stake, which implied in turn that hostilities would be
pursued with a rigour and belligerence hitherto unheard of in the century of *lumières*. Implied, too, was the prospect of a mass mobilisation
in which categories not usually much affected by hostilities between
states (merchants, Grand Tourists, *savants*, migrant craftsmen, etc.) would
all be enlisted into the war effort.

---

[1] Langford, *A Century of Birmingham Life*, i, pp. 489–90, 'A POETICAL EFFUSION
On the Writings and Political Principles of Dr Priestley. Presumptious man! Can thy
electric flash / Oppose the great artill'ry of the sky, / And mock the rolling thunder?
Can thy streams / Of philosophic sulphur dim the blaze / Of light celestial?'

[2] E. Sparrow, *Secret Service: British Agents in France, 1792–1815* (Woodbridge:
Boydell, 1999), p. xi.

The abolition by the French National Convention of all learned academies, including the Académie des Sciences, in the summer of 1793 administered a swift corrective to Priestley's confidence. Since the sciences were tainted with aristocracy, the new republic could manage very well without them – or so the *académiciens* were informed. Antoine-Laurent Lavoisier, one of the principal adornments of the old Académie, would fall foul of this chilling logic before the year was out. Arrested and incarcerated for the political sin of being an *ancien-régime* tax farmer, he was guillotined in May 1794 – just as Priestley and his family were heading off across the Atlantic in search of a haven in the New World. Although no fan of aristocracy, or indeed of Lavoisier's own self-proclaimed revolution in chemistry, James Watt concluded that the French revolutionaries had 'murdered philosophy'.[3]

The strains arising from this encounter between polite science, radical political revolution and ideologically motivated warfare provide the theme for the present chapter. It sets out to explain how these decidedly unpolite pressures impacted upon the Republic of Letters as constituted in the late Enlightenment decades. However, the chapter will also show that Watt's gloomy prognostication of the death of natural philosophy was in large measure misplaced. The scientific world that had been fashioned in the 1770s and 1780s would never recover from the twin shocks of revolution and war, to be sure. Instead, it was reshaped into a socio-economic environment more conducive to the rapprochement of science and technology. Nowhere is this more apparent than in France, where the revolution brought *savants* and politicians into a partnership unlike anything witnessed in Europe before.[4] Whether it also forged an enduring partnership between *savants* and *fabricants* is a more open question, although Margaret Jacob, for one, believes that the events of the 1790s and 1800s turned that country firmly in an industrial direction.[5] What is indisputable, however, is that the French Revolution facilitated an extraordinary flowering of techno-science which, in many instances, turns out to have been built on the *savant* foundations of the Republic of Letters.

---

[3] BCL MS 3219/4/124 J. Watt snr to W. Roebuck, Birmingham, 19 April 1795.

[4] See Horn, *The Path Not Taken*, pp. 127–67.

[5] Jacob, *Scientific Culture and the Making of the Industrial West*, p. 182; Horn, *ibid.*, also identifies the thorough-going social and political revolution of the 1790s as the event which facilitated a rerouting of French industrialisation. However, he insists that this development was temporarily arrested by regressive policies pursued during the Napoleonic Empire, and he doubts whether the reorientation was driven by a shift in 'scientific culture'.

Trading in *liberté*

Commerce, industry and scientific enquiry were certainly moving into closer alignment in the final quarter of the eighteenth century, as we have already had occasion to note. The correspondence of *savant-fabricants* such as Boulton, Watt or Keir was neither exclusively mercantile nor exclusively philosophical. For analytical purposes, however, it helps to explore these themes as though they were largely independent areas of activity. As far as the manufacturers of Birmingham and the West Midlands were concerned, the age of freedom began to dawn in 1786, with the signing of the long-awaited trade treaty with Bourbon France. Since Matthew Boulton was one of the largest exporters to the Continent, he was kept abreast of the negotiations by William Eden in a private capacity. But the Birmingham Commercial Committee also sent a representative to Paris with a watching and reporting brief (see Chapter 2). In the meantime the button, buckle and cut-steel trinket workshops took on more labour, and the whole town became a spectacle of near-manic energy. It was the same in the north Staffordshire Potteries, where Wedgwood and his fellow manufacturers were stock-piling goods in anticipation of the lowering of customs duties, and in Manchester likewise. Birmingham's eighteenth-century prosperity would reach a final crescendo in the years 1786, 1787 and 1788. When John Wesley[6] visited the town again in early 1789, he noted that trade had subsided to its usual level and there was even some unemployment.

Matthew Boulton and James Watt were able to take the measure of the opportunities for commercial and *savant* intercourse that were now opening up first hand. In November 1786 they travelled to Paris as guests of a French government which was preparing to embark upon root-and-branch fiscal and institutional reform. The trade treaty was a part, but only a part, of this programme and the stated purpose of their visit was to consult on the repair or replacement of the Machine de Marly. This hydraulic installation raised water from the River Seine to an aqueduct supplying the palaces of Versailles and Marly using 225 forcing pumps, but it was supplying barely half the volume of water produced when it was first set in motion in 1688. In reality, however, it seems that Charles-Alexandre de Calonne, the Controller-General, and Comte de Vergennes, the Foreign Minister, were seeking to buy into their knowledge as metal and steam technologists – probably with a view to encouraging a permanent move to France. Aimé Argand, the Swiss distiller and lamp inventor, acted as go-between and was

---

[6] Ward and Heitzenrater, *The Works of John Wesley*, xxiv, pp. 124–5.

handsomely rewarded for his success in persuading Boulton to interrupt his supervision of the firm's Cornish mine interests and cross the
Channel. On their arrival in the French capital they were feted, not as
businessmen but as inventors and natural philosophers of international
repute. James Watt found the experience quite intoxicating – literally
so. 'To tell you the truth I was much out of my element at Paris', he
informed the chemist Grossart de Virly on returning to Birmingham,
'constantly running about after my superiors & constantly drunk
with Burgundy & undeserved praises.'[7] It is true that 'dress'd with our
Bags & Swords & and our little silk Chapeau Bras',[8] they would have
appeared an odd couple to anyone who knew them from the streets
of Birmingham, or even the coffee houses of London. Dress swords had
ceased to be worn in England, and Matthew Boulton was mortified to
discover on arrival that the swords they had had made specially in a
Birmingham workshop were not of the highest taste, since 'les lames
plattes ne sont plus à la mode'.[9]

Apart from inspecting the Machine de Marly and the Paris pumping stations, Calonne insisted that the pair visit the metalware works at
La Charité in the Berry, which had been set up a generation earlier by
another Birmingham entrepreneur, Michael Alcock. Although it was a
losing concern by the 1780s, the Minister was thinking of relaunching
the venture using his own capital and technological expertise supplied
by Boulton & Watt. Like the Midlands manufacturers, the French, too,
were looking for ways of profiting from the huge increase in trade that
was expected to flow from the signing of the treaty of commerce. For
most of their six-week sojourn in France the partners remained in Paris,
however, enjoying the attention and esteem of fellow natural philosophers as the Republic of Letters materialised around them. At the
Académie they met Berthollet, Laplace, Lavoisier and Monge, with whom
they drank tea. Berthollet, who was 'said to be one of ye best chymists in
france,'[10] afterwards demonstrated to them his chlorine bleaching experiments, and they met him again over dinner at Jacques – Constantin Périer's.
Lavoisier extended an invitation to dine, too, as did the wallpaper manufacturer Jean-Baptiste Réveillon. To judge from Boulton's pocket book,
the pair were also introduced to the editor of the *Journal de physique*,

---

[7] BCL MS 3219/4/123 J. Watt snr to Virly, Birmingham, 9 April 1787.

[8] Mason, *The Hardware Man's Daughter*, p. 77.

[9] BCL MS 3782/12/32 Pradeaux to M. Boulton, Paris, 18 January 1787.

[10] BCL MS 3782/12/108/49 M. Boulton: diaries and notebooks, 1786–7; also P.
M. Jones, 'Les Inventeurs et l'activité inventive dans les archives de Soho', in M.-S. Corcy,
C. Douyère-Demeulenaere and L. Hilaire-Pérez (eds), *Les Archives de l'invention: écrits,
objets et images de l'activité inventive* (Toulouse: CNRS, 2006), pp. 209–10.

Lamétherie, to Sage (at the Hôtel de la Monnaie) and to Vandermonde, then the Keeper of the King's Models. The botanist Pierre Broussonet and Louis-Bénigne Bertier, the Intendant of Paris, who had visited Soho two and a half years earlier, hastened to renew their acquaintance, as did Grossart de Virly. The only notable French chemist to remain beyond reach was Guyton de Morveau, for, as Watt mentioned in a letter to de Virly, the partners had not been able to find the time to travel out to the Sèvres porcelain manufactory.

Controller-General Calonne's fall from power in April 1787 stymied any prospect of technology transfer through official channels, and a contract to fit the Machine de Marly with steam-powered pumps would not be awarded for another twenty years. Calonne's loss of office following the debacle of the Assembly of Notables wrecked any lingering prospect that the firm might secure an exclusive licence to manufacture the Watt steam engine in France, as well. But if the reform-minded ministers of the Bourbon monarchy extracted next to nothing in return for the 1,000 *louis d'or* expended to bring over to France Europe's most celebrated engineers, the trip was not without its benefits for Matthew Boulton and James Watt. With Argand's help they were able to collect from Périer the balance of the monies still owing for the two engines supplied in 1779–80. They were able to vindicate their right of priority in the design of the improved steam technology, despite the misinformation sedulously propagated by Périer and his associates; and of course they had been enabled to make contacts in the Republic of Letters that would last a lifetime. Watt also returned home with a good understanding of Berthollet's new bleaching process, whilst Boulton's encounter with the engraver and tool-maker Jean-Pierre Droz at the Paris Mint convinced him that he possessed the wherewithal to strike coins at a fraction of the usual cost if only Droz could be persuaded to bring his new press and his know-how to Soho. Although Matthew Boulton acknowledged the cultural and institutional impediments to the application of scientific knowledge in pre-revolutionary France, he arrived back in Birmingham with a healthy regard for the speed with which French manufacturers were catching up. Relaying a conversation he had had with both Watt and Boulton on this subject, Samuel Garbett reported: 'their account of the progress the French of [*sic*] made in many of our English Manufactures clearly shew that we are still in possession & that we shall keep it if we are allowed to go to their Market with a Duty not exceeding ten per cent, and that they will get possession if we are not allowed that liberty'.[11]

[11] BCL 510639 S. Garbett to Lord Lansdowne, Birmingham, 6 February 1787.

As one door closed, another opened. Among the entrepreneurs whom Boulton and Watt had met at La Charité was a relative of the Calonnes, Guillaume Foucault, who was involved in procurement for the army. He visited Soho in the late summer of 1789 and was the first to alert Matthew Boulton to the rich pickings to be had from the revolution that was now taking shape in France. He ordered buttons for troop uniforms and buckle chapes. In fact, when the National Assembly introduced anti-sumptuary legislation in a vain attempt to remedy the fiscal deficit, he advised Boulton to expect large orders for copper and copper-gilt items as patriotic citizens cast off their silver shoe buckles. Over the course of the ensuing decade Soho would supply large quantities of buttons for the National Guard, cheap copper medallions depicting the heroes and martyrs of the Revolution, and a small-denomination token currency. Boulton would even be approached to engrave *assignat* plates for *émigré* counterfeiters. He indignantly refused, although in 1803 an order from 'Monsieur' (the Comte de Provence and future Louis XVIII) to manufacture buttons bearing the *fleur de lys* symbol was accepted.

The token currency venture was a particularly risky speculation, and one which proved costly for both Matthew Boulton and his associates in France, the Monneron banking family.[12] It originated in the need to find gainful employment for the mint which Boulton had erected alongside his manufactory in 1787–88. With steam power at his command and a substantial investment in the services and know-how of the *monnaieur* Droz to recoup, it seemed obvious to the Birmingham entrepreneur that the cost and quality advantages of the new technology would quickly secure the market for coin. It is likely that the capitalistic Monneron brothers were thinking along similar lines in 1790 and 1791, for France, too, was desperately short of small-denomination currency – not to mention a currency befitting the new regime. Although supplies of bell-metal were superabundant, the Académie's chemists and metallurgists were encountering difficulties in finding an efficient method of refining the alloy, which would not be overcome before 1794. Moreover, the National Assembly was busily engaged in the institutional restructuring of the kingdom and the moment seemed propitious for root-and-branch currency reform.

What neither party sufficiently calculated were the political sensitivities attaching to coining – particularly in France, where the issuing of tradesmen's tokens was not widely practised. Having failed to secure a

[12] For this episode, see P. M. Jones, ' "England expects . . .": trading in liberty in the age of Trafalgar', in M. Crook, W. Doyle and A. Forrest (eds), *Enlightenment and Revolution* (Aldershot: Ashgate, 2004), pp. 187–203.

regal coinage contract for Great Britain, Matthew Boulton started off by trying to interest the new rulers of France in buying his improved technology lock, stock and barrel (coining presses, cutting-out presses, rolling mill, smelter, engines, etc.). Early in 1791 he sent over to Paris the chameleon natural philosopher and commercial agent Dr Franz Swediaur, whom we have encountered before, with a mandate to negotiate with the committees of government and the more prominent deputies in the National Assembly. The scheme to set up Soho – style mints across the length and breadth of France quickly foundered. Instead, it was replaced with a more modest but still risky venture to strike low-denomination token coins and ship them to France in partnership with the Monnerons. This was risky because the legal status of such coins upon their entry into France was unclear. Inscribed as 'médailles de confiance', the items were styled in such a way that they could either be traded as tokens (with a face value of two or five *sols*) or as medallions. Between October 1791 and August 1792 Soho struck and shipped over six million of these *monnerons*. They entered day-to-day circulation quite easily in Paris and other large cities, just as the partners had anticipated, but without the sanction of government. Only in the aftermath of the uprising of 10 August 1792 and the termination of the experiment with constitutional monarchy was the trade explicitly banned. Boulton was left with a huge stock of cake copper on his hands, which had to be sold at a loss, plus the cost of recalling shipments of coin that were already in transit.

Even in a time of peace, trading in *liberté* was not a business for the faint-hearted, then. A world of privileges and exemptions, patronage and cronyism was fast disappearing. Boulton & Watt's contacts in Paris warned them to drop any idea of franchising the manufacture and erection of steam engines in France by means of an exclusive 'privilege' (i.e., patent). 'Ce mot bless tellement les oreilles régénérées que vous-mêmes ne seriez probablement pas admis à faire valoir vos prétentions',[13] advised one correspondent. Argand, too, fell foul of the wheel of political fortune when his distilling monopoly, supported by Calonne, Vergennes and Breteuil, was overtaken by events, and his French patent for the cylinder lamp became unenforceable. Indeed, the whole edifice of Anglo-French trade would collapse when the revolutionaries repudiated the 1786 commercial treaty in January 1793 and the continental war widened to include Britain a few weeks later. Previous wars may have impeded, but they did not halt the flow of traffic between the two countries. When Jacques-Constantin Périer placed an order for two Watt engines on behalf of

[13] BCL MS 3147/3/391 A. Guyot to J. Watt snr, Paris, 21 February 1791.

the Paris Waterworks Company in December 1778, Britain and France had been engaged in hostilities for the previous five months. Yet Boulton & Watt interceded with the British government to secure shipment papers for what were machine parts notwithstanding, and James Keir, the factory manager at Soho, cheerfully dispatched engine components for loading the following year. This, despite the start of a privateering war and reports that a Franco-Spanish invasion fleet had been sighted off the north Cornish coast. The only difficulties experienced by Périer occurred in November 1779, when the British vessel transporting his precious cargo was denied permission to proceed up the Seine to Rouen and had to unload at Honfleur instead.

The limited and still-genteel character of international conflict prior to the wars of the Revolution and the Empire is underlined further if the Périer episode is juxtaposed with the tribulations of Jan Daniël Huichelbos van Liender when he tried to import a Watt engine into the Netherlands in 1807. Bonaparte's Continental System had made the Dutch coastline very hard to penetrate, and van Liender arranged for carriage in a neutral ship, with strict instructions that it should only set sail from Hull upon news that an import licence had been granted. The old Republic was by now a satellite kingdom within the Grand Empire, albeit one with little enthusiasm for the trade blockade, and a sixth Anglo-Dutch War was under way. In the event, the vessel departed without either insurance or a landing permit. Damaged in a storm, it had to put into the port of Terschelling, where the cargo was confiscated together with the vessel. In a throw-back to the *ancien régime*, van Liender had to use influence at Court to secure the engine's release via the personal intervention of King Louis-Napoléon. But the damage caused by saltwater had still to be made good, and it was not in place and pumping on the Katwijk canal until the autumn of the following year.

Regular trade with revolutionary France stopped abruptly in the spring of 1793, with the consequences for Birmingham and its district that we have already explored. Matthew Boulton sent in his accounts for the Monneron medal and token speculation on 4 March 'as the commerce with France [is] now at a stand'.[14] In the years that followed, revolutionary expansionism gradually squeezed British merchants from continental and Mediterranean markets. Boulton and his fellow manufacturers endeavoured to reroute their exports to American consumers, whilst at the same time seeking out fresh commercial opportunities in the North. But no sooner had new markets been found in

---

[14] BCL MS 3782/12/38 M. Boulton to Bourdieu, Cholet & Bourdieu, Soho, 4 March 1793.

Scandinavia and the Baltic than French power encroached, or commercial frictions with neutral states threatened to boil over. By 1796 Birmingham's trade with the north German towns had been almost completely wiped out, according to a letter written from Städtfeld near Eisenach by Matthew Robinson Boulton's old tutor. Later that year Samuel Garbett confided to Lord Lansdowne that remittances from Holland, Flanders, Spain and Italy had all drained away as well. In fact 1796 and 1797 proved to be crisis years at every level. From backwoods Pennsylvania, Priestley predicted that old England was about to be brought to her knees by economic strangulation, crushing taxation and mutinous radicalism. Meanwhile, the Birmingham Quaker Charles Lloyd was shocked to discover, on visiting the City of London early in March 1797, that his bank notes could no longer be exchanged for cash.

The abiding, indeed increasing, strength of the steam-engine business helped to insulate Boulton & Watt from these difficulties. But Boulton's personal financial embarrassment was exacerbated by an incautious undertaking he had made to Empress Catherine II to supply St Petersburg with a brand new mint. This undertaking – given in 1796 – was intended to spearhead a major reorientation of Soho's manufacturing output in the direction of the Baltic. Very rapidly, however, the risks inherent in such a commercial strategy became apparent. On his mother's sudden death, Tsar Paul I moved to suspend the contract and to cut all ties with Matthew Boulton. In February 1797 the technicians and apprentices who had been sent over to Soho to learn the art of steam-powered coining were instructed to return to Russia forthwith. The mint project would soon be reinstated, thanks, it seems, to behind-the-scenes activity by Boulton's friend, the ambassador Vorontsov. But it remained a losing concern if viewed from a strictly commercial point of view. In the meantime, however, Boulton found his trading strategy in the Baltic and Scandinavia undercut by Britain's worsening relations with the neutral powers – Denmark in particular. This quarrel arose out of Britain's insistence on its right to stop and search neutral merchantmen during a time of war. In the case of the Danes, it was grounded in the strong suspicion that they were abusing their neutral status and allowing belligerent vessels to sail under their flag. When the Danes sought the support of Tsar Paul in the summer of 1800, a fresh League of Armed Neutrality was formed, which was extended to embrace Sweden and Prussia as well as Denmark and Russia.

For Matthew Boulton the next six months or so threatened disaster as Paul impounded British goods and ships and closed the English trading factories in St Petersburg. A tit-for-tat trade war ensued which prompted Boulton to exclaim that he had switched his activities to the northern markets 'little thinking that ye Kings of the Earth would make war upon the private property of individuals by forbidding them to pay their debts to foreigners'. He stood to lose remittances worth £20,000 in the Danish and Norwegian markets alone, 'unless our own Gov^t are pleased to mitigate it by allotting a portion of the Danish property they have seized'.[15] Monies owed by Swedish and Russian merchant houses were likewise frozen. The log-jam was broken by two events: a *coup d'état* against Paul in March 1801 which resulted in the Russian Emperor's death, and the naval action of Admirals Parker and Nelson against the Danish fleet off Copenhagen at the start of the following month. Hugely relieved, Boulton set off to take the waters in Cheltenham on 17 April; and in July his Scandinavian agent, Andrew Collins, reported that he was working his way up the coast of Norway collecting in all debts.

'The sciences are never at war'

Philosophers, even more than merchants, tried to rise above the storm and stress of civil commotions and war. Indeed, there is a persistent thread in the historiography of the sciences which asserts that they were largely successful in doing just that. Commenting on the conditions prevailing towards the end of the eighteenth century, A. Hunter Dupree insists that 'no one saw in the science of that day, however useful, the key to military power by weapons research'. In common with other writers, he cites the remark of Edward Jenner, the physician who demonstrated to the world the efficacy of vaccination against smallpox, that 'the sciences are never at war'.[16] The problem with the argument to the effect that cosmopolitanism and professional solidarity 'soared above the noise of battle'[17] even in an age of visceral nationalism is not that it lacks evidential support but that the balance of the evidence points in a rather different direction. Historians who are inclined to accept the self-image of the Republic of Letters as an intellectual organisation transcending the bonds of religion, nationhood, faction and party tend to focus on what men said rather than on how they behaved. Yet even the correspondence of Sir Joseph Banks, the long-serving President of the Royal Society, reveals, when studied in the round, a tension between the ideal of scientific discourse and the day-to-day reality.

[15] BCL MS 3782/12/46 [draft of] M. Boulton to H. Legge, n.d. [January 1801].
[16] Hunter Dupree, 'Nationalism and science', p. 37; also C. C. Gillispie, *Science and Polity in France: the Revolutionary and Napoleonic Years* (Princeton: Princeton University Press, 2004), pp. 134–5.
[17] Hunter Dupree , 'Nationalism and science', p. 37.

Even before the Republic of Letters was put to the test of the French Revolution and the wars of Napoleon, it could be found wanting, as Giuliano Pancaldi[18] points out in his reconstruction of Alessandro Volta's manoeuverings to secure recognition. Nearer to home, Joseph Priestley discovered the Royal Society less than transparent to deal with on two occasions. In 1771 he responded positively to an informal invitation to join Captain Cook's second voyage to the South Seas (albeit as an astronomer). The invitation, if ever it was issued, was soon withdrawn – leading Priestley to insinuate in a letter to Banks that he had been blackballed on grounds of religious Nonconformity. Nearly two decades later the Royal Society declined to elect the *savant-fabricant* Thomas Cooper – again for reasons of religion – despite a galaxy of accredited backers which included Priestley, Kirwan, Crawford and Watt, not to mention Boulton and Wedgwood. Joseph Priestley would exclaim that Cooper's knowledge of chemistry even exceeded his own. In this connection it is significant that professional support for Priestley during his own hour of need came chiefly from continental natural philosophers. Over 100 in France alone deplored the actions taken against him during the Birmingham riots of 1791. Even very ordinary members of the Republic of Letters with no particular interest in pneumatic chemistry were shocked by the fate that had befallen his library and laboratory. The Baron de Sainte-Croix, a correspondent of the Avignon antiquarian Esprit Calvet, claimed that he had been unable to sleep for several nights on receiving the news.[19] Yet the Royal Society responded with churlish silence, and when the *savants* of the Manchester Literary and Philosophical Society displayed a reluctance to show solidarity, several members, including Thomas Cooper and James Watt junior, resigned from that body in protest.

The political threat to the integrity of the Republic of Letters was brought to bear more insidiously at first, however. All over Europe, but particularly in France, the pursuits of natural philosophy were overtaken by a more immediate and tangible agenda focused on the reform of institutions. To the surprise and dismay of English *savants*, the spectacle of France's slide into full-blown political revolution transfixed philosophers, in common with nearly every other branch of Europe's intelligentsia. Calvet's web of correspondents may have practised a studied detachment, but the *académiciens* were closer to the scene of the action and experimental work rapidly ground to a halt. One of Sir Joseph Banks's most reliable Paris correspondents was Pierre Broussonet and

[18] Pancaldi, *Volta: Science and Culture in the Age of the Enlightenment*, pp. 104, 151, 169–76.
[19] Brockliss, *Calvet's Web*, p. 348.

he would report as early as January 1789 that science had given way to politics. As the first year of revolution drew to a close, Gaspard Monge confirmed this judgement, and the following year James Watt complained to the Manchester *savant-fabricant* Charles Taylor that he had heard very little from his French chemist friends because they were too absorbed in the affairs of state to be bothered with natural philosophy experiments. Only Berthollet held out for a time and continued to service the Republic of Letters. With rare single-mindedness he began a fresh round of bleaching and dyeing experiments even as the Bastille was being demolished, and would publish his findings in the *Annales de chimie* that same year. Having narrowly avoided a lynching during the first frenetic spasm of revolution, Lavoisier had turned his attention to financial matters, according to one of Marc-Auguste Pictet's correspondents. Pictet, too, had turned away from experimental natural philosophy and in the direction of journalism, owing to the need to make a living following the loss of his investments in the French funds.

There were other reasons for the harvest shortfall in scientific news, of course. In 1791 the secretary of the Royal Society, Joseph Planta, attributed the dearth of information being laid before the Fellows to the recent sprouting of more specialised scientific societies.[20] Nevertheless, it seems indisputable that revolution in France was having a damaging impact on the public output of science even before the war severed communications and put scientific sociability to the test. The Birmingham *savants* relied principally on Swediaur in order to know what was going on at the Académie, although reports of the jubilation with which Black and Kirwan's defection to the anti-phlogistonian camp had been received in Paris reached them via Alexandre Guyot. Early in 1792, however, Thomas Cooper and James Watt junior travelled to the French capital on a thinly disguised mission of revolutionary fraternisation. They gravitated towards the political Left, where they found most of the chemists aligned. After visiting La Rochefoucauld, Fourcroy, Guyton de Morveau, Hassenfratz 'and other first rate chemists' at Lavoisier's house, young Watt reported to his father, 'but not a word of Chemistry was there spoken, they are all mad with politics'.[21] We know, too, that Berthollet had stopped work, or rather that he had been elected a Justice of the Peace and deployed to other duties. As everyone awaited the news of the outbreak of a war between France and the German

---

[20] H. Hecht, *Briefe aus G. Chr. Lichtenbergs englischen Freundkreis* (Göttingen, 1925), pp. 28–9.
[21] BCL MS 3219/4/13 J. Watt jnr to J. Watt snr, Paris, 22 March 1792; also P. M. Jones, 'Living the Enlightenment and the French Revolution: James Watt, Matthew Boulton and their sons', *Historical Journal*, 42 (1999), 157–82.

Powers in April 1792, he announced to the Dutch *savant* Martinus van Marum that scientific activity was virtually paralysed.

Europe remained at war from 1792 until 1814, apart from a twenty-month truce known as the Peace of Amiens (1801–3). It is scarcely surprising, therefore, that the functioning of the Republic of Letters should have been disrupted. But the Revolutionary and Napoleonic Wars cut communications in a more fundamental way, as the states embroiled in the conflict with France strove to insulate themselves from the ideological contamination of revolution. This placed natural philosophers in an unenviable situation. If the 'ping-pong' of the Republic of Letters did not altogether cease, it became extremely hit and miss. And when philosophers did manage to sustain some semblance of slow-motion play, they became vulnerable to accusations of disloyalty. Unlike any previous period of hostilities, the British government took steps to control the movement of foreigners in and out of the country, whilst a traitorous Correspondence Act passed in May 1793 endeavoured to control other forms of communication and to prevent British subjects from travelling to France, or residing there without a permit. The contrast with the relaxed attitudes prevailing during earlier conflicts could not have been starker. In Birmingham the flow of visitors to Soho (see Figure 3.1) fell sharply from the spring of 1793. Parties of *émigrés* continued to arrive at the factory gates, but the movements of other French nationals were subject to restrictions imposed by the Alien Office. The flow of scientific correspondence seems to have diminished, too, although it is difficult to know how far letters were being intercepted, or lost in transit. The editors of Pictet's extant correspondence estimate that perhaps 30 per cent of letters dispatched from Britain to Geneva during these years never arrived.[22]

As President of the Royal Society, Sir Joseph Banks did his best to keep lines of communication open, but in 1794 and 1795 conditions were scarcely propitious. The old Académie des Sciences had been abolished, and at the height of the Terror the Robespierrist Convention passed savage legislation requiring the execution of British and Hanoverian prisoners of war on the spot. Those who survived encounters on the battlefield or on the high seas were often interrogated by agents of the Comité de Salut Public for useful knowledge about technological processes. The *Transactions* of the Royal Society remained undelivered; meanwhile the Birmingham *savants* complained that French scientific journals could not be obtained at any price. This paralysis of the Republic of Letters eased slightly in 1796 and early 1797, thanks

---

[22] *Marc-Auguste Pictet, Correspondance*, iii, p. xxi.

in part to several high-profile cases in which Banks played the honest broker between warring governments. Having secured the release of the French naturalist J.-J. La Billardière's specimen collection, which had been sent to Britain and impounded following the surrender of his vessel to the Dutch in Java, Banks expressed the sentiment that 'the science of two Nations may be at Peace while their Politics are at war'.[23] This was in June 1796, but the collapse of peace negotiations at the start of the following year brought the atmosphere of partial *détente* to a speedy close. In November 1797 the London papers reported that the French Directory had established an 'Army of England' for a prospective invasion, and with the Jacobins in the ascendant once more, all English speakers, whether British, Irish or Anglo-American, were given notice of expulsion.

Dr Joseph Priestley and Thomas Cooper observed these events from afar, for they had emigrated to America in common with several hundred other English dissenters in religion and politics. A scheme mooted by Joseph Priestley junior, Cooper, Robert Southey and Samuel Taylor Coleridge to establish an agrarian commune for Rational Christians in north-central Pennsylvania quickly foundered, leaving old Priestley with little option but to do what he alone knew best. From his distant outpost in the Republic of Letters, he reworked the scriptural prophesies and refought the controversies that had divided the chemical community in the 1780s and early 1790s, apparently unaware that the French natural philosophers, at least, were now being enlisted into the war effort. It is true that what little philosophical news made its way across the Atlantic and up the Susquehanna River was generally out of date. 'I never was so far behind hand in philosophical intelligence',[24] he confided in a letter to Theophilus Lindsay – not an English newspaper, book or pamphlet having reached him in the course of 1799. His interventions in the world of letters lacked cogency, in consequence. Indeed, they are chiefly revealing as pointers to his own intellectual journey. In an open letter to the French chemists on the subject of phlogiston, he employed metaphors drawn from the Revolution in urging the case for free debate and the avoidance of scientific absolutism. Persuasion alone could establish consensus; by this route 'your power will be universally established, and there will be no Vendée in your dominion'.[25]

---

[23] D. R. Dawson (ed.), *The Banks Letters* (London, 1958), p. 906.
[24] Rutt, *Life and Correspondence of Joseph Priestley*, ii, p. 421.
[25] *Open Letter to the French Chemists, 15 June 1796*, cited in *Autobiography of Joseph Priestley: Memoirs written by Himself.* Introduction by Jack Lindsay (Bath: Adams, 1970), p. 44.

The signing of Peace Preliminaries with France in October 1801, followed by a definitive treaty some six months later, made it safe to travel on the high seas once more. Joseph Priestley senior could have returned to the European science fray at this point had there been anything to return to. His New Meeting lieutenant, William Russell, whose preoccupations were mostly biblical and humanitarian rather than scientific, certainly quit his American asylum at this point with the intention of returning to Britain by way of France. The immediate by-product of the Peace, however, was a resumption of trade, a dramatic increase in visitor flows across the Channel (see Figure 3.1) and, in consequence, a re-energising of the Republic of Letters. The British Minister in Paris issued over 3,000 travel warrants between June 1802 and April 1803,[26] and the repercussions were soon felt in Soho. Birmingham manufacturers had been preparing to flood the reopened European market since the previous autumn, in fact, although they were to be disappointed in respect of France. Bonaparte's Consular regime was protectionist in outlook and showed no interest in negotiating an open-door trade treaty to replace the one repudiated in 1793. Nothing could be as bad as the dark months of the winter of 1800–1, however, and Matthew Boulton remained confident as he showed the new visitors around his rebuilt mint: 'although the French government may prohibit the Manufactories of England they are not so absurd as to prohibit English knowledge or so illiberal as to reject an Invention because it happen'd to be mine'.[27]

The continental tour of James Watt's youngest son, Gregory, can be used as a measure of the revival of the Republic of Letters. He set off in September 1801 and accessed the Continent by way of Hamburg, since France and Holland were still out of bounds to English travellers. However, he encountered the French geologist Déodat de Dolomieu whilst staying at an inn in Lausanne. Dolomieu had not forgotten Banks's efforts to secure his release, or at least to ease his confinement, when a prisoner of Britain's ally the King of Naples, and he helped the young man to obtain a passport for Paris. Gregory was therefore able to do the rounds of the French capital in December 1801, just as his half-brother had done in 1792 and his father in 1786–87. Apart from Volta's demonstrations of his electric pile at the Institut National there was little to report, and most of his time seems to have been spent refurbishing the links in the philosophers' network. By this date epistolary correspondence between the nodes of the Republic of Letters had also been

[26] J. D. Grainger, *The Amiens Truce: Britain and Bonaparte, 1801–1803* (Woodbridge: Boydell, 2004), pp. 130–1.

[27] BCL MS 3782/12/47 [copy of] M. Boulton to H. Herisse, Soho, 1 October 1802.

reactivated. Matthew Boulton managed to dispatch a gift of coins struck in his new mint to Berthollet, for which he received cordial thanks in late September, and Argand made contact, after a long silence, from Versoix on the Swiss border in December.

Many of England's reformers and natural philosophers were ardent admirers of Napoleon Bonaparte (Russell, Cooper, Priestley, Blagden, etc.). There was a real sense of shock, in consequence, when the unappetising reality of the First Consul's approach to state power and scientific progress became apparent. But the British were guilty of genteel hypocrisy in matters to do with scientific knowledge transfer and technology as well. For all the protestations of undying amity, neither side regarded the Peace of Amiens as anything more than a pause in an unfinished conflict. As the first institutional contact with the Royal Society for many years, Sir Charles Blagden's arrival in Paris in March 1802 was feted, but Bonaparte soon lost interest in him and by the time of his departure some thirteen months later Blagden stood accused of having visited France in order to carry out a spying mission. The British, too, had lost much of the bonhomie with which they had treated inquisitive visitors in the 1780s, and the Alien Office kept a close watch on some of the new arrivals. The young mining engineer and *polytechnicien* Auguste-Henri de Bonnard secured access to James Watt senior by tendering a letter of introduction signed by Gaspard de Prony, but his was scarcely a courtesy call predicated on the uninhibited exchange of knowledge. Bonnard toured the country's mining regions in the company of Erik Svedenstierna, calculating that he was less likely to attract attention, and refusals, if travelling with a Swedish metallurgist.[28] As the peace began to unravel and his activities to provoke suspicion, he hastened back to France.

Bonaparte's largely functional attitude towards the Republic of Letters and the civilities of enlightened discourse became painfully apparent on 23 May 1803, when an order was made to round up and detain all British subjects, military and civilian, who were then residing or travelling in France, or in territories controlled by France. The measure was promulgated five days after the Royal Navy had begun attacking French vessels, and three days after the news of the resumption of the war became widely known in Paris. Whilst not entirely without precedent, this blurring of the status of combatant and non-combatant amounted to a rewriting of international law. Anxious as always to maintain the distinction between philosophers and ordinary belligerent mortals, Sir Joseph Banks nonetheless labelled the measure in a letter to the

---

[28] Grainger, *The Amiens Truce*, pp. 134–5.

secretary of the Institut National as 'manifestly subversive of the mutual interest of civilised nations'.[29] The French authorities proceeded to detain some 7,500 British hostages, or so they claimed, to which number many thousands of prisoners of war were added once hostilities had resumed in earnest. Even if no more than 1,000 non-combatant Britons were permanently deprived of their freedom of movement, as seems probable, the figure still amounted to a spectacular erosion of the consensual assumptions on which warfare had previously rested. Conscious that a line had been crossed, the British government adamantly refused to exchange French prisoners of war for the hostages, lest it confer an aura of validity on their detention.

The Russells, father and son, who were residing on an estate which they had purchased near Caen, were caught by Bonaparte's 'hostage' law. But since both claimed to be American citizens and were known to be French sympathisers and refugees who had fled England in 1794, they were soon exempted from its provisions. Besides, they would both secure French citizenship in 1807 and 1809 respectively. More serious was the case of the Edgeworths. Richard Lovell Edgeworth, the erstwhile Lunar member, had brought his family to Paris in October 1802. He attended sessions of the Institut, where his enthusiasm for the First Consul rapidly cooled, while his daughter Maria was a welcome guest in the salons as the recognised author of *Practical Education* (1798). Tipped off that the war was likely to resume, the family headed for home the following March. However, Maria's elder brother, Lovell, was residing in Geneva and did not receive his father's warning in time. In the rush to quit the city in May 1803, he was apprehended and marched to Verdun, where he was detained for six years. 'Poor Lovel! Alas! He is still in the clutches of the detestable tyrant, Buonaparte',[30] wrote Anna Seward to one of her correspondents. When finally allowed to leave France in 1814, he returned a stranger to his family.

As the contest for the domination of the western world entered its final and most aggressive phase, the internationalism underpinning the Republic of Letters broke down almost completely. Sir Joseph Banks interceded in a personal capacity on behalf of Fellows of the Royal Society and others with scientific credentials who had been apprehended, but his efforts were not appreciated by a home government that was preoccupied by contingency planning to meet an invasion threat. To hard-headed ministers, petitions to release French prisoners of war as

---

[29] G. de Beer, *The Sciences were never at War* (Edinburgh: Nelson, 1960), p. 136.
[30] *Letters of Anna Seward written between the years 1784 and 1807*, 6 vols (Edinburgh, 1811), v, p. 206.

a *quid pro quo* for easing the plight of English men of letters made no sense at all. The Birmingham *savants* received pleas for help, too. In 1810 the *académicien* Pierre Lévêque, whose corn mill company had sought an engine from Boulton & Watt at the start of the Revolution, urged James Watt to intercede on behalf of his son, who was held as a parole prisoner in Lichfield. Three years later the offspring of the original partners were contacted by their old tutor, pastor Reinhard of Stadtfeld, with the request that they interest themselves in the fate of the son of the Baron von Boyneburg, a neighbour and a mutual acquaintance, who had been incarcerated on the island of Ibiza. All they could do, or were willing to do, was to make enquiries and to refer the matter to ministers. Watt senior did at least go through the motions, aware perhaps that Lévêque had been instrumental in securing his election two years earlier as a corresponding member of the Institut. He rounded off his reply with the usual refrain: 'if I had any Philosophical news I should trouble you with them on this occasion, but having none permit me . . .'[31]

The visit of Sir Humphry Davy (and his assistant Michael Faraday) to France in the autumn of 1813 is sometimes instanced as evidence of Bonaparte's transcendent commitment to the sciences. Yet the trip was an anachronism, notwithstanding the urgings of the Institut, and it was criticized on both sides. *The Times* newspaper fulminated at the prospect of Davy setting foot on enemy soil, and when the party arrived at the cartel port of Morlaix the local authorities initially refused to accept the authenticity of their passports. Since 1806 all formal contact between Britain and Napoleonic Europe had been shut down. Bonaparte's Berlin Decree (21 November) even terminated postal services as well as human intercourse, whilst Britain's counter-measures (the Orders-in-Council of 7 January 1807) targeted neutral states trading with France and launched a blockade of French ports. For the next five years Britain stood isolated and desperate. In such conditions scientific knowledge exchange appeared an irrelevant luxury, unless it could be channelled into the war effort. Fearful lest Denmark's fleet fall into French hands, the Royal Navy bombarded Copenhagen in September 1807. This reckless action, which saw Sir William Congreve's high-tech rockets deployed effectively for the first time, was widely denounced as the bullying of a small and neutral country. For Thomas Bugge, the Danish astronomer, it marked a sad end to the Scientific Enlightenment. In a letter to Martinus van Marum[32] he recounted, in French, how the

---

[31] BCL MS 3219/4/120 J. Watt snr to P. Lévêque snr, Heathfield, 14 March 1810.
[32] Forbes, Lefebvre and Bruijn, *Martinus van Marum*, vi, p. 63.

'perfidious English' had caused 305 houses to be razed to the ground, including his own, with the loss of 7,000 books, maps and a collection of mathematical instruments – in short, a lifetime's work.

Towards techno-science

The rocket designer Congreve's experiments and trials at the laboratory in the Woolwich Arsenal were known to Matthew Boulton, although he seems only to have visited Soho in 1816 as part of the entourage of Grand Duke Nicholas of Russia. Neither Boulton nor any of the other West Midlands *savant-fabricants* were formally enlisted into the war effort. The Birmingham gun-makers received large orders directly from the Board of Ordnance, it is true, but by and large the know-how and engineering capacity of the Birmingham manufacturers were mobilised on a *laissez-faire* basis and without any attempt to interfere with production methods. One of the windfalls of the Revolution had been the emigration of 80,000 French nationals, among whom numbered several talented military engineers and artillery specialists. One such was A.-P.-D. de Loyauté, who persuaded Boulton in 1795 to build him a new kind of mortar or grenade launcher, which was subsequently trialled at Carlton House gardens. Soho was the first port of call for many a military inventor, in fact, although we should be wary of assuming that they were all activated by patriotic or nationalistic motives. Robert Fulton, the American pioneer of steam-powered boats, only turned to James Watt junior for technological backing in 1804, when the French government showed a lack of appreciation of the potential of his submarine vessel. In view of his provenance, the firm responded to his enquiries with a caution bordering on disdain. Utilitarianism now increasingly prevailed at the two Soho manufacturing sites, but it would be going too far to discern a shift to a species of techno-science fuelled by the needs of the war. Instead, Boulton's retreat from the ornamental and the fashionable – like the late-century retreat from speculative natural philosophy – formed part of a much broader cultural transition which can be documented in other parts of Europe, too. In all likelihood the practice of science would have evolved in a similar manner in France also, had it not been for the outbreak of political revolution.[33]

[33] According to Horn in *The Path Not Taken*, the revolution made possible in France a unique institutional synthesis rooted in political liberalism and state interventionism to promote technological advance. He identifies the Consulate (1800–4) as the period in which these strands began to be combined productively.

Whilst quitting England in the summer of 1794 William Russell, his two daughters and his son had been taken captive in the Channel by a French frigate. In an episode heavy with irony and not a little danger, they were held for four months on a hulk in Brest harbour within sight of the guillotine. When, in December, the Comité de Salut Public took notice of their existence, they were released with instructions to proceed forthwith to Paris 'pour conférer sur des objets d'industrie manufacturière'.[34] Once in the capital, William was interrogated at the behest of the Committee: What did he know about the manufacture of English steel? How was enamelling undertaken? How was Bristol brass made? What could he tell them about the screw-cutting machinery employed by the Wyatt brothers at their mill near Birmingham? How was coal tar extracted ('. . . on nous a dit que Milord Dundonald avoit établi des fourneaux pour cette opération'),[35] etc., etc. Clearly, French intelligence-gathering agents had done their work well over the previous fifteen years. The embattled Republic had discovered, too, that it could not manage without scientists. The natural knowledge of Fourcroy, Hassenfratz, Guyton-Morveau (who had dropped his seigneurial *particule*), Monge, Berthollet and Laplace was enlisted for the war effort. These individuals have been described as 'techno-jacobins',[36] as if to emphasise the extent to which natural philosophers became a part of the governing elite of France as a result of the Revolution. Yet the term is scarcely apt, for they served all regimes and were loaded with the trappings of power as a consequence. Fourcroy, Monge and Berthollet all became Counts of the Empire, and Laplace a Restoration peer. Only Jean-Henri Hassenfratz truly deserves the title of 'jacobin'.

Nevertheless, something had happened in France which happened nowhere else in Europe at that time. Natural philosophers and engineers were absorbed into government and invited to bring their scientific knowledge to bear on technical problems which politicians and planners had prioritised for solution. If the paternity of the *savant-fabricant* in France remains an unresolved issue, the Revolution unquestionably gave birth to the phenomenon of the *savant-politicien*. However, this outcome was not as straightforward and predictable as some accounts seem to suggest.[37] Unlike England, France was not ineluctably embarked on

---

[34] S. H. Jeyes, *The Russells of Birmingham in the French Revolution and in America, 1791–1814* (London: Allen, 1911), p. 99; also P. M. Jones, ' "Fraternising with the enemy": problems of identity during the French Revolution and the Napoleonic Wars', in J. Kalman, I. Coller and H. Davies (eds), *French History and Civilization. Papers from the George Rudé Seminar* (Melbourne, 2005), pp. 38–44.

[35] British Library Add. MSS 44992 William Russell papers, vol. 1, item 108.

[36] K. Alder, *Engineering the Revolution*, p. 282.

[37] See, in particular, Gillispie, *Science and Polity in France*.

the road to utilitarian science as the *ancien régime* drew to a close, and nor was French technology bound to take a theoretically informed and statist turn after 1789. As we have already had occasion to remark, there are grounds for supposing that the gap between the natural sciences and the mechanical arts was still substantial on the eve of the Revolution. According to Christian Licoppe,[38] indeed, it may even have been widening. Matthew Boulton had sensed this paradox when chronicling all the establishments devoted to the propagation of the sciences in Paris during his 1786–87 visit. Cultivation of knowledge and the business of putting it to work were not at all the same thing.

However, once France found herself at war with the rest of Europe and once the revolutionaries had resolved their internal political divisions, the situation began to change quite rapidly. In the autumn of 1793 a committee of the legislative body – the Comité de Salut Public – emerged as the first in a series of war governments. It ruthlessly reorganised and conscripted so as to ensure that the Republic possessed the material wherewithal to defeat its enemies. Whereas the Board of Ordnance in London invited tenders and placed contracts, the Comité de Salut Public in Paris sought to revamp the nation's entire arms-manufacturing economy, and with impressive results. Louis-Bernard Guyton-Morveau would claim in a report presented to the legislature in 1795 that the capital's small-arms workshops were producing 9,000 muskets and pistols a year before September 1793, an output which rose to around 145,600 over the next thirteen months.[39] Political sympathies apart, French chemists were accustomed to carrying out the tasks of government, for this was the basis on which the old Académie had functioned, unlike the Royal Society. Mass production of side-arms chiefly mobilised craft skills, of course, but the work undertaken into propellants, ballistics, aeronautics or, for that matter, the extraction of sugar from beet all presupposed experimental research. It was in these areas that the Comité and its successors tried hard to bridge the science–technology interface, and with some degree of success.

Yet this was war work pursued in secrecy – a concept inimical to the Republic of Letters and the whole character of Europe's Enlightenment. Sir Joseph Banks, who was neither an experimentalist nor a manufacturer, nor at the beck and call of government, could afford to take the moral high ground. In a remark triggered by William Wollaston's initial refusal to disseminate the results of his own investigations into

[38] See Chapter 3, p. 116.
[39] Alder, *Engineering the Revolution*, p. 288; also Horn, *The Path Not Taken*, p. 142 and note 36.

palladium, he declared in 1805: 'the keeping of secrets among men of science is not the custom here; & those who enter into it cannot be considered as holding the same situation in the scientific world as those who are open & communicative'.[40] Manufacturing *savants* such as Boulton and Watt had already faced this dilemma, as we know, and the Comité de Salut Public showed no compunction whatsoever about installing its research chemists and technicians in a top-secret experimental testing station at Meudon, just outside Paris. If there had been any such thing as an international conversation going on between natural philosophers by this date, one can only wonder what they would have found to talk about. Perhaps it was just as well that James Watt was no longer in letter contact with Berthollet, Virly and Monge.

The aerostatic experiments which had seemed so exciting and fashionable in the 1780s were taken up again at Meudon, but this time with a view to military use. After the science of high-volume hydrogen production and storage had been optimised, a great deal of ingenuity was brought to bear on the practical side of manufacturing balloons so that they could be kept aloft in a tethered position for aerial reconnaissance. Different varnish formulae were tried and Alexandre Vandermonde, the mathematician, who had moved into weapons research, was sent to the silk-weaving city of Lyons to ensure that sufficient quantities of fabric would be forthcoming. Transporting all the apparatus for use *in situ* by the Armée du Nord proved no easy matter, though. Nevertheless, the deployment of a tethered balloon, with *aérostiers* in a gondola reporting enemy positions during the battle of Fleurus (26 June 1794), was pronounced a success. There were few, if any, other occasions when reconnaissance balloons were used in combat by the revolutionaries or by Napoleon's field commanders. Nevertheless, in 1813 *The Times* would unhesitatingly condemn ballooning on the ground that it was a Frenchified science.

As the questions directed towards William Russell suggested, the main thrust of the revolutionaries' techno-science in these years was metallurgical, however. In the 1790s, still, the French were not able to match the quality of English steel. Matthew Boulton would normally send cast-steel billets to France when he needed dies engraving rather than trust to locally produced, or what was called 'German', steel. The onset of war exacerbated the problem: in 1800 Augustin Dupré, the *graveur-général des monnaies*, complained that supplies brought in from Germany were not fit for purpose, and when European markets were altogether closed to British trade from 1806–7 the situation became much worse. Cast-steel

---

[40] Gascoigne, *Science in the Service of Empire*, p. 147.

orders reaching the Huntsman firm in Sheffield from the Continent virtually dried up. Hence the urgency with which the revolutionaries set about tackling the bottleneck. Although Dupré thought that the hardening of his dies after tempering was due to their loss of phlogiston, the French chemists had accurately explained the role of carbon in the manufacture of steel some years earlier. The problem was, rather, to connect the science to the technology. This was achieved, or rather attempted, when Vandermonde, Berthollet and Monge (the original authors of the 1786 *Mémoire sur le fer*) drew up a practical manual at the behest of the Comité de Salut Public which was specifically aimed at the ironmasters and forge workers whose job it was to produce the steel. This thirty-four page illustrated *Avis aux ouvriers en fer sur la fabrication de l'acier* was distributed in 15,000 copies throughout the metal-working districts of the Republic. Whether it achieved the desired result may be questioned, however. Although targeted at those possessing craft skills only, the old problem of finding an appropriate language, which had taxed Charles-Augustin Coulomb, intervened. 'Ne croyez pas qu'il soit possible à des ouvriers en fer de faire de l'acier à l'aide du seul mémoire que vous avez fait distribuer', *représentant-en-mission* Pierre Roux-Fazillac informed the Comité from the mines and forges of the Dordogne, 'il est trop savant et intelligible seulement par des ouvriers qui savant en faire'.[41]

The issue of bell-metal is worth considering again in this context, for the revolutionaries were not unaware of the difficulties that Matthew Boulton foresaw in the refining process. On the other hand, they were well supplied with able research chemists whose time and labours could be recruited in the hunt for solutions. The principal copper works had been set up at Romilly-sur-Andelle near Rouen before the Revolution, with the aid of know-how and skilled foundry-men brought over from Britain. But Romilly existed chiefly to roll and hammer copper strip for ships' hulls – it did not smelt and had little experience of refining bell-metal alloys. As we know, it was coining which incited the first attempts to discover a method that would recover the copper from bell-metal in industrial quantities. Throughout 1790 and 1791 various techniques were tried to remove the 30 to 40 per cent of tin in the alloy,

---

[41] D. Woronoff, *L'Industrie sidérurgique en France pendant la Révolution et l'Empire* (Paris: EHESS, 1984), p. 253; see also Horn, *The Path Not Taken*, pp. 147–55. The author provides an informative account of the steel-making initiatives of the Comité de Salut Public to buttress his conclusion that 'a strong state governing a rich nation undergoing a Revolutionary crisis *could* jump start industrial production and compete technologically at the highest international level (p. 167)'. Representative Roux-Fazillac's deflating response to the Comité is not mentioned, however.

using an oxidant, in the reverberatory furnaces at Romilly. Boulton and the Monnerons, meanwhile, moved into the market for low-denomination copper coin. It was the war crisis of 1793 and the urgent need for field artillery which really spurred these efforts, however. Gun-metal, unlike copper strip for coining, required the retention of some of the tin in the molten bronze, which in turn presupposed a consider-able amount of foundry skill in knowing when to arrest the recovery process. Once the procedure had been perfected, in 1794, the Comité hastened to disseminate it in a craft manual, or *Instruction sur l'art de séparer le cuivre du métal des cloches*. Again, thousands of copies were printed. The war had interrupted the importation of cake copper, just as it had closed off access to good-quality cast-steel, and the French Republic had to fend for itself, using its own resources and ingenuity.

In an atmosphere of international *détente* Sir Joseph Banks was elected a foreign associate of the Institut National, the body which had replaced the Académie des Sciences, in December 1801. Even though peace was impending, his acceptance of this French-bestowed honour provoked criticism at home. For all the stress and strain caused by revolution and war, natural philosophers were hugely reluctant to suspend the protocols of the Republic of Letters, or to concede that the 'public' version of science pioneered by the Enlightenment might have had its day. In May 1802 (two months after the signing of the definitive peace treaty between Britain and France), Blagden would even entertain, in a letter to Banks, the idea that the First Consul be elected a Fellow of the Royal Society – a proposal that would have looked grotesque a year or so later, had it ever become known.[42] For all his conviction that natural philosophy had been 'murdered' by the French revolutionaries and his lack of illusions about Bonaparte, James Watt, too, found him-self the recipient of French scientific honours. One day in July 1808 an American visitor turned up at Soho carrying the certificate of his election as a corresponding member of the Institut.[43] It was a measure of the disarray into which the Republic of Letters had fallen, however, that the bearer was unknown, and that Watt was embarrassed to know how to respond. He eventually penned a formal letter of thanks and passed it over to Banks for onward transmission. But even two years later he was unsure whether it had actually been delivered in Paris. Not until the very end of 1810 was indirect contact re-established. Samuel Widmer,

[42] G. de Beer, 'The relations between the Fellows of the Royal Society and French Men of Science when France and Britain were at war', *Notes and Records of the Royal Society of London*, 9 (May 1952), 276.

[43] BCL MS3219/4/33 J. Watt jnr to J. Watt snr, Soho, 27 July 1808.

the nephew of the textile printer Oberkampf, obtained Napoleon's permission to cross the Channel on a factory inspection tour, and he presented himself at Soho with a letter of recommendation signed by Count Berthollet. It was through this medium that James Watt was able to inform the oldest of his French philosopher acquaintances that he had largely abandoned chemistry in favour of mechanics. Indeed, he was now working on a stone-cutting machine 'which promises to be useful in the imitative arts'.[44]

Lavoisier's execution did not signal the eclipse of natural philosophy, as it turned out, then. On the contrary, the partnership between *savants* and political actors which the Comité de Salut Public improvised as a war-time measure would usher in a golden age of French scientific achievement. Some historians have therefore concluded that France's entire scientific culture was altered as a result of the Revolution and the Empire. Margaret Jacob, for instance, argues that 'by 1810 the French had put in place the elements of a new scientific culture that glorified application as much as it championed the entrepreneur'.[45] The juxtaposition of Britain and France invites a more nuanced conclusion, however, as Jeff Horn has pointed out.[46] There was certainly plenty of rhetoric in circulation glorifying the progress made in bridging the arts and the sciences after 1789. A scientist-statesman of no less a calibre than Jean-Antoine Chaptal proudly recorded how, in his wake, 'beaucoup d'autres chimistes ont formé de grands établissements et c'est à cette heureuse révolution que nous devons la conquête de plusieurs arts et le perfectionnement de tous'.[47] Indeed, it is in the emblematic career and influence of Chaptal that Horn finds the most compelling evidence of the effectiveness of France's new state-sponsored route to industrialization after 1815.

Yet this kind of self-congratulation was commonplace on the morrow of the revolution, and in Horn's account it is not at all clear what Chaptal actually achieved. Most of the initiatives with which he was associated seem more evocative of the institutions being nurtured by Bourbon *dirigisme* in the 1780s. We would do better to concentrate on the evidence in the workshop. This evidence suggests that the gulf between the two countries in terms of the theory and application of science was widening in the 1790s, and continued to widen into the 1800s and 1810s.

---

[44] BCL MS 3219/4/120 J. Watt snr to Comte Berthollet, Heathfield, 26 December 1810.

[45] Jacob, *Scientific Culture and the Making of the Industrial West*, p. 181.

[46] Horn, The Path Not Taken, especially pp. 194–216.

[47] J. Pigeire, *La Vie et l'oeuvre de Chaptal, 1756–1832* (Paris: Spès, 1932), p. 103; also Gillispie, 'The natural history of industry', 398–9.

Whilst in England and Lowland Scotland Industrial Enlightenment was beginning to blur into Industrial Revolution, in France there remained, in practice, a considerable credibility gap between the *savant* and the *fabricant.*

Bridging this gap required more than simply a harnessing of state will-power and the market. Indeed, it is arguable whether a proactive state should be considered the critical ingredient for industrial progress at all. But even in this sphere the post-revolutionary regime in France pursued contradictory objectives. Napoleon personally expressed the Empire's preoccupation with economic development by visiting industrial premises (Oberkampf's vast workshops at Jouy in 1806 and 1810; Benjamin Delessert's beet sugar refinery at Passy in 1812). Yet at the same time the Continental System starved France of British know-how and technology, whilst ruthlessly manipulating the economies of subject states to suit the perceived needs of 'la Grande Nation'. Marc-Auguste Pictet, whose own city-state had long since been annexed to France, seemed to grasp what was happening better than most. Congratulating Davy in 1813 on his *Elements of Chemical Philosophy* (1812), he remarked: 'the work is worthy of your name, and of your country, in which the sciences are now cultivated with more speed and success than anywhere else, on account of the tranquillity you enjoy while Europe is upside down'.[48] Only after 1814, when the sea lanes and the ports reopened and visitors began to beat a path to the West Midlands and the industrial north of England once more, did France's reconstituted elite of semi-professional *savants* truly come to appreciate the size of the gulf that had opened up.

What of the Republic of Letters? Few scholars have attempted to follow the 'conversations' going on between members of Europe's intelligentsia across the revolutionary watershed – no doubt for good reasons. As we have seen, communication between the Birmingham philosophers and their peers on the Continent came to a virtual standstill for a period in the mid- and late 1790s, and again after 1806. On the basis of his study of Esprit Calvet's network of correspondents, Lawrence Brockliss[49] concludes that the 'Republic' did not unravel as a consequence of the Revolution in France, even if it went very quiet during the Terror. Letter writing resumed after 1795, cautiously at first and then more vigorously once Napoleonic stabilisation began to take effect. However, the post-revolutionary construct – viewed through the lens of Calvet's correspondence – lacked the international flavour and federal structure of the old Republic of Letters. Chronology apart, our study offers no real

[48] *Marc-Auguste Pictet, Correspondance,* iii, p. xxiii.
[49] Brockliss, *Calvet's Web,* pp. 354–69.

ground for dissent from these conclusions. Even before 1789 there had been tensions between philosophers, rivalries between experimental communities, and competing scientific methodologies. The older generation of *savants* to which Matthew Boulton, James Watt and James Keir belonged would probably have preferred to forget about the posturings of the 1790s and 1800s, had that option been available to them. In 1814 they made a conscious effort to rethink the Republic of Letters as they had known it in middle age. Indeed, Watt was expecting a long-delayed visit from Count Berthollet in the summer of 1819 when he succumbed to his final illness. Boulton, of course, died a bed-bound 'spectator in this deranged world',[50] without ever seeing the conclusion of the duel between Britain and France. They were no longer in charge when the peace finally came, though, and the new generation, epitomised by the younger Watt and his partner Matthew Robinson Boulton showed, little interest in reactivating their geographical corner of the Republic of Letters. The projectors of the Soho Foundry were businessmen, not *savant-fabricants*.

[50] BCL MS 3782/12/48 [draft of] M. Boulton to R. Ramsden, 8 December 1803.

7

Conclusion

I nvited to comment on the business plan of a London acquaintance who had just launched a factory to produce domestic furnishings, Matthew Boulton finally allowed what those around him had accepted for some time. After fifty years as a merchant-manufacturer, he concluded that there was little money to be made in fashion goods, quite the opposite in fact: 'it is better to work for the gross mass of the people of the world, than for the lords and princes of it'. As a result he had given up those branches of his manufactory 'which depend on fashion & tast such as Golden toys or ormolu ornaments, paintings etc. & in lieu thereof is building iron furnaces & foundrys which he knows is more perminant & more profitable in proportion to their being more usefull to the publick'. These lessons of experience, he intimated, had been passed on to his son in the form of advice 'never to engage in any manufactory that depends on Fashion, tast, Caprice & Fancy of lords and ladies but to confine his persuits to things usefull rather than ornamental'.[1] It is true that 1796 – the year in which this advice was proffered and taken – would mark a difficult passage in Soho's fortunes. But Boulton's candid self-appraisal also acknowledged that he and his fellow Birmingham manufacturers were caught up in a more far-reaching adjustment that can be described as a retreat from some of the core cultural values associated with the English Enlightenment.

Most of the output of the Soho Manufactory had been ornamental, in fact. As such it signalled Matthew Boulton's life-style ambition to identify with the polite and cosmopolitan culture of the second half of the eighteenth century, and to gather around him like-minded individuals who were keen to 'live' this Enlightenment and to preach its virtues to the other inhabitants of the West Midlands. Fortunately the manufacture

[1] BCL MS 3782/12/41 [draft of] M. Boulton to E. G. Eckhardt, 1796.

of buttons and buckles enabled him both to project his ambitions and to remain in profit; it subsidised the less successful excursions into the ornamental and the tasteful: ormolu, silversmithing and mechanical paintings. The move in the direction of the utilitarian had started in 1774 with the arrival on the scene of James Watt and the successful bid to extend the patent on his improved steam engine. Although another decade would pass before the commercial potential of the machine became fully apparent, Boulton could certainly afford, by 1796, to adopt a deprecating tone towards his earlier endeavours. By this date, indeed, the steam engine had become an integral part of the Soho enterprise, and the decision to concentrate on the functional rather than the ornamental was less a choice than a necessity. Yet it was a decision which brought momentous consequences in its wake. By 1796 Watt's patent had only four more years to run and, if competitors in the steam-power business were to be forestalled, an integrated foundry and engineering works would need to be established. The Soho Foundry was set up on an eighteen-acre site about a mile distant from the old manufactory, in consequence, and by the time it was fully fitted out – in 1803 – something over £30,000 had been ploughed into the venture. By 1826 the total capital expenditure on the site had risen to £60,253.[2] In order to protect this investment from prying eyes, both the Soho Manufactory and the Soho Foundry were closed to visitors from 1802 – in theory if not always in practice. Whilst Boulton could see the sense of these entrepreneurial decisions, there is sufficient indirect evidence to show that he accepted them with some reluctance. The old partnership had been restructured in 1794 so as to bring on board the sons, and he was no longer alone in the driving seat. Nothing captures this change of regime more vividly than the contrasting architectural styles between 'old' and 'new' Soho. Whereas the old manufactory was an eye-catching neo-Palladian building, the design for the new foundry was severely utilitarian (see Figure 2.5). Not a penny was spent on ornamentation, or on facilities for sightseers.

At the end of the eighteenth century 'utility' was a concept with several connotations, as we have already had occasion to observe. For a Joseph Priestley the utility of natural philosophy extended far beyond its role as a signifier of polite culture. Indeed, he viewed the sciences essentially as a vehicle for the revelation of God's Creation, although he would not have neglected their capacity to generate useful knowledge, for all that. No doubt these were the reasons why he felt so acutely

[2] J. R. Immer, 'The Development of Production Methods in Birmingham, 1760–1851' (DPhil dissertation, University of Oxford, 1954), p. 56.

his separation from the Lunar Society, for that body remained wilfully, even playfully, non-dogmatic in matters to do with natural philosophy, as in matters to do with religious faith. Members certainly discussed topics of immediate practical relevance, but they did not confine themselves to such topics, and there is no sound reason for supposing that they devoted the bulk of their convivial hours to such discussions either. It would be quite wrong as well as anachronistic, therefore, to envisage the Lunar Society as little more than a technological 'think tank' for the Industrial Revolution. Yet a cultural shift in the direction of 'utility' as it would be understood by the Victorians was undoubtedly taking place by the century's end. The Lunar Society gracefully faded away and it was replaced, in Birmingham, by a new institution whose remit was more improving than speculative.

This was the Philosophical Society. Edward Thomason, a Soho apprentice made good, was one of the founders and he described in his memoirs how the body came into being in 1800 as a private society consisting of six members with a mission to improve one another's knowledge and skills in the fields of electricity, pneumatics and mechanics. By 1803 the Society embraced twenty members and had been put on a more formal footing, and over the ensuing decade it went from strength to strength. By 1812 there were about 200 subscribers, and a move was afoot to purchase and fit out dedicated premises. The Society also changed its name to the Birmingham Philosophical Institution, in emulation of the Royal Institution – a clear pointer to how the role of science in a rapidly industrialising provincial environment was shaping up. The aim was to purvey useful knowledge in genteel surroundings, by means of lectures rather than table-talk and discussion, to a second generation of well-heeled Birmingham manufacturers and professionals. The emphasis was placed on dissemination rather than discovery, and on objects rather than theories. The new premises opened up in 1814 presupposed an emphatically non-participatory audience arranged in semi-circular fashion on crimson-cushioned seats.

Analysis of the membership of the Philosophical Society indicates scarcely any overlap with the Lunar generation, although a polite invitation was issued in 1807 to the bed-bound Boulton. On the other hand, Samuel Galton junior's son Tertius became a stalwart of the new organisation, and Matthew Robinson Boulton – old Boulton's son – is recorded as having attended the lectures also. A sense of the transition of generations that was now in progress, as well as some understanding of the shifting boundaries of science and technology, was expressed by Francis Horner, the Whig politician, when he visited the West Midlands in 1809 as a house guest of the Galtons. Following a tour of Birmingham and an afternoon spent examining geological specimens collected by James Keir as a by-product of his Black Country mining operations, he mused in a letter to Lord Webb Seymour:

> my short excursion into Warwickshire proved very agreeable. I made the acquaintance of several persons whom I was curious to see, and some of whom I shall be very happy to see again. The remnant of the Lunar Society, and the fresh remembrance in others of the remarkable men who composed it, are very interesting; the impression which they made is not yet worn out, and shows itself, to the second and third generations, in a spirit of scientific curiosity and free enquiry, which even yet makes some stand against the combined forces of Methodism, Toryism, and the love of gain.[3]

The exchange of knowledge, whether for fun, or driven by curiosity, the desire for human betterment, or by the conviction that it would help to improve existing technologies, has been the central preoccupation of this book. Most of the evidence for the enquiry has been gleaned from two overlapping sources: the records of visitors to Matthew Boulton's Soho Manufactory during the second half of the eighteenth century, and the correspondence files of members of what might be termed the West Midlands branch of the Republic of Letters. The conceptual frame which has contributed most to our reading of what was taking place in this regional theatre is Joel Mokyr's notion of an Industrial Enlightenment. It invites us to explore the knowledge dynamic which he locates at the heart of the Industrial Revolution on the hypothesis that the build-up of 'useful' knowledge would be critical to the unleashing of a self-sustaining cycle of modernisation in the western world. This study has only explored the initial stage of the process outlined by Mokyr, that is to say, the stage where the knowledge-generating and disseminating capacity of the European Enlightenment interacted with sites of potential technological creativity to provide the fuel for a chain reaction of innovation. On the other hand, the book has strayed beyond the strict requirements of a verification of Mokyr's thesis in some respects. We have seen, for example, how Boulton and his coterie withheld knowledge as well as exchanged knowledge; also how sensitive knowledge sometimes escaped their powers of control altogether. His teasing remark to a Dutch correspondent underlines the different qualitative levels at which the knowledge economy operated by the century's end: 'if I was to take you into my Mint you wou'd be none the Wiser for you wou'd see 8 improv'd Coining Presses at work without any visible Cause or Assistance from any human Being, & they are so constructed as to be incomprehensible

---

[3] L. Horner (ed.), *Memoirs and Correspondence of Francis Horner MP edited by his Brother Leonard Horner Esq. FRS*, 2 vols (London: Murray, 1843), ii, p. 2.

to the best Mechanic by merely seeing them'.[4] The evolving etiquette of knowledge dissemination is also illustrated in this quotation, and it constitutes another area in which our study has moved outside the parameters of Mokyr's thesis.

But how do Joel Mokyr's contentions fare when confronted with the findings of a case study? It is clear that the sharpness with which he formulates the steps leading to the production of 'useful knowledge' – the critical ingredient which Industrial Enlightenment bequeathed to the Industrial Revolution – cannot be neatly evidenced. As stated in Chapter 1, the bracketing of oral and 'hands-on' wisdom alongside 'pure' scientific knowledge seems arbitrary; or at least it makes sense only if we assume that eighteenth- and early nineteenth-century folk knowledge was rapidly codified. In Mokyr's terms, that it was swiftly incorporated into the sum total of propositional knowledge. On the whole, however, the evidence of our study suggests that this was not the case. There are good grounds for concluding, too, that Mokyr does not allow sufficiently for the extent to which socio-cultural 'context' shaped the nature and content of technical knowledge, or even impeded its transmission altogether. Nevertheless, the overall dynamic of useful knowledge generation by the process of cross-fertilisation, or conversion, rings true and finds powerful support in this study. The same may be said of Mokyr's feedback hypothesis, according to which advances in technological understanding provoked, in turn, further additions to the propositional knowledge base. 'Industrial Enlightenment' is a valuable addition to our conceptual toolkit, then, whether it is understood as a characterisation of a particular kind of society gestated in the interstice between the Scientific and the Industrial Revolutions, or as a model of the technological preconditions for economic growth.

Chapter 2 of our study depicted a particular kind of society, or emblematic site of interaction, for Industrial Enlightenment. It is unlikely that Birmingham and its district were unique in this regard. Yet the fact remains that the primary sources required in order to mount an investigation of this type are far more plentiful for the West Midlands than they are for Manchester and its district, or for Lowland Scotland. The role of the Birmingham *savants* in helping both to generate and to manage the flow of experimental scientific knowledge during the second half of the eighteenth century formed the subject of Chapter 3. It explored the links and overlaps between the popular market for science facts, discoveries and inventions, the Lunar group of natural philosophers, and the wider international web of knowledge purveyors. The formal codes which ostensibly governed behaviour within the Republic of Letters

---

[4] BCL MS 3782/12/48 M. Boulton to H. de Heus, Soho, 31 March 1803.

were illustrated by reference to the Soho Manufactory and Matthew Boulton's understanding of the obligation of civility.

The longest and perhaps the most important investigation to be undertaken in this book came next. For it was in Chapter 4 that the mechanics of communication between possessors of natural knowledge and possessors of technical know-how were subjected to close scrutiny. In the course of this scrutiny we found it more helpful to elide Mokyr's categories of *savant* and *fabricant*, for the empirical evidence undoubtedly points in this direction, and not just for the West Midlands. Moreover, the elision largely overcomes the problem which preoccupies Mokyr – namely the documenting of the process of communication. It is nonetheless true that the science–technology interface could not be automatically bridged in this fashion. Much depended on cultural and institutional contexts, and when we look to Europe for comparators it is evident that formidable barriers to *savant* communication continued to subsist well into the nineteenth century. Indeed, the failure to communicate and wilful non-communication of knowledge 'secrets' remained a besetting problem even during the high decades of the European Enlightenment. It could put men such as Matthew Boulton and James Watt who asserted a claim to the status of *savants* as well as manufacturers in an ambivalent, not to say contradictory, position. Once the retreat from the values associated with the high Enlightenment had been sounded, this difficulty became acute, moreover. Knowledge transfer via osmosis and emulation faltered, and more aggressive forms of industrial espionage replaced genteel intelligence gathering. Embedded knowledge – in men and machines – posed a particular challenge. The persistence of enticement and the growth of skilled labour mobility throughout Europe after 1820 give the lie to the notion that artisanal practices were swiftly encoded and hand tools easily replicated.

It is significant that Francis Horner should have mentioned Methodism when reflecting on his visit to the West Midlands and the challenges confronting the spirit of free enquiry. By the 1800s most of Birmingham's workshops were 'infected' by Methodism, to judge from our sources, and the Evangelical Revival has often been depicted as inimical to the pursuit of pure science. Erasmus Darwin, indeed, had been caught up in the politico-religious backlash against those holding non-orthodox views since the mid-1790s, and prior to his departure for America Priestley would complain that Dissenting Sunday schools were being accused of 'making the common people too knowing'.[5] Nevertheless, there is little evidence that Methodism was weakening Birmingham's enterprise

---

[5] Rutt, *Life and Correspondence of Joseph Priestley*, ii, pp. 207–8, letter addressed to Mr Gough, Clapton, 25 August 1793.

culture during these years, or diminishing the inventive capacity of the craft workers of the West Midlands. It is true that John Wesley had been unenthusiastic, if not hostile, towards the deductive sciences. But speculative natural philosophy was no longer in fashion, and he would doubtless have endorsed the improving thrust of what passed for science in the Birmingham Philosophical Institution. In Chapter 5 our study explored the relationship between religious beliefs, scientific enquiry and industrial activity in an effort to reach some broadly applicable conclusions. In this area, however, we can only agree with John Brooke[6] that general theses about the interaction of science and religion are extraordinarily difficult to sustain when put to the test of case-study evidence.

Neither Robert Merton nor Max Weber (Chapter 5) offers a convincing explanation of why the ingredients of Industrial Enlightenment should be present in such abundance in Birmingham and the Black Country and not elsewhere. Whilst we were able to document the reality of protestant Dissent throughout the region, a claim that Dissenters contributed disproportionately to the expansion of the epistemic base in the late seventeenth and the eighteenth centuries would be entirely speculative. This judgement must apply to the conversion process by which technologically useful knowledge was generated also. The *savant-fabricant* was not by nature a Dissenter. Those who were nonconformist in religion were, by the second half of the eighteenth century, remarkably conforming in most other respects. Polite culture transcended sectarian difference by and large, and in Birmingham at least Dissenters were almost completely integrated into the system of local government – however rudimentary it may have been. Only the Quakers sought to maintain an existence on the margin. But even their sense of apartness weakened as the century unfolded and Birmingham's affluent and consumerist Enlightenment began to take its toll on them. In any case, Quaker prowess in science and industry probably owed more to their moral outlook and tight-knit social organisation than to the specifics of their religious beliefs. The shock of the 1791 riots enabled opponents of the Dissenters to label them as dangerous scientific dabblers, it is true, but the charge was gratuitous, and of course it overlooked the nonpartisan character of the town's preoccupation with natural philosophy at every social level.

The riots did curtail Birmingham's experiment with Enlightenment as an aspiration towards human emancipation, however. Or to put it another way, they interrupted the cultural trajectory on which the town's elite had been embarked since the 1760s. The anachronism of the term

6 Brooke, *Science and Religion*, p. 5.

'Enlightenment' presents a problem for researchers, whether they use it to descry a Europe-wide phenomenon or one with discrete national or regional characteristics.[7] It is unlikely that any of the West Midlands intelligentsia brought back to life in these pages made use of the term as a noun. Nevertheless, it is a reasonable assumption that all would have recognised themselves as belonging to a generation that was making unprecedented moral and material progress; and some at least would have fashioned a role for themselves as participant members of a wider philosophical community that was actively engaged in thinking about the mechanics of human betterment.

The growth of the West Midlands as a highly integrated region with Birmingham as its hub helped to foster this process. In Chapter 2 we charted the development of the town as a transport node – a trend which bound Birmingham and the Black Country metal-working sites ever more tightly together whilst serving to differentiate the district from Coventry and the Midlands towns to the east. It was the expanding demographic and industrial presence of Birmingham on the route map of provincial England that drove the mercantile and professional bourgeoisie to endow the town with commensurate cultural institutions from the 1760s onwards. In the process they succeeded in domesticating the Enlightenment as a form of polite culture for a time, even if the riots eventually exposed the limits of the exercise. Cultural institutions could not engineer social cohesion on their own, and we can surmise that many a Birmingham button-stamper or pin-header would have regarded polite culture with indifference or impatience. In the final analysis, however, it was the town's leading citizens who would undermine their own creation – by falling out over matters of religion.

The affront to middle-class self-esteem administered by the events of 1791 was all the greater in that it was accompanied by the realisation that the French Revolution was not the practical triumph of philosophy after all. On receiving the news of the September 1792 prison massacres in France, Charles Burney spoke for every member of the English liberal intelligentsia when he asked rhetorically: 'is this the end of the 18th century, so enlightened & so philosophical?'[8] James Watt's commitment to measured parliamentary reform was tested by the defection of his eldest son to the revolutionary camp along with Thomas Cooper and Joseph Priestley junior, and it was found wanting. Both partners, in fact, would play a role in damping down the sparks of artisan

[7] See Robertson, *The Case for the Enlightenment*, pp. 10–44.

[8] J. Gascoigne, *Joseph Banks and the English Enlightenment: Useful Knowledge and Polite Culture* (Cambridge: Cambridge University Press, 1994), p. 240.

radicalism in the Birmingham of the 1790s. But when the French revolutionaries turned from annihilating one another to the systematic
demolition of the *ancien régime* across the face of Europe, the Republic of
Letters found itself cruelly exposed. As the penultimate chapter of this
study makes clear, a *savant* discourse committed to the free exchange
of information and rooted in an honour code borrowed from the nobility could scarcely have expected to survive unscathed. By 1794 the very
building blocks of the Republic of Letters – academies, reading clubs
and transnational correspondence networks had all become deeply suspect to governments. The circulation of technical knowledge in pre-
1789 Europe had never been frictionless, to be sure, and nor had the
theory and the practice of intercourse between natural philosophers
always perfectly coincided. But the French revolutionaries brought a
radically new approach to the eighteenth-century knowledge economy
into play, and for a time it produced significant results in terms of knowledge conversion and feedback. In conditions of revolution, war and
national embitterment, then, it is more surprising, perhaps, that the
Republic of Letters managed to survive intact for as long as it did.

After repeated journeys to London and the constant jolting of his
kidneys on the cobblestones of the capital, Matthew Boulton's health
broke down in his seventy-fourth year. After 1802 he rarely left Soho
and was bed-bound for most of the time. That spring he began to call
in his funds from the country banks, observing wryly: 'my doctors say
my only chance of continuing in this World depends on my living quiet
in it'.[9] He would die on 17 August 1809. As a token of respect the 500
or so employees of the Manufactory and the Foundry were given the
day off, and a remarkably secular funeral medal was struck at the Soho
Mint to record the event. It is said that thousands lined the route taken
by the cortège to the parish church of Handsworth. Old James Watt
retired from business with a huge sigh of relief in 1795–96. His health
had always been parlous, but the decision to withdraw from active management of the several industrial concerns operating from Soho seems
to have given him a fresh lease of life. He would outlive his erstwhile
partner by ten years. The day-to-day running of the Foundry, which by
now was the chief money-making component of Boulton's legacy, fell
on the shoulders of James Watt junior, and until the 1830s this engine-
building business appears to have prospered. The old Manufactory
slipped into the doldrums, however. No longer visited and increasingly
neglected, workshop space was leased to other companies. A pocket
guide to Birmingham published in 1849 described its operations as 'of

[9] BCL MS 3782/12/47 M. Boulton to T. Hart & Sons, Soho, 28 March 1802.

comparatively little importance'.[10] When Johann Conrad Fischer,[11] the Swiss ironmaster, visited yet again in 1851, he was taken aback to find that the buildings were semi-derelict. His old friend James Watt junior had passed away three years earlier and there was no one left to provide continuity. Between 1858 and 1863 the site was cleared and the land sold for redevelopment. Whilst Soho House, Matthew Boulton's welcoming private residence, still stands, it looks out over a sea of terraced red-brick houses. Scarcely any trace of the Soho Manufactory remains.

[10] *A Pictorial Guide to Birmingham being a Concise, Historical, and Descriptive, Account of the Great Midland Metropolis* (Birmingham: Allen & Son, 1849), p. 167.

[11] Henderson, *J. C. Fischer and his Diary*, p. 12.

Bibliography

Manuscript primary sources

British Library, London (Manuscripts)

Add. MSS 44992–45022 William Russell (1740–1818): correspondence and family papers.

Birmingham City Archives (Birmingham Central Library)

MS 3147 Boulton & Watt Collection

MS 3147/3 correspondence and papers, 1769–1895.
MS 3147/3/5 letters from M. Boulton to J. Watt snr, 1781.
MS 3147/3/391 general correspondence, G, 1785–1795.
MS 3147/3/485 letters from A. Argand, 1785–1799.
MS 3147/3/509 letters from J.-H. Magellan, 1777–1785.
MS 3147/3/510 Marly, French patent, 1778–1787.
MS 3147/3/516 letters and papers relating to Périer and Motteux, 1777–1786.

MS 3219 The Papers of James Watt and Family

MS 3219/4/38–54 James Watt snr, incoming correspondence, 1796–1819.
MS 3219/4/56; 61–23; 66 James Watt snr, incoming correspondence, 1764–1776.
MS 3219/4/78; 80B; 86; 88–90 James Watt snr, incoming correspondence, 1774–1799.
MS 3219/4/91; 93–98 James Watt snr, incoming correspondence, 1781–1805.
MS 3219/4/99–102; 104; 111; 113 James Watt snr, incoming correspondence, 1784–1809.
MS 3219/4/117–124 James Watt snr, copy press letter books, 1782–1819.
MS 3219/4/125–126 James Watt snr, outgoing correspondence, unbound letters, 1779–1796.

MS 3219/4/141–172 James Watt snr, notebooks and cash memoranda books, 1779–1818.

MS 3219/4/267–271 James Watt snr, personal papers, letters to Ann Watt, 1780–1793.

MS 3219/6/6–13 James Watt jnr, copy letter books, 1792–1816.

MS 3219/7/1–4 Gregory Watt, incoming letters, special correspondents, 1792–1804.

MS 3219/7/6 Gregory Watt, correspondence, letter book, 1802–1804.

MS 3782 Matthew Boulton Papers

MS 3782/12/1–9 Matthew Boulton, letter books, 1766–1792.

MS 3782/12/23–55 Matthew Boulton, general correspondence files, 1758–1809.

MS 3782/12/56–57; 60; 65; 75; 77–79 Matthew Boulton, special correspondence files, 1764–1806.

MS 3782/12/91 Matthew Boulton, special subject files: French coinage, 1791–1793.

MS 3782/12/98 Matthew Boulton, special subject files: Paris, Marly waterworks, 1777–1789.

MS 3782/12/107–108 Matthew Boulton, diaries and notebooks, 1774–1808.

Miscellaneous

263547–48 Withering family letters, 2 vols.

331068 compensation claim: W. Hutton [1791].

386813 minute book of the Birmingham Police Committee, 1789–90.

510639 photostatic copies of letters from Samuel Garbett to Lord Lansdowne, 4 vols, 1766–1802.

MS 218 diary of Julius Hardy, button maker of Birmingham, 1788–93.

MS 263924 J. Bisset, commonplace book.

MS 3101/C/D/10/9 Galton papers.

MS 661782 Russell family of Moseley.

MS 399801 Church of the Messiah 238 'Inventory of the House and Goods of Dr Joseph Priestley which were destroyed during the Birmingham Riots of 1791'.

Archives of the Birmingham Meeting (Bull Street, Birmingham)

Register of members, 1789–1807.

Cornwall Record Office (Truro)

AD/1583/1–12 Boulton & Watt and Thomas Wilson Correspondence, 1780–1800.

Manchester Patent Library (Manchester)

MS 608 'A list of Patents granted to 1852 to persons resident in Manchester'.

Deutsches Museum (Munich)

Handschriftenslg. Des DM. 8277; HS 6168 Tagebuch von Georg von Reichenbach, 1791.

Websites

http://linnaeus.c18.net/letters The Linnaean correspondence.
www.histpop.org/ohpr Online historical population reports.

Postgraduate theses

Bebbington, P. S. 'Samuel Garbett, 1717–1803: a Birmingham Pioneer'. M. Comm dissertation, University of Birmingham, 1938.
Bushrod, E. 'The History of Unitarianism in Birmingham from the Middle of the Eighteenth Century to 1893'. MA dissertation, University of Birmingham, 1954.
Cumberland, A. G. 'Protestant Nonconformity in the Black Country, 1662–1851'. MA dissertation, University of Birmingham, 1951.
Immer, J. R. 'The Development of Production Methods in Birmingham, 1760–1851'. DPhil dissertation, University of Oxford, 1954.
Robson, G. 'Religion and Irreligion in Birmingham and the Black Country'. PhD dissertation, University of Birmingham, 1998.
Whitehead, D. 'Georgian Worcester'. MA dissertation, University of Birmingham, 1976.

Printed primary sources

A Pictorial Guide to Birmingham being a Concise, Historical, and Descriptive, Account of the Great Midland Metropolis. Birmingham: Allen & Son, 1849.
A Sketch of the Life of James Keir Esq. F.R.S. with a selection from his Correspondence. London: Taylor, n.d. [1859].
Annals of Agriculture, 16 (1791).
Aris's Birmingham Gazette.
Autobiography of Joseph Priestley: Memoirs written by Himself. Introduction by Jack Lindsay. Bath: Adams, 1970.
Beckmann, J. *Anleitung zur Technologie.* Göttingen, 1777.
Bicknell, J. *Musical Travels through England by Joel Collier.* London, 2nd edn, 1775.
Bisset, J. *A Poetic Survey Round Birmingham With Brief Description of the Different Manufactories of the Place.* Birmingham: The Author, 1800.
Blanqui, A. *Voyage d'un jeune français en Angleterre et en Ecosse pendant l'automne de 1823.* Paris, 1824.
Burns, J. H. (ed.), *The Collected Works of Jeremy Bentham: Correspondence*, 11 vols. London: Athlone Press, 1968–2000.

Carlid, G. and Nordström, J. (eds), *Torbern Bergman's Correspondence.* Volume 1: *Letters from Foreigners to Torbern Bergman.* Stockholm: Almqvist & Wiksell, 1965.

Carvalho, J. de. 'Correspondência científica dirigida a João Jacinto de Magalhães', *Revista da Faculdade de Ciências da Universidade de Coimbra,* 20 (1951), pp. 93–283.

Cavallo, T. *The History and Practice of Aerostation.* London: Dilly, 1785.

Dawson, D. R. (ed.), *The Banks Letters.* London, 1958.

Dupin, C. *Voyages dans la Grande-Bretagne entrepris relativement aux services publics de la Guerre, de la Marine, et des Ponts et Chaussées en 1816, 1817, 1818 et 1819,* 6 vols in 3. Paris: Fain, 1820–24.

Elias, R. H. and Finch, E. D. (eds), *Letters of Thomas Attwood Digges, 1742–1821.* Columbia: University of South Carolina Press, 1982.

Epistolario di Alessandro Volta. Edizione nationale sotto gli auspice dell'Istituto Lombardo di scienze et lettere e della società italiana di fisic, 5 vols. Bologna, 1949–55.

Faujas de Saint-Fond, B. *Description des expériences de la machine aérostatique de MM. de Montgolfier.* Paris, 1784.

Faujas de Saint-Fond, B. *Voyages en Angleterre, en Ecosse et aux Iles Hébrides,* 2 vols. Paris: Jansen, 1797.

Faujas de Saint-Fond, B. *Travels in England, Scotland, and the Hebrides,* 2 vols. London: Ridgway, 1799.

Faujas de Saint-Fond, B. *A Journey through England and Scotland to the Hebrides in 1784,* 2 vols. Glasgow: Hopkins, 1907.

Forbes, R. J., Lefebvre, E. and Bruijn, J. G. de (eds), *Martinus van Marum: Life and Work,* 6 vols. Haarlem: Tjeenk Willink & Zoon, 1969–76.

Forster, G. *Voyage philosophique et pittoresque en Angleterre et en France fait en 1790 suivi d'un essai sur l'histoire des arts dans la Grande-Bretagne.* Paris: Buisson, an IV.

Goede, C. A. G. *The Stranger in England or Travels in Great Britain,* 3 vols. London, 1807.

Gury, J. (ed.), *Marc de Bombelles: Journal de voyage en Grande-Bretagne et en Irlande 1784.* Studies in Voltaire and the Eighteenth Century, 269, Oxford: Voltaire Foundation, 1989.

Hecht, H. *Briefe aus G. Chr. Lichtenbergs englischen Freundkreis.* Göttingen, 1925.

Horner, L. (ed.), *Memoirs and Correspondence of Francis Horner MP edited by his Brother Leonard Horner Esq. FRS,* 2 vols. London: Murray, 1843.

Hutton, W. *An History of Birmingham to the End of the Year 1780.* Birmingham: Rollason, 1781.

Hutton, W. *Court of Requests: their Nature, Utility, and Powers Described with a variety of Cases, determined in that of Birmingham.* Birmingham: Pearson and Rollason, 1787.

Hutton, W. *An History of Birmingham.* Birmingham: Thomas Pearson, 3rd edn, 1795.

Keir, J. *The First Part of a Dictionary of Chemistry.* Birmingham: Pearson and Rollason, 1789.

King-Hele, D. (ed.), *The Letters of Erasmus Darwin.* Cambridge: Cambridge University Press, 1981.

King-Hele, D. (ed.), *The Collected Letters of Erasmus Darwin.* Cambridge: Cambridge University Press, 2007.

Kroker, W. von. *Wege zur Verbreitung technologischer Kenntnisse zwischen England und Deutschland in der zweiten Hälfte des 18 Jahrhunderts.* Berlin: Duncker & Humboldt, 1971.

Lalande, J. *Journal d'un voyage en Angleterre 1763, publié avec introduction par Hélène Monod-Cassidy.* Oxford: Voltaire Foundation, 1980.

Letters of Anna Seward written between the years 1784 and 1807, 6 vols. Edinburgh, 1811.

Letters of Wedgwood, 3 vols. Manchester and Stoke-on-Trent: privately printed, n.d.

Levere, T. H. and L'E. Turner, G. *Discussing Chemistry and Steam: the Minutes of a Coffee House Philosophical Society, 1780–1787.* Oxford: Oxford University Press, 2002.

Lichtenberg's Visits to England as Described in his Letters and Diaries. Translated and annotated by Margaret L. Mare and W. H. Quarrell. Oxford: Clarendon Press, 1938.

Marc-Auguste Pictet, 1752–1825. Correspondance: sciences et techniques, 3 vols. Geneva: Slatkine, 1996–2000.

Memoirs of Richard Lovell Edgeworth Esq Begun by Himself, and Concluded by his Daughter Maria Edgeworth. London: Bently, 3rd edn, 1844.

Morgan, K. (ed.), *An American Quaker in the British Isles: the Travel Journal of Jabez Maud Fisher, 1775–1779.* Records of Social and Economic History, new series XVI. Published for the British Academy by Oxford University Press, 1992.

Pratt, S. J. *Harvest-Home: consisting of supplementary Gleanings, original Drama and Poems, contributions of literary Friends and select republications*, 3 vols. London: Richard Phillips, 1805.

Price, J. *An Historical Account of Bilston: from Alfred the Great to 1831.* Bilston, 1835.

Priestley, J. *A Free Address to Protestant Dissenters as Such.* London: G. Pearch, 1769.

Raistrick, A. (ed.), *The Hatchett Diary: a Tour through the Counties of England and Scotland in 1796 Visiting their Mines and Manufactories.* Truro: Bradford Barton, 1967.

Relazioni di Marsilio Landriani sui progressi delle manufatture in Europa alla fine dell Settocento a Cura di Mario Pessina. Introduzione di Aldo de Maddalena. Milan: Edizione Il Polifilo, 1981.

Rutt, J. T. *Life and Correspondence of Joseph Priestley*, 2 vols. London: Hunter and Eaton, 1831–32.

Schofield, R. E. (ed.), *A Scientific Biography of Joseph Priestley, 1733–1804: Selected Scientific Correspondence.* Cambridge, Mass: MIT Press, 1966.

Scott, W. *Stourbridge and its Vicinity.* Stourbridge: Heming, 1832.

Simond, L. *Voyage d'un français en Angleterre pendant les années 1810 et 1811*, 2 vols. Paris, 1816.

Sir Edward Thomason's Memoirs during Half a Century, 2 vols. London, 1845.

Southern, J. *A Treatise upon Aerostatic Machines containing Rules for calculating their Powers of Ascension*. Birmingham: Pearson and Rollason, 1785.

Tann, J. (ed.), *The Selected Papers of Boulton & Watt*. Volume 1: *The Engine Partnership*. Cambridge, Mass: MIT Press, 1981.

The Birmingham, Wolverhampton, Walsall, Dudley, Bilston, and Willenhall Directory; or Tradesman's Useful Companion. Birmingham, 1780.

The New Birmingham Directory, and Gentleman and Tradesman's Compleat Memorandum Book: Containing a Brief Description of the Town of Birmingham. Birmingham and London: Swinney, n.d.

Travels of Carl Philipp Moritz in England. London: Milford, 1924.

Verbruggen, J. A. (ed.), *The Correspondence of Jan Daniël Huichelbos van Liender (1732–1809) with James Watt (1736–1819) and Boulton & Watt, supplemented by a few related Documents compiled and annotated by Jan A. Verbruggen*. Privately printed, 2005.

Walker, A. *Remarks Made in a Tour from London to the lakes of Westmoreland in the Summer of M,DCC,XCI*. London, 1792.

Ward, W. R. and Heitzenrater, R. P. (eds), *The Works of John Wesley*, 24 vols. Nashville: Abingdon Press, 1988–2003.

Zimmermann, E. A. W. *A Political Survey of the Present State of Europe*. London, 1787.

Zorzanello, G. 'L'inedita correspondenza del diplomatico veneziano Simon Cavelli con Matthew Boulton (1779–1786)', *Archivo Veneto*, 122 (1984), pp. 35–64.

Secondary sources

A History of the County of Warwick. Volume VII: *The City of Birmingham*. Oxford: Oxford University Press, 1964.

Adey, K. R., 'Seventeenth-century Stafford: a county town in decline', *Midland History*, 2 (1974), pp. 152–66.

Ågren, M. (ed.), *Iron-Making Societies: Early Industrial Development in Sweden and Russia, 1600–1900*. New York: Berghahn, 1998, reprinted 2003.

Alder, K. *Engineering the Revolution: Arms, Enlightenment, and the Making of Modern France*. Princeton: Princeton University Press, 1997.

Allen, R. C. 'An alternative community in North-East England: Quakers, morals and popular culture in the long eighteenth century', in Berry, H. and Gregory, J. (eds), *Creating and Consuming Culture in North-East England, 1660–1830*. Aldershot: Ashgate, 2004, pp. 98–140.

Andrews, S. *Unitarian Radicalism: Political Rhetoric, 1770–1814*. Basingstoke: Palgrave, 2003.

Argent, A. 'The founding of the London Missionary Society and the West Midlands', in Sell, A. P. F. (ed.), *Nonconformists and the West Midlands of England*. Keele: Keele University Press, 1996, pp. 13–41.

Ashton, T. S. *The Industrial Revolution, 1760–1830*. Oxford: Oxford University Press, 1948.

Barraclough, K. C. *Steelmaking before Bessemer*, 2 vols. London: The Metals Society, 1984.

Bayly, C. A. *The Birth of the Modern World, 1780–1945*. Oxford: Blackwell, 2004.

Bayne-Powell, R. *Travellers in Eighteenth-Century England*. London: Murray, 1951.

Beer, G. de. 'The relations between the Fellows of the Royal Society and French Men of Science when France and Britain were at war', *Notes and Records of the Royal Society of London*, 9 (May 1952), pp. 244–99.

Beer, G. de. *The Sciences were never at War*. Edinburgh: Nelson, 1960.

Behrens, H. *Mechanikus Franz Dinnendahl (1775–1826), Erbauer der ersten Dampfmaschinen an der Ruhr: Leben und Wirken aus zeitgenössischen Quellen*. Cologne: Rheinisch-Westfälischen Wirtschaftsarchiv, 1970.

Beresford, M. W. and Jones, G. R. J. (eds), *Leeds and its Region*. Leeds: BAAS, 1967.

Beretta, M. 'The grammar of matter: chemical nomenclature during the XVIII century', in Chartier, R. and Corsi, P. (eds), *Sciences et langues en Europe*. Paris: EHESS, 1996, pp. 109–25.

Berg, M. 'In pursuit of luxury: global history and British consumer goods in the eighteenth century', *Past and Present*, 182 (February 2004), pp. 85–142.

Berg, M. *Luxury and Pleasure in Eighteenth-Century Britain*. Oxford: Oxford University Press, 2005.

Berg, M. and Bruland, K. (eds), *Technological Revolutions in Europe: Historical Perspectives*. Cheltenham: Elgar, 1998.

Berman, M. *Social Change and Scientific Organization, The Royal Institution, 1799–1804*. London: Heinemann, 1978.

Bernard Cohen, I. (ed.), *Puritanism and the Rise of Modern Science: the Merton Thesis*. New Brunswick: Rutgers University Press, 1990.

Berry, H. and Gregory, J. (eds), *Creating and Consuming Culture in North-East England, 1660–1830*. Aldershot: Ashgate, 2004.

Birmingham and its Regional Setting: a Scientific Survey prepared for the Meeting held in Birmingham 30th August–6th September 1950. Birmingham: British Association for the Advancement of Science, 1950.

Blanken, R. 'The diffusion of coke smelting and puddling in Germany, 1796–1860', in Evans, C. and Rydén, G. (eds), *The Industrial Revolution in Iron: the Impact of British Coal Technology in Nineteenth-Century Europe*. Aldershot: Ashgate, 2005, pp. 55–74.

Borsay, P. *The English Urban Renaissance: Culture and Society in the Provincial Town, 1660–1770*. Oxford: Oxford University Press, 1989.

Bradley, J. E. *Religion, Revolution and English Radicalism. Nonconformity in Eighteenth-Century Politics and Society*. Cambridge: Cambridge University Press, 1990.

Bret, P. 'Genèse et légitimation patrimoniale d'une invention: les archives de l'Artillerie à l'origine d'une innovation cruciale dans la Marine au XIXe siècle', in Hilaire-Pérez, L. and Garçon, A.-F. (eds), *Les Chemins de la nouveauté: innover, inventer au regard de l'histoire*. Paris: Editions CTHS, 2003, pp. 385–410.

Brockliss, L. W. B. *Calvet's Web: Enlightenment and the Republic of Letters in Eighteenth-Century France*. Oxford: Oxford University Press, 2002.

Broman, T. 'The Habermasian Public Sphere and "Science *in* the Enlightenment"', *History of Science*, 36 (1998), pp. 123–49.

Brooke, J. H. *Science and Religion: some Historical Perspectives*. Cambridge: Cambridge University Press, 1991.

Brown, S. C. *Benjamin Thompson Count Rumford*. Cambridge, Mass: MIT Press, 1979.

Bruland, K. (ed.), *Technology Transfer and Scandinavian Industrialisation*. New York: Berg, 1991.

Bruland, K. 'Skills, learning and the international diffusion of technology: a perspective on Scandinavian industrialisation', in Berg, M. and Bruland, K. (eds), *Technological Revolutions in Europe: Historical Perspectives*. Cheltenham: Elgar, 1998, pp. 161–87.

Busch, W. 'Joseph Wright of Derby: art, science, and the validity of artistic language', in Shea, W. R. (ed.), *Science and the Visual Image in the Enlightenment*. Canton: Science History Publications, 2000, pp. 25–37.

Butler, M. *Maria Edgeworth: a Literary Biography*. Oxford: Clarendon Press, 1972.

Cantor, G. *Quakers, Jews, and Science: Religious Responses to Modernity and the Sciences in Britain, 1650–1900*. Oxford: Oxford University Press, 2005.

Cardwell, D. S. L. 'Science, technology and industry', in Rousseau, G. S. and Porter, R. (eds), *The Ferment of Knowledge: Studies in the Historiography of Eighteenth-Century Science*. Cambridge: Cambridge University Press, 1980, pp. 449–83.

Chalklin, C. W. *The Provincial Towns of Georgian England: a Study of the Building Process, 1740–1820*. London: Arnold, 1974.

Chevalier, J. 'La Mission de Gabriel Jars dans les mines et les usines britanniques en 1764', *Transactions of the Newcomen Society*, 26 (1947–48), pp. 57–68.

Christensen, D. Ch. *Det Moderne Projekt: Teknik & Kultur I Danmark-Norge, 1750–(1814)–1850*. Copenhagen: Gyldendal, 1996.

Clark, P. (ed.), *The Cambridge Urban History of Britain*. Volume 2: *1540–1840*. Cambridge: Cambridge University Press, 2000.

Clark, W., Golinski, J. and Schaffer, S. (eds), *The Sciences in Enlightened Europe*. Chicago: Chicago University Press, 1999.

Coley, N. G. 'John Warltire, 1738/9 – 1810: itinerant lecturer and chemist', *West Midlands Studies: a Journal of Industrial Archaeology and Business History*, 3 (1969), pp. 31–44.

Court, W. H. B. *The Rise of the Midlands Industries, 1600–1838*. Oxford: Oxford University Press, 1938.

Cross, A. G. *'By the Banks of the Thames': Russians in Eighteenth-Century Britain*. Newtonville: Oriental Research Partners, 1980.

Cross, A. G. *By the Banks of the Neva: Chapters from the Lives and Careers of the British in Eighteenth-Century Russia*. Cambridge: Cambridge University Press, 1997.

Darnton, R. *The Business of the Enlightenment: a Publishing History of the Encyclopédie, 1776–1800*. Cambridge, Mass: Harvard University Press, 1979.

Daston, L. 'The ideal and reality of the Republic of Letters in the Enlightenment', *Science in Context*, 4:2 (1991), pp. 367–86.

Daston, L. 'Afterword: the ethos of the Enlightenment', in Clark, W., Golinski, J. and Schaffer, S. (eds), *The Sciences in Enlightened Europe*. Chicago: Chicago University Press, 1999, pp. 495–8.

Daston, L. 'Are you having fun today?', *London Review of Books*, 23 September 2004, pp. 29, 31.

Dear, P. 'Cultural history of science: an overview with reflections', *Science, Technology and Human Values*, 20 (1995), pp. 150–70.

Dent, R. K. *Old and New Birmingham: a History of the Town and its People*, 2 vols. East Ardsley, Wakefield: The Scholar Press reprint, 1973.

'Der Curieuse Passagier': Deutsche Englandreisende des achzehnten Jahrhunderts als Vermittler kultureller und technologischer Anregungen. Colloquium der Arbeitsstelle 18. Jahrhundert Gesamthochschule Wuppertal Universität Münster. Münster vom 11–12. Dezember 1980. Heidelberg, 1983.

Dilworth, D. *West Bromwich before the Industrial Revolution.* A Black Country Society Publication, 1973.

Dolan, B. *Josiah Wedgwood: Entrepreneur to the Enlightenment.* London: Harper, 2004.

Dyck, W. von. *Georg von Reichenbach.* Deutsches Museum Lebensbeschreibungen und Urkunden, Munich, 1912.

Dyer, A. 'Midlands', in Clark, P. (ed.), *The Cambridge Urban History of Britain.* Volume 2: *1540–1840.* Cambridge: Cambridge University Press, 2000, pp. 93–110.

Ede, J. F. *History of Wednesbury.* Wednesbury: Wednesbury Corporation, 1962.

Evans, C., Jackson, O. and Rydén, G. 'Baltic Iron and the British Iron Industry in the Eighteenth Century', *Economic History Review*, 55:4 (2002), pp. 642–65.

Everett, J. 'Réseaux épistolaires: le cas du Québec dans les années trente', in Melançon, B. (ed.), *Penser par lettre. Actes du colloque d'Azay-le-Ferron, mai 1997.* Québec: Fides, 1998, pp. 125–37.

Flinn, M. W. 'The travel diaries of Swedish engineers of the eighteenth century as sources of technological history', *Transactions of the Newcomen Society*, 31 (1957–58), pp. 95–109.

Frängsmyr, T. *A la recherche des Lumières: une perspective suédoise.* Pessac: Presses universitaires de Bordeaux, 1999.

Gascoigne, J. *Joseph Banks and the English Enlightenment: Useful Knowledge and Polite Culture.* Cambridge: Cambridge University Press, 1994.

Gascoigne, J. *Science in the Service of Empire: Joseph Banks, the British State and the Uses of Science in the Age of Revolution.* Cambridge: Cambridge University Press, 1998.

Gay, P. *The Enlightenment: an Interpretation.* 2 vols. New York: Vintage, 1966–69.

Gill, C. *History of Birmingham.* Volume 1: *Manor and Borough to 1865.* Oxford: Oxford University Press, 1952.

Gillispie, C. C. 'The natural history of industry', *Isis*, 48 (1957), pp. 398–407.

Gillispie, C. C. *Science and Polity in France: the Revolutionary and Napoleonic Years.* Princeton: Princeton University Press, 2004.

Golinski, J. 'Science *in* the Enlightenment', *History of Science*, 24 (1986), pp. 411–24.

Golinski, J. *Science as Public Culture: Chemistry and Enlightenment in Britain, 1760–1820.* Cambridge: Cambridge University Press, 1992.

Grainger, J. D. *The Amiens Truce: Britain and Bonaparte, 1801–1803.* Woodbridge: Boydell, 2004.

Granovetter, M. 'The strength of weak ties', *American Journal of Sociology*, 78 (1973), pp. 1360–80.

Gresley, W. *Colton Green, a Tale of the Black Country.* London, 1847.

Guttery, D. R. *From Broad Glass to Cut Glass: a History of the Stourbridge Glass Industry.* London: Hill, 1956.

Hackwood, F. W. *History of Tipton in Staffordshire.* Studley: Brewin reprint, 2001.

Hahn, R. *The Anatomy of a Scientific Institution: the Paris Academy of Sciences, 1660–1803.* Berkeley: University of California Press, 1971.

Hamilton, H. *The English Brass and Copper Industries to 1800.* London: Longman, 1926.

Hankins, T. A. Science and the Enlightenment. Cambridge: Cambridge University Press, 1985.

Hann, A. 'Industrialisation and the service economy', in Stobart, J. and Raven, N. (eds), *Towns, Regions and Industries: Urban and Industrial Change in the Midlands, c. 1700–1840.* Manchester: Manchester University Press, 2005, pp. 42–61.

Harris, J. R. *The Copper King: a Biography of Thomas Williams of Llanidan.* Liverpool: Liverpool University Press, 1964.

Harris, J. R. 'The diffusion of English metallurgical methods to eighteenth-century France', *French History*, 2 (1988), pp. 22–44.

Harris, J. R. *Industrial Espionage and Technology Transfer: Britain and France in the Eighteenth Century.* Aldershot: Ashgate, 1998.

Heal, F. *Hospitality in Early Modern England.* Oxford: Oxford University Press, 1990.

Heilbron, J. 'Experimental natural philosophy', in Rousseau, G. S. and Porter, R. (eds), *The Ferment of Knowledge: Studies in the Historiography of Eighteenth-Century Science.* Cambridge: Cambridge University Press, 1980, pp. 358–88.

Henderson, W. O. *Britain and Industrial Europe, 1750–1870: Studies in British Influence on the Industrial Revolution in Western Europe.* Liverpool: Liverpool University Press, 1954.

Henderson, W. O. *J. C. Fischer and his Diary of Industrial England, 1814–51.* London: Frank Cass, 1966.

Herman, A. *The Scottish Enlightenment. The Scots' Invention of the Modern World.* London: Fourth Estate, 2001.

Hills, R. L. *James Watt.* Volume 1: *His Time in Scotland, 1736–1774.* Ashbourne: Landmark, 2002.

Hills, R. L. *James Watt.* Volume 2: *The Years of Turmoil, 1775–1785.* Ashbourne: Landmark, 2005.

Hills, R. L. *James Watt.* Volume 3: *Triumph through Adversity, 1785–1819.* Ashbourne: Landmark, 2006.

Home, R. W. 'Volta's English connections', in Belvilacqua, F. and Fregonese, L. *Nuovo Voltiana. Studies in Volta and his Times.* Volume One. Milan: Hoepli, 2000, pp. 115–32.

Hopkins, E. *Birmingham: the First Manufacturing Town in the World, 1760–1840.* London: Weidenfeld & Nicolson, 1989.

Hopkins, E. 'The Birmingham economy during the Revolutionary and Napoleonic wars, 1793–1815', *Midland History*, 23 (1998), pp. 111–20.

Horn, J. *The Path Not Taken: French Industrialization in the Age of Revolution, 1750–1830.* Cambridge, Mass: MIT Press, 2006.

Hufbauer, K. *The Formation of the German Chemical Community, 1720–1795.* Berkeley: University of California Press, 1982.

Hunter Dupree, A. 'Nationalism and science: Sir Joseph Banks and the wars with France', in Pinkney, D. H. and Ropp, T. (eds), *A Festschrift for Frederick B. Artz.* Durham: Duke University Press, 1964, pp. 37–51.

Inkster, I. and Morrell, J. B. (eds), *Metropolis and Province: Science in British Culture, 1780–1850.* London: Hutchinson, 1983.

Isichei, E. *Victorian Quakers.* Oxford: Oxford University Press, 1970.

Jacob, J. R. and Jacob, M. C. 'The Anglican origins of modern science: the metaphysical foundations of the Whig constitution', *Isis*, 71 (1980), pp. 251–67.

Jacob, M. C. *The Newtonians and the English Revolution, 1689–1720.* Ithaca: Cornell University Press, 1976.

Jacob, M. C. *Scientific Culture and the Making of the Industrial West.* New York and Oxford: Oxford University Press, 1997.

Jacob, M. C. and Kadane, M. 'Missing now found in the eighteenth century: Weber's Protestant capitalist', *American Historical Review*, 108 (2003), pp. 20–49.

Jacob, M. C. and Stewart, L. *Practical Matter: Newton's Science in the Service of Industry and Empire, 1687–1851.* Cambridge, Mass: Harvard University Press, 2004.

Jeyes, S. H. *The Russells of Birmingham in the French Revolution and in America, 1791–1814.* London: Allen, 1911.

Jones, E. *Les Voyageurs français en Angleterre de 1815 à 1830.* Paris, 1930.

Jones, P. M. 'Living the Enlightenment and the French Revolution: James Watt, Matthew Boulton and their sons', *Historical Journal*, 42 (1999), pp. 157–82.

Jones, P. M. '"England expects . . .": trading in liberty in the age of Trafalgar', in Crook, M., Doyle, W. and Forrest, A. (eds), *Enlightenment and Revolution.* Aldershot: Ashgate, 2004, pp. 187–203.

Jones, P. M. '"Fraternising with the enemy": problems of identity during the French Revolution and the Napoleonic wars', in Kalman, J., Coller, I. and Davies, H. (eds), *French History and Civilization. Papers from the George Rudé Seminar.* Melbourne, 2005, pp. 38–44.

Jones, P. M. 'Les Inventeurs et l'activité inventive dans les archives de Soho', in Corcy, M.-S., Douyère-Demeulenaere, C. and Hilaire-Pérez, L. *Les Archives de l'invention: écrits, objets et images de l'activité inventive.* Toulouse, CNRS, 2006, pp. 203–10.

King, R. 'The sociability of the trades guilds of Newcastle and Durham, 1660–1750: the urban renaissance revisited', in Berry, H. and Gregory, J. (eds), *Creating and Consuming Culture in North-East England, 1660–1830*. Aldershot: Ashgate, 2004, pp. 57–71.

Klemm, F. *A History of Western Technology*. London: Allen & Unwin, 1959.

Klingender, F. D. *Art and the Industrial Revolution*. New York: Kelley 2nd edn, 1968.

Landes, D. *The Unbound Prometheus: Technological Change and Industrial Development in Western Europe from 1750 to the Present*. Cambridge: Cambridge University Press, 1969.

Langford, J. A. *A Century of Birmingham Life or a Chronicle of Local Events from 1741 to 1841*, 2 vols. Birmingham: More & Co., 1870.

Langford, P. *Englishness Identified: Manners and Character, 1650–1850*. Oxford: Oxford University Press, 1992.

Laudan, R. *From Mineralogy to Geology: the Foundations of a Science, 1650–1830*. Chicago: University of Chicago Press, 1987.

Lawley, G. T. *A History of Bilston, in the County of Stafford*. Bilston: Price, 1893.

Letts, M. *As the Foreigner Saw Us*. London: Methuen, 1935.

Licoppe, C. *La Formation de la pratique scientifique: le discours de l'expérience en France et en Angleterre, 1630–1820*. Paris: La Découverte, 1996.

Linder, B. and Smeaton, W. A. 'Schwediauer, Bentham and Beddoes: translators of Bergman and Scheele', *Annals of Science*, 24 (1968), pp. 259–73.

Lindqvist, S. *Technology on Trial: the Introduction of Steam Power Technology into Sweden, 1715–1736*. Stockholm: Almqvist & Wiksell, 1984.

Lloyd, S. *The Lloyds of Birmingham with some Account of the Founding of Lloyds Bank*. Birmingham: Cornish Bros, 1907.

Lux, D. S. and Cook, H. J. 'Closed circuits or open networks? Communicating at a distance during the Scientific Revolution', *History of Science*, 36 (1998), pp. 179–211.

Lynn, M. R. *Popular Science and Public Opinion in Eighteenth-Century France*. Manchester: Manchester University Press, 2006.

McInnes, A. 'The emergence of a leisure town: Shrewsbury, 1660–1760', *Past and Present*, 120 (1988), pp. 53–87.

Mackensen, L. von. 'The introduction of English steam engine and metallurgical technology into Germany during the Industrial Revolution prior to 1850', in *L'Acquisition des techniques par les pays non-initiateurs. Pont-à-Mousson, 28 juin–5 juillet 1970*. Paris: CNRS, 1973, pp. 429–53.

MacLeod, C. 'James Watt, heroic invention and the idea of the Industrial Revolution', in Berg, M. and Bruland, K. (eds), *Technological Revolutions in Europe: Historical Perspectives*. Cheltenham: Elgar, 1998, pp. 96–116.

Malone, D. *The Public Life of Thomas Cooper, 1783–1839*. Columbia: South Carolina University Press, 1961.

Mason, S. *The Hardware Man's Daughter: Matthew Boulton and his 'Dear Girl'*. Chichester: Phillimore, 2005.

Matheson, P. E. *German Visitors to England, 1770–1795*. The Taylorian Lecture. Oxford: Clarendon Press, 1930.

Mayer, J. P. (ed.), *A. de Tocqueville, Journeys to England and Ireland*. London: Faber, 1958.

Merton, R. K. *Science, Technology and Society in Seventeenth-Century England* (originally published in *Osiris*, 4 (1938), pp. 360–632). New York: Harper, 1970.

Miller, D. P. ' "Puffing Jamie": the commercial and ideological importance of being a "Philosopher" in the case of the reputation of James Watt (1736–1819)', *History of Science*, 38 (2000), pp. 1–24.

Miller, D. P. 'True myths: James Watt's kettle, his condenser, and his chemistry', *History of Science*, 42 (2004), pp. 333–60.

Miller, D. P. *Discovering Water: James Watt, Henry Cavendish and the Nineteenth-Century 'Water Controversy'*. Aldershot: Ashgate, 2004.

Moilliet, A. (ed.), *Elizabeth Anne Galton (1808–1906): a Well-Connected Gentlewoman*. Hartford: Léonie Press, 2003.

Mokyr, J. *Industrialisation in the Low Countries, 1795–1850*. New Haven: Yale University Press, 1976.

Mokyr, J. (ed.), *The British Industrial Revolution*. Boulder: Westview Press, 2ⁿᵈ edn, 1999.

Mokyr, J. *The Gifts of Athena: Historical Origins of the Knowledge Economy*. Princeton: Princeton University Press, 2002.

Mokyr, J. 'The intellectual origins of modern economic growth', *Journal of Economic History*, 65 (2005), pp. 285–343.

Money, J. 'Taverns, coffee houses and clubs: local politics and popular articulacy in the Birmingham area, in the age of the American Revolution', *Historical Journal*, 14 (1971), pp. 15–47.

Money, J. *Experience and Identity: Birmingham and the West Midlands, 1760–1800*. Montreal: McGill-Queen's University Press, 1977.

Money, J. 'Joseph Priestley in cultural context: philosophic spectacle, popular belief and popular politics in eighteenth-century Birmingham: part one', *Enlightenment and Dissent*, 7 (1988), pp. 57–81.

Money, J. 'Joseph Priestley in cultural context: philosophic spectacle, popular belief and popular politics in eighteenth-century Birmingham: part two', *Enlightenment and Dissent*, 8 (1989), pp. 69–89.

Money, J. 'Science, technology and dissent in English provincial culture: from Newtonian transformation to agnostic incarnation', in Wood, P. (ed.), *Science and Dissent in England, 1688–1945*. Aldershot: Ashgate, 2004.

Muirhead, J. *The Life of James Watt with Selections from his Correspondence*. New York: Appleton, 1859.

Mulligan, L. 'Civil War politics, religion and the Royal Society', *Past and Present*, 59 (1973), pp. 92–116.

Munck, T. *The Enlightenment: a Comparative Social History, 1721–1794*. London: Arnold, 2000.

Musson, A. E. (ed.), *Science, Technology and Economic Growth in the Eighteenth Century*. London: Methuen, 1972.

Musson, A. E. and Robinson, Eric. *Science and Technology in the Industrial Revolution*. Manchester: Manchester University Press, 1969.

Pancaldi, G. *Volta: Science and Culture in the Age of Enlightenment.* Princeton: Princeton University Press, 2003.

Parish, C. *History of the Birmingham Library: an Eighteenth-Century Proprietary Library as described in the Annals of the Birmingham Library, 1779–1799.* London: The Library Association, 1966.

Payen, J. *Capital et machine à vapeur au XVIIIe siècle: les frères Périer et l'introduction en France de la machine à vapeur de Watt.* Paris: Mouton, 1969.

Peck, T. W. and Wilkinson, K. D. *William Withering of Birmingham M. D., F. R. S., F. L. S.* Baltimore: Williams and Wilkins, 1950.

Pickering, A. (ed.), *Science as Practice and Culture.* Chicago: Chicago University Press, 1992.

Pigeire, J. *La Vie et l'oeuvre de Chaptal, 1756–1832.* Paris: Spès, 1932.

Porter, R. 'Science, provincial culture and public opinion in Enlightenment England', *British Journal for Eighteenth-Century Studies*, 3 (1980), pp. 20–46.

Porter, R. *Enlightenment: Britain and the Creation of the Modern World.* London: Penguin, 2000.

Porter, R. (ed.), *The Cambridge History of Science.* Volume 4: *Eighteenth-Century Science.* Cambridge: Cambridge University Press, 2003.

Pounds, N. J. G. *The Upper Silesian Industrial Region.* Bloomington: Indiana University Publications, 1958.

Pratt, D. H. *English Quakers and the First Industrial Revolution.* New York: Garland, 1985.

Prosser, R. B. *Birmingham Inventors and Inventions being a Contribution to the Industrial History of Birmingham.* Birmingham, 1881.

Quickenden, K. 'Boulton and Fothergill Silver: business plans and miscalculations', *Art History*, 3 (September 1980), pp. 274–92.

Raistrick, A. *Dynasty of Iron Founders: the Darbys and Coalbrookdale.* London: Longman, 1953.

Raistrick, A. *Quakers in Science and Industry being an Account of the Quaker Contributions to Science and Industry during the 17th and 18th Centuries.* Newton Abbott: David and Charles, 1968.

Ram, R. W. 'Influences on the patterns of belief and social action among Birmingham dissenters between 1750 and 1870', in Bryman, A. (ed.), *Religion in the Birmingham Area: Essays in the Sociology of Religion.* University of Birmingham Institute for the Study of Worship and Religious Architecture, n.d. [1975], pp. 29–44.

Raspe, R. E. *Singular Travels, Campaigns and Adventures of Baron Munchausen.* London: Cresset, 1948.

Raven, N. and Stobart, J. 'Networks and hinterlands: transport in the Midlands', in Stobart, J. and Raven, N. (eds), *Towns, Regions and Industries: Urban and Industrial Change in the Midlands, c. 1700–1840.* Manchester: Manchester University Press, 2005, pp. 80–101.

Robertson, J. 'The Enlightenment above national context: political economy in eighteenth-century Scotland and Naples', *Historical Journal*, 40:3 (1997), pp. 667–97.

Robertson, J. *The Case for the Enlightenment: Scotland and Naples 1680–1760.* Cambridge: Cambridge University Press, 2007.

Robinson, E. 'The Lunar Society: its membership and organisation', *Transactions of the Newcomen Society*, 35 (1962–63), pp. 153–77.

Roll, E. *An Early Experiment in Industrial Organisation being a History of the Firm Boulton & Watt, 1775–1805.* London: Longman, 1930.

Rose, R. B. 'The Priestley Riots of 1791', *Past and Present*, 18 (1960), pp. 68–88.

Rousseau, G. S. 'Science books and their readers in the eighteenth century', in Rivers, I. (ed.), *Books and their Readers in Eighteenth-Century England.* Leicester: Leicester University Press, 1982, pp. 197–255.

Rowlands, M. B. *A History of Industrial Birmingham.* Birmingham: City of Birmingham Education Department, 1977.

Ryland, W. H. (ed.) *Reminiscences of Thomas Henry Ryland.* Birmingham: The Midland Counties Herald Limited, 1904.

Sayers, R. S. *Lloyd's Bank in the History of English Banking.* Oxford: Clarendon Press, 1957.

Scarfe, N. *Innocent Espionage: the La Rochefoucauld Brothers' Tour of England in 1785.* Woodbridge: Boydell, 1995.

Schofield, R. E. *The Lunar Society of Birmingham: a Social History of Provincial Science and Industry in Eighteenth-Century England.* Oxford: Clarendon Press, 1963.

Schwarz, L. D. 'On the margins of industrialisation: Lichfield', in Stobart, J. and Raven, N. (eds), *Towns, Regions and Industries: Urban and Industrial Change in the Midlands, c. 1700–1840.* Manchester: Manchester University Press, 2005, pp. 176–92.

Seed, J. 'Gentlemen dissenters: the social and political meanings of rational dissent in the 1770s and 1780s', *Historical Journal*, 28 (1985), pp. 299–325.

Shea, W. R. (ed.), *Science and the Visual Image in the Enlightenment.* Canton: Science History Publications, 2000.

Smiles, S. *Lives of the Engineers: the Steam-Engine, Boulton and Watt.* London: Murray, 1874.

Smith, B. D. 'The Galtons of Birmingham: Quaker gun merchants and bankers, 1702–1831', *Business History*, 9 (1967), pp. 132–50.

Smith, C. U. M. and Arnott, R. (eds), *The Genius of Erasmus Darwin.* Aldershot: Ashgate, 2005.

Smith, J. 'Industrialisation and social change: Wolverhampton transformed, 1700–1840', in Stobart, J. and Raven, N. (eds), *Towns, Regions and Industries: Urban and Industrial Change in the Midlands, c. 1700–1840.* Manchester: Manchester University Press, 2005, pp. 134–46.

Snelders, H. A. M. 'The new chemistry in the Netherlands', *Osiris*, 4 (1988), pp. 121–45.

Sparrow, E. *Secret Service: British Agents in France, 1792–1815.* Woodbridge: Boydell, 1999.

Stanton, G. S. *On and Off the Campus.* Minneapolis: University of Minnesota Press, 1938.

Stewart, L. and Weindling, P. 'Philosophical threads: natural philosophy and public experiment among the weavers of Spitalfields', *British Journal for the History of Science*, 28 (1995), pp. 37–62.

Stobart, J. *The First Industrial Region: North-West England c. 1700–60*. Manchester: Manchester University Press, 2004.

Stobart, J. and Raven, N. (eds), *Towns, Regions and Industries: Urban and Industrial Change in the Midlands, c. 1700–1840*. Manchester: Manchester University Press, 2005.

Stobart, J. and Trinder, B. 'New towns of the industrial coalfields: Burslem and West Bromwich', in Stobart, J. and Raven, N. (eds), *Towns, Regions and Industries: Urban and Industrial Change in the Midlands, c. 1700–1840*. Manchester: Manchester University Press, 2005, pp. 121–7.

Sturges, R. P. 'The membership of the Derby Philosophical Society, 1783–1802', *Midland History*, 4 (1978), pp. 212–19.

Tann, J. 'Two knights of pandemonium: a worm's eye view of Boulton, Watt & Co', *History of Technology*, 20 (1998), pp. 47–72.

Tawney, R. H. *Religion and the Rise of Capitalism: a Historical Study*. Holland Memorial Lectures, 1922. London: Murray, 1926.

Thackray, A. 'Natural knowledge in cultural context: the Manchester model', *American Historical Review*, 79 (June 1974), pp. 672–709.

Thorpe, H. *Lichfield: a Study of its Growth and Function*. n.p., n.d.

Tildesley, N. W. *A History of Willenhall*. Willenhall: Willenhall Urban District Council, 1951.

Timmins, S. (ed.), *The Resources, Products, and Industrial History of Birmingham and the Midland Hardware District: a Series of Reports, collected by the Local Industries Committee of the British Association at Birmingham in 1865*. London: Hardwicke, 1866.

Torstendahl, R. 'Knowledge, its transfer and reproduction in occupations', in Ågren, M. (ed.), *Iron-making Societies: Early Industrial Development in Sweden and Russia, 1600–1900*. New York: Berghahn, 2003, pp. 276–306.

Trainor, R. H. *Black Country Elites: the Exercise of Authority in an Industrialised Area, 1830–1900*. Oxford: Clarendon Press, 1993.

Trogan, R. and Sorel, P. *Augustin Dupré, 1748–1833: graveur-général des Monnaies de France*. Paris: Paris Musées, n.d. [2000].

Underdown, P. T. 'Religious opposition to licensing the Bristol and Birmingham theatres', *University of Birmingham Historical Journal*, 6 (1957–58), pp. 149–60.

Vann, R. T. and Eversley, D. *Friends in Life and Death: the British and Irish Quakers in the Demographic Transition, 1650–1900*. Cambridge: Cambridge University Press, 1992.

Venturi, F. *The End of the Old Regime in Europe: the First Crisis, 1768–1776*. Princeton: Princeton University Press, 1989.

Viennet, O. *Une Enquête économique dans la France Impériale. Le voyage du hambourgeois Philippe-André Nemnich, 1809*. Paris, 1947.

Villas-Boas, M. *Jacinto de Magalhães. Um empreendedor científico na Europa do Século XVIII*. Aveiro: Fundação João Jacinto Magalhães, 2000.

Vries, J. de. 'The Industrial Revolution and the industrious revolution', *Journal of Economic History*, 54 (1994), pp. 249–70.

Vries, J. de. 'Between purchasing power and the world of goods: understanding the household economy in early modern Europe', in Brewer, J. and Porter, R. (eds), *Consumption and the World of Goods*. London: Routledge, 1993, pp. 98–132.

Walvin, J. *The Quakers: Money and Morals*. London: Murray, 1997.

Watts, M. R. *The Dissenters*. Volume 1: *From the Reformation to the French Revolution*. Oxford: Oxford University Press, 1978.

Weber, M. *The Protestant Ethic and the Spirit of Capitalism*. Translated by T. Parsons. London: Allen & Unwin, 1930.

Weber, W. *Innovationen im frühindustriellen deutschen Bergbau und Hüttenwesen: Friedrich Anton von Heynitz*. Göttingen: Vandenhoeck & Ruprecht, 1976.

Webster, C. *The Great Instauration: Science, Medicine and Reform, 1626–1660*. London: Duckworth, 1975.

Widmalm, S. 'Instituting science in Sweden', in Porter, R. and Teich, M. (eds), *The Scientific Revolution in National Context*. Cambridge: Cambridge University Press, 1992, pp. 240–62.

Wolfe, J. J. *Brandy, Balloons and Lamps: Ami Argand, 1750–1803*. Carbondale: Southern Illinois University Press, 1999.

Wood, P. (ed.), *Science and Dissent in England, 1688–1945*. Aldershot: Ashgate, 2004.

Woronoff, D. *L'industrie sidérurgique en France pendant la Révolution et l'Empire*. Paris: EHESS, 1984.

Wrigley, E. A. *Continuity and Change: the Character of the Industrial Revolution*. Cambridge: Cambridge University Press, 1988.

Wykes, D. L. 'James II's Religious Indulgence of 1687 and the early organisation of dissent: the building of the first Nonconformist meeting-house in Birmingham', *Midland History*, 16 (1991), pp. 86–102.

Wykes, D. L. ' "A finished monster of the true Birmingham breed": Birmingham Unitarians and the 1791 Priestley Riots', in Sell, A. P. F. (ed.), *Nonconformists and the West Midlands of England*. Keele: Keele University Press, 1996, pp. 43–69.

Zorzanello, G. 'Il diplomatico veneziano Simon Cavalli et le sua legazione in Inghilterra (1778–1782)', *Ateno Veneto*, 22 (1984), pp. 226–48.

Index